GW00578589

Credit:

THE COMPLETE GUIDE TO PRICING, HEDGING AND RISK MANAGEMENT

Credit:

THE COMPLETE GUIDE TO PRICING, HEDGING AND RISK MANAGEMENT

Angelo Arvanitis and Jon Gregory

Published by Risk Books, a division of the Risk Waters Group.

Haymarket House
28–29 Haymarket
London SW1Y 4RX
Tel: +44 (0)20 7484 9700
Fax: +44 (0)20 7484 9758
E-mail: books@riskwaters.com
Website: www.riskbooks.com

Every effort has been made to secure the permission of individual copyright
holders for inclusion.

© Risk Waters Group Ltd 2001

ISBN 1 899 332 731

British Library Cataloguing in Publication Data
A catalogue record for this book is available from the British Library

Risk Books Commissioning Editor: Emma Elvy
Project Editor: Sarah Jenkins

Typeset by Special Edition Pre-press Services

Printed and bound in Great Britain by Bookcraft (Bath) Ltd, Somerset

About the Authors

Angelo Arvanitis is head of the risk department at Egnatia Bank in Greece. He is on the board of directors of the bank's portfolio management subsidiary, as well as being a member of the assets and liabilities management committee and the audit committee. Prior to that, Angelo headed the quantitative credit, insurance and risk research at Paribas worldwide, which he founded in 1997. His responsibilities included the development of pricing, hedging and risk management models for credit derivatives, convertible bonds and insurance derivatives. He was also responsible for analysing the economic capital of the fixed income division, covering market, credit and operational risks. Previously, he was a vice president in the derivatives and the emerging markets departments at Lehman Brothers in New York. He has also spent time in structured products at BZW in London, specialising in tax arbitrage. He has had various papers published in both professional and academic journals, his main subject being the management of credit and insurance risks. Angelo gained a BA in physics at the University of Athens. He continued his studies at the University of California, the London School of Economics and the doctoral programme in finance at the University of Chicago.

Jon Gregory is global head of credit derivatives research at BNP Paribas, based in London. His team has provided the quantitative foundations for the rapid growth of the BNP Paribas credit derivative desks in London, New York, Hong Kong and Tokyo since the BNP and Paribas merger in 2000. Jon joined Paribas in 1997 and was responsible for the development of the internal model for analysing the economic capital of the fixed income division. In addition to his work on capital management, he has worked on pricing models for the interest-rate derivative and equity derivative desks. He has also been involved in developing models for insurance derivatives. His main interest lies in reconciling theoretical and practical approaches for pricing, hedging and managing credit risk. Jon gained a BSc from the University of Bristol in 1993 and was awarded his PhD from Cambridge University in 1996. He worked in the Fixed Income division of Salomon Brothers (now Salomon Smith Barney) prior to joining Paribas.

Contents

PART II – PRICING AND HEDGING OF CREDIT RISK

Introduction

In this book, we aim to provide a comprehensive treatment of credit, without artificial barriers, while developing the links between pricing, hedging and risk management. Study of this book should provide readers with the tools necessary for addressing the credit problems they face in their own areas of specialisation. We first develop the fundamental framework, and then apply this to a broad range of products. We hope that this common denominator will be apparent and prevent this book being approached as a series of independent studies. Our focus is mainly capital markets rather than corporate banking products, because this is our area of concentration, and because only limited material is available in the financial literature, with the exception of academic papers.

We believe that the timing of this book is right. On the one hand, credit derivative products are being used more, while, on the other, the need to measure and guard against credit risk is heightened. There is also increased regulatory pressure for the banks to control and manage their aggregate credit exposure. The banks have started to view their credit risk globally, and this is the approach that we follow here.

This book has been written with the practitioner in mind. Our main audience comprises chief risk officers, credit risk managers, researchers, quantitative credit analysts, portfolio managers, senior credit derivative and interest rate traders and marketers, as well as anyone else interested in the subject. We do not intend this to be a book on mathematical finance with an emphasis on credit. We have avoided unnecessary use of complex mathematics, while keeping the book self-sufficient by providing technical appendices where needed. The material should be accessible to the non-technical reader, but analytical aptitude and knowledge of standard derivatives, calculus and statistics are helpful. Selectively, it can also be used as a textbook for MBA and advanced undergraduate students majoring in economics or business.

In Chapter 1, after reviewing some of the fundamental concepts in credit risk management, we demonstrate how the normal approximation of the credit loss distribution can lead to gross errors in the computation of various statistics, even for simple loan portfolios. The normal distribution does not capture the skewness in typical credit portfolios, and this leads to underestimation of the tail probabilities. We discuss the scarcity of historical time series, and briefly review some of the available data for default and credit migration probabilities, default correlation and recovery rates. At the end of this chapter, we critically review and compare the commercially available models: JP Morgan's CreditMetrics, Credit Suisse Financial Products' CreditRisk+, KMV's Portfolio Manager and McKinsey Company's Credit Portfolio View.

Chapter 2 introduces the concept of stochastic exposures for fixed-income instruments, which, unlike loan portfolios, are marked-to-market. In the following chapters, we demonstrate how stochastic exposures complicate the computation of the credit loss distribution, and show how approximating by a constant exposure, quite often referred to as "loan equivalent", can provide erroneous results. The credit exposure is defined as the percentile of the distribution of the future present value of a particular transaction at a certain confidence level. This idea is closely related to the credit lines, which are commonly used by financial institutions in controlling their exposure to each counterparty they transact with.

Chapter 3 builds on Chapter 2 and couples the exposure distribution with the default process, introducing the concept of credit portfolio management. It provides standard material for the computation of credit loss distributions and the simulation of binary default events. The first part of the chapter is based on work originally presented in the CreditMetrics framework. In the second part, we discuss a few other related topics. We expand the standard model so that the recovery rate is driven by the severity of default. We show how we can use default correlation as an input to the simulation, rather than asset return correlation. We investigate the sensitivity of the economic capital to default correlation, stochastic recovery rates, stochastic exposures and multiple periods.

Chapter 4, which expands on Chapter 3, is probably the most technical chapter in the book. The reader who is not interested in computational techniques can skip most of the material without loss of continuity. We present analytical techniques for computing capital under rather restrictive assumptions, Monte Carlo speeding-up techniques and extreme value theory for fitting the tails of the credit loss distribution. An important subject that we cover is the computation of risk contributions and portfolio optimisation, while the normality assumption is being relaxed. Lastly, we present a model for the evolution of the term structure of the credit spreads. This model can be used for marking-to-market the portfolio's credit spread when computing the credit loss distribution.

Chapters 5, 6 and 7 constitute the main credit pricing (as opposed to risk management) chapters of this book. In Chapter 5, we discuss the pricing and hedging of credit derivatives. First, we explore standard interpolation techniques for deriving a credit-spread curve from the market quotes of liquid default swaps. We analyse various products on single underlyings, such as credit spread options, credit contingent contracts, cancellable swaps and quanto default swaps. Next, we expand the analysis to cover multiple underlying credit derivative products, with particular emphasis on baskets – ie, "worst of" and first m or last k to default in a basket of n assets. We decided to focus on this product class because of both its complexity and its importance in structured credit derivative transactions. We show how these products relate to standard collateralised debt obligations. We explore different hedging strategies and show how traditional delta hedging can result in poorly managed positions. A multitude of examples for pricing and hedging various types of portfolios have been provided to clarify the theoretical ideas.

Chapters 3 and 4 covered the computation of the credit loss distribution of a derivative portfolio, assuming that counterparty risk is not hedgeable. We pointed out the importance of economic capital, in order for the financial institution to sustain potential future defaults without disruption of its operations. In Chapter 6, we use standard default swaps as the fundamental instruments for hedging counterparty default and credit spread risk. This approach provides a link between two areas that have developed independently within the financial community: credit risk management and credit derivatives trading. If credit risk is assumed to be non-hedgeable, the credit spread of a new transaction should compensate for its marginal contribution to the financial institution's capital, while if it is hedgeable, it should cover its expected loss. We consider pricing risky transactions on a "stand-alone" and on a "portfolio" basis. In the latter case, existing deals within a master agreement are taken into account, as they are netted in the event of default. Finally, we extend the hedging techniques developed in the credit derivative chapters with the aim of immunising a portfolio against defaults and credit spread volatility.

In Chapter 7, we incorporate a credit element to the pricing of convertible bonds. The importance of the US convertible high yield market along with the expected growth of a similar market in Europe with the advent of the euro have been the motivation behind this work. We present two models: the Credit Spread and the Firm Value model. In the former, the credit spread is mainly driven by the value of the firm's stock, while in the latter we model the process followed by the value of the firm explicitly. The pros and cons of each approach are explored in detail.

In the last chapter we discuss three topics that are related to credit, even though for simplicity the first two applications are presented in an equity context: impact of market illiquidity, non-continuous rebalancing of hedging portfolios and asymmetric information among market participants. The discussion is rather brief and our purpose has been only to introduce these topics and the underlying fundamental economic ideas. Even though we have not yet applied these ideas to credit, we believe that they can provide more realistic models that emulate more closely the functioning of the real market. We realise that the models' complexity and difficult calibration issues could limit their applicability.

In the Appendix we have reprinted articles from either *Risk* magazine or Risk Books that we consider important, and they are complementary to the material covered in the book.

We would like to thank our colleagues, academics and conference participants, where we have presented much of this work, for stimulating discussions. Special thanks are due to Jean-Michel Lasry, Jean-Paul Laurent and Olivier Scaillet. Angelo Arvanitis would like to thank Darrell Duffie for numerous discussions on the fundamentals of pricing credit. We thank Douglas Long for refereeing Chapter 4. We express our appreciation to Conrad Gardner, Head of Risk Books Publishing, for his enthusiasm in undertaking this project. We are also grateful to Nick Dunbar for initial discussions regarding the subject matter and focus of this book. Special thanks go to Sarah Jenkins for her tireless work in coordinating the whole process.

While writing this book we have used C++ to implement all the models that are presented and we have used the software to produce the examples in the book. In the near future, we intend to provide companion software. This will give readers the opportunity to experiment with and challenge the models we describe.

We have independently implemented full versions of all of the models described here. These models have been used exclusively for all of the examples presented. We have been careful to implement numerically efficient algorithms which have been tested thoroughly. Needless to say, we are fully responsible for any errors. We hope that this book will trigger discussions and further work on the subjects we have addressed.[1]

---

1   If readers would like to contribute any comments or ideas, the authors can be contacted at: angelo_arvanitis@hotmail.com; jon-gregory@supanet.com.

Part I

Credit Risk Management

Overview of Credit Risk

Measuring and managing credit risk, whether for loans, bonds or deriva-tive securities, has become a key issue for financial institutions. The risk analysis can be performed either for stand-alone trades or for portfolios of deals. The latter approach takes into account risk diversification across trades and counterparties. As will be shown later, ignoring risk diversifi-cation can lead to erroneous risk management decisions, increasing rather than reducing the risk exposure of the financial institution. Diversification occurs both at the counterparty (obligor) level and at a more global level. At the counterparty level, diversification is the result of the offsetting of the exposures of different trades with the same transacting counterparty. Portfolio diversification also arises across counterparties, since different firms do not default at the same time. As a result, the equity that must be held against defaults for a well-diversified portfolio is only a fraction of the total exposure of the portfolio.

Traditionally, credit risk encompasses two distinct risk types: counter-party risk and issuer risk. Counterparty risk is relevant for loans and derivative transactions, whereas issuer risk refers mostly to bonds. This book deals mainly with the former. Credit derivative contracts are subject to both types of risk. Counterparty risk is analysed over a long time hori-zon, as the positions are illiquid and it is difficult (if at all possible) to trade out of them. Issuer risk for bonds is computed over a time horizon of a few days – similarly to traditional market risk. Bonds are considered liquid – ie, they can be traded easily if the need arises; in practice, however, this is not always the case.

Consider a portfolio with market value V. In order to assess the market risk of this portfolio over a certain time horizon, we need to estimate the worst value of V over this period. This value could be negative if cashflows are exchanged between the two transacting counterparties, as is the case in an interest rate swap. Market risk is generally driven by the variability of continuous market variables, such as interest rates and stock prices. The period over which market risk should be assessed is often only a few days, since it is usually possible to trade out of positions over this time horizon. For example, a liquid stock that has plummeted in value can usually be sold fairly easily (albeit at a loss), whereas credit-risky assets, such as loans, are not often traded on the secondary market. Derivative contracts, such as swaps, are even more illiquid, since it is not usually possible to trade or even unwind them.

If V is negative, there is no loss or gain to the holder of this position if his counterparty defaults, since the same amount of money is still to be paid. It is important to stress that credit risk is still present, even though most likely reduced, since it is still possible that V becomes positive over the life of the deal. Credit risk is more significant when V is positive, as monies owed at default will not be paid in full. Only the recovery value will be received. Therefore credit risk is driven by two components: the overall value of the positions and the actual "credit state" of the counterparty. The first is similar to market risk (although in the opposite direction) and has the same underlying variables driving the exposure. The second is particular to credit risk and can be simply thought of as default or no-default. This introduces a binary element into credit risk, which is not an element of market risk. The "credit state" can be enriched by assigning credit ratings, which are characterised by the default probabilities and the credit migration matrix.

As will be shown in the following chapters, the characterisation of a credit portfolio's risk allows the identification of concentration in credit exposures, which leads naturally to the active management of credit risk through trading in the secondary markets, if they exist, use of credit derivatives and securitisation.

1.1 COMPONENTS OF CREDIT RISK

Credit risk arises from potential changes in the credit quality of a counterparty in a transaction. It has two components: default risk and credit spread risk.

Default risk
Default risk is driven by the potential failure of a counterparty to make promised payments, either partly or wholly. In the event of default, a fraction of the obligations will normally be paid. This is known as the recovery value.

Credit spread risk
If a counterparty does not default, there is still risk due to the possible widening of the credit spread or worsening in credit quality. We make the distinction between two components of credit spread risk:

❑ *Jumps in the credit spread.* These may arise from a rating change (ie, an upgrade or a downgrade). It will usually be firm-specific and may result from some adverse or positive information becoming available in the market.

❑ *Credit spread volatility* (continuous changes in the credit spread). This is more likely to be driven by the market's appetite for certain levels of risk. For example, the spreads on high-grade bonds may widen or tighten, although this need not necessarily be taken as an indication that they are more or less likely to default.

If the credit spread of a portfolio is not marked-to-market, only default risk is important, since it represents the sole immediate loss. However, if a portfolio's credit spread is marked-to-market, then an increase in the credit spread will lead to an immediate realised loss, due to the expected future losses being increased. In Chapter 5 we discuss in detail the discounting of future risky cashflows. Loan portfolios are not usually marked-to-market. Consequently, the only important factor is whether or not the loan is in default today (since this is the only credit event that can lead to an immediate loss). Capital market portfolios are marked-to-market. This means that a transaction with a counterparty whose credit quality has worsened (though not defaulted) will be marked at a loss. The reason for this is that the future cashflows with that counterparty are now more "risky" and should therefore be discounted at a higher discount rate.

1.2 FACTORS DETERMINING THE CREDIT RISK OF A PORTFOLIO

Three groups of factors are important in determining the credit risk of a portfolio, as illustrated in Figure 1.1:

❑ deal-level factors corresponding to a single transaction;
❑ counterparty-level factors corresponding to a portfolio of transactions with a single counterparty; and
❑ portfolio-level factors corresponding to a portfolio of transactions with more than one counterparty.

These are depicted in Figure 1.1

1.2.1 Deal level

Exposure

It is important to model the variability of the future exposure in a derivative transaction, since the related market risk of a dynamic exposure is much harder to manage than that of a static one. It is therefore necessary to compute the distribution of the future exposures (present value (PV) discounted at the risk-free rate) at the deal level at all possible default times. This exposure can change dramatically over time, so it is vital to capture the future variability of such a deal. In fixed-income instruments this variability is driven by the evolution of the underlying variables, ie, interest rates and foreign exchange rates. Crucial parameters are the volatilities and the correlation of the above variables.

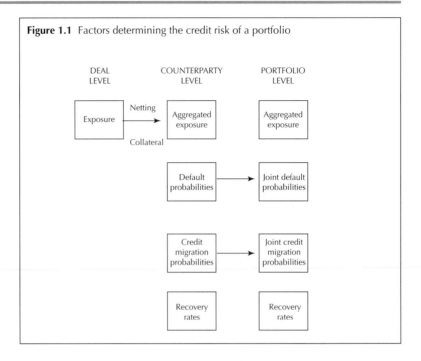

Figure 1.1 Factors determining the credit risk of a portfolio

Default probabilities
The default probability is the likelihood that a counterparty will be bankrupt or will not honour its obligations at the times when they become due over a given period. Since exposures can vary significantly with time, it is useful to have a series of marginal default probabilities over some reasonably fine intervals, such as three months. The marginal default probability gives the probability of default in a certain period (eg, six to nine months).

Credit migration probabilities
Losses may also occur as a result of less drastic deterioration in the credit quality of a counterparty, such as a downgrade to a lower rating. Although a downgrade does not mean that the counterparty will fail to make a payment (as in the event of default), it does mean that all future cashflows should be discounted at a higher risky rate, or, equivalently, that the expected future losses will have increased. For this reason, if a position is marked-to-market, a downgrade will result in a decrease in the PV and a loss. In some circumstances, it may not be appropriate or even possible to value a deal or a portfolio (eg, an illiquid loan), and hence credit migration events may not be considered. Furthermore, the severity of losses due to credit migration is generally lower than that of losses due to default (although the corresponding probabilities are almost always greater). On the other hand, there are reasonable situations where losses due to credit

deterioration can be of substantial magnitude. (This is addressed in Chapter 3.)

Recovery rates
Even in the event of default, there will normally be some recovery on the position. This is defined by the recovery rate. As we will present later, historical recovery rates have had a very large variability, spanning the whole interval between zero and one.

Correlation of exposure and default parameters
A final point to consider is whether a high exposure to a counterparty implies an increase in its default probability (or vice versa). Such an effect would significantly increase the expected loss. There are clearly extreme circumstances where this may be the case, such as when a company sells a put on its own equity. In this case, there is clearly a non-zero correlation between the probability of default and the exposure. There has been little empirical research relating market variables to default parameters, and it is generally ignored in modelling. In Chapter 5, we will present a simple way to model this effect.

1.2.2 Counterparty level
Aggregated exposure
Moving from the deal level to the counterparty level, we must aggregate the possible future exposure of all deals with the counterparty in question. This aggregation must take into account netting agreements and collateral, which we discuss briefly in the next section.

1.2.3 Portfolio level
Joint default probabilities
Even if we know the values of the default probabilities of each counterparty in a portfolio, the distribution of defaults and, in particular, the tail of this distribution will still depend on the joint default probabilities. If we have individual default probabilities p_1 and p_2, the joint default probability (probability that both default) is only $p_1 \times p_2$ if the events are independent. Historically, default rates have varied substantially from year to year. There are two potential interpretations of this observation, as outlined below.

1. The default probabilities themselves are random quantities that depend on a set of underlying variables. The underlying variables driving the default probabilities depend to some extent on the nature of the counterparty in question (eg, geographical location, industry), but also on more general factors (eg, the state of the economy). The default probabilities decrease (increase) under "good" (bad) economic conditions.

This is the approach taken by KMV, CreditRisk+ and McKinseys, as described later in this chapter.

2. Although the probabilities do not change, the underlying events are themselves correlated. A counterparty specific part (idiosyncratic or firm-specific risk) and country/industry contributions determine this correlation. A high correlation will occur among counterparties in similar countries or industries while unrelated entities will have only a small correlation. CreditMetrics advocates this approach.

The second assumption is the one we will follow in most of our analysis – hence we will now describe default events as being correlated rather than default probabilities being stochastic. However, the estimation of default correlation is a rather difficult issue. In equity markets, correlation can be easily measured by observing liquid stock prices. However, for relatively infrequent default events, this is much more difficult, and the confidence intervals on the estimated parameters will be high.

Joint credit migration probabilities

Following on from the above discussion of joint default probabilities, it seems reasonable to assume that if default events are correlated, then so are changes in credit quality. For example, in the case of an investment grade portfolio, even if there are no defaults, there may be a significant chance that a rather high proportion of the counterparties will be downgraded. This would lead to a large mark-to-market loss in the portfolio. In another example, suppose that two counterparties, believed to be very highly correlated, have different default probabilities, so they cannot always default at the same time. However, given that they are so highly correlated, the default of one counterparty should surely imply that there is some effect on the other one. The answer to this may be that the second counterparty may be downgraded if the first one defaults. For estimation and implementation, it would therefore seem natural that the same model should be used for generating both joint defaults and joint credit migrations.

1.3 TRADITIONAL APPROACHES TO MANAGING CREDIT RISK

The advent of the secondary markets for loans and other debt securities, together with the growth of the credit derivatives market and the development of securitisation techniques, has opened up new opportunities for active credit risk management. For completeness, we review some of the traditional approaches to credit risk management, which are still commonly used, such as credit limits, netting agreements and collateral arrangements.

1.3.1 Credit limits

Traditionally, credit limits have been used to control the amount of exposure a financial institution can have to each transacting counterparty. In particular, there has been a cap on the total exposure, the value of which depends on the credit rating of the counterparty. However, this is at odds with the "Banker's Paradox", since it implies that a financial institution should stop transacting with a counterparty with whom it has a very good relationship, but high exposure. This is the case because the risk of a position will increase with increasing exposure. Although it is likely that a bank will have a number of large exposures with certain clients, these must be controlled where possible, and the returns made must truly reflect the risks taken. Looking at credit risk from a portfolio perspective allows the risks and returns of each position to be properly quantified. This approach is safer and more efficient than the somewhat arbitrary approach of credit lines, as the latter considers counterparties on an individual basis and not their contributions to the portfolio as a whole.

1.3.2 Netting agreements
Netting is relevant only when there is more than one transaction with a counterparty. A netting agreement is a contract that is legally binding through the existence of a signed master agreement. It allows exposures under the master agreement to be aggregated in the event of default. The amount owed by a defaulted counterparty can be offset against any amount that is to be received and only the net outstanding amount needs to be paid. This will reduce the overall loss. Without a master agreement, all money owed to a counterparty must be paid, while a fraction of all money owed will be received.

1.3.3 Collateral agreements
A way to reduce a credit exposure is to take collateral from the counterparty, as this can be liquidated in the event of default and set aside against any losses incurred. However, there is still the risk that the exposure at the time of default will be more than the market value of the collateral. There may, therefore, also be postings of collateral to account for the change in the exposure of the position. Even then, there remains the risk that the exposure will rise and default will occur before a required margin call. To model the effect of collateral appropriately, we should first consider the initial threshold (or "haircut") which determines the cushion with respect to the initial exposure. The probability that more collateral will be needed then depends on the volatility of the exposure. The minimum call amount (and the time between a margin call and the due payment) will influence the amount that can be lost between margin calls. Finally, we should also consider the correlation between the exposure and the collateral value. If these values are positively correlated, the credit risk on the position will be further decreased, as the value of the collateral is likely to increase with the exposure. For example, if the collateral for a cross-currency swap position

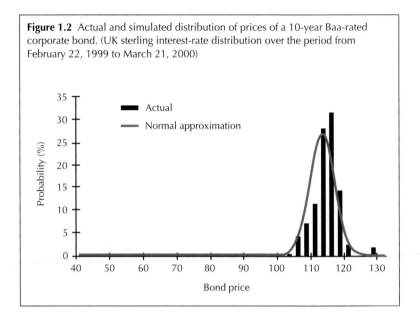

Figure 1.2 Actual and simulated distribution of prices of a 10-year Baa-rated corporate bond. (UK sterling interest-rate distribution over the period from February 22, 1999 to March 21, 2000)

is denominated in the currency we receive, we are better protected against the strengthening or weakening of that currency. In Chapter 8 we discuss collateral liquidation in an illiquid market, which is a situation that is quite often encountered in practice.

1.4 MARKET RISK VERSUS CREDIT RISK

A major difference between credit risk and market risk lies in their respective return distributions. For simplicity, we demonstrate this effect through an illiquid corporate bond. Very illiquid bonds could in principle be (and quite often are) included in the computation of the global credit exposure. Consider a corporate bond of face value 100 and maturity 10 years, paying a semi-annual coupon of 7.5% issued by a Baa-rated corporate. In

Table 1.1 Data used to calculate credit returns

Rating	Transition probability	Spread	Bond price
Aaa	0.02%	5bps	110.0
Aa	0.33%	10bps	109.6
A	5.95%	20bps	108.9
Baa	86.93%	50bps	106.7
Ba	5.30%	200bps	96.8
B	1.17%	400bps	85.4
Caa	0.12%	1000bps	60.2
Default	0.18%	–	44.1

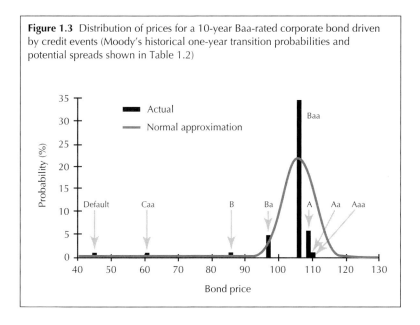

Figure 1.3 Distribution of prices for a 10-year Baa-rated corporate bond driven by credit events (Moody's historical one-year transition probabilities and potential spreads shown in Table 1.2)

Figure 1.2, we show a histogram of the distribution of market prices for this bond, based on the actual UK sterling interest rate distribution from February 22, 1999 to March 21, 2000. We see that the actual distribution is fairly well approximated by a normal distribution.

Next, we investigate the impact of credit risk on the price of this corporate bond, using historical data on ratings changes and some potential values of the credit spread in each rating class, as shown in Table 1.1. This dataset is discussed in the next section. This table shows that, for example, there is a 5.95% probability that a Baa- rated bond will be upgraded to an A, resulting in the spread tightening from 50bps to 20bps and leading to an increase in its price. We assume that in the event of default, the recovery value is 40% of the bond price just before the default event. In Figure 1.3, we show the distribution of returns due to credit migration and default for this bond. It is clear that a normal distribution is not a good approximation, since it does not capture the large losses that can occur. The normal distribution is symmetric, while the actual one has a fat tail to tail to left.

An obvious question to ask is whether the normal approximation, although not valid for a single bond, will be a reasonable approximation for a large portfolio. We will see that, usually, the answer to this question is that it will not. Unlike market returns, credit returns are not well approximated by a normal distribution. In Figure 1.4, we show typical market and credit returns for a portfolio consisting of a large number of assets. The credit-return distribution is characterised by a large negative skew, which arises from the significant (albeit small) probability of incurring a large loss.

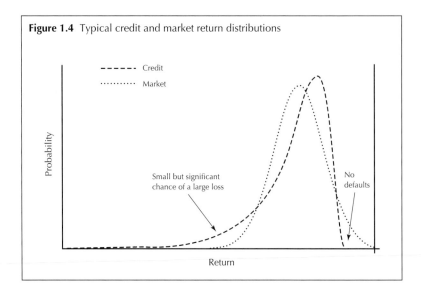

Figure 1.4 Typical credit and market return distributions

This is also true for a relatively homogeneous, well-diversified portfolio with small individual exposures.

1.4.1 Time horizon

Another important difference between credit risk and market risk is the relevant time horizon. For market risk, regulatory guidelines state that this need only be 10 days. Positions can usually be liquidated within such a period, assuming that there is enough liquidity in the market. For credit risk, the period to use is less clear, but must be considerably longer, as credit risk is not readily tradable.

It is becoming a convention that credit risk measurement is done on an annual time horizon, in part because budgets are annual. However, the actual time horizon used should reflect the security type, liquidity, maturity and credit worthiness of the underlying exposures. An interest rate swap may have a peak exposure several years in the future, which would give rise to the biggest risk, so it should therefore be risk-managed with respect to a longer horizon. A high-grade institution may have only a slight chance of default over a short period, but, because of the possibility of deterioration of its credit quality, it may be more likely to default over a longer horizon. In practice, more than one time horizon should be used, and they should be chosen following a detailed analysis of the portfolio of the financial institution.

1.5 HISTORICAL DATA
1.5.1 Default and credit migration probabilities

Historical transition matrices, such as those provided by Moody's (1997a),

Table 1.2 Moody's one-year transition matrix

	Aaa	Aa	A	Baa	Ba	B	Caa	Default
Aaa	93.4%	5.94%	0.64%	0.00%	0.02%	0.00%	0.00%	0.00%
Aa	1.61%	90.55%	7.46%	0.26%	0.09%	0.01%	0.00%	0.02%
A	0.07%	2.28%	92.44%	4.63%	0.45%	0.12%	0.01%	0.00%
Baa	0.05%	0.26%	5.51%	88.48%	4.76%	0.71%	0.08%	0.15%
Ba	0.02%	0.05%	0.42%	5.16%	86.91%	5.91%	0.24%	1.29%
B	0.00%	0.04%	0.13%	0.54%	6.35%	84.22%	1.91%	6.81%
Caa	0.00%	0.00%	0.00%	0.62%	2.05%	4.08%	69.20%	24.06%

provide average rating transition probabilities sampled over many thousands of firm years of data. The transition probabilities are obtained by analysing time-series data of credit-rating transitions for many different firms. A Moody's one-year transition matrix is shown in Table 1.2. The first column represents the initial rating and the first row the final one. For example, the probability of a Baa-rated company being downgraded to Ba in one year is 4.76%. The last column represents the default probabilities. The probability of a Baa defaulting in one year is estimated to be 0.15%.

There are clearly some inconsistencies in the above transition matrix. For example, the probability of default of an A-rated counterparty is zero; yet there is a non-zero probability that a supposedly more credit-worthy Aa-rated counterparty will go bankrupt. Such inconsistencies are clearly a result of the scarcity of data for these extremely unlikely events. We also note that, regardless of category, the most likely outcome is that the credit rating remains unchanged. Moody's (1997a) also make available transition matrices for longer periods. It is also possible to construct, by modification of a one-year matrix under certain assumptions, transition matrices for any period required. In this case, there are certain properties that such a computed transition matrix should be required to have. For example, it is reasonable to require that low-rated firms are always more risky. Note also that there is seemingly a "mean-reversion" effect in credit ratings, since good ratings (Aaa, Aa, A) are more likely to get worse rather than better, whereas poor ratings (Ba, B, Caa) have a greater probability of improving (assuming they do not default first!).

1.5.2 Recovery rates

Studies of recovery data have shown that the recovery value, in case of default, can vary substantially, depending on the seniority of the underlying debt. For example, Table 1.3 shows the recovery rates as reported by Moody's (1997b). There is clearly a large variance around the mean value, even within the same debt class. It is important to incorporate this uncertainty in the recovery rate to account for the fact that a worst case scenario

Table 1.3 Moody's (1997b) recovery rates based on debt seniority

Seniority	Mean	Standard deviation
Senior secured	53.80%	26.86%
Senior unsecured	51.13%	25.45%
Senior subordinated	38.52%	23.81%
Subordinated	32.74%	20.18%
Junior subordinated	17.09%	10.90%

may correspond to an especially low recovery rate, even if the expected recovery rate is high.

1.5.3 Default correlation

One of the most challenging tasks in credit risk management is the modelling of the correlation among default events. High default correlation can drastically increase the severity of the losses in a portfolio of many assets. Historical observations over many years can also be used to show that default events and credit movements among different firms are, in general, positively correlated. These correlations are mostly influenced by macroeconomic factors and depend on the general state of the economy. For example, see CreditMetrics (1997) for a convincing argument for the existence of positive default correlation and estimates of the correlation between counterparties according to ratings.

The main implication of positive default correlation is the increased probability of suffering abnormally large losses due to multiple "bad" credit events. Indeed, we will later show that this effect can be very substantial. There are two issues with modelling default correlations. First, there is the introduction of correlation among binary variables and the simulation from this distribution; unlike for a multivariate normal distribution, this is not a trivial issue. Second, there is the estimation of the required parameters.

The estimation of default correlations can be made directly from historical data or indirectly using an approach such as the KMV "Asset Value Model" (KMV, 1996). The advantage of the latter treatment is that company-specific information, such as industry and region, is naturally captured in the correlation estimation. Alternatively, we can enrich the historical data with some sort of macroeconomic analysis, such as in the model used by McKinsey & Company (Wilson, 1997) to incorporate the current state of the economy. At the end of this chapter, we will review the different approaches that have become standard in the industry.

Given the importance of default correlation, we will discuss it in detail in the next chapter. We will show how correlation between credit migration events and recovery rates can also be incorporated in one unified framework.

1.6 AN EXAMPLE OF DEFAULT LOSS DISTRIBUTION

1.6.1 A simple loan portfolio

In this section, we present an example of the quantification of credit risk for a simple hypothetical portfolio, making some important observations. By greatly simplifying matters, we aim to highlight the main features of credit risk that are important from a risk management perspective. We will keep the mathematics simple. For a further study of the relevant mathematics, the reader should consult any standard textbook on statistics.

Suppose we have a portfolio of n loans of the same maturity and notional values denoted by X_i. Assume that there is a probability p_i that the ith loan will not be repaid at maturity. We use a binary variable d_i to denote whether or not the ith loan is to be repaid. For this analysis, we ignore credit migration. We assume that there is no recovery in case of default.

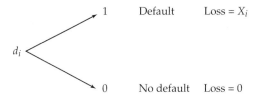

The distribution of d_i is such that, if we draw a large number of realisations, their average value will be p_i. In other words, the expected value of d_i is p_i or $E[d_i] = p_i$.

1.6.2 Expected loss

We can now define the loss, L_p, on the portfolio of loans as:

$$L_p = \sum_{i=1}^{n} X_i d_i \tag{1}$$

depending on the realised values of d_i. Since the X_is are constant we can rewrite the above expression as:

$$EL_p = E\left[L_p\right] = E\left[\sum_{i=1}^{n} X_i d_i\right] = \sum_{i=1}^{n} X_i E\left[d_i\right] = \sum_{i=1}^{n} X_i p_i \tag{2}$$

We now simplify further, and assume that the notional amounts and probabilities of default are all equal, ie,

$$p_i = p \ \forall i \ \text{ and } X_i = X \ \forall i$$

Table 1.4 Loss probabilities corresponding to $n = 100$, $X = 100$ and $p = 0.01$

k	L_p	$\binom{n}{k}$	$p^k(1-p)^{n-k}$	$\Pr(L_p = kX)$
0	0	1	0.366	0.366
1	100	100	0.004	0.370
2	200	4,950	$\sim 10^{-5}$	0.185
3	300	161,700	$\sim 10^{-7}$	0.061
4	400	3,921,225	$\sim 10^{-9}$	0.015
5	500	$\sim 10^7$	$\sim 10^{-11}$	0.003
6	600	$\sim 10^9$	$\sim 10^{-13}$	$\sim 10^{-4}$
7	700	$\sim 10^{10}$	$\sim 10^{-15}$	$\sim 10^{-5}$
8	800	$\sim 10^{11}$	$\sim 10^{-17}$	$\sim 10^{-6}$
9	900	$\sim 10^{12}$	$\sim 10^{-19}$	$\sim 10^{-7}$
10	1000	$\sim 10^{13}$	$\sim 10^{-21}$	$\sim 10^{-8}$
20	2000	$\sim 10^{20}$	$\sim 10^{-41}$	$\sim 10^{-20}$
30	3000	$\sim 10^{25}$	$\sim 10^{-61}$	$\sim 10^{-35}$
40	4000	$\sim 10^{28}$	$\sim 10^{-81}$	$\sim 10^{-53}$
50	5000	$\sim 10^{29}$	$\sim 10^{-101}$	$\sim 10^{-72}$

In this case, the expected loss is simply given by:

$$EL_p = np$$

1.6.3 Distribution of losses

We further assume that the default events of the various loans are independent. Therefore the probability of a given number of defaults k, resulting in a portfolio loss of kX, is given by the binomial distribution:

$$\text{Prob}\left(L_p = kX\right) = \binom{n}{k} p^k (1-p)^{n-k} \tag{3}$$

Number of combinations

Probability that k loans default

Probability that other $n-k$ loans do not default

The number of combinations represents the number of ways of achieving k defaults. It is given by:

$$\binom{n}{k} = \frac{n!}{k!(n-k)!}$$

Suppose that there are a total of 100 loans ($n = 100$), each of which has a notional value of 100 ($X = 100$), and also that the probability of default of each loan is 1% ($p = 0.01$). In Table 1.4, we show the probability of suffering various losses as given by the binomial distribution.

Figure 1.5 Loss distribution for $n = 100$, $X = 100$ and $p = 0.01$

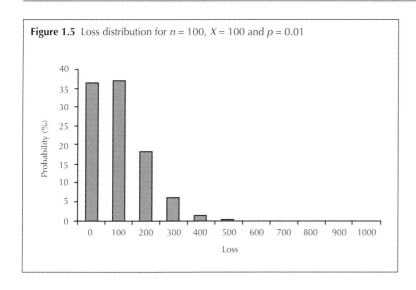

As the loss increases, the probability of achieving the required number of defaults ($p^k(1 - p)^{n-k}$) decreases, but the number of possible ways to achieve them, $\binom{n}{k}$, increases. However, the former effect is dominant, so the probability of more than 10% of the portfolio defaulting is very small. In fact, it is so small that it can be neglected. We can represent the losses in a simpler manner as in the frequency distribution shown in Figure 1.5. This is a direct consequence of the assumption that the default correlation is zero. If the default correlation was positive, then the occurrence of large losses would be a lot more likely. This would result in a longer tail for the distribution shown in Figure 1.5.

The expected loss for this portfolio is 100 and the probability of this loss occurring is 37%. The probability of losing more than the expected loss is 26%. Indeed, the probability of losing four times the expected loss is still significant at 1.5%. The expected loss alone is not sufficient for us to characterise the risk of the portfolio. We need, in addition, to have some measure of the deviation of the potential losses around the mean.

The variability of a distribution of n losses around the mean value can be characterised by the standard deviation that is the square root of the variance of the distribution. This is given by:[1]

$$\sigma\left(L_1, L_2, ..., L_n\right) = \frac{\sqrt{\sum_{j=1}^{n}\left(L_j - L\right)^2}}{n} \qquad (4)$$

We can compute the standard deviation using the above expression:

$$\sigma\left(L_p\right) =$$

$$\sqrt{0.366\times(0-100)^2 + 0.185\times(200-100)^2 + 0.061\times(300-100)^2 + ...}$$

$$= 99.5$$

For demonstration purposes, we also compute the standard deviation using properties of the binary distribution which should give the same result. As $\sigma^2(d_i) = p_i(1-p_i)$ and as the total variance is simply the sum of each individual one, we write:

$$\sigma^2\left(L_p\right) = \sigma^2\left(\sum_{i=1}^{n} X_i\, d_i\right)$$

$$= \sum_{i=1}^{n}\sigma^2\left(X_i\, d_i\right) = \sum_{i=1}^{n} X_i^2 p_i\left(1-p_i\right) = X\sqrt{np\left(1-p\right)} = 99.5 \qquad (5)$$

It is a straightforward task to calculate the standard deviation of a portfolio, even when the notionals and the default probabilities are not the same for each asset.

1.6.4 The normal approximation
The Central Limit theorem states that the sum of a large number of independent random variables converges to a normal distribution. A normal distribution is characterised entirely by its mean μ and variance σ^2 (or standard deviation).

The probability density function of a normal distribution is given by:

Table 1.5 Accuracy of the normal approximation of the credit loss distribution for $n = 100$, $X = 100$ and $p = 0.01$

L_p	Actual	Normal
0	0.366	0.242
100	0.370	0.401
200	0.185	0.242
300	0.061	0.053
400	0.015	0.004
500	0.003	$\sim 10^{-4}$
600	$\sim 10^{-4}$	$\sim 10^{-6}$
700	$\sim 10^{-5}$	$\sim 10^{-9}$
800	$\sim 10^{-6}$	$\sim 10^{-9}$
900	$\sim 10^{-7}$	$\sim 10^{-15}$
1000	$\sim 10^{-8}$	$\sim 10^{-19}$

$$\frac{1}{\sigma\sqrt{2\pi}}\exp\left[-\frac{1}{2}\left(\frac{x-\mu}{\sigma}\right)^2\right]$$

The probability of a value lying within one standard deviation of the mean is 66%. This means that the probability of experiencing a loss of more than one standard deviation from the mean is 16%. We can calculate the probability of exceeding any loss by computing the necessary number of standard deviations. For example, a loss that is exceeded no more than 1% of the time corresponds to 2.33 standard deviations.

The normal distribution seems to give a reasonable approximation around the mean of the credit loss distribution. However, when we consider the values shown in Table 1.5 for the tail (far right-hand side) of the distribution, this is clearly not the case. For example, we would underestimate the probability of a loss of 500 by a factor of 23 and underestimate the probability of a loss greater than 500 by over 100 times. This is clearly a crucial point and the normal approximation, although a very powerful and convenient tool, must be used with extreme caution when analysing credit portfolios. The approximation will perform even more poorly if the default correlation is positive, which will be the case for most portfolios.

1.6.5 Percentiles

The normal approximation is inadequate, as it can give completely inaccurate estimates of the probabilities of experiencing certain losses, especially in the tail of the distribution, where the biggest losses occur. The normal distribution does not capture the skews in typical credit portfolios, and this leads to an underestimate of the tail probabilities.

However, instead of the standard deviation, we can use a percentile as a measure of the variability of losses. The kth percentile of the distribution corresponds to a loss L_k, such that $\Pr(L_p > L_k) = \alpha$ or equivalently $\Pr(L_p < L_k) = 1 - \alpha$. This means that the probability of exceeding a loss of L_k is $1 - \alpha$. The percentile therefore gives either the true probability that a given loss will be exceeded or the maximum loss for a given confidence level, without making any assumptions about the underlying distribution.

Table 1.6 Accuracy of the normal approximation in percentile estimation

Percentile	Actual loss	Normal approximation
95th	400	263.7
99th	400	331.5
99.9th	500	407.5
99.97th	600	441.5

Figure 1.6 Ratio of the unexpected loss at the 99.9% confidence level of a homogeneous portfolio as estimated by the portfolio variance (3.09 standard deviations) and the actual percentile

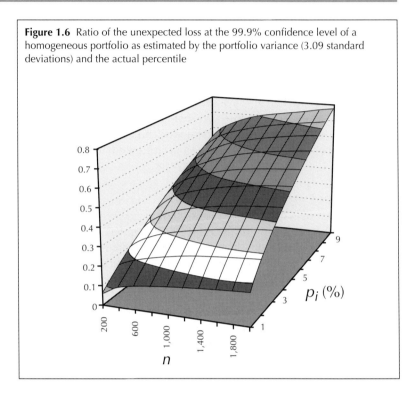

In Table 1.6 we illustrate some percentiles for the distribution of losses in the above example, and compare them to the normal approximation.[2]

From Table 1.6 we see that the normal approximation leads to an underestimate as expected. A legitimate question to ask is when the normal approximation is valid. This is illustrated in Figure 1.6, where we compare the ratio of the 99.9th percentile, as estimated using the portfolio variance (3.09 standard deviations), to the true 99.9th percentile for various homogeneous portfolios (ie, one in which the correlations, default probabilities and effective notionals are equal). We can see that as the number of assets in the portfolio and the default probability increase, the ratio slowly approaches one. However, given that the average default probability for a typical portfolio is low, it is clear that this measure will substantially underestimate the true unexpected loss.

Finally, we also notice that for this portfolio, the 95th and 99th percentiles are equal; this is due to the fact that the distribution we are looking at is highly discrete. In practice, for large portfolios this is rarely an issue. However, there are certain circumstances where we need to be aware of this drawback. We will need to address this point in Chapter 4 when we discuss a method for credit portfolio optimisation.

1.7 CREDIT RISK MODELS

During recent years, specialist teams in major financial institutions have developed several models that have either remained proprietary or become commercially available. In this section we review the latter models that have attracted a lot of attention from the financial community: JP Morgan's CreditMetrics, Credit Suisse Financial Products' CreditRisk[+] (1997), KMV's Portfolio Manager and McKinsey & Company's Credit Portfolio View (Wilson, 1997). In this section we review these models and point out both their commonalities and differences. (See also Koyluoglu and Hickman, 1998.)

1.7.1 KMV/CreditMetrics

These models use Merton's firm value model (1974) to calculate default probabilities based on the firm's capital structure and the asset return volatility. The Merton model states that a firm defaults when the value of its assets is lower than that of its liabilities when its debt matures.

In this model, sampling from a multivariate normal distribution, which represents the asset returns of the firm, can generate default events.

The Merton model uses an option valuation framework based on Black and Scholes (1973). The firm's assets are assumed to follow a lognormal random walk. Under the assumption that the firm will default when its liabilities exceed its assets, the default probability is given by[3]

$$p = N\left(-\frac{\ln\left(A_0 / X\right) + \left(r - \frac{1}{2}\sigma^2\right)T}{\sqrt{\sigma^2 T}}\right) \qquad (6)$$

where A_0 is the asset value of the firm today, X is the "strike" or face value of the firm's debt, σ is the asset volatility, T is the maturity of its debt and r is the risk-free rate. The above model is known to underestimate default probabilities, since default can often occur before a firm's assets exceeds its liabilities. KMV therefore use a modified approach to create an empirical estimate of default probabilities based on the distance to default (DD), given by:

$$DD = \frac{1 - \left(\text{Default point} / \text{Asset value}\right)}{\text{Asset volatility}} \qquad (7)$$

Firms with a higher volatility or gearing will therefore have a shorter DD, and a higher default probability. The default probability is obtained by comparing the DD to KMV's proprietary database of empirically observed DDs for companies that have actually defaulted. KMV claim that this relationship is stable across time and in different environments.

CreditMetrics adopts a similar approach to KMV, but rather than esti-mate default probabilities directly, it uses historical data based on ratings (see Chapter 3). By adding additional thresholds, credit migrations (tran-sition between ratings, ie upgrades and downgrades) may also be incorporated.

1.7.2 Correlation structure in KMV/CreditMetrics

The KMV/CreditMetrics framework is very powerful, since the joint default probability for a pair of assets:

$$p_{12} = \Phi\left(N^{-1}\left(p_1\right), N^{-1}\left(p_2\right); \lambda\right) \tag{8}$$

where Φ denotes the cumulative bivariate normal density function that is computationally tractable (see Chapter 3). More generally, the probability of the assets one to k defaulting (note that this is not the probability of k defaults) is an integral over the multivariate normal distribution:

$$p_{12\ldots k} = \Phi\left(N^{-1}\left(p_1\right), N^{-1}\left(p_2\right), \ldots, N^{-1}\left(p_k\right); \lambda\right) \tag{9}$$

The above formulae require an estimate of the asset return correlation, λ, among all pairs of assets. The assets returns are calculated using easily observable equity returns. Although this method has the drawback of over-looking the differences between equity and asset correlations, it is more accurate than using a fixed correlation, and is based on data that are more readily available than, say, credit spreads or actual rating changes.

It is inefficient to produce correlations for every pair of obligors that a user might need, this is because of the scarcity of data for some obligors, and the resulting size of the correlation matrix. CreditMetrics therefore use cor-relations within a set of indices and a mapping scheme to build the obligor-by-obligor correlations from the index correlations. There are two steps, as follows:

1. Use industry indices in particular countries to construct a matrix of cor-relations between these industries (so one particular element might be the correlation between UK finance and US steel).
2. Map individual obligors by industry participation. For example, a com-pany might be mapped as 80% UK and 20% US, 70% steel and 30% finance. By multiplying out, we have: 56% UK steel, 24% UK finance, 14% US steel, 6% US finance.

CreditMetrics uses the following:

$$r = \underbrace{w_0 r_0}_{\substack{\text{Company} \\ \text{idiosyncratic}}} + \underbrace{w_1 r_1 + \cdots + w_k r_k}_{\text{Sectorial}} \tag{10}$$

Table 1.7 Number of defaults at the 99.97% confidence level for a homogeneous portfolio of 50 assets with default probabilities of 0.1% using KMV/CreditMetrics model for different asset return correlations

	0%	30%	50%	70%
Default correlation, ρ	0.0%	1.39%	5.33%	15.87%
Number of defaults	2	5	10	17

in which r and the (r_i) are Gaussian of mean 0 and variance 1; r is the normalised asset return of the company, r_0 is the specific risk and the remaining rs are the normalised asset returns of the country/industry indices that affect the obligor in question. The random variable r_0 is uncorrelated with all the others, while the remaining rs we have $\mathrm{Corr}(r_i, r_j) = \rho_{ij}$. The obligor specific risk (OSR) is related to w_0 by

$$\mathrm{OSR} = 1 - \sqrt{1 - w_0^2}$$

and is a "given parameter". Let α_i denote the participation ratios of the obligor in the various sectors (in the example above, these were 56%, 24%, 14%, 6%), and σ_i denote the sector volatilities. The remaining weights (w_i) are given by the equation

$$w_i = \frac{\alpha_i \sigma_i}{\sqrt{\sum_{i,j=1}^{n} \alpha_i \alpha_j \sigma_i \sigma_j \rho_{ij}}} \times (1 - \mathrm{OSR}) \tag{11}$$

Note that

$$w_0^2 + \sum_{i,j=1}^{n} w_i w_j \rho_{ij} = 1$$

which must be so if r is to have unit variance. KMV adopts a similar but more complex strategy.

$$[\text{Firm return}] = \begin{cases} [\text{Firm-specific effect}] \\ + [\text{Country-specific effects}] \\ + [\text{Industry-specific effects}] \\ + [\text{Industry sector effects}] \\ + [\text{Regional economic effects}] \\ + [\text{Global economic effects}] \end{cases}$$

The full details of the estimation procedure are proprietary parts of the

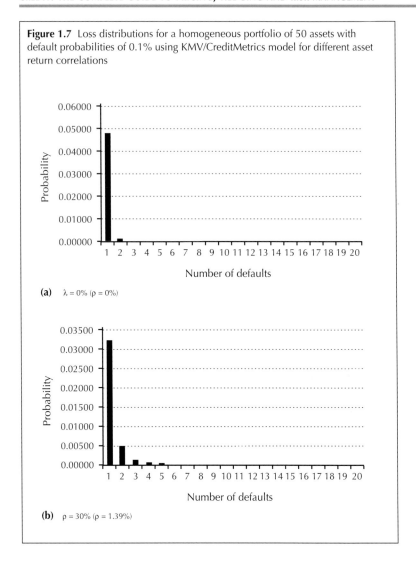

Figure 1.7 Loss distributions for a homogeneous portfolio of 50 assets with default probabilities of 0.1% using KMV/CreditMetrics model for different asset return correlations

KMV software. Table 1.7 and Figure 1.7 illustrate the loss distributions for different values of the asset return correlation. Below, we summarise the advantages and disadvantages of the KMV/CreditMetrics approaches.

The advantages are that:

❑ a Monte Carlo simulation is easy to perform;
❑ credit migration can be incorporated; and
❑ it is relatively easy to estimate the underlying multivariate Gaussian structure.

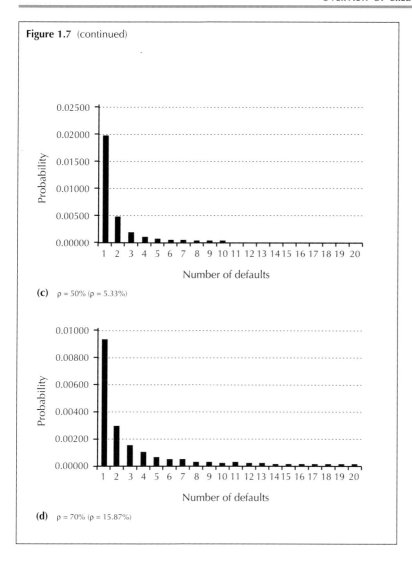

Figure 1.7 (continued)

(c) $\rho = 50\%$ ($p = 5.33\%$)

(d) $\rho = 70\%$ ($p = 15.87\%$)

The disadvantages are that::

❑ the model is analytically intractable – we must use a simulation to compute loss distribution;
❑ there is uncertainty as to whether probability of multiple defaults is realistic, or not; and
❑ for large portfolios, the computational load scales as $O(N^2)$.

1.7.3 Credit Portfolio View
The McKinsey model is an econometric model that takes the current

macroeconomic environment into account. Rather than using historical default rate averages calculated from decades of data, the McKinsey model uses default probabilities that are conditional on the current state of the economy.

The default probability of a particular obligor is obtained from the (normally distributed) macroeconomic "explanatory" variable by the logistic transformation:

$$p = \frac{1}{1+e^y} \tag{12}$$

The independent macroeconomic factors used as explanatory variables in the model are then simulated to create numerous possible states of the economy over the horizon. These outcomes are then used to determine the expected default rates.

The model is fitted using the historical average default rates and economic data for different rating, industry and country pairings. One practical difficulty is the lack of data with which to calibrate the model. As the data are further refined to make them more granular (eg, by increasing the number of rating classes, industries or geographical regions), the observations become more sparse and the standard error of the estimates increases. It becomes difficult to verify the accuracy of such an economic model other than by observing default probabilities increasing during economic downturns. Another problem is model risk itself: does the model correctly simulate the default process based on the selected economic factors? Are these factors correctly modelled? Few institutions can predict interest rates, let alone the resulting default rates based on these.

1.7.4 CreditRisk+

This is an actuarial model, which means that it is based on probabilities alone and does not infer an underlying causality or default process. Default probabilities are assigned to rating classes that are then mapped to individual exposures. CreditRisk+ also uses the volatility (standard deviation) of default rates as an input. A certain type of correlation structure is imposed; the parameters of this can be inferred from the default rate volatility. This produces the tail of the portfolio. The CreditRisk+ documentation recommends a volatility approximately equal to the default rate itself. Neither the theory nor the documentation provide an insight into the appropriate value.

The correlation structure is obtained as follows. The loss from the whole portfolio is assumed to follow a Poisson distribution with parameter K (ie, if there are n unit exposures each with default probability p, then $K = np$) which is itself a random variable. In that case the number of defaults M has the distribution

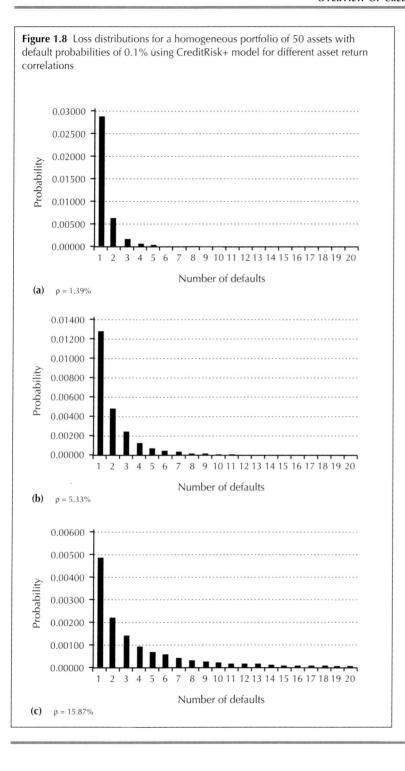

Figure 1.8 Loss distributions for a homogeneous portfolio of 50 assets with default probabilities of 0.1% using CreditRisk+ model for different asset return correlations

Table 1.8 Number of defaults at the 99.97% confidence level for a homogeneous portfolio of 50 assets with default probabilities of 0.1% using CreditRisk+ model for different default correlations

Default correlation, ρ	0.0%	1.39%	5.33%	15.87%
Number of defaults	2	4	9	17

$$P(M=r) = \int \frac{e^{-k}k^r}{r!} dG(k) \tag{13}$$

where G is the distribution function of K. If K has a $\Gamma(v_K, \alpha_K)$ distribution, as CreditRisk+ recommends, then

$$P(M=r) = \int_0^\infty \frac{e^{-k}k^r}{r!} \frac{e^{-\alpha_K k}\alpha_K^{v_K} k^{v_K-1}}{\Gamma(v_K)} dk$$

$$= \frac{\alpha_K^v}{(\alpha_K+1)^{r+v}} \frac{\Gamma(r+v_K)}{r!\Gamma(v_K)} \tag{14}$$

For a finite number of assets, it is more convenient to work with the distribution of $p = K/n$, which will also have a Gamma distribution, but with parameters $v = v_K/n$ and $\alpha = \alpha_K$. The probability that one particular asset defaults is v/α, and the probability that two particular assets default is $v/\alpha^2 + (v/\alpha)^2$ (these being the first two moments of the Gamma distribution). The default correlation is therefore $\rho = 1/(v - \alpha)$.

One possible objection to this treatment is that the distribution of the default probability should be bounded above by 1. Therefore, the Beta distribution would be a more appropriate choice. This has the same analytical tractability as the Gamma case discussed above. For, if p is B (a, b)-distributed, then the number of defaults follows this distribution:

$$P(M=r) = \int_0^1 \frac{p^{a-1}(1-p)^{b-1}}{B(a,b)} \binom{n}{r} p^r (1-p)^{n-r} dp$$

$$= \frac{B(a+r, b+n-r)}{B(a,b)} \binom{n}{r} \tag{15}$$

where B $(,)$ denotes the Beta function. Further, the probability that one particular asset defaults is $\bar{p} = a/(a + b)$ and the probability that two particular assets default is $a(a + 1)/(a + b)(a + b + 1)$. The default correlation is $\rho = 1/(a + b + 1)$. Hence $a = \bar{p}(1/\rho - 1)$ and $b = (1 - \bar{p})(1/\rho - 1)$.

To compare the results with those of KMV/CreditMetrics (see Table 1.7, Figure 1.7), we have used the same default correlations ρ, and present the same results as shown previously (see Table 1.8, Figure 1.8).

1.8 CONCLUSION

Credit risk encompasses counterparty risk for loan and derivative portfolios as well as issuer risk for bonds. In this book, we will cover the former, with a few references to the latter where appropriate. The traditional approach to managing credit risk is the use of credit limits, netting agreements and collateral. These techniques, although useful, have proved inadequate for the plethora of capital market products that are traded. Internal models have been developed during recent years by major financial institutions. New mathematical and statistical techniques have been introduced which were not required for developing market risk models. The two main differences between market and credit risk are as follows.

1. The analysis of credit risk is performed over a longer time horizon than market risk. This is driven by the illiquidity of the corresponding positions. It requires more refined simulation techniques for the evolution of the market exposure.
2. The credit loss distribution is highly asymmetric and the normal approximation produces erroneous results. It is characterised by a large negative skew, which arises due to the significant (albeit small) probability of incurring a large loss.

Derivative portfolios are distinguished from loan portfolios by the fact that their exposures are random over time, since they are marked-to-market. In order to compute the credit loss distribution of a derivative portfolio, we need to model:

1. The evolution of the underlying market variables, ie, interest rates, FX rates, and stock prices driven by the underlying volatilities and correlations; and
2. the credit parameters, ie, default and credit migration events, driven by default and credit migration probabilities, correlation and recovery rates.

One of the most crucial parameters that drive the tails of the credit loss distribution is the default correlation matrix. The financial industry has placed particular emphasis on estimating this matrix. Various packages, such as KMV/CreditMetrics, Credit Portfolio View and CreditRisk+, are commercially available. KMV/CreditMetrics are option-based models that calculate the default probabilities based on the firm's capital structure and the asset return volatility. Credit Portfolio View is an econometric model that takes into account the current macroeconomic environment. CreditRisk+ is an actuarial model. It is based on probabilities alone and it does not infer an underlying causality or default process.

1 Commonly, in order to derive an unbiased estimator, the denominator in this expression is $n - 1$ instead of n. In this case, as the mean of the distribution is known, it is appropriate to use n.

2 The probabilities for the normal distribution can be determined by $\mu + c\sigma$, ie, a certain number of standard deviations away from the mean. The values of c required in the above example are 1.644, 2.326, 3.090 and 3.432 respectively.

3 This is actually under the risk-neutral measure. Under the historical measure, we should substitute μ (the actual return) for r in the above expression.

BIBLIOGRAPHY

Black, F., and M. Scholes, 1973, "The Pricing of Options and Corporate Liabilities", *Journal of Political Economy* 81, pp. 637–59.

Carty, L., and D. Lieberman, 1996a, "Corporate Bond Defaults and Default Dates 1938–1995", Moody's Investor Services, *Global Credit Research*, January.

Carty, L., and D. Lieberman, 1996b, "Defaulted Bank Loan Recoveries", Moody's Investor Services, *Global Credit Research*, November.

Credit Suisse Financial Products, 1997, *CreditRisk+ – A Credit Risk Management Framework.*

Gupton, G. M., C. C. Finger and M. Bhatia, 1997, CreditMetrics – Technical Document, Morgan Guaranty Trust (New York: JP Morgan).

Jarrow, R., and D. R. van Deventer, 1999, "Practical Use of Credit Risk Models in Loan Portfolio and Counterparty Exposure Risk Management", in D. Shimko (ed), *Credit Risk: Models and Management* (London: Risk Books), pp. 301–9.

JP Morgan & Co. Incorporated, 1997, CreditMetrics.

Keenan, S. C., L. V. Carty and D. T. Hamilton, 1999, "An Empirical Analysis of Corporate Rating, Migration, Default and Recovery", in *Derivative Credit Risk: Further Advances in Measurement and Management,* Second Edition (London: Risk Books), pp. 37–51.

KMV Corporation, 1996, "Portfolio Manager Description, Usage and Specification, Version 4.0", San Francisco.

Koyluoglu, H. U., and A. Hickman, 1998, "Reconcilable Differences", *Risk,* October, pp. 56–62.

Merton, R., 1974, "On the Pricing of Corporate Debt: The Risk Structure of Interest Rates", *Journal of Finance,* 29, pp. 449–70.

Moody's Investor Services, 1997, "Rating Migration and Credit Quality Correlation, 1920–1996", *Global Credit Research,* July [http://www.moodysqra.com/research].

Standard and Poor's, 1997, "Ratings Performance 1996: Stability and Transition", Special Report, February [http://www.standardandpoors.com/ResourceCenter/index.html].

Wilson, T., 1997(a), "Portfolio Credit Risk, Part I", *Risk,* September, pp. 111–17.

Wilson, T., 1997(b), "Portfolio Credit Risk, Part II", *Risk,* October, pp. 56–61.

Exposure Measurement

2.1 INTRODUCTION

A traditional and well-used credit risk management technique is controlling the underlying market exposure to each counterparty. Banks require that there be a credit line for each counterparty they transact with. The credit line, set and controlled by a credit officer, will determine the maximum exposure that is allowed at a series of points in the future. The credit line will, therefore, limit the amount that could be lost at default. The size of the credit line must be set with a number of factors in mind. One of the most important factors is the probability of default. If this is low, a larger limit will be more tolerable than for a riskier counterparty. Other determining factors are collateralisation, netting agreements and the characteristics of the underlying transactions, ie, liquidity, complexity, etc. These factors may also determine the length of the credit line. For example, for transactions that would be hard to trade out of, were credit quality to deteriorate, the financial institution may decide to extend the line only up to a certain point, thereby effectively limiting the maturity of the allowed trades. The main drawback of this approach is that it can be overly conservative and difficult, if not impossible, to quantify for a portfolio consisting of deals with more than one counterparty. Also, it fails to take into account the diversification effect, ie the fact that default correlation is not equal to one.

To utilise credit lines for effective credit risk management, there needs to be a sensible method for consistently calculating the potential future exposure on all deals. The potential exposure describes the projected worst-case change in the present value of a deal, or several deals under a master agreement. Since credit risk needs to be assessed over a relatively long horizon, the variation of the potential exposure over time is important, since it shows the potential loss if default occurs at any point in the future. The potential exposure is a useful measure that incorporates both the average value of a deal, or a portfolio of deals, and their future variability.

Two general factors are important in determining the credit exposure at some point in the future, and therefore the peak exposure, for a single transaction or a portfolio of transactions with the same counterparty.

1. Over time, there will be greater variability/uncertainty in the market variables, resulting in greater exposure as time progresses.
2. For a multitude of transactions, cashflows will be paid over time, causing the outstanding "notional" to decrease, eventually dropping to zero at maturity. Known as "pull-to-par", this is the case for an interest rate swap.

These two effects act in opposite directions, the former increasing the credit exposure over time and the latter decreasing it. It is, therefore, possible that the peak credit exposure will occur at some point between the inception and the maturity of the deal. Different instruments generate completely different credit exposure profiles. An instrument with roughly equal payments throughout its lifetime will have a smaller exposure than one with a large payment made at maturity. An instrument whose value depends on a market variable that is mean-reverting, such as interest rates, will have a smaller future credit exposure due to the mean-reversion. The future exposure profile of a contract is crucial for determining its credit risk. In this chapter, we show typical exposure profiles over time for a number of different products. The exposure is simply the percentile of the future PV of a particular transaction at a certain confidence level. Of course, this means that the precise definition of exposure is somewhat arbitrary. In the examples presented in this chapter, we use the 84th percentile, which, for a normal distribution, represents one standard deviation from the forward or the expected value. We do not use the standard deviation directly, since exposure distributions can deviate significantly from normality, particularly for derivative products.

In the computation of value-at-risk (VAR) for market risk, a common assumption is to use the sensitivity of the portfolio to each of the under-lying market variables (the so-called "delta approximation"), instead of performing the full-blown simulation. This approximation can on occa-sions be dubious, since financial products, especially derivatives, tend to be inherently non-linear. For market risk, where the measurements are only over a period of a few days, this linear approximation is possibly justifiable, whereas for credit risk, where we consider much longer periods, it is not.

A common way to generate potential exposures is to use Monte Carlo simulation based on some assumption regarding the joint distribution of the underlying variables. By simulating many realisations of interest rates, FX rates and equity paths, transactions can be valued, on a deal-by-deal basis, at a number of time-points on these paths. The full correlation matrix of the underlying variables is introduced into the simulation, resulting in correlated simulated exposures. The exposure data is then aggregated. The aggregation is often on a counterparty basis, in compliance with active netting agreements. Netting agreements, such as the International Swaps and Derivatives (ISDA) Master Agreement, are legal contracts that allow liabilities to a counterparty to be offset against exposures to that same counterparty in the case of default. A netting agreement decreases the exposure in case of default to the net difference between the liabilities in both directions. The exposures need to be further adjusted to account for any collateral held against various positions. The treatment of collateral is a complex problem that should take the following into account:

❑ that the value of the collateral will not be perfectly correlated with that of the underlying position; and
❑ its amount will not change continuously to match the exposure, since it is called in blocks.

2.2 EXPOSURE SIMULATION

As we will show in the next chapter, one of the most significant factors driving the capital of a typical credit portfolio is the process followed by the underlying market variables. This process determines the evolution of the exposure of the portfolio at hand across time. We need financial models, appropriately calibrated, that will then allow the financial institution to capture the uncertainty of the future exposure, since greater uncertainty will lead to greater risk. Note that generating exposures is inherently different from arbitrage pricing or risk-neutral valuation. For risk management, we are interested in the distribution of the actual exposure in the future. For the technically minded, we point out that the computations are performed under the historical probability and not under the risk-neutral, which is the case for pricing.

The future exposure of a financial instrument will be driven by one or more market variables. Next, we briefly discuss simple standard models for the evolution of interest rates and FX rates. We also discuss the pros and cons of using rather simple models for the evolution of the underlying compared to using more sophisticated ones.

2.2.1 Interest rates

We outline the important attributes that a model for generating a realistic evolution of the interest rates for our purposes should have.

❑ It should match the current yield curve, in order to price correctly linear interest rate products today, eg, spot and forward interest rate swaps. In other words, the model should not allow arbitrage.
❑ It must account for different possible yield curve movements in the future (parallel shifts, steepenings and inversions).

The model should exhibit a realistic volatility structure. The volatility parameters should be calibrated either on historical or market data, depending on the application. In the second approach, the parameters should be set such that the model correctly prices the fundamental instruments that will be used for pricing and hedging. For the purposes of this analysis, these instruments will be standard European caps and swaptions.

Probably the simplest possible model[1] that meets the above criteria is the one-factor Hull and White (or extended Vasicek) model (Hull and White, 1990). The "short rate" (ie, short-term interest rate) follows the stochastic process:

$$dr = [\theta(t) - ar]dt + \sigma_r dW_t \tag{1}$$

In this model, r follows a normal random walk with mean-reversion. The instantaneous volatility depends on the level of the interest rate. Because of mean-reversion, when the short rate is above a certain "mean" level, it reverts back to its "mean". The speed of mean-reversion is determined by a. The mean-reversion level $\theta(t)$ is time-dependent. This allows this model to be fitted to the initial yield curve. The parameters a and σ_r need to be estimated either from historical or market data. Although the yield curve is not modelled directly, it can be "reconstructed" at any point, knowing $\theta(t)$, a, σ_r and the current short rate r_t. The basic yield curve movements observed in practice (parallel shifts, steepenings and inversions) can be obtained, although more complex changes in the shape of the yield curve cannot.

In the Hull and White model, the standard deviation at time t of a zero-coupon bond maturing at time T is given by:

$$\sigma\left(B(t,T)\right) = \sigma_r \left[\frac{1 - \exp\left(-a(T-t)\right)}{a(T-t)} \right] \tag{2}$$

If we can estimate the standard deviation (volatility) of zero-coupon bond prices of various maturities, we can imply estimated values of σ_r and a (eg, by least squares). We observe that, from the above equation, if the zero-coupon bond price volatility is increasing with maturity, then the mean-reversion will be negative. This is not a particularly pleasant situation, since it implies that the interest rates are exploding. A conservative way to get around this is to set the mean-reversion to zero and the volatility to be the maximum of the observed bond price volatilities.

The advantages of using the above model are that it is easy to implement as a Monte Carlo simulation or tree (Hull and White, 1993). It allows a fair degree of analytical tractability, eg, explicit formulae for the values of caps/floors and interest rate swaptions can be derived; the model also has the ability to value interest rate and cross-currency swaps (as the yield curve can be reconstructed at any point). It is also easy to extend to multiple currencies, since we model each currency as described above, however, we must take into account correlations among the interest rates of each currency and among the interest rates and FX rates. These values can be readily estimated using historical data. The model is also simple to explain as a basic, but reasonably realistic, description of interest rate behaviour.

Criticisms of the above model are that it allows negative interest rates, since the shocks to the yield curve follow a normal distribution, and it is restrictive in the possible yield curve movements that it captures. In regard to the former point, negative interest rates have occasionally been experienced. However, the probability of having negative rates in this model will almost certainly be too high, especially when the interest rates are low, such as for the Japanese yen. With the yield curve restricted in the way it can move, we may feel that we will "miss" some of the risk. However, our experience has been that only under quite extreme circumstances can this be the case.

A one-factor interest rate model, as described above, cannot account for all of the variability in yield curve movements that is observed historically. A common alternative model used for simulation of interest rates is a multi-factor simulation of the principal factors in describing yield curve movements. Historically, most of the observed movements in yield curves can be explained in terms of three principal factors. These factors correspond to parallel shifts, twists and butterfly movements. The advantage of using such a model is clearly that it is more flexible and realistic. The disadvantages are that the implementation is more difficult, as the dimensionality is increased and the calibration is more complex. There will be no analytical tractability within such a model. Finally, the extension to multiple currencies is more complex; we now need to estimate the correlations between the different principal factors for each yield curve, rather than simply the correlation between the short-term interest rates.

Our own preference is to use the simpler and more transparent approach with fewer parameters rather than the more complex model. To highlight our reasons, consider – for example – analysing the risk of a single currency portfolio. In the one-factor model we described above, there is only one parameter that drives the risk, namely the volatility of the interest rate and mean reversion (a). If a risk manager is concerned with the risk of his portfolio, it is easy to do a sensitivity analysis with respect to this parameter, and maybe choose a conservative value for the risk management. Such an approach will probably be better appreciated than a long theoretical discussion on how to explain the risk within a more complex multi-factor model. In short, it is better to have a simple model that can be easily understood by senior management or risk managers than a more complex model that cannot.

It can be shown, using principal component analysis, that yield curve movements can be largely explained using two or three factors (eg, see Rebonato, 1998). An obvious way to model the yield curve is to model directly the first n factors (eg, $n = 3$) that account for almost all the variance in yield curve movements. An example of this is described by Jamshidian and Zhu (1997). Such an approach would be expected to be more realistic than the one-factor approach. However, we have not found the latter model to significantly underestimate the risk, and furthermore note that in the Jamshidian and Zhu paper, the results when using two factors or three factors are virtually identical, even though the third factor accounts for between 3% and 10% of the variance (depending on the currency).

2.2.2 FX rates

The FX rates are modelled as lognormal variables according to the following process:

$$dX = \mu(t)Xdt + \sigma_{FX}XdW_t \qquad (3)$$

This ensures that the FX rates are always positive. The drift function, $\mu(t)$, can be calibrated to the forward FX rates, ie, it is uniquely determined by the spot FX and the shape of the two yield curves. For the analysis we are performing, a very important parameter is the FX volatility, σ_{FX}. We also need to estimate the correlation between the FX rates and the spot interest rates. For n different currencies, there will be a total of $2n - 1$ rates to be modelled (n interest rates and $n - 1$ FX rates) and we therefore need to estimate a correlation matrix of dimension $2n - 1$.

One criticism of the above model is that there is no mean-reversion as there was for interest rates. This means that there is a chance that the FX rates will become unrealistically large or small, especially for long time horizons. However, since the omission of mean-reversion represents a conservative assumption, we do not try to incorporate it. A further problem is that the estimation of mean-reversion in FX rates is difficult and unstable.

2.3 TYPICAL EXPOSURES

This section demonstrates the exposure profiles for various standard fixed-income instruments.

2.3.1 Standard interest rate swaps – same payment dates

Usually, the fixed rate on an interest rate swap will be set so that the initial PV (and therefore exposure) is zero. Depending on the movement of interest rates, it is possible that the future exposure becomes positive or negative. Of course, only positive exposures are of importance for assessing credit risk, since negative exposures do not lead to a loss in the event of default.

Consider a five-year payer interest rate swap, where we pay fixed amounts and receive floating payments, all quarterly, in US dollars. The exposure and the forward value for this swap are shown in Figure 2.1. The peak exposure occurs at about 1.75 years. Under simplified assumptions,

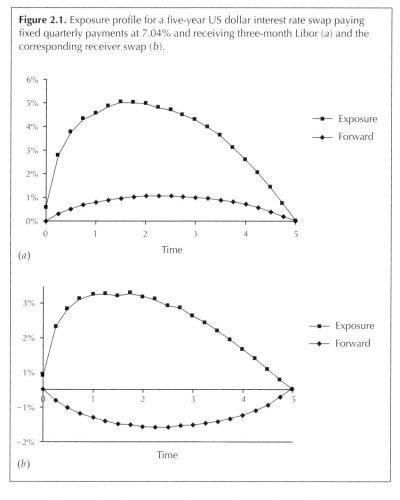

Figure 2.1. Exposure profile for a five-year US dollar interest rate swap paying fixed quarterly payments at 7.04% and receiving three-month Libor (*a*) and the corresponding receiver swap (*b*).

(*a*)

(*b*)

it is well known that this can be shown to be one third of the maturity of the swap. This is a result of a balance between payments being made and effectively decreasing the notional at risk and the greater uncertainty of the underlying yield curve evolution over time.

In Figure 2.2, we see the exposure of the corresponding receiver swap (ie, pay floating, receive fixed). We notice that the exposure is not quite as high in this case. The reason for this is that the yield curve is upward-sloping, which means that the swap rate is greater than the spot interest rate. We therefore expect the first fixed payment to be greater than the first floating payment. This will create a greater exposure for the payer swap than for the receiver swap. Of course, for payments near the end of the life of the swap, this effect is likely to be reversed, but the exposure here is driven by the large uncertainty as to the shape of the yield curve in several

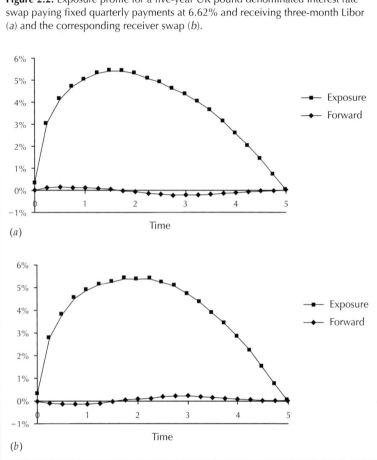

Figure 2.2. Exposure profile for a five-year UK pound denominated interest rate swap paying fixed quarterly payments at 6.62% and receiving three-month Libor (a) and the corresponding receiver swap (b).

years time. In general, for upward-sloping yield curves, a payer swap has a higher exposure than a receiver swap, while the opposite is true if the yield curve is downwards sloping.

For humped yield curves, it is unclear which swap carries more risk. Consider the UK pound example shown in Figure 2.2. The humped yield curve means that the forward value of the payer swap is initially positive and then it becomes negative (and vice versa for the receiver). The overall effect of this is that the swaps themselves are almost "equally risky".

The last point we note is the effect of maturity on the exposure of an interest rate swap. In Figure 2.3, we show that the exposure of an interest rate swap increases with maturity. This is due to the increased number of payments and increased uncertainty of the magnitude of the later payments on the floating leg.

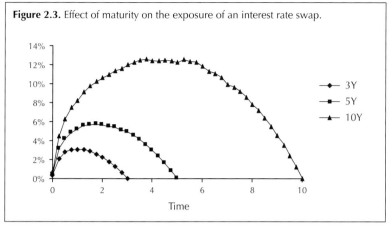

Figure 2.3. Effect of maturity on the exposure of an interest rate swap.

2.3.2 Swaps with unequal payment frequencies

In the above example, we considered a swap where the payments had the same frequency. However, it is common for the frequencies of the two legs to be unequal. This can have a substantial impact on the exposure. In Figure 2.4*a*, we compare the exposure of a standard payer swap to that of a swap where the fixed rate is paid semi-annually rather than quarterly. This has the effect of decreasing the exposure, as half of the payments have effectively been moved forward by three months and they make their positive contribution to the exposure three months later. Note that at six-monthly intervals, the exposures of the two swaps are almost exactly the same (yet not exactly, since the swap rates are slightly different).

We would expect the receiver swap to observe the opposite effect, and this is indeed the case as shown in Figure 2.4*b*. As half the payments received are effectively moved forward by three months, if default occurs in this three-month period, we stand to lose this amount as well as all the other future cashflows.

2.3.3 Principal amortising swaps

We next consider an amortising swap, which is the same as the standard swap presented in 2.3.1, except for the fact that the notional amortises (decreases) by 2% after every payment is made. Not surprisingly, the effect of this is to decrease the exposure, compared to the standard swap (Figure 2.5), since the future cashflows are paid on a reduced notional. For an accreting swap, the effect is reversed.

2.3.4 Cross-currency swaps

In a cross-currency swap there is an exchange of fixed or floating payments in two different currencies and an exchange of notional at inception and at maturity. In Figure 2.6, we show the exposure for such a contract, where

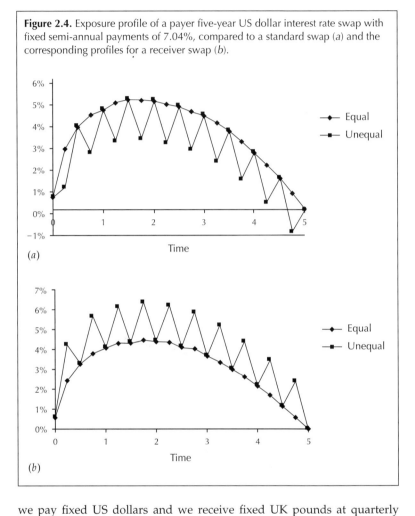

Figure 2.4. Exposure profile of a payer five-year US dollar interest rate swap with fixed semi-annual payments of 7.04%, compared to a standard swap (a) and the corresponding profiles for a receiver swap (b).

we pay fixed US dollars and we receive fixed UK pounds at quarterly intervals for five years. We can see that unlike an interest rate swap, the exposure does not decay to zero towards maturity, but instead it increases steadily, due to the FX risk introduced by the notional exchange at maturity, which is clearly much greater than the interest rate risk. The exposure is much larger in percentage of notional than in the interest rate swap, since at maturity, payments based on the entire notional are exchanged and the FX volatility is much higher than the interest rate volatility.

We also show the exposure for the opposite swap. This exposure is slightly smaller. The reason for this is that we are receiving the discount currency and have greater FX risk, as it is more likely that we will receive a larger payment than we make at maturity. An alternative way to explain this is that the forward value of the swap is negative.

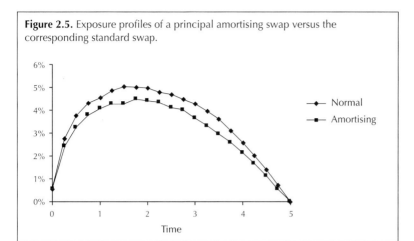

Figure 2.5. Exposure profiles of a principal amortising swap versus the corresponding standard swap.

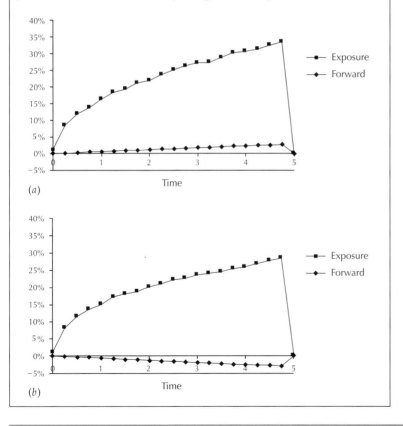

Figure 2.6. Exposure profile for a five-year cross-currency swap paying fixed quarterly payments in US dollars at 7.04% and fixed quarterly payments in UK pounds at 6.62% (*a*) and the corresponding receiver swap (*b*).

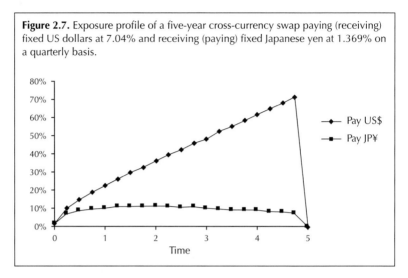

Figure 2.7. Exposure profile of a five-year cross-currency swap paying (receiving) fixed US dollars at 7.04% and receiving (paying) fixed Japanese yen at 1.369% on a quarterly basis.

The asymmetry due to the different yield curves is most pronounced when the forward interest rates are furthest apart. Consider the US dollar/ Japanese yen example shown in Figure 2.7. Here, there is a huge exposure close to the notional amount in one direction, but an exposure an order of magnitude lower in the other direction, due to the fact that yen interest rates are so low.

2.3.5 Caps and floors
We consider caps and floors, where the premium is paid upfront, which is most common. For periodic premiums, the exposure would be considerably reduced.

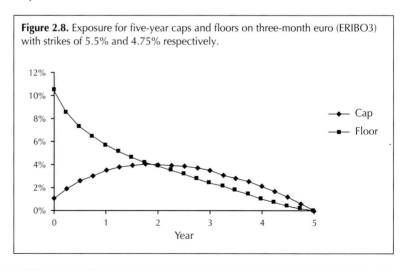

Figure 2.8. Exposure for five-year caps and floors on three-month euro (ERIBO3) with strikes of 5.5% and 4.75% respectively.

Figure 2.8 shows the exposure for a five-year interest rate cap on three-month euro rates with a strike of 5.5%. This exposure peaks at around two years. Since the yield curve is upward-sloping, the short-maturity caplets are out of the money. The caplets near maturity are in the money, but there is less notional at risk. Hence, similar to the case of an interest rate swap, the peak exposure is at an intermediate maturity.

In Figure 2.8, we also show the exposure for a floor with strike 4.75% on the three-month euro rate. The short-maturity floorlets are now in the money, so the exposure peaks at the inception of the deal.

For a downward-sloping yield curve, the above results will be reversed, ie, a cap will have a high initial exposure, while the exposure of a floor would peak at an intermediate point.

2.3.6 Swaptions and cancellable swaps
In Figure 2.9 we show the exposure profile for an at-the-money interest rate swaption with physical delivery (we enter into a risky swap at the swaption maturity). It is useful to compare this to the corresponding forward swap. While the swaption is alive, it always has a higher exposure than the forward swap, since its PV under any scenario must, by definition, be greater than the PV of the forward swap. However, after the exercise date, the exposure of the forward swap will always be greater, since there will be some scenarios under which the swaption is not exercised. This effect is the same as a cancellable swap as after the first cancellation date there will be some scenarios under which the swap has no credit exposure (the cancellation option has been exercised). This will be covered in more detail in Chapter 6.

Figure 2.9. Exposure profile of a one-year swaption with strike 7.5% on a five year interest rate swap, giving the holder the right to make fixed quarterly payments and to receive three month Libor. Also shown is the corresponding forward swap.

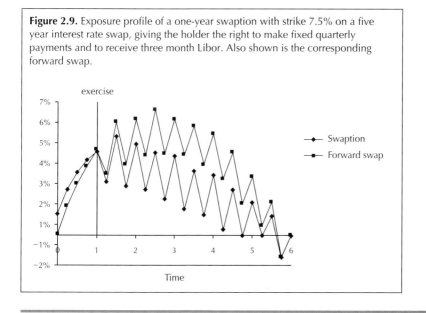

Note that the exposure profile for a cash-settled swaption (where a cash payment equal to the positive value of the swap is made at the swaption maturity) will be almost the same as a swap-settled or physical delivery swaption up to the exercise point and zero thereafter. As previously mentioned, there are disadvantages when quantifying for portfolios with deals with more than one counterparty.

2.4 CONCLUSION

Credit lines have been used to control the exposure of financial institutions to the various counterparties they transact with. The disadvantage of this approach is described in the introduction. We define the credit exposure as the percentile of the future PV of a particular transaction at a certain confidence level. To generate the exposure distribution, we need to simulate the underlying variables, ie, various interest rates and FX rates. It is important to introduce a well-estimated correlation matrix to perform this analysis. Two conflicting factors determine the credit exposure profile over time. On one hand, the volatility of the underlying variables increases over time, while on the other the underlying notional decreases over time. These two effects result in a humped exposure curve. The risk on an interest rate swap depends on the shape of the yield curve. In an upward (downward) sloping yield curve, the payer (receiver) swap is more risky than the corresponding receiver (payer) one. The exposure of a cross-currency swap increases over time and we do not observe a humped shape. The reason for this is that the exposure is mainly driven by the exchange of principal at maturity.

1   The simplest possible arbitrage-free model of this type is the Ho and Lee model, which corresponds to the Hull and White model with zero mean-reversion and constant volatility. However, this model allows only parallel shifts in the yield curve and not changes in the shape, making it unrealistic.

BIBLIOGRAPHY

Derivative Credit Risk: Advances in Measurement and Management, 1999, Second Edition (London: Risk Books).

Hull, J., 1996, *Options, Futures and Other Derivatives*, Third Edition (New Jersey: Prentice-Hall).

Hull, J., and A. White, 1990, "Pricing Interest Rate Derivative Securities", *Review of Financial Studies* 3(4), pp. 573–92.

Hull, J., and A. White, 1993, "One-Factor Models and the Valuation of Interest-Rate Derivative Securities", *Journal of Financial and Quantitative Analysis* 28, pp. 235–54.

Jamshidian, F., and Y. Zhu, 1997, "Scenario Simulation: Theory and Methodology", *Finance and Stochastics* 1, pp 43–67.

Rebonato, R., 1998, *Interest-Rate Option Models*, Second Edition (New York: John Wiley).

3

A Framework for Credit Risk Management

This chapter examines the important points in determining a portfolio credit loss distribution and it develops the fundamental framework for estimating that distribution. We consider mainly transactions whose exposures are stochastic. This analysis is thus applicable to derivative portfolios as well as loan portfolios.

As we discussed in Chapter 1, there are several methods for quantitative analysis of portfolio credit risk. The formulation we have chosen is the one we believe to be flexible with model parameters that can be estimated if we have sufficient data. In terms of the commercial models we discussed in Chapter 1, it is most similar to CreditMetrics, but with an emphasis on derivatives. We will describe in simple terms the equations governing the distribution of credit losses and give details of how such a distribution can be computed using Monte Carlo simulation. We will expand on the original CreditMetrics model in several directions.

Having described the computation of a portfolio credit loss distribution, we will then take a hypothetical example and consider the effect of different factors on the shape of this distribution. Most important is the "tail region", which defines both the unexpected loss and the portfolio's economic capital. We show that the unexpected loss is very sensitive to a number of important factors, namely uncertain exposures, stochastic recovery rates and correlated default events. Without an accurate treatment of these effects, the economic capital may be severely underestimated.

3.1 CREDIT LOSS DISTRIBUTION AND UNEXPECTED LOSS

As shown in the first chapter, when managing a portfolio subject to credit risk, characterisation of the credit loss distribution (Figure 3.1) is of fundamental importance. One of its main applications in the financial industry is the computation of the economic capital required to support a business. Combined with revenue data, it is useful in identifying business areas that achieve the highest return on risk-adjusted economic capital (RAROC). The latter topic is covered in more detail in Chapter 8. The credit loss distribution also leads to other useful techniques, such as marginal risk calculations, portfolio analysis and portfolio optimisation, which we will cover in the next chapter.

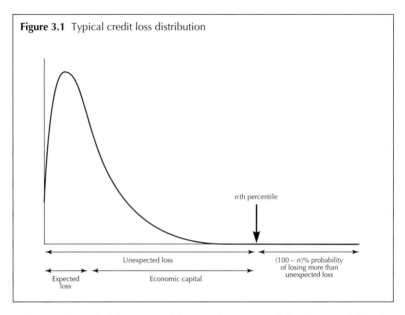

Figure 3.1 Typical credit loss distribution

Economic capital for credit risk must be estimated by characterising the expected and unexpected losses of a portfolio, as it is simply the difference between the two. The unexpected loss could be incurred in a particularly bad year and capital must be set aside to cover such a possibility and avoid bankruptcy. For reasons discussed in Chapter 1, a percentile is generally used to estimate the unexpected loss, instead of a certain multiple of the standard deviation. The $(1 - \alpha)^{th}$ percentile defines the point on the loss distribution where the probability that the incurred loss exceeds that value is $\alpha\%$. The economic capital is taken to be equal to the unexpected loss reduced by the expected loss as the return on a portfolio should always cover at least the expected loss. This is the minimum spread that a financial institution should charge in order to guarantee that at least it breaks even. The computation of this spread is discussed in Chapter 6. A financial institution should allocate economic capital against a percentile that reflects its desired credit rating. For example, the probability of default on an A-rated institution is 0.1%. It is therefore appropriate that an A-rated institution estimates its economic capital at the 99.9% confidence level. Other confidence levels are 99.99% for Aaa and 99.97% for Aa. For this analysis we use confidence levels of 99%, 99.9% and 99.97%, which are generally quite far apart in the tail of the distribution.

3.1.1 Portfolio default loss distribution
Our initial analysis will consider only the default events, since for most portfolios they account for the majority of the severe losses that determine the tail of the loss distribution. If we only consider defaults, we assume no

mark-to-market of the credit spread. In Chapter 1, we derived a simplified expression for the expected value and the standard deviation of the loss for a portfolio of n loans where defaults are independent. The actual loss incurred depends on the realised values of the binary default variables d_i and the size of the loans X_i. This expression only holds under the rather restrictive assumptions outlined below. The goal of this chapter will be to relax the following assumptions.

❏ The exposures (X_i) are constant. For a standard bullet loan this is not an issue (assuming the drawdown in the event of default is known) since the interest rate part is generally not marked-to-market and therefore the exposure does not change with interest rates. However, there is a plethora of corporate banking instruments for which the exposure over the analysis horizon would be random. This is even more pronounced for fixed-income instruments, where portfolios are always marked-to-market (eg, a swap has an initial exposure of zero, but this can easily change as interest rates move). We therefore need to relax the assumption of constant exposure.

❏ The default events are uncorrelated. As discussed in the previous chapter, defaults tend to cluster, reflecting adverse market-wide conditions. As will be shown later on in the analysis, the default correlation is crucial in determining the tail of the credit loss distribution. We will show how to introduce such correlation in the simulation.

❏ The recovery rate in the event of default is zero. Normally, there will be some recovery on a defaulted asset, and we must model this as a random quantity since historical recovery rates have a high variability.

❏ We introduce a concept of time horizon. First, this will allow us to discount all expected losses in the future at the appropriate risk-free rate. Secondly, it allows a specification of the default probabilities. For example, if the time horizon is several years, then we may consider the default probabilities to evolve over time, depending on the underlying credit quality. We will discuss this in more detail.

With the above comments in mind, we state a more general expression for the loss distribution of a credit-sensitive portfolio. A crucial assumption underlying this analysis is that the exposures and default events are uncorrelated. To incorporate such correlation would be very difficult computationally; also, there is little data to use to parameterise such a model. We will face this issue again in Chapter 6, where we present a solution to the problem.

For a portfolio consisting of n assets or netted positions (we shall refer to them as assets from now on), the portfolio loss distribution in a single period $[0, T]$ (eg, up to one year) due to defaults only is given by:

$$L_p(T) = \sum_{i=1}^{n} X_i(T)^+ d_i(0,T) \left[1 - \delta_i(T)\right] B(0,T) \qquad (1)$$

Since we are initially considering losses for only one period, we will simplify the above by removing the time dependence:

$$L_p = \sum_{i=1}^{n} X_i^+ d_i \left[1 - \delta_i \right] B\left(0, T \right) \tag{1*}$$

Each term in Equation (1*) is outlined below.

❑ X_i represents the exposure of the ith underlying at time T, which is simply given by the PV in the future, which is a random quantity. If the PV is negative, default does not lead to any change in the overall position, since anything owed to the defaulted entity must still be paid. However, a loss up to the whole exposure can be incurred when the PV is positive, which leads to the term $X_i^+ = \max(X_i, 0)$ in the above equation. The current loss should be computed by discounting the future loss at the risk-free rate. We discount at the risk-free rate, instead of the risky, because we have already accounted for the possibility of defaults. The proof is included in an appendix to Chapter 7.

❑ d_i is a binary default variable that is 1 in the case of default and 0 otherwise. The expected value of this binary variable should be equal to the probability of default p_i, ie, $E[d_i] = p_i$. If these events are correlated, we cannot assume that $E[d_i d_j] = p_i p_j$, ie, that the joint default probability of assets i and j is equal to the product of their individual default probabilities.

❑ $[1 - \delta_i]$ represents the loss given default. δ_i is the recovery rate as a percentage.

❑ $B(0, T)$ is the risk-free discount factor.

3.2 GENERATING THE LOSS DISTRIBUTION
3.2.1 Introduction
We now proceed to estimate the loss distribution, which gives the probability of incurring a loss of any given magnitude over a certain time horizon. For a general portfolio, it is not possible to derive an analytical expression of the credit loss distribution without major simplifications. We will proceed with two distinct ways to address this problem.

Use Monte Carlo simulation
As pointed out in the first chapter, the number of possible default combinations is extremely large for a sizeable portfolio. By sampling a reasonable number of scenarios, we aim to achieve an acceptably accurate result. Indeed, Monte Carlo simulation of the loss distribution will converge to the real distribution as the number of simulations increases. Unfortunately, it is possible that Monte Carlo convergence can be very slow. This can be particularly true for high grade portfolios, since we may need to perform

many simulations in order to observe just one default event. For example, if the default probability for a given asset is 1% then, on average, only one default event will be generated in every 100 simulations – the other 99 simulations essentially tell us nothing. This is in contrast to market risk, where in every simulation there would be a change in the value of each underlying asset. An analogy to this is pricing very "out of the money" options by Monte Carlo, where most paths of the underlying will not result in a payoff. An additional difficulty arises from the fact that we are generally interested in extreme percentiles of the loss distribution, which further increase the required number of simulations. Despite these difficulties, the attraction of the Monte Carlo approach for credit risk management is that we do not need to make any approximations and the resulting framework will allow us to incorporate more complex effects, such as credit migration, stochastic recovery rates, etc.

Derive analytical approximations
The resulting computations are much faster than Monte Carlo, but the restrictive assumptions can introduce substantial errors for many portfolios of interest. In the next chapter, we provide an introduction to the subject and show how these can be useful in practice. In particular, we will also show that a combination of Monte Carlo and analytical approximations can be a powerful technique.

3.2.2 Default events

The simplest way to simulate the binary default events is to draw random numbers between 0 and 1 from a uniform distribution (uniform deviates). We draw a random number U_i and set the default variable to 1 if $U_i \leq p_i$ and 0 otherwise. We can represent this using the indicator function as follows:

$$d_i = 1_{U_i \leq p_i} \tag{2}$$

The indicator function, $1_{U_i \leq p_i}$, is 1 if the expression is true and 0 if it is false. For a reasonably large number of simulations, the number of defaults divided by the number of simulations will be close to the required default probability p_i, which is a result of the following:

$$\lim_{M \to \infty} \left(\frac{1}{M} \sum_{k=1}^{M} d_i^k \right) = p_i \tag{3}$$

The number of simulations required to achieve a reasonable convergence depends on the actual values of p_i. If the default probabilities were particularly small, we would expect to require a greater number of simulations simply to generate a reasonable number of defaults. For example, it is not unreasonable for an asset of very high credit quality to have an annual default probability of 0.02%. On average, we would expect such an asset to "default" only once in every 5,000 simulations.

It is also possible to draw from alternative distributions in order to generate binary variables. For example, instead of a uniform deviate, it is common practice to use a normal deviate, ie, a random number Y_i drawn from a normal distribution with mean 0 and standard deviation 1. Its pdf is

$$\frac{1}{\sqrt{2\pi}} \exp\left(-\frac{x^2}{2}\right) \tag{4}$$

As before, we need to choose a threshold k_i on the normal distribution in order to determine when default occurs, ie, $d_i = 1_{Y_i \le k_i}$.

When using a uniform deviate, it is clear that the threshold that defined the default was simply the default probability itself, while for a normal deviate it requires further analysis. The area under the unit normal is equal to 1 by definition:

$$\int_{-\infty}^{\infty} \frac{1}{\sqrt{2\pi}} \exp\left(-\frac{x^2}{2}\right) dx = 1$$

The threshold k_i is determined such that the area bounded to its left is equal to the probability of default:

$$\int_{-\infty}^{k_i} \frac{1}{\sqrt{2\pi}} \exp\left(-\frac{x^2}{2}\right) dx = p_i \tag{5}$$

The above integral is the cumulative density function for a standard normal variable (mean 0 and variance 1) and it is often denoted by $\Phi(\cdot)$. For any function, the cumulative density function is given by $F(x) = \Pr(X \le x)$. To explicitly calculate k_i, we require the inverse cumulative normal distribution function, ie,

$$k_i = \Phi^{-1}(p_i) \tag{6}$$

This is illustrated in Figure 3.2.

In Table 3.1, we show an example of default event simulation using both the uniform variable method and the normal variable method. We have chosen the two sets of number to exactly correspond to one another, eg, $0.897 = \Phi(1.265)$.

Note that good approximations for $\Phi^{-1}(\cdot)$ are widely available. It may seem that this procedure is unnecessarily complicated when compared to the basic method using uniform deviates. While this is true, we will see in

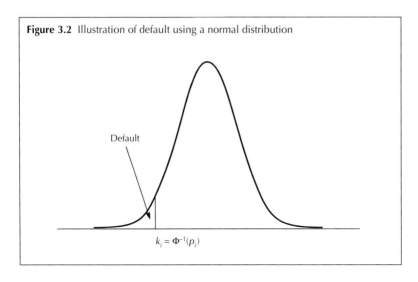

Figure 3.2 Illustration of default using a normal distribution

$$k_i = \Phi^{-1}(p_i)$$

the next section that the normal variables are very useful when we need to incorporate correlation into the analysis.

3.2.3 Correlated default events

The entire correlation structure among binary variables is not completely specified by the pairwise correlations. Consider three assets in a portfolio with probabilities of default p_1, p_2 and p_3. The correlation matrix will give the pairwise correlations ρ_{12}, ρ_{13} and ρ_{23}, which will allow us to calculate the probability of any two defaults occurring, p_{12}, p_{13} and p_{23}. However, there is still one piece of vital information missing, namely the probability that all three assets default, p_{123}. Although this number can be substantially

Table 3.1 Simulation of binary default variables using uniform and normal variables. $p_i = 20\%$ and the corresponding $k_i = -0.8416$. The numbers shown are equivalent

Simulation	Uniform	Normal	Outcome
1	0.897	1.265	No default
2	0.439	−0.154	No default
3	0.616	0.294	No default
4	0.180	−0.917	Default
5	0.624	0.315	No default
6	0.767	0.730	No default
7	0.244	−0.695	No default
8	0.197	−0.851	Default
9	0.270	−0.613	No default
10	0.667	0.432	No default

larger than the product of the three individual default probabilities, most likely it will be negligible for this simple portfolio. However, for a larger portfolio, multiple default probabilities are vital, since there are multiple combinations of assets. As we discussed earlier, they are crucial in determining the shape of the tail of the loss distribution and hence the portfolio capital. Therefore, the way in which the multiple defaults are generated will have a large impact on the portfolio capital. In practice, it is very difficult to estimate pairwise default probabilities and almost impossible to estimate default probabilities of higher order. The only alternative is for the latter to be imposed by the model at hand. Various models will give varying probabilities for multiple defaults and economic capital. A model for generating multiple defaults should have at least the following properties:

❏ it should have a reasonable economic structure;
❏ it should be relatively straightforward to implement; and
❏ it should be in principle possible to estimate its parameters.

We will make the assumption that the default structure can be determined from a multivariate normal distribution. The multivariate normal distribution has the attractive property that its entire correlation structure is defined by its covariance matrix, so all the higher order default probabilities are uniquely determined by the pairwise correlations and the problem mentioned above does not arise.

As described above, in this structure, we map the probability of default $p_i \in (0, 1)$ to a normal variable $k_i \in (-\infty, \infty)$ by $k_i = \Phi^{-1}(p_i)$, where Φ is the standard normal probability function.

The joint default probability of two assets is now given by integrating the bivariate normal pdf:

$$\Phi(k_i, k_j, \lambda_{ij}) =$$

$$\int_{-\infty}^{k_i} \int_{-\infty}^{k_j} \frac{1}{2\pi\sqrt{1-\lambda_{ij}^2}} \exp\left(-\frac{y_i^2 + y_j^2 - 2\lambda_{ij}\, y_i\, y_j}{2(1 - \lambda_{ij}^2)}\right) dy_i\, dy_j \qquad (7)$$

This function is plotted in Figure 3.3 to show the two scenarios with correlations of 0% and 50%. The area bounded by the two normal variables, $k_i = \Phi^{-1}(p_i)$ and $k_j = \Phi^{-1}(p_j)$, defines the probability of joint default of assets i and j. As the correlation increases, the density function is "squashed" along the diagonal, increasing the joint default probability.

Considering again the above problem, the correlation structure would be completely defined by a trivariate normal distribution. The probability of three defaults occurring p_{123} would be uniquely determined within the model by the individual default probabilities and the pairwise default correlations. A disadvantage of this approach is that even though the input

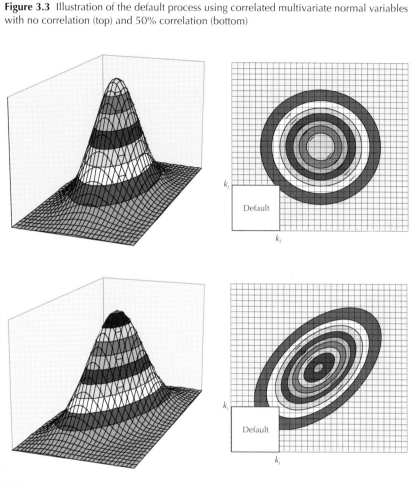

Figure 3.3 Illustration of the default process using correlated multivariate normal variables with no correlation (top) and 50% correlation (bottom)

parameters (the default probabilities and the pairwise default correlations) may be reasonable, the implied value of p_{123} could be unreasonable. Since it is unlikely that we can estimate p_{123}, the best we can expect is a reasonable implied value.

We now need to relate the correlations among the normal variables (λ_{ij}) to the correlations between binary variables (ρ_{ij}). This can be achieved by equating the expectation of pairs of joint binary events to the joint probability given by the bivariate normal distribution: $E[d_i d_j] = \Phi(\lambda_{ij}, k_i, k_j)$. From the definition of covariance, the binary default correlation is given by $\rho_{ij} = \sigma_{ij}/\sigma_i \sigma_j$ where σ_{ij} is the covariance between the default events and σ_i and σ_j are their standard deviations. Since they are binary events, the standard deviation is equal to $\sigma = \sqrt{p(1-p)}$. This means that from the

Figure 3.4 Maximum value of the default correlation as a function of the default probabilities

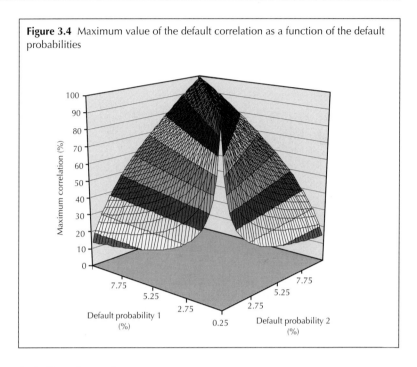

definition of covariance:

$$\rho_{ij} = \frac{E[d_i\, d_j] - E[d_i]\, E[d_j]}{\sqrt{p_i(1-p_i)\, p_j(1-p_j)}} = \frac{\Phi(\lambda_{ij},\, k_i,\, k_j) - p_i\, p_j}{\sqrt{p_i(1-p_i)\, p_j(1-p_j)}} \tag{8}$$

thereby establishing a relation between ρ_{ij} and λ_{ij} that can be solved numerically (using numerical integration or an analytical approximation to the double integral). We can therefore use historical estimates of default correlations (ρ_{ij}) in the analysis. The alternative is to estimate the "asset return" correlations (λ_{ij}) directly. This is the approach used by KMV and CreditMetrics as described in Chapter 1.

It is important to understand the full implication of Equation (8). Without loss of generality, assume that $p_i \leq p_j$. Then $\Phi(\lambda_{ij}, k_i, k_j) \leq p_i \leq p_j$ (as the probability of a pair of events occurring is no more than either of their individual probabilities), and so:

$$\rho_{ij} \leq \sqrt{\frac{p_i(1-p_j)}{p_j(1-p_i)}} \tag{9}$$

which shows that the default correlation can reach unity if and only if the individual probabilities are equal. The maximum value of the pairwise

Figure 3.5 Implied pairwise correlations, λ_{ij}, between the normal variables as a function of the default probabilities for a constant default correlation of $\rho_{ij} = 10\%$

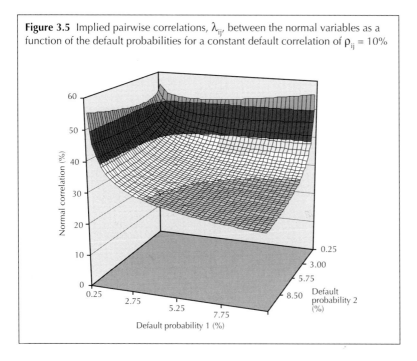

default correlation as a function of the individual probabilities is shown in Figure 3.4.

As expected, if two assets are perfectly correlated ($\lambda_{ij} = 100\%$), but have unequal default probabilities, it is still possible that only one of the two defaults. Hence, the default correlation (ρ_{ij}) can only be 100% if the assets have the same probability of default. Figure 3.5 shows the variation of λ_{ij} as the individual default probabilities change for a constant default correlation of 10%. When at least one probability of default is small, λ_{ij} can become very large. For example, for default probabilities of 0.1% and 10%, it is meaningless to specify a default correlation above 9.5%, since the inequality in Equation (9) is no longer satisfied.

To simulate the correlated binary (default) events, we draw from the following correlated multivariate normal distribution:

$$\tilde{\mathbf{Y}} = \begin{pmatrix} \tilde{Y}_1 \\ \vdots \\ \tilde{Y}_n \end{pmatrix} \sim N\left(\begin{pmatrix} 0 \\ \vdots \\ 0 \end{pmatrix}, \begin{pmatrix} 1 & & \lambda_{ij} \\ & \ddots & \\ \lambda_{ij} & & 1 \end{pmatrix} \right) \sim N(0, \Lambda) \qquad (10)$$

It must be stressed that the underlying correlation matrix represents the correlation among the multivariate normal variables and not the default events themselves. It can be shown (eg, Morrison, 1976) that if a random vector $\mathbf{Y}$ has a multivariate normal distribution $N(0, \mathbf{I})$ ($\mathbf{I}$ is the identity matrix, so this is just a vector of uncorrelated normal variables), then $\tilde{\mathbf{Y}} = \mathbf{AY}$ has a multivariate normal $N(0, \mathbf{AA}')$ distribution. Therefore, to simulate normal variables according to Equation (10), we need to factorise the normal correlation matrix according to $\Lambda = \mathbf{AA}'$. This can be done using, for example, Cholesky decomposition or eigenvalue decomposition (see Press et al, 1992). We then only need to multiply a vector of uncorrelated normal variables $\mathbf{Y}$ by the matrix $\mathbf{A}$. One way to simulate normal random variables is to simply invert the uniform deviates using such an approximation. However, a more favoured approach is the Box–Muller method (eg, see Press et al, 1992). The correlated default variables are then given by $d_i = 1_{\tilde{Y}_i \le k_i}$.

3.2.4 Credit migrations

We now show how to incorporate credit migration into the framework. There are two reasons why we may wish to do this. First, if we are considering losses over multiple periods, then credit migrations will modify the future default probabilities. This is important – for example, for assets of high credit quality that over one year have a very small default probability – but as there can be a significant chance of deterioration in the credit quality, the longer term default probabilities increase exponentially. Second, if we are marking-to-market the credit spread, we can use credit migration as a way to incorporate changes in the credit spread into the model. We leave the discussion of this second point for the next chapter and for now concentrate on the former point.

As we discussed in Chapter 1, historical data on credit rating changes is commonly reported in a transition matrix representing a one-year period (as shown in Table 3.2). For example, the probability of a Baa being downgraded to a B is 0.71%, the probability of an A being upgraded to an Aaa is 0.07% and the probability of an Aa defaulting is 0.02%.

Consider the Baa transition probabilities in Table 3.2. The probability of default is 0.15%, which implies that the default threshold is $\Phi(k_{\text{Baa, Default}}) = p_{\text{Baa, Default}}$ or $k_{\text{Baa, Default}} = \Phi^{-1}(p_{\text{Baa, Default}}) = -2.968$. Consider that we wish to add further thresholds to define the credit migration probabilities. Since we are working with the cumulative normal distribution, if we need to find the next threshold which corresponds to downgrade to rating Caa, we need to solve the following equation:

$$\Phi(k_{\text{Baa, Caa}}) - \Phi(k_{\text{Baa, Default}}) = p_{\text{Baa, Caa}} \tag{11}$$

Since we have already positioned the previous threshold such that $\Phi(k_{\text{Baa, Default}}) = p_{\text{Baa, Default}}$, this can be rewritten:

$$\Phi(k_{\text{Baa, Caa}}) = p_{\text{Baa, Caa}} + p_{\text{Baa, Default}} \tag{12}$$

$$k_{\text{Baa, Caa}} = \Phi^{-1}(p_{\text{Baa, Caa}} + p_{\text{Baa, Default}}) \tag{13}$$

Table 3.2 Moody's one-year transition matrix (see Carty and Lieberman, 1997)

	Aaa	Aa	A	Baa	Ba	B	Caa	Default
Aaa	93.40%	5.94%	0.64%	0.00%	0.02%	0.00%	0.00%	0.00%
Aa	1.61%	90.55%	7.46%	0.26%	0.09%	0.01%	0.00%	0.02%
A	0.07%	2.28%	92.44%	4.63%	0.45%	0.12%	0.01%	0.00%
Baa	0.05%	0.26%	5.51%	88.48%	4.76%	0.71%	0.08%	0.15%
Ba	0.02%	0.05%	0.42%	5.16%	86.91%	5.91%	0.24%	1.29%
B	0.00%	0.04%	0.13%	0.54%	6.35%	84.22%	1.91%	6.81%
Caa	0.00%	0.00%	0.00%	0.62%	2.05%	4.08%	69.20%	24.06%

A general expression for the computation of the threshold $k_{i,j}$ corresponding to the transition from rating i to j is

$$k_{i,j} = \Phi^{-1} \left(\sum_{l=j}^{K} p_{i,l} \right)$$

(14)

where K represents the total number of states (K is the default state). Using the above, we can calculate the thresholds corresponding to Table 3.2, which are shown in Table 3.3 – eg, drawing a normal variable of -2.0 will lead to downgrade to A for an asset originally rated Aa.

In Figure 3.6, we show the position of the thresholds for an asset rated initially Baa. Most probably, this asset will retain its Baa rating, which is seen by the large area in the middle of the distribution.

Intuitively, the normal distribution can be thought of as the "asset returns" of the counterparty. This is the principal behind the method for estimating joint credit quality moves advocated by KMV and CreditMetrics, as described in Chapter 1. A large asset return would lead to an upgrade, whereas a small asset return would lead to a downgrade or default. In the

Table 3.3 Thresholds corresponding to mapping the transition matrix in Table 3.2 onto a normal distribution

	Aaa	Aa	A	Baa	Ba	B	Caa	Default
Aaa	$+\infty$	-1.506	-2.478	-3.540	-3.540	$-\infty$	$-\infty$	$-\infty$
Aa	$+\infty$	2.142	-1.416	-2.669	-3.036	-3.432	-3.540	-3.540
A	$+\infty$	3.195	1.986	-1.625	-2.524	-3.012	-3.719	$-\infty$
Baa	$+\infty$	3.290	2.737	1.570	-1.580	-2.349	-2.834	-2.968
Ba	$+\infty$	3.540	3.195	2.583	1.585	-1.444	-2.162	-2.229
B	$+\infty$	$+\infty$	3.353	2.929	2.452	1.471	-1.358	-1.490
Caa	$+\infty$	$+\infty$	$+\infty$	$+\infty$	2.506	1.933	1.495	-0.704

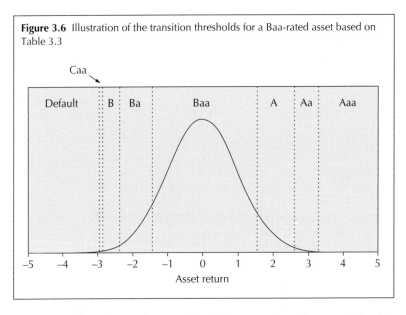

Figure 3.6 Illustration of the transition thresholds for a Baa-rated asset based on Table 3.3

simulation, if we draw a large and positive normal random variable, this may lead to an improvement in credit quality, while a large negative one may lead to a downgrade or default. The fact that the asset returns are correlated means that they are more likely to default or deteriorate in credit quality together. We want to stress that the mathematical formulation we have presented does not rely on this argument. This is just a convenient way to add economic meaning to the mathematical computations.

The second reason for including credit migration is for portfolios that are marked-to-market; here, we should include changes in the P&L as a result of a change in the credit spread of a given counterparty. In certain circumstances, not necessarily extreme, this component can dominate the loss due to default. We illustrate this with an example. Consider computing the credit risk of a 10-year swap at a one-year horizon. If there is default in the first year and there has not been a substantial interest rate move, the loss will be moderate, since sufficient time has not yet passed for the PV to become dramatically positive. However, consider that the spread at one-year has widened significantly due to a credit migration (downgrade). If we mark-to-market this swap, then the loss from the credit migration will be the loss arising from revaluing the remaining nine-year swap at the higher spread. This latter effect can easily be greater than the former. We discuss marking-to-market in Chapter 7.

We emphasise that in the extended model, the correlation among default events will also apply to the credit migrations. For example, there is more chance that two counterparties will jointly downgrade or that their credit quality will improve together. This is likely to be observed in practice.

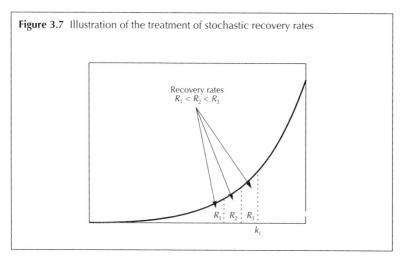

Figure 3.7 Illustration of the treatment of stochastic recovery rates

Of course, the joint probabilities representing multiple changes in credit migration are determined by the default correlation inputs. As mentioned before, very little data is available on this kind of correlation. It is convenient to be able to express the correlation between all possible moves in credit quality (including default) for two obligors in terms of a single number. This is an advantage of the "asset value" approach.

3.2.5 Recovery rates

Recovery rates have been estimated from historical data for US debt issues (see Carty and Lieberman, 1996) and were discussed in Chapter 1. We can incorporate stochastic recovery rates into the model by extending the default and credit migration framework. Consider that, in the event of default, the recovery rate is defined by a series of further thresholds below the default threshold as illustrated in Figure 3.7. The intuition here is that the extent by which the "asset return" falls below the default threshold determines the severity of default and consequently the recovery rate.

This approach has two attractive properties. Firstly, it is efficient since the stochastic recovery rates are introduced without drawing a further set of random numbers. Secondly, it introduces correlation among the recovery rates. The default correlation matrix determines the recovery rate correlation structure. This can be a realistic assumption, since estimating the correlation of recovery rates from historical data would be an impossible task. During a recession when default correlation is high, we expect defaults to be quite "severe", resulting in below average recovery rates. When defaults are driven by idiosyncratic factors, the recovery rates would be expected to be uncorrelated.

Denoting the recovery rates by R_i, the thresholds are determined by the probability of each recovery rate occurring (p_j). The probabilities can be

Table 3.4 Recovery rate estimates for different classes of debt (see Carty and Lieberman, 1996)

Class	Mean	Standard deviation
Senior secured	53.8%	26.9%
Senior unsecured	51.1%	25.5%
Senior subordinated	38.5%	23.8%
Subordinated	32.7%	20.2%
Junior subordinated	17.1%	10.9%

calibrated to the historical mean (μ) and variance (σ^2):

$$\mu = \sum_{j=1}^{N} p_j R_j, \quad \sigma^2 = \sum_{j=1}^{N} p_j (R_j)^2 - \mu^2, \quad 1 = \sum_{j=1}^{N} p_j \quad (15)$$

Table 3.4 gives estimates of the mean and standard deviation of recovery rates.

For example, from Equation (15), if we choose the historical recovery rates for subordinated debt and three recovery rates of 15%, 30% and 75%, the probabilities can be calculated to be 34%, 49% and 17% respectively. If the default probability is 1%, then the three thresholds required would be:

$$\Phi^{-1}(100\% \times 1\%) = -2.326, \quad \Phi^{-1}(83\% \times 1\%) = -2.395,$$

$$\Phi^{-1}(34\% \times 1\%) = -2.707$$

so that a normal variable between -2.326 and -2.395 corresponds to a recovery rate of 75%, between -2.395 and -2.707 to a recovery rate of 30%, and any value less than -2.707 to a recovery rate of 15%. Note that the first threshold coincides with the default threshold.

Since there are only three constraints given above, only three recovery rates can be matched uniquely. If more information on the historical distribution is known, then more recovery rates can be matched.

An alternative way to incorporate recovery rates into the analysis is to use a beta distribution, as was originally proposed in CreditMetrics. Any value for the recovery rate is possible with a non-zero probability. The pdf of the beta distribution is given by:

$$f(x) = \begin{cases} x^{\alpha-1} (1-x)^{\beta-1} \dfrac{\Gamma(\alpha+\beta)}{\Gamma(\alpha)\Gamma(\beta)} & \text{for } 0 < x < 1 \\ 0 & \text{for } x < 0 \text{ and } x > 1 \end{cases} \quad (16)$$

This has the required property that the recovery is bounded by 0 and 1. The parameters can be computed since the mean (μ) and variance (σ^2) of a beta

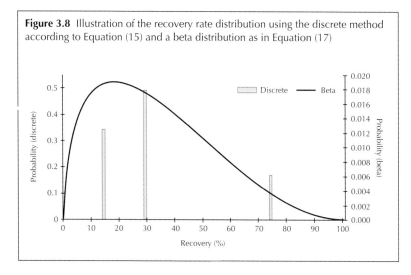

Figure 3.8 Illustration of the recovery rate distribution using the discrete method according to Equation (15) and a beta distribution as in Equation (17)

distribution are given by:

$$\mu = \frac{\alpha}{\alpha + \beta} \quad \text{and} \quad \sigma^2 = \frac{\alpha\beta}{(\alpha + \beta)^2 (\alpha + \beta + 1)} \tag{17ab}$$

Using the above, it is possible to calculate values for α and β according to:

$$\alpha = \eta\beta \quad \text{and} \quad \beta = \frac{\left[1/\sigma^2 - \eta - 1/\eta - 2\right]}{\left[\eta^2 + 3\eta + 1/\eta + 3\right]}, \quad \eta = \frac{\mu}{1 - \mu} \tag{18ab}$$

In Figure 3.8, we show the probability density functions for subordinated debt corresponding to the discrete method of matching the historical mean and variance to the probabilities of three discrete recovery rates and compare this to the method using a beta distribution. The figure illustrates the high degree of randomness present in recovery rates.

Note that we can also incorporate a beta distribution for the recovery rates into our simulation framework. By assuming that the recovery rates are given by a beta distribution, we can use as many discrete thresholds as required. Rather than simply matching the mean and variance, as in Equation (15), we can match the thresholds to the cumulative probability density function of the beta distribution directly (in a similar way as for credit migration as shown in Equation 14). For example, suppose we wish to use 100 discrete thresholds. The relevant probabilities can be obtained from Equation (16) (with α and β matched to the required mean and variance) and then mapped to thresholds in a similar way to Equation (14). This method has the advantage that the recovery rates are correlated without restricting the number of attainable values.

3.3 EXAMPLE – ONE PERIOD MODEL

We now apply the methodology developed in the previous sections to a hypothetical example, in order to demonstrate the effect of the various factors on the shape of the loss distribution and the economic capital. We construct a large derivatives portfolio, which has been devised as a good example for illustrating the various effects. We emphasise that there is a multitude of factors that determine the shape of the loss distribution (ie, product types, maturities, default correlations, default probabilities, etc) and therefore the results presented here should be considered only as an example, as they could differ for other portfolios. Nevertheless, we believe the main qualitative conclusions drawn to be generally valid. For reference, we have included a simple example of a simulation algorithm in Appendix B.

3.3.1 Portfolio description

The portfolio was generated randomly using information on ratings and exposures for standard instruments. The portfolio consists of 500 counterparties, with each assigned an associated rating. The rating scheme we use is that of Moody's. Each counterparty has 1–10 deals, which are assumed to be covered by a single master agreement. This data is summarised in Table 3.5.* To start with, we will assume that the exposure is constant and equal to the expected exposure of each instrument one year from now. The expected exposure corresponds to $E[\max(PV_1, 0)]$, ie, the expected value of the positive PV in the future (see the Appendix A for a more thorough

Table 3.5 Overview of hypothetical portfolio used in computations

Rating	Counterparties	Total notional	Original maturity (weighted average)	Remaining maturity (weighted average)	Recovery rate	Products
Aaa	100	US$25,000m	8.1 years	5.3 years	60%	IR swaps CC swaps IR swaptions caps/floors
Aa	100	US$10,000m	10.2 years	9.2 years	50%	IR swaps CC swaps
A	150	US$12,500m	9.4 years	6.5 years	40%	IR swaps
Baa	75	US$7,500m	7.9 years	5.2 years	35%	IR swaps
Ba	50	US$500m	10.0 years	8.3 years	30%	Loans
B	15	US$75m	6.8 years	4.1 years	25%	Loans
Caa	10	US$50m	7.1 years	5.5 years	20%	Loans

*The exposures have been generated using the approach described in Chapter 2.

Table 3.6 Transition matrix used in the computations (numbers in bold have been modified from the official Moody's values)

	Aaa	Aa	A	Baa	Ba	B	Caa	Default
Aaa	93.39%	5.94%	0.64%	0.00%	0.02%	0.00%	0.00%	**0.02%**
Aa	1.61%	90.55%	7.46%	0.26%	0.09%	0.01%	0.00%	0.05%
A	0.07%	2.28%	**92.34%**	4.63%	0.45%	0.12%	0.01%	**0.10%**
Baa	0.05%	0.26%	5.51%	88.48%	4.76%	0.71%	0.08%	0.15%
Ba	0.02%	0.05%	0.42%	5.16%	86.91%	5.91%	0.24%	1.29%
B	0.00%	0.04%	0.13%	0.54%	6.35%	84.22%	1.91%	6.81%
Caa	0.00%	0.00%	0.00%	0.62%	2.05%	4.08%	**78.25%**	**15.00%**
Default	0.00%	0.00%	0.00%	0.00%	0.00%	0.00%	0.00%	100.00%

discussion of the reasons for this). We have modified the transition matrix in Table 3.2 as shown in Table 3.6, making all default probabilities non-zero so as to be conservative.

3.3.2 Impact of default correlation
We first investigate the impact of default correlation. The default correlation matrix used was constructed from data provided in CreditMetrics (1997) and it is reproduced in Table 3.7, which provides historical estimates for rating classes Aa, A, Baa, Ba and B, along with the corresponding default probabilities. From these default correlations, we calculate the corresponding "asset return" correlation according to Equation (8). We impose the correlation between Aaa to be equal to that between Aa and the correlations between Caa to be equal to that between B rated assets. The cross correlations are calculated as simply the average of the two relevant numbers, ie, $\lambda_{ij} = (\lambda_{ii} + \lambda_{jj})/2$. We hope these numbers present a reasonable estimate of the correlation for a fairly well diversified portfolio. Naturally,

Table 3.7 Asset return correlations used for the computations calculated from the historical default correlation estimates in CreditMetrics

	ρ_{ii}	ρ_i	Aaa	Aa	A	Baa	Ba	B	Caa
Aaa			28%	28%	26%	24%	20%	19%	19%
Aa	0.33%[a]	0.01%[a]		28%[b]	26%	24%	20%	19%	19%
A	1.00%[a]	0.13%[a]			24%[b]	22%	18%	17%	17%
Baa	0.69%[a]	0.13%[a]				20%[b]	16%	15%	15%
Ba	1.40%[a]	1.42%[a]					11%[b]	11%	11%
B	3.27%[a]	7.63%[a]						10%[b]	10%
Caa									10%

a. From CreditMetrics.
b. Calculated using Equation (8).

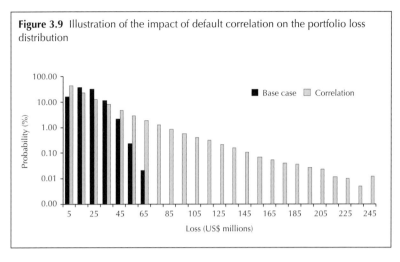

Figure 3.9 Illustration of the impact of default correlation on the portfolio loss distribution

a portfolio heavily concentrated in one or more geographical regions or industries would have higher correlations. The derived asset return correlation matrix is shown in Table 3.7.

We plot a histogram of the loss distribution by taking a series of bins and using the Monte Carlo simulation to calculate the probability of a loss falling in each bin. Furthermore, since the distribution has such heavy tails, we plot the probabilities on a lognormal scale. This allows us to see the whole distribution, and in particular the tail region corresponding to very small probabilities.

In Figure 3.9, we show the impact of default correlation on the shape of the loss distribution. The tail of the distribution becomes much fatter as the probability of multiple defaults becomes more likely. This effect could be

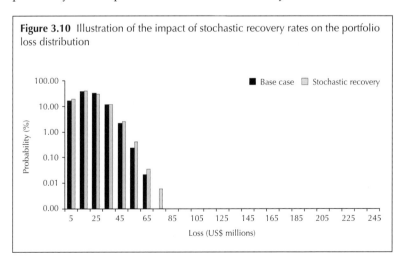

Figure 3.10 Illustration of the impact of stochastic recovery rates on the portfolio loss distribution

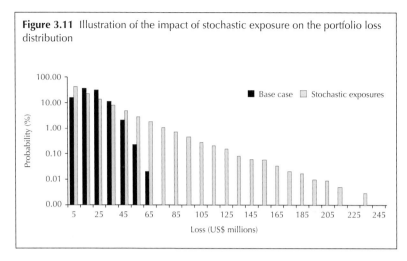

Figure 3.11 Illustration of the impact of stochastic exposure on the portfolio loss distribution

even more pronounced for an under-diversified portfolio, since the correlation matrix we have used is effectively averaged across geographical regions and sectors.

3.3.3 Impact of stochastic recovery rates
In an earlier chapter, we discussed the high variability that has been observed historically in the recovery rates. We consider the impact on the portfolio loss distribution of assuming a beta distribution for the recovery rates with mean given by the corresponding entry in Table 3.5 and the standard deviation fixed at 25%, which is a reasonable estimate given the data in Table 3.4. The effect of incorporating stochastic recovery rates is reasonably small, although there is still a moderate increase of the tail of the loss distribution.

3.3.4 Impact of stochastic exposures
We now consider the impact of stochastic exposures on the loss distribution. Rather than using the fixed expected exposure (LEQ1 derived in Appendix A), we draw from the distribution of possible exposures at default time. In each simulation path, the actual loss may be greater or lower than that under the constant exposure scenario. Figure 3.11 shows the impact of stochastic exposures to be very significant. This has important implications for loan equivalent methodologies, as we shall see later. Using constant exposures can significantly underestimate the true unexpected loss.

3.3.5 Summary
Table 3.8 summarises our findings, showing the increase in the 99th, 99.9th and 99.97th percentiles for the effects studied. Note that the expected loss

Table 3.8 Impact of various assumptions on the unexpected loss (all numbers in US$ millions)

	Expected loss	99th percentile	99.9th percentile	99.97th percentile
Base case	19.13	43.63	53.51	58.02
Default correlation	19.13	112.86	192.66	242.92
Stochastic recovery rates	19.13	45.75	56.40	61.73
Stochastic exposures	19.14	99.63	162.82	196.38
All effects	19.14	177.35	380.90	476.41

does not change. When all effects are considered, the unexpected loss at the 99.9th percentile increases by more than 600% compared to the naïve base case.

3.4 MULTIPLE PERIOD MODEL

We have so far restricted our analysis to a single period model. The next step will be to extend this model into a multi-period framework. There are two important effects to consider:

❑ stochastic exposures become even more important than in the one-period model, since the variance of the underlying variables increases over time; and
❑ default probabilities vary over time.

For demonstration purposes, we extend the one-year example of the previous section into a two-year period.

3.4.1 Drift in default probabilities

Credit migration introduces a drift in default probabilities due to rating changes. By raising the transition matrix to the appropriate power, it is possible to calculate cumulative transition probabilities for any period.

Table 3.9 Transition matrix in Table 3.2 squared to compute two-year transition probabilities

	Aaa	Aa	A	Baa	Ba	B	Caa	Default
Aaa	87.31%	10.94%	1.63%	0.05%	0.04%	0.00%	0.00%	0.04%
Aa	2.97%	82.26%	13.67%	0.82%	0.21%	0.03%	0.00%	0.11%
A	0.17%	4.19%	85.69%	8.40%	1.04%	0.27%	0.02%	0.22%
Baa	0.10%	0.60%	10.00%	78.79%	8.42%	1.52%	0.16%	0.41%
Ba	0.04%	0.12%	1.05%	9.10%	76.16%	10.16%	0.51%	2.86%
B	0.00%	0.08%	0.29%	1.28%	10.93%	71.39%	3.12%	12.91%
Caa	0.00%	0.00%	0.05%	1.16%	3.67%	6.75%	61.31%	27.04%
Default	0.00%	0.00%	0.00%	0.00%	0.00%	0.00%	0.00%	100.00%

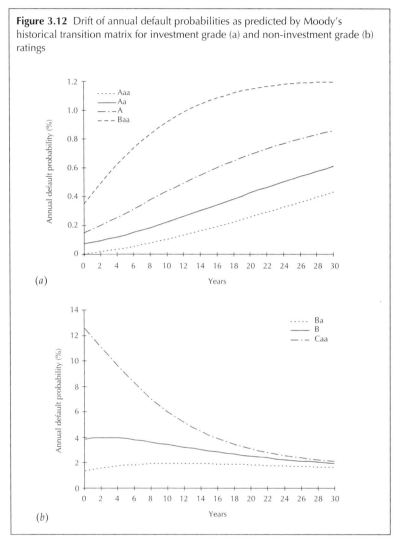

Figure 3.12 Drift of annual default probabilities as predicted by Moody's historical transition matrix for investment grade (a) and non-investment grade (b) ratings

The difference between transition matrices for successive periods will then give the default probability between those periods. In Figure 3.12, we show the evolution of annual default probabilities as predicted by the Moody's historical transition matrix (Table 3.2). An important observation is that the default probability is not constant, but can change significantly over time. The reason for this is that a company with a good credit rating has higher chance of downgrade than of upgrade and vice versa (mean reversion in credit ratings). This means that default probabilities of investment grade companies increase over time, reflecting the fact that they may be downgraded to a state where the default probability is higher. By contrast,

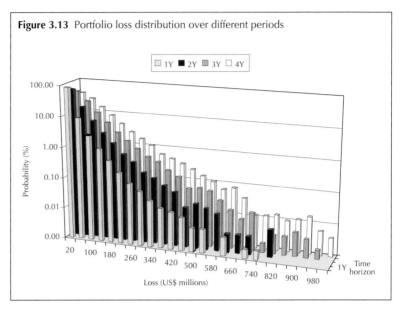

Figure 3.13 Portfolio loss distribution over different periods

non-investment grade ratings that do not default are more likely to improve than deteriorate in credit quality, and, therefore, the default probability decreases with time.

3.4.2 Change in exposure

The other effect when considering the portfolio loss distribution over different periods is the change in the exposure. For a bond or loan, this effect could be insignificant, while for a swap, for example, the exposure at two-years can show significantly more variation than that at one-year. (See the previous chapter for more details.)

Of course, this effect depends on the remaining and overall maturity of each deal. This can clearly have a significant impact in a derivatives portfolio. Figure 3.13 shows the evolution of the loss distribution for different time horizons and Table 3.10 shows the increase in the unexpected loss as the time horizon increases. Although the expected loss increases approxi-

Table 3.10 Expected and unexpected losses for different time horizons (all numbers in US$ millions)

	Expected loss	99th percentile	99.9th percentile	99.97th percentile
One year	19.35	163.41	340.24	483.86
Two years	38.87	239.44	449.54	568.83
Three years	58.96	326.83	562.45	695.19
Four years	79.08	408.88	669.78	886.60

mately linearly, as we would expect, the capital does not increase by as much, only approximately doubling as the time horizon is changed from one to four years.

3.5 LOAN EQUIVALENTS

Loan equivalents have been proposed and used by certain financial institutions for approximating the stochastic exposure of derivative portfolios by a single number. The advantage of this approach is that the computations are significantly simplified and it is possible to use loan portfolio calculators for analysing derivative exposures. Following this approach, it becomes easy to integrate the traditional loan portfolios with derivative products for risk analysis purposes. The main drawback of this approach is that it makes the crucial assumption that the unexpected loss can in some way be matched by the expected loss or the portfolio variance. For the majority of financial instruments, this is not the case. We will illustrate how loan equivalents can introduce substantial errors even for simple portfolios.

Consider a portfolio of 500 assets with the same probability of default of 0.5% and zero recovery rates. The exposures of each of the assets are taken to correspond to different maturities of interest rate swaps, each with notional US$10million. Initially, we will consider no correlation between the default events. We then consider changing the parameters, first, changing the probability of default to 1%; second, incorporating a homogeneous "asset return" correlation of 25%; and, third, changing the exposure distributions from swap to caps (which also have notionals of US$10million and different strikes and maturities). The results are shown in Table 3.11. LEQ1 refers to the loan equivalent computed via the expected loss, while LEQ2 refers to the loan equivalent computed via the variance. The formulas are given below:

$$LEQ1_i = E[X_i^+], \qquad LEQ2_i = \sqrt{LEQ1^2 + \mathrm{Var}[X_i^+]/(1 - p_i)}$$

$$(19ab)$$

The derivations of the above are given in Appendix A.

LEQ1 generally underestimates the unexpected loss with the notable exception of case (b), in which it (perhaps by chance) shows good agreement. However, it is not surprising, since we have already showed that stochastic exposure increases the tail of the loss distribution and that, consequently, if we ignore this randomness and replace it with only the expected value, we would expect to underestimate the tail. This is particularly true for case (d). However, for the swap portfolios, LEQ2 consistently overestimates the percentiles. The effect of correlation is very significant: comparing (a) and (b), we see that LEQ2 is a much greater overestimate when default correlation is present. This can be quantified since, in the event of multiple defaults, we will always lose a positive amount when we

Table 3.11 Expected and unexpected losses estimated using loan equivalent methods (all numbers in US$millions)

a) $p = 0.5\%$, $\lambda = 0\%$, swap exposures

	Actual	LEQ1	LEQ2
Expected loss	0.456	0.459	1.041
99th percentile	1.997	1.287	2.919
99.9th percentile	2.795	1.655	3.753
99.97th percentile	3.072	1.655	3.753

b) $p = 0.5\%$, $\lambda = 25\%$, swap exposures

	Actual	LEQ1	LEQ2
Expected loss	0.453	0.455	1.031
99th percentile	5.136	5.481	10.842
99.9th percentile	10.680	11.033	25.021
99.97th percentile	16.681	16.734	37.948

c) $p = 1\%$, $\lambda = 0\%$, swap exposures

	Actual	LEQ1	LEQ2
Expected loss	0.921	0.918	2.081
99th percentile	2.930	2.023	4.587
99.9th percentile	3.755	2.391	5.421
99.97th percentile	4.302	2.574	5.838

d) $p = 1\%$, $\lambda = 0\%$, cap exposures

	Actual	LEQ1	LEQ2
Expected loss	0.825	0.833	1.283
99th percentile	3.408	2.338	3.600
99.9th percentile	4.583	3.006	4.628
99.97th percentile	5.192	3.006	4.628

adopt a loan equivalent methodology, whereas in reality some default would result in losses, while others would not (negative exposures). Finally, we can see that for the cap portfolio, where the exposure distribution is more highly skewed than for the swap portfolio, both LEQ1 and LEQ2 underestimate the true unexpected loss at the 99.97th percentile.

Our conclusion is, therefore, that the use of loan equivalents to approximate the credit risk on a derivatives portfolio is suspect. We cannot have a good idea of the extent to which the loan equivalent calculation will over or under-estimate the true unexpected loss; the two measures cannot even give upper and lower bounds to the true unexpected loss. The error in using loan equivalents is sensitive to the nature of the exposures to be approximated: the value of default correlation, the percentile used and to a lesser extent the default probabilities in the portfolio.

3.6 CONCLUSION

We have presented a comprehensive framework for simulating the credit loss distribution and computing the economic capital of any type of portfolio using Monte Carlo. It is not possible to simulate directly binary default events, and the simulation has to be performed using a transformation of the binary distribution into a normal. Employing a normal distribution has become standard, but it is possible to use other continuous distributions through a different transformation. The corresponding normal distribution can be thought of as the "asset return" distribution, even though this is not necessary. Following this line of thought, default correlation is mapped into the corresponding asset return correlation.

Historical data can be used to estimate default probabilities and pairwise default correlations. Higher order default correlations are almost impossible to estimate due to the scarcity of multiple defaults. The transformations mentioned above uniquely determine the probabilities of multiple defaults (more than two). The latter figures will differ among various models and it is important that they are intuitively acceptable to the model's user. These figures are crucial for capital computation, since they determine the tail of the loss distribution. This is particularly true for portfolios with many assets.

We have placed major emphasis on derivative portfolios, which have not been the focus of past studies. It is clear that ignoring the variability of future exposures can severely underestimate the economic capital. This is true whether we use naïve approaches or more sophisticated loan equivalent methodologies. Over multiple periods the impact of stochastic exposures becomes even more severe. We have investigated the evolution of default probabilities over time using Moody's data. The set of numbers we have used imply that highly rated assets will tend to deteriorate in credit quality, while low rated assets that do not default will improve.

APPENDIX A. DERIVATION OF THE FORMULAS FOR LOAN EQUIVALENT EXPOSURES.

In Equation (1), we gave the formula for the loss on a credit portfolio at a given time T:

$$L_p = \sum_{i=1}^{n} X_i^+ d_i \left(1 - \delta_i\right) B(0, T) \qquad \text{(A1)}$$

where $X_i^+ = \max(X_i, 0)$. Let us simplify this formula by assuming that the recovery rate is constant, which is reasonable, since the effect of stochastic recovery rates is much smaller than that of stochastic exposures. We further simplify by removing the discount factor:

$$L_p = \sum_{i=1}^{n} X_i^+ d_i \qquad \text{(A2)}$$

The expected loss is given by (under the assumption that the exposure and default probabilities are independent as discussed in the main text):

$$E[L_p] = E\left[\sum_{i=1}^{n} X_i^+ d_i\right] = \sum_{i=1}^{n} E[X_i^+ d_i] = \sum_{i=1}^{n} E[X_i^+] p_i \quad \text{(A3)}$$

with p_i representing the default probability over the period of interest. Suppose that to simplify the problem of dealing with the stochastic variables X_i, we would like to represent them by fixed quantities LEQ1. One way in which to identify these quantities is via the expected loss of each expression. If the exposure is constant then the expected loss is simply:

$$E[L_p] = \sum_{i=1}^{n} LEQ1_i \, p_i \quad \text{(A4)}$$

By comparing this to Equation (A3), we can see that the loan equivalent amount is simply the expected exposure at the time horizon t, $LEQ1_i = E[X_i^+]$. We would use this to approximate the portfolio loss distribution by:

$$L_p = \sum_{i=1}^{n} LEQ1_i \, d_i \quad \text{(A5)}$$

ie, we replace the stochastic quantity representing the future exposure by its expected value. However, the problem with this is that by taking only the average exposure, we will miss the high exposures that we would expect to (at least in part) drive the tail of the distribution. We would therefore expect the above approximation to underestimate the true unexpected loss. This is often – but not always – the case.

So, in order to incorporate the uncertainty of the future exposure into the computations, we could, instead of using the expected loss, base the calculations on the variance of the loss distribution under the assumptions that the assets are independent (no covariance between the exposures). Since the variance of the loss distribution will be the sum of the individual variance of each asset, we can work at the asset level.

We make use of the definition of the variance of a random variable Y as being the expectation of the square of Y less the square of the expected value of Y, $E[Y^2] - E[Y]^2$. The variance of the loss for asset i can therefore be written as

$$\text{Var}[X_i^+ d_i] = E\left[(X_i^+ d_i)^2\right] - E\left[(X_i^+ d_i)\right]^2$$

$$= E\left[(X_i^+)^2\right] E\left[(d_i)^2\right] - E\left[(X_i^+)\right]^2 E\left[(d_i)\right]^2$$

$$= E\left[(X_i^+)^2\right] p_i - E[X_i^+]^2 \, p_i^2$$

$$= \left(\text{Var}[X_i^+] + E[X_i^+]^2 \right) p_i - E[X_i^+]^2 p_i^2$$

$$= p_i \text{Var}[X_i^+] + p_i(1-p_i) E[X_i^+]^2 \tag{A6}$$

Suppose we would like to write the variance of the loss distribution in terms of a constant loan equivalent amount. We would write the variance for a single asset as:

$$\text{Var}[LEQ2_i d_i] = LEQ2_i^2 \, p_i(1-p_i) \tag{A7}$$

ie, the constant amount multiplied by the variance of the probability of default. From Equations (A6) and (A7), we can identify the loan equivalent by:

$$LEQ2_i = \sqrt{E[X_i^+]^2 + \text{Var}[X_i^+]/(1-p_i)}$$

$$= \sqrt{LEQ1^2 + \text{Var}[X_i^+]/(1-p_i)} \tag{A8}$$

The intuition behind the above formula is to collapse the exposure distribution into a single value, which is given, by the expected exposure plus a factor depending on the variance of the exposure distribution. So, a very uncertain exposure will have a large loan equivalent to reflect the greater risk due to this uncertainty.

We finally note that sometimes a different version of a loan equivalent is used:

$$LEQ_i = E[X_i] + \sigma[X_i] \tag{A9}$$

where $\sigma[X_i] = \sqrt{\text{var}[X_i]}$ is the standard deviation of the exposure. Comparing this to Equation (8), we see that it is similar (at least "in spirit") in that it has a term corresponding to the average exposure and one to the variability of the exposure.

APPENDIX B. EXAMPLE SIMULATION ALGORITHM

Having described all the elements required to generate a loss distribution, we outline a simple simulation algorithm below.

1. Generate vector of exposures for each asset according to the time horizon, using – for example – a Monte Carlo simulation, as described in the previous chapter.
2. Obtain thresholds for each asset from individual default probabilities, according to $k_i = \Phi^{-1}(p_i)$.
3. Generate the $n \times n$ correlation matrix by either estimating the "asset returns" directly (eg, by using equity returns as a proxy) or from estimated default probabilities using Equation (8).

4. Perform decomposition of the correlation matrix, eg, $\Lambda = \mathbf{AA}'$.

5. Your simulation is:

For s = 1 to NumSims

   loss = 0

   Draw a vector of gaussian random numbers Y_i (uncorrelated normal variables)

   $\tilde{Y} = AY$ (obtain vector of correlated variables from uncorrelated ones)

   For a = 1 to NumAssets

      If $Y_i < k_i$ then (default has occurred)

         draw = int (rand() * NumExposures)+1 (random exposure)

         recovery = BetaDist (MeanRecovery, StdevRecovery) (random recovery)

         loss = loss + max (Exposure[draw], 0) * (1 – recovery)

               (add loss for this simulation)

      End if

   Next a

   TotalLoss[s] = loss (record total loss)

Next s

6. Calculate statistics of distribution of losses given by the vector *TotalLoss(s)*.

BIBLIOGRAPHY

Arvanitis, A., and J. Gregory, 1999, "A Credit Risk Toolbox", in *Credit Risk. Models and Management* (London: Risk Publications), pp. 283–9.

Carty, L. V. and D. Lieberman, 1996, *Defaulted Bank Loan Recoveries*, Moody's Investor Services, Global Credit Research, November.

Carty, L. V. and D. Lieberman, 1997, *Historical Default Rates of Corporate Bond Issuers 1920–1996*, Moody's Investor Services, Global Credit Research, July.

Credit Suisse Financial Products, 1997, *CreditRisk+, A Credit Risk Management Framework.*

JP Morgan & Co Incorp, 1997, *CreditMetrics* (New York, NY: JP Morgan).

Hull, J., 1993, *Options, Futures and Other Derivative Securities*, Second Edition (Englewood Cliffs, NJ: Prentice-Hall International).

Johnson N. L., S. Kotz and N. Balakrishnan, 1995, *Continuous Univariate Distributions*, Volumes I and II (New York, NY: John Wiley).

KMV Corporation, 1996, *Portfolio Manager, Description, Usage and Specification, Version 4.0*, CD-ROM (San Francisco: KMV Corporation).

Mark, R. M., 1999, "Integrated Credit Risk Management", in D. Shimko (ed), *Credit Risk: Models and Management* (London: Risk Books), pp. 3–35.

Meadows, R., 2000, "Haircuts for Hedge Funds", *Risk* 13(1), pp. 96–9.

Morrison, D. F., 1976, *Multivariate Statistical Methods*, Second Edition (New York, NY: McGraw-Hill).

Press, W. H., S. A. Teukolsky, W. T. Vetterling and B. P. Flannery, 1992, *Numerical Recipes in C*, Second Edition (Cambridge: Cambridge University Press).

4

Advanced Techniques For Credit Risk Management

In this chapter we present extensions to the framework developed in Chapter 3. This requires some mathematical detail, which the non-technical reader can skip without loss of continuity. First, we discuss analytical techniques that are based on the Edgeworth expansion and the saddle-point approximation for computing the credit loss distribution of a portfolio under certain restrictive assumptions. We then show how the Monte Carlo convergence can be improved using some well-known acceleration techniques – namely low-discrepancy or quasi-random sequences, importance sampling and control variates. Next, we apply extreme value theory to estimate events that are far into the tail of the credit loss distribution. To assess risk contributions we break down the unexpected loss into components corresponding to each underlying in the portfolio. This leads us to portfolio optimisation, where we generalise the traditional Markowitz mean–variance approach to credit portfolios. We minimise the expected shortfall for a given expected loss. Finally, we present a model of the term structure of the credit spread. This is based on a credit migration process and is used to mark-to-market the credit spread when computing economic capital. Special attention is given to the estimation of the model.

4.1 ANALYTICAL APPROXIMATIONS TO THE LOSS DISTRIBUTION
If we consider only defaults, the credit loss distribution is defined by 2^n possible outcomes, which cannot all be computed except for rather small portfolios. This is the reason for resorting to Monte Carlo simulation. An alternative approach is to obtain analytical approximations to the loss distribution under restrictive assumptions. These analytical expressions do not allow the full flexibility of Monte Carlo simulation, but they can be useful for very large portfolios, where simulation is not a viable option. Also, they can be used as a control variate to reduce the variance of the Monte Carlo estimator.

4.1.1 The Edgeworth expansion
The central limit theorem states that the sum of a large number, n, of independent random variables has an approximately normal distribution.

Although this is true as $n \to \infty$, the convergence can be slow, particularly if we are interested in estimating a high percentile of the distribution. For simplicity, we consider computing the loss distribution for a portfolio with equal exposures and recovery rates, so that the quantity of interest is the number of defaults, $Y = \sum_{i=1}^{n} d_i$. The approximation furnished by the central limit theorem may be improved if one expands the probability density function (pdf) of a random variable as an asymptotic series in n. The first term in the resulting series is the familiar central limit theorem, while higher terms give corrections that vanish in the limit as $n \to \infty$. This is known as the Edgeworth series (Abramowitz and Stegun, 1972). Its derivation uses the higher-order moments of the distributions of the constituent variables (d_i) and information that is contained in the cumulants. For a normal distribution, the first two cumulants are the mean and variance and the others are all zero. The higher cumulants give quantitative information about the non-normality of a distribution (eg, whether it is skewed or has fat tails). The Edgeworth expansion states that if (d_i) are independent random variables with means (p_i), standard deviations (σ_i) and cumulants $(\kappa_{i,r})_{r=1}^{\infty}$, the probability density function of the random variable $Y = \sum_{i=1}^{n} d_i$ is given by

$$f_Y(y)\,dy =$$

$$\frac{e^{-\frac{1}{2}t^2}\,dt}{\sqrt{2\pi}}\left[1+\frac{\kappa_3 He_3(t)}{3!\sigma^3}n^{-\frac{1}{2}}+\left(\frac{\kappa_4 He_4(t)}{4!\sigma^4}+\frac{\kappa_3^2 He_6(t)}{2!3!^2\sigma^6}\right)n^{-1}+\cdots\right]$$

(1)

with

$$t=\frac{y-p}{\sigma\sqrt{n}}, \quad p=\frac{1}{n}\sum_{i=1}^{n}p_i, \quad \sigma^2=\frac{1}{n}\sum_{i=1}^{n}\sigma_i^2, \quad \kappa_r=\frac{1}{n}\sum_{i=1}^{n}\kappa_{i,r} \quad (2)$$

Here $He_r(t)$ is the rth Hermite polynomial, which is given by successive differentiations of the function $e^{-\frac{1}{2}t^2}$ (so that, for example, the third and fourth Hermite polynomials are $He_3(t) = t^3 - 3t$ and $He_4(t) = t^4 - 6t^2 + 3$). The leading term in Equation (1) is the normal distribution, and the first and second correction terms adjust the skewness (asymmetry of the distribution) and kurtosis (fatness of the tails). We would expect that the inclusion of these two terms will greatly improve the approximation to the loss distribution by incorporating the skew and fat tails.

To apply these results when estimating the percentile of a loss distribution, we need to know the (κ_r). The rth cumulant of a random variable V is the coefficient of $s_r/r!$ in the power-series expansion of the logarithm of its moment-generating function, ie, in the expansion of $\log E[e^{sV}]$. For a binary random variable with underlying probability p, the rth cumulant is given

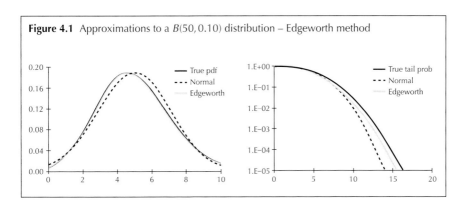

Figure 4.1 Approximations to a $B(50, 0.10)$ distribution – Edgeworth method

for $r \geq 1$ by the equation

$$\kappa_r = \left(p(1-p)\frac{d}{dp} \right)^{r-1} p \qquad (3)$$

so that the first four cumulants are p, $p(1 - p)$, $p(1 - p)(1 - 2p)$ and $p(1 - p) \times (1 - 6p + 6p^2)$.

Figure 4.1 shows the results for a simple case where Y corresponds to the well-known binomial distribution, which is denoted by $B(n, p)$. Taking $n = 50$ and $p = 0.10$, we have plotted the true pdf, the normal approximation and the results obtained by taking the first two correction terms from the Edgeworth series. The normal approximation does not take the skew and kurtosis into account and severely underestimates the tail of the distribution. The first two correction terms in the Edgeworth expansion from Equation (1) produce a better approximation.

In Figure 4.2 we consider an even more skewed distribution with $p = 0.01$. The Edgeworth approximation with four terms is better than the normal approximation, but it becomes less accurate further into the tail.

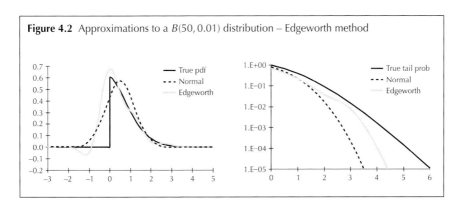

Figure 4.2 Approximations to a $B(50, 0.01)$ distribution – Edgeworth method

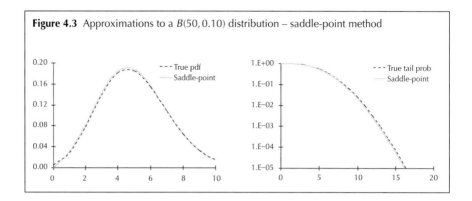

Figure 4.3 Approximations to a $B(50, 0.10)$ distribution – saddle-point method

The approximation is also poor to the left of the origin, where the true pdf vanishes. For example, the estimation of the unexpected loss at the 99.9th percentile corresponds to a tail probability of 0.001. The normal approximation underestimates the true value by 40% and the Edgeworth approximation (with four terms) underestimates it by 14%.

4.1.2 Saddle-point approximation

When considering sums of independent random variables, it is convenient to consider the moment-generating functions (mgf). The mgf of a random variable V is (see, eg, Morgan, 1984)

$$M_V(s) = E\left[e^{sV}\right] = \int_{-\infty}^{\infty} e^{st} p_V(t)\, dt \tag{4}$$

The mgf can be thought of the Fourier transform of the pdf. When independent distributions are added, their mgf are multiplied. For the example we are considering, which is a sum of binary variables (with weights w_i), the mgf is

$$M_Y(s) = \prod_{i=1}^{n} p_i + p_i\, e^{w_i s}$$

The next step is to "undo" the transform – ie, to obtain the pdf of $Y = \sum_{i=1}^{n} V_i$ from its mgf, $M_Y(s) = \prod_{i=1}^{n} M_{V_i}(s)$. This can be achieved by an inversion integral similar to Equation (4). By suitably approximating the shape of the integrand, one obtains an analytical approximation to the density function of Y. The technique is known as the method of steepest descents or saddle-point method (Bender and Orszag, 1978; Davison and Hinckley, 1988). The method also allows one to obtain analytical approximations to the tail probability without having to integrate the density function. The saddle-point method does not make any prior assumption about the shape of the distribution. The shape of the approximated pdf may be fat- or thin-tailed, symmetric or asymmetric, unimodal or multi-

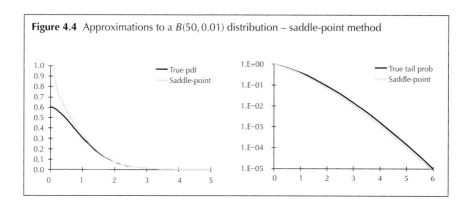

Figure 4.4 Approximations to a $B(50, 0.01)$ distribution – saddle-point method

modal and may have bounded or unbounded support.[1] Figures 4.3 and 4.4 compare the saddle-point approximation with the true distribution for $B(50, 0.1)$ and $B(50, 0.01)$. It is apparent that the saddle-point method gives better results than the normal and Edgeworth approximations in the tails, although it can be poor elsewhere. This is the region where the normal and Edgeworth approximations are worst. If we consider the $B(50, 0.01)$ example and estimate the tail probability of 0.001, we find that the saddle-point method underestimates its value by only 3% – a big improvement on the four-term Edgeworth expansion (14%) and the normal approximation (40%).

The computations we have presented can be extended to take into account unequal (and stochastic) exposures and recovery rates. However, it is not possible to include correlation in the analysis. For the above analytical techniques to be useful, it is necessary to make approximations to the portfolio in question. Despite this drawback, they are computationally undemanding and can provide a very efficient method for calculating tail probabilities. As we shall see in the next section, they can also be used as control variates for improving the convergence of the Monte Carlo simulation.

4.2 MONTE CARLO ACCELERATION TECHNIQUES

As discussed in Chapter 3, a large number of simulations are usually required to obtain a good estimate of the unexpected loss and the capital for a credit portfolio. This is because the tail events (multiple defaults) are rare and the percentile required is normally quite high – ie, far into the tail of the distribution. In this section we discuss various numerical techniques for enhancing the convergence of the Monte Carlo simulation, meaning that fewer simulations will be required to achieve a given level of accuracy. A useful way of gauging the improvement such techniques provide is to keep track of other Monte Carlo estimators for known quantities, such as the average loss or default probabilities. We also discuss the use of low-discrepancy sequences and importance sampling.

Figure 4.5 Estimation of economic capital for the example in Table 3.5 using standard Monte Carlo using a Sobol sequence

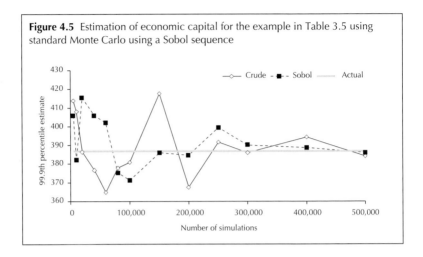

4.2.1 Low-discrepancy sequences

A problem with standard Monte Carlo simulation is that it leads to an error which decreases as $S^{-1/2}$, where S is the number of simulations. Therefore, to improve a Monte Carlo estimate by a factor of 10, we need to perform 100 times as many simulations. The crude or standard Monte Carlo approach simply uses standard random numbers to generate each simulation. As computers cannot generate true random numbers, algorithms have been devised to generate pseudo-random numbers, which are used in the standard method.

Other techniques have been developed to speed up simulation. One such approach is to use low-discrepancy sequences (also known as quasi-random numbers). These methods are no longer random and do not attempt to be random. Examples of quasi-random numbers or low-discrepancy sequences are Sobol, Holton and Faure (Press *et al*, 1992). The idea of a low-discrepancy sequence is to generate points that fill the space more uniformly. We will illustrate their efficiency by using Sobol, a well-known quasi-random sequence. It is an easy technique to implement and works well in high dimensions. To assess the accuracy of the Sobol sequence, we consider the computation of capital for the portfolio used in the last chapter (Table 3.5). We include all the effects – stochastic exposures, default correlation and stochastic recovery rates. We compare the 99.9th percentile estimator given by the basic Monte Carlo method with the results obtained when a Sobol quasi-random sequence is used. Figure 4.5 shows the two estimators of the economic capital at the 99.9th percentile level with increasing number of simulations. The Sobol method gives better and more stable convergence than the crude approach. Indeed, we have found it to give reasonable improvement in a variety of cases.

It is easy to see why a quasi-random sequence such as Sobol can be

Figure 4.6 Generation of 5,000 points in two-dimensional space using a purely random sequence (*left*) and a Sobol quasi-random sequence (*right*)

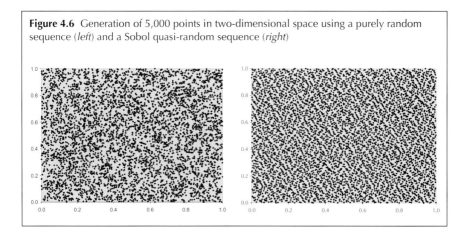

useful. Consider, for example, generating the default events for two uncorrelated underlyings. We could do this by picking a large number of points in two-dimensional space, as shown in Figure 4.6. The Sobol sequence clearly gives superior filling of the space. This means that when generating the default of both underlyings the Sobol sequence is less likely to over- or under-sample the specific region. For example, in Figure 4.6, when considering individual default probabilities of 10%, the probability of joint default (ie, the percentage number of points in the lower left-hand corner) is estimated to be 0.82% using standard Monte Carlo and 1.00% with the Sobol sequence. The latter value is clearly the answer we would expect.

4.2.2 Importance sampling

Importance sampling is a commonly used technique for speeding up convergence in Monte Carlo. Loosely speaking, rather than generating purely random paths, it involves simulating paths that are more relevant in determining the quantity that is being estimated. This should allow us to concentrate the simulations in the regions of most interest, although, as we shall see, we must be sure to correct for any bias introduced into the simulation.

The problem with estimating tail events is that, by their very nature, they are extremely rare since they arise from a far greater than average number of defaults. A way of improving efficiency would therefore be to artificially increase the default probabilities for some, or all, counterparties in the simulation while correcting for this bias. As discussed in Chapter 3, the default events are generated by drawing an n-dimensional vector of correlated normal variables $\tilde{Y}_i$, where n represents the number of underlyings in the simulation. If one of these variables is below a certain threshold of default, k_i, default occurs. These thresholds are directly related to the default probabilities, p_i, according to $k_i = \Phi^{-1}(p_i)$. We can change the individual default

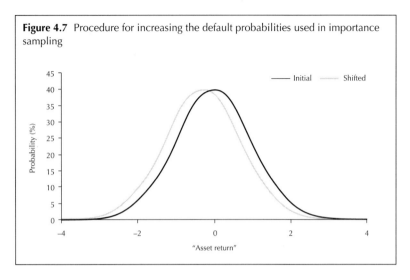

Figure 4.7 Procedure for increasing the default probabilities used in importance sampling

probabilities by applying a shift, ε_i, to each normal random variable. This means that we are drawing from a distribution $N(\varepsilon_i, 1)$ rather than $N(0,1)$. If ε_i is negative, the corresponding default probability is increased. This is also true for the probabilities of downgrade: by applying negative shifts to some or all of the counterparties in the simulation, more defaults and downgrades are produced. The simulation is therefore biased into the region where losses are high. This procedure is illustrated in Figure 4.7. For example, for a default probability of $p_i = 1\%$, we obtain $k_i = -2.326$; if we apply a shift of $\varepsilon_i = -0.3$ when we simulate these default variables, the actual default frequency is $p_i^* = \Phi(-2.326 + 0.3) = 2.14\%$.

The above procedure is of no use unless we can "correct" for the shift that causes a change in the underlying default probabilities. Mathematically, the process of shifting the normal variables corresponds to a change of probability measure. The Cameron–Martin theorem can be used to quantify this change of measure. This is similar to the application of Girsanov's theorem in the asset pricing literature to compute the change in probability measure with the aim of linking the historical and the risk-neutral measures. The Cameron–Martin theorem is applied as follows:

$$\frac{dQ}{dP} = \exp\left(-\frac{1}{2}\sum_{i=1}^{n}\mu_i^2 + \sum_{i=1}^{n}\mu_i \tilde{Y}_i \right) \tag{5}$$

where the μ_is are computed by solving the set of non-linear equations

$$\varepsilon_i = \sum_{l=1}^{n}\sigma_{il}\,\omega_l\,\mu_l \tag{6}$$

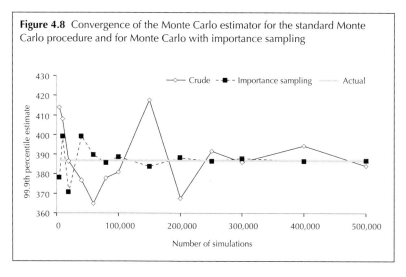

Figure 4.8 Convergence of the Monte Carlo estimator for the standard Monte Carlo procedure and for Monte Carlo with importance sampling

In Equation (5), $\tilde{Y}_i$ represents the standard normal variables under the original measure P and σ_{ii} and ω_i are, respectively, the eigenvalues and eigenvectors of the correlation matrix. Applying this change of measure ensures that the shifted standard variables have mean zero and unit variance under the new probability measure, Q. This means that we should weight each simulation by dQ/dP, whose value is dependent on the shift and the random numbers drawn in the simulation. For simulations with many defaults the value of dQ/dP will be small, reflecting the fact that this outcome is unlikely. If the shifts are chosen well, the sampling of the tail of the distribution will be improved, increasing the accuracy of the Monte Carlo estimator of the percentile.

Provided that it is implemented carefully, importance sampling can provide an excellent improvement in the speed of Monte Carlo simulation. However, the choice of shift is very important. If the shift is too large and negative, convergence can be worsened. We have found that the best procedure is to apply shifts only to the counterparties with the best credit quality and/or highest exposure. It can also aid convergence if counterparties with high probabilities of default are shifted by a positive amount so as, effectively, to reduce their probability of default. In doing this we are in a sense making the portfolio more homogeneous.

The improvement in speed of convergence is typically between five and 10 times. An example illustrating this for the portfolio in Chapter 3 is shown in Figure 4.8.

4.2.3 Control variates

As discussed in the first section, we have derived a number of analytical formulae that have been shown to give extremely accurate and fast estimation of the loss distribution under certain restrictions. Although such expressions cannot account for the completely general case, they would seem to be good candidates to act as control variates for Monte Carlo simulation. A random variable (estimator) $\hat{C}$ is a control variate for the (Monte Carlo) estimator, $\hat{P}$, of P if it is correlated with $\hat{P}$ and if its expectation, C, is known. The control variate can be used to construct an estimator $\hat{P}_\theta$ with a smaller variance than the original estimator $\hat{P}$ as follows:

$$\hat{P}_\theta = \hat{P} - \theta(\hat{C} - C)$$ (7)

where $\hat{P}$ is the Monte Carlo estimator of P, $\hat{C}$ is the Monte Carlo estimator of C (under the same simulation), C is the actual (known) value of the control variate and $\hat{P}_\theta$ is the unbiased estimator of P based on the control variate.

The variance of the estimator $\hat{P}_\theta$ will be smaller than that of $\hat{P}$ provided that θ is chosen appropriately. The optimum value of θ is $\rho_{\hat{P}\hat{C}} \times \sigma_{\hat{P}}/\sigma_{\hat{C}}$, where ρ denotes correlation and σ denotes standard deviation. In this case the reduction in variance is given by

$$\text{var}\left[\hat{P}_\theta\right] = \left(1 - \rho^2_{\hat{P}\hat{C}}\right)\text{var}[\hat{P}]$$ (8)

It is possible to estimate θ, but often the easiest and fastest approach is simply to take $\theta = 1$.

The saddle-point approximation described earlier is a good way to estimate the loss distribution analytically, although it can only be used under the assumption that there is no correlation between default events. If the percentiles of the loss distributions calculated with zero and positive default correlation are highly correlated, the analytical expression for computing the former can be used to construct an efficient control variate for the latter. The control variate estimator of the unexpected loss would then be

$$UL^{\text{Correlation}} = UL^{\text{Correlation}}_{\text{Monte Carlo}} - \theta\left(UL^{\text{No correlation}}_{\text{Monte Carlo}} - UL^{\text{No correlation}}_{\text{Saddle-point}}\right)$$ (9)

Note that since the correlated normal variables are generated from a set of independent normal variables, it is a simple matter to calculate the distributions with and without default correlation in the same simulation ($UL^{\text{Correlation}}_{\text{Monte Carlo}}$ and $UL^{\text{No correlation}}_{\text{Monte Carlo}}$). One beneficial feature of using control variates is that because the additional computation time is small they will almost always improve the efficiency of the Monte Carlo simulation, although the speed-up can be negligible. Figure 4.9 shows the improvement gained by using the control variate described above to compute the unexpected loss for the portfolio in Chapter 3.

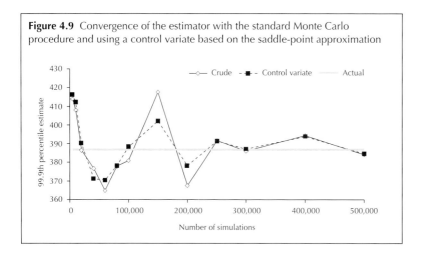

Figure 4.9 Convergence of the estimator with the standard Monte Carlo procedure and using a control variate based on the saddle-point approximation

4.3 EXTREME VALUE THEORY

4.3.1 Overview

Extreme value theory (EVT) deals with the modelling of extreme and rare events. It has been applied to disciplines such as hydrology and climatology and, more recently, to insurance (Embrechts, Klüppelberg and Mikosch, 1997). EVT has also been identified as a possible too! for market risk VAR computations (Danielsson and de Vries, 1998). Given that it is the study of extreme events, such as multiple defaults, EVT would seem ideal for use in credit risk management, as discussed by Ong (1999). The normal distribution governs the limiting behaviour of common events as dictated by the central limit theorem or the Edgeworth expansion. As we shall see, there is another family of distributions that proves to be important in the study of the limiting behaviour of extreme events. As highlighted in the last two chapters, one of the main concerns in credit risk management is the estimation of the probability that a loss will exceed a high threshold, UL_α. For a given confidence level, α, this threshold is defined such that

$$\Pr(UL_\alpha > L_p) = \alpha \qquad (10)$$

The random variable L_p denotes the loss due to credit events and the threshold UL_α represents a quantity that will be exceeded with probability α. We also described how the estimation of such a threshold can be difficult because the required probability is generally quite small. Since EVT supposedly gives information about the form of the distribution in this low-probability (tail) region of the loss distribution, it should be a useful tool for the estimation of such thresholds and, therefore, for the computation of the unexpected credit loss and capital. As far as the theory of EVT is concerned, we will restrict ourselves to presenting the important

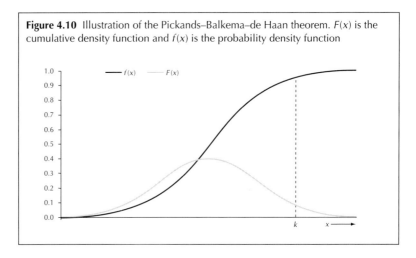

Figure 4.10 Illustration of the Pickands–Balkema–de Haan theorem. $F(x)$ is the cumulative density function and $f(x)$ is the probability density function

theoretical results that are useful for applying EVT to credit risk management. An important result of EVT which we are going to use is the
Pickands–Balkema–de Haan theorem (Balkema and de Haan, 1974, and
Pickands, 1975). This theorem states that, for a large class of distributions,
losses above a high threshold follow a generalised Pareto distribution.
Clearly, when estimating the tails of credit loss distributions it would be
useful to know the actual limiting distribution that governs the extreme
losses. The other significant result in EVT is the Fisher–Tippett theorem,
which describes the limiting behaviour of sampled maxima and is akin to
the central limit theorem. Finally, we illustrate the results with a practical
example.

4.3.2 Generalised Pareto distribution
In its simplest form, the generalised Pareto distribution (GPD) is commonly
expressed as the density function

$$G_{\xi,\mu,\sigma}(x) = \begin{cases} 1-\left(1+\xi\dfrac{x-\mu}{\sigma}\right)^{-1/\xi} & \text{if } \xi \neq 0 \\[2em] 1-\exp\left(-\dfrac{x-\mu}{\sigma}\right) & \text{if } \xi = 0 \end{cases} \qquad (11)$$

where ξ is the shape parameter, μ is the location parameter and σ is the tail
index. The GPD family of distributions includes three other distributions:
the Gumbel ($\xi = 0$), the Fréchet ($\xi > 0$) and the Weibull ($\xi < 0$). The
Pickands–Balkema–de Haan theorem states that above a certain threshold,
k, a distribution function will be well approximated by $F_k(x) \approx G_{\xi,\mu,\sigma}(x)$.
This is illustrated in Figure 4.10, which shows a threshold above which a

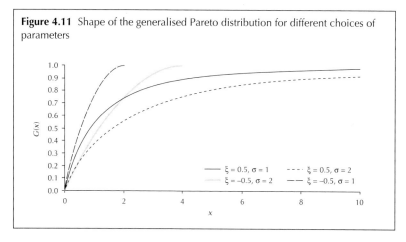

Figure 4.11 Shape of the generalised Pareto distribution for different choices of parameters

distribution may exhibit GPD behaviour. Figure 4.11 shows the shape of the GPD distribution for different combinations of shape parameter, ξ, and tail index, σ.

4.3.3 Sample mean excess function

The main hindrance in the application of EVT is the selection of the threshold parameter. We need to know the point above which we can accurately approximate an unknown distribution with a generalised Pareto distribution. If the threshold is too low, the distribution will not be GPD-like above this point; if the threshold is too high, we will have few relevant data with which to determine the GPD parameters. We need some way of estimating the optimal threshold, k. One method is to use the mean excess function, which is defined as

$$\hat{e}(k') = \frac{\sum\limits_{i=1}^{n} \left(L_i - k' \right)^+}{\sum\limits_{i=1}^{n} 1_{\{L_i > k'\}}} \qquad (12)$$

That is, we sum all the excesses above a certain threshold k' and divide the result by the total number of data points that exceed the threshold. It is, therefore, the conditional expectation of the variable L_i (ie, the expected value of L_i) given that it is greater than k'. For GPD distributions, the mean excess function can be written as

$$e(k') = \frac{\sigma + \xi k'}{1 - \xi} \qquad (13)$$

which is a linear function of the threshold k'. Therefore, a plot of the mean excess function given by Equation (12) should be approximately linear above a certain point. This point should be chosen as the threshold, k, so that we can be reasonably sure that above k the distribution is GPD-like. A positive gradient in the mean excess function is indicative of heavy tails. It is clearly desirable to be able to estimate the lowest threshold above which the distribution is indeed GPD-like since this will give the maximum amount of data for fitting. At the current time there is no satisfactory algorithm for non-subjective estimation of the threshold in EVT, but a number of tools, mostly graphical, are available for this purpose. Examples of these tools include QQ-plots – where quantiles of the sample are plotted against those of a GPD distribution – and mean excess plots (as described above). With both an approximately straight line is an indication that the data closely follow a GPD.

4.3.4 Example

We will now illustrate the application of mean excess plots for estimating the tail of a credit loss distribution. The portfolio we analyse consists of loans to counterparties of different ratings; details are given in Table 4.1. Since most of the default probabilities are small, the tail of the distribution will be rather heavy. Moreover, we have included default correlation in the analysis, which, as discussed in the last chapter, will fatten the tail further. The use of constant exposures can be expected to make the analysis harder as the distribution is likely to be less smooth. This means that the estimation of high percentiles will be difficult unless a large number of Monte Carlo simulations are run.

We performed a Monte Carlo simulation with 50,000 scenarios to obtain an approximation to the loss distribution for the portfolio. From these simulations we calculated the sample mean excess function, which is shown in Figure 4.12. This shows approximately linear behaviour up to a loss of US$250 million, between US$250 million and US$600 million, and again above US$600 million – although in the last case we see random errors arising from the sparseness of the data in this region.

Given the trend shown in Figure 4.12, we performed a least-squares fit of

Table 4.1 Portfolio used in example

Number of loans	Exposure (US$ million)	Rating	Default probability (%)	Recovery (%) Mean	Std dev
25	100	Aaa	0.02	30	25
20	75	Aa	0.05	30	25
20	60	A	0.10	30	25
15	50	Baa	0.15	30	25
10	25	Ba	1.29	30	25
5	20	B	6.81	30	25
5	10	Caa	24.06	30	25

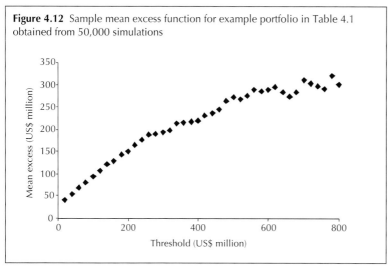

Figure 4.12 Sample mean excess function for example portfolio in Table 4.1 obtained from 50,000 simulations

the loss data above the US$600 million threshold (a total of 28 data points). The results are shown in Figure 4.13, where they are compared with those obtained using a very large Monte Carlo simulation (50,000,000 simulations). The distribution with 50,000 simulations is clearly quite jagged compared with the distribution obtained using the large simulation. However, the Pareto fit to the data from the smaller simulation agrees very well with the distribution obtained with 1,000 times as many scenarios. This shows the power of EVT if used correctly.

We also applied the same procedure using different parameterisations and found similar behaviour for all thresholds above US$400 million. The power of EVT can be illustrated if we calculate very high exceedance probabilities for the example portfolio, as shown in Figure 4.14 for a loss of

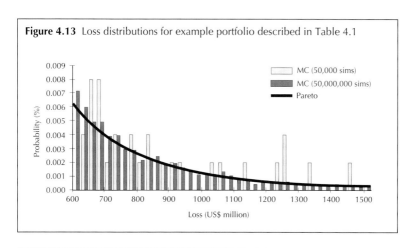

Figure 4.13 Loss distributions for example portfolio described in Table 4.1

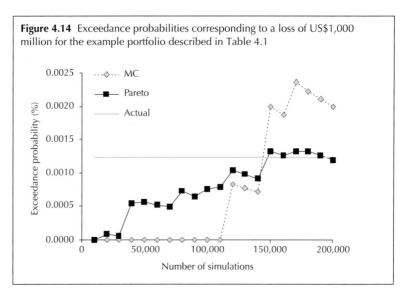

Figure 4.14 Exceedance probabilities corresponding to a loss of US$1,000 million for the example portfolio described in Table 4.1

US$1,000 million. In a Monte Carlo simulation with just 50,000 scenarios we can only estimate a probability with a resolution of 0.002% (the biggest loss out of 50,000), which shows why this provides such a poor estimate of the probability. However, EVT converges much faster to the actual probability. In practice the estimation of such a small probability may be needed for an institution with very good credit quality.

4.4 MARGINAL RISK

Until now we have dealt with the estimation of the unexpected loss or economic capital for a credit portfolio, and so far in this chapter we have fine-tuned the computational techniques presented in Chapter 3. The next step is to understand and then to control the risk contained in a credit portfolio.

To achieve this we start by determining which underlyings contribute most to the portfolio's total risk, which can be done by ranking them according to their marginal risk. This enables one to decide which positions should be reduced to achieve the most effective reduction of the portfolio's aggregate risk and improve its return on capital. It should be emphasised that the underlyings with the highest marginal risk will not necessarily be those with the highest default probabilities as exposure concentration is also a significant factor. It is even possible for an underlying with a low default probability to dominate the portfolio and have the greatest marginal risk contribution. Marginal risk also provides a useful measure for efficient computation of the increase in portfolio capital when a new instrument is added. These ideas will be important in optimising the portfolio's risk-adjusted returns.

4.4.1 Risk sensitivities

We now consider the computation of the marginal risk of an asset in a portfolio, assuming that the loss distribution is generated from a Monte Carlo simulation. Otherwise the analysis is completely general so that it is compatible with any framework and not just the one described in the last chapter.

In any Monte Carlo simulation we generate a large number of portfolio losses for many different scenarios. These losses can be used to approximate the loss distribution, as described in the previous chapter. We can therefore express the loss on the portfolio in a given scenario as

$$L_p = \sum_{i=1}^{n} w_i L_i \tag{14}$$

where L_i is the random loss on underlying i in the scenario and w_i is the weight of that underlying in the portfolio. Suppose that we have calculated the unexpected loss for a portfolio of n underlying credit exposures to be $UL_{\alpha,n}$. Recall that the unexpected loss is defined by a percentile of the portfolio loss distribution according to

$$\Pr\left[UL_{\alpha,n} > L_p\right] = \alpha \tag{15}$$

where α represents the confidence level (eg, 0.1%). How can we now analyse this unexpected loss? Can one find a mathematical definition of the marginal risks? It would seem desirable to be able to write the unexpected loss as follows:

$$UL_{\alpha,n} = \sum_{i=1}^{n} w_i UL_{\alpha,i} \tag{16}$$

where $UL_{\alpha,i}$ is interpreted as the marginal contribution to the unexpected loss for the ith underlying in the portfolio. Indeed, such a decomposition is possible as a direct consequence of Euler's theorem, which states that if F is a real, n-variable homogeneous function of degree k, then

$$\sum_{j=1}^{n} x_j \frac{\partial F(x)}{\partial x_j} = x_1 \frac{\partial F(x)}{\partial x_1} + x_2 \frac{\partial F(x)}{\partial x_2} + \ldots + x_n \frac{\partial F(x)}{\partial x_n} = kF(x) \tag{17}$$

Since the unexpected loss is homogeneous of degree one, Equation (16) can be re-written as

$$UL_{\alpha,n} = \sum_{i=1}^{n} w_i \frac{\partial UL_{\alpha,n}}{\partial w_i} \tag{18}$$

where the $\partial UL_{\alpha,n}/\partial w_i$ term represents the sensitivity of the unexpected loss to a change in exposure to the underlying. We will therefore refer to this term as the "risk sensitivity". Clearly, if the risk sensitivity associated with a particular underlying is high, we can expect that underlying to contribute a significant amount to the total portfolio risk, and vice versa. Risk sensitivities have the appealing property that they aggregate linearly into the total diversified risk (the unexpected loss). Equation (18) therefore suggests a natural way to apportion the portfolio risk to each underlying while respecting its individual weight. Garman (1996 and 1997) provides a more detailed discussion of marginal risk measures under multivariate normal assumptions. Hallerbach (1999) discusses computations without any distributional assumptions.

The economic capital to the same confidence level α, $EC_{\alpha,n}$, is simply the difference between the unexpected and expected losses:

$$EC_{\alpha,n} = UL_{\alpha,n} - EL_n \qquad (19)$$

The analysis for the unexpected loss can be easily extended to the economic capital. From Equation (19) we get

$$\frac{\partial EC_{\alpha,n}}{\partial w_i} = \frac{\partial UL_{\alpha,n}}{\partial w_i} - \frac{\partial EL_n}{\partial w_i} \qquad (20)$$

We see that the sensitivity of the economic capital is equal to the difference between the sensitivity of the unexpected loss and the sensitivity of the expected loss, knowing that the portfolio loss is equal to the unexpected loss and the sensitivity of its unconditional expected loss. We will consider the risk sensitivity of the economic capital from now on, although we note that this should be similar to the risk sensitivity of the unexpected loss since the expected loss is, by comparison, generally quite small.

4.4.2 Estimation of derivatives
The first derivatives for the expected loss in Equation (20) are given by

$$\frac{\partial EL_n}{\partial w_i} = E[L_i] \qquad (21)$$

The most obvious way to estimate the derivative representing the marginal unexpected loss in Equation (18) is by using a finite-difference method such as

$$\frac{\partial UL_{\alpha,n}}{\partial w_i} = \frac{UL_{\alpha,n}(w_i + \varepsilon) - UL_{\alpha,n}(w_i - \varepsilon)}{2\varepsilon} \qquad (22a)$$

or

$$\frac{\partial UL_{\alpha,n}}{\partial w_i} = \frac{UL_{\alpha,n}\left(w_i + \varepsilon\right) - UL_{\alpha,n}}{\varepsilon} \tag{22b}$$

which means that we must compute the loss distribution once or twice for each sensitivity with a sufficiently small change, ε, in the weight of the relevant underlying. The "shift" ε needs to be large enough to cause a change in the unexpected loss (a very small change in the weight may lead to numerical error). Clearly, this procedure can be quite slow and would also be expected to lead to significant errors. Even if we store the simulation data, we still need to aggregate it again – ie, sum each loss to find the overall loss in a given simulation with the corresponding weight changed from w_i to $w_i + \varepsilon$. Furthermore, since the estimated unexpected loss can have quite a large confidence interval, we would expect the estimated first derivative to exhibit an even larger statistical error. Rather than a finite-difference approach to computing the derivative, we could instead try to use the fact that this derivative can be written as a conditional expectation (Gouriéroux, Laurent and Scaillet, 1999):

$$\frac{\partial UL_{\alpha,n}}{\partial w_i} = E\left[L_i \,\middle|\, L_p = UL_{\alpha,n}\right] = \frac{E\left[L_i 1_{\left\{L_p = UL_{\alpha,n}\right\}}\right]}{E\left[1_{\left\{L_p = UL_{\alpha,n}\right\}}\right]} \tag{23}$$

This formula looks as if it will be difficult to compute because the probability that $L_p = UL_{\alpha,n}$ is extremely small. However, instead of attributing all the weight to any observations L_p that are exactly equal to the unexpected loss $UL_{\alpha,n}$, we can spread across all observations close to this point by using the function $K((L_p - UL_{\alpha,n})/h)$ so as to smooth the estimator. The function $K(\cdot)$ is a "kernel" – a real, symmetric function that integrates to unity – and the parameter h is the "bandwidth". As h tends to zero, the kernel tends towards the indicator function in Equation (23).

Suppose that the vector of simulated losses for each underlying in the portfolio for a total of S simulations is given by $L_j = (L_{j,1}, \ldots, L_{j,S})$, $j = 1, \ldots, n$. They are all stored in memory. We note that this will require the storage of a total of $n \times S$ numbers. The portfolio loss for a given simulation path, k, will be

$$L_p^k = \sum_{j=1}^{n} w_j L_{j,k} \tag{24}$$

so that Equation (23) now becomes

$$\frac{\partial UL_{\alpha,n}}{\partial w_i} = \frac{\dfrac{1}{nS}\displaystyle\sum_{k=1}^{S} L_{i,k}\,1_{\{L_p^k = UL_{\alpha,n}\}}}{\dfrac{1}{nS}\displaystyle\sum_{k=1}^{S} 1_{\{L_p^k = UL_{\alpha,n}\}}} \tag{25}$$

Finally, the kernel estimator for the first derivative of the unexpected loss in (23) can be written as

$$\frac{\partial UL_{\alpha,n}}{\partial w_i} = \frac{\dfrac{1}{nS}\displaystyle\sum_{k=1}^{S} L_{i,k}\, K\!\left(\dfrac{L_p^k - UL_{\alpha,n}}{h}\right)}{\dfrac{1}{nS}\displaystyle\sum_{k=1}^{S} K\!\left(\dfrac{L_p^k - UL_{\alpha,n}}{h}\right)} \tag{26}$$

Indeed, it can be shown that the above expression converges towards Equation (23) as $S \to \infty$ and $h \to 0$, ie, as the number of underlying simulations increases and the bandwidth shrinks. The kernel estimator is a weighted average of the simulated losses and, unlike the finite-difference approach described above, does not involve any differentiation. Furthermore, such numerical differentiation of the empirical percentile will result in an unstable estimation of the sensitivity because the percentile is not a smooth function of the weights in the portfolio. The kernel estimator is a smooth function.

There are a number of different candidates for the kernel, $K(\cdot)$. An obvious contender is the normal distribution function, which will clearly give a lot of weight to observations lying close to the unexpected loss but much less to those further away. Other kernels can be used, such as triangular or uniform distributions, but here we will consider only a normal kernel. It can be shown that the optimal bandwidth in such a problem (if "optimal" is defined in the sense of minimising the mean squared-error function) is proportional to $S^{-1/5}$ (Scaillet, 2000). We will therefore use the expression $h = \sigma_p S^{-1/5}$, where σ_p is the standard deviation of the portfolio losses. If the tail of a loss distribution is fat, this will be partially reflected in a larger standard deviation and, therefore, a larger bandwidth. This is desirable as the simulated losses will be more spread out.

4.4.3 Example of kernel estimation
We will compute the risk sensitivities for the following stylised, hypothetical portfolio. We consider all combinations of exposures of 100, 150, 200, 250 and 300, and default probabilities of 0.5%, 1.0%, 1.5%, 2.0% and

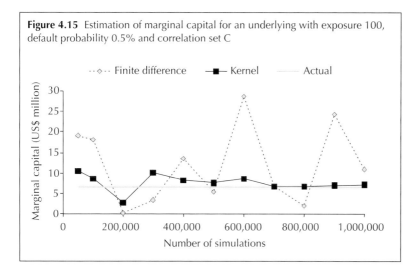

Figure 4.15 Estimation of marginal capital for an underlying with exposure 100, default probability 0.5% and correlation set C

2.5%, giving a total of 25 possibilities. The recovery rates are all 50%. We created three sets, A, B and C, of these 25 underlyings with different correlations of 10%, 20% and 30%, respectively. The cross-correlations between these sets are the average of the corresponding correlations in each individual set (for example, the cross-correlation between A and B is 15%). We investigate the variation of the risk sensitivities as a function of the exposure, the default probability and the correlation. This should provide a good test of the procedure as the results should be fairly smooth. First, we test the accuracy of the estimation of the risk sensitivity as the number of Monte Carlo simulations is increased. Each underlying has exposure 100, default probability 0.5% and the correlation set is C (Figure 4.15). We compare the finite-difference estimator in Equation (22b) with the kernel estimator in Equation (26). The finite-difference estimator is very unstable, even with a large number of simulations, whereas the kernel estimator gives far better convergence. We have also found the latter to be reasonably stable as the bandwidth is changed.

The results discussed below are based on a total of 500,000 simulations. In all, $75 \times 500{,}000 = 37{,}500{,}000$ numbers need to be stored for the kernel estimation procedure. In fact, as long as the default probabilities are low, it is more efficient to store only those simulations in which there was a loss, even though this requires three numbers: the loss, the simulation number and a reference identifying the underlying. Typically, this requires only about 5–20% of the capacity needed to store all simulation losses. We have found that even if it is necessary to store the data in a file format, computation of the risk sensitivity (and indeed the whole loss distribution) can be done quickly. This may be important for an institution with a large portfolio since it means that it is possible to run one large Monte Carlo simulation

Table 4.2 Basic statistics of the loss distribution of the hypothetical portfolio computed using 500,000 Monte Carlo simulations

Statistic	Estimate
Mean	113.3
Standard deviation	204.7
99th percentile	951.7
99.9th percentile	1699.9

(perhaps overnight) and then perform numerous fast computations on the portfolio with no need to re-run the simulation.

For the stylised portfolio considered here we estimated the basic quantities given in Table 4.2. Based on 500,000 simulations, the economic capital was estimated to be 838.4 and 1586.6 at the 99th and 99.9th percentiles, respectively. We will compute the risk sensitivity divided by the expected loss of each underlying (probability of default times the exposure). The reason for doing this is that it allows a fair comparison between the relative risks of the underlyings – ie, the amount of unexpected loss (or, more precisely, economic capital) for each unit of expected loss. This shows which underlying is, relatively speaking, the biggest user of capital. In Figure 4.16 we show this for all 75 underlyings at the 99th and 99.9th percentile levels.

The results in the figure are reasonably smooth with respect to changes in the exposure and default probability (except for the diagram at top right, where the irregularity is probably a result of random error from the Monte Carlo simulation). This supports our claim that the kernel estimation procedure can be performed to good accuracy with a reasonable number of simulations. Looking at the results more closely, we observe that an increase in exposure generally increases the adjusted marginal capital. This is not surprising as one would expect two exposures of 100 to be less risky than one exposure of 200. A reduction in the default probability also relatively increases the marginal capital – ie, an underlying with default probability 1.0% has less than double the marginal capital of one with 0.5% default probability. Finally, as we would expect, the marginal capital contributions increase consistently with increasing correlation because high correlation extends the tail of the distribution. The breakdown of marginal capital is fairly similar when either the 99th or the 99.9th percentiles is considered as a confidence level. The only noticeable difference is that as default probability decreases, the relative marginal capital increases more at the 99.9th percentile level than at the 99th percentile. A possible interpretation of this is that at a higher confidence level we are effectively more risk-averse and care more about the skew and fat tails in the distribution.

Figure 4.16 Risk sensitivities (based on economic capital) divided by the expected loss corresponding to (*left*) the 99th percentile and (*right*) the 99.9th percentile for all 75 underlyings in the hypothetical portfolio for correlation set A (*top*), B (*middle*) and C (*bottom*)

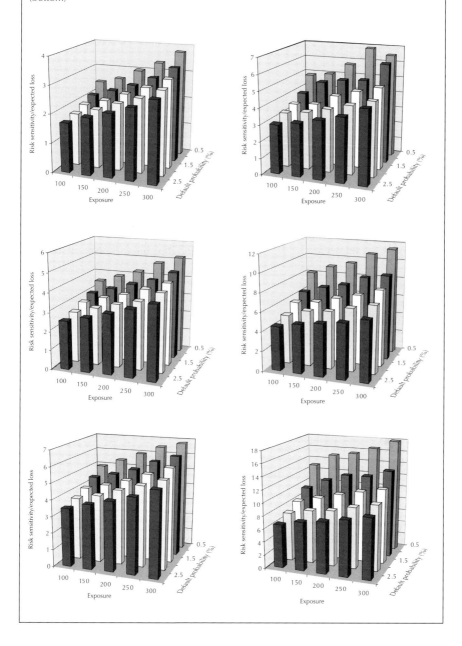

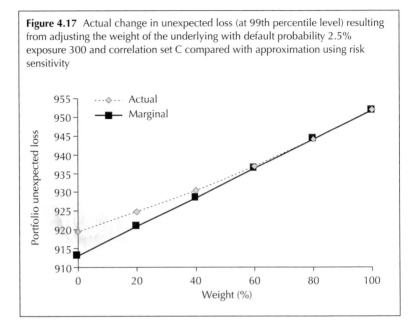

Figure 4.17 Actual change in unexpected loss (at 99th percentile level) resulting from adjusting the weight of the underlying with default probability 2.5% exposure 300 and correlation set C compared with approximation using risk sensitivity

4.4.4 Risk contribution

The expression for the marginal risk in Equation (23) is a partial derivative and is valid only for small changes in the underlying exposure. Suppose we consider the change in the unexpected loss when removing an underlying completely (100% of the exposure). We will refer to that quantity as the "total marginal risk". We calculated these numbers for all 75 underlyings in the portfolio and found that they sum to 814.5, which is considerably less than the total unexpected loss (at the 99th percentile) of 951.7. This implies that the marginal risk is valid only for small changes in each underlying. In Figure 4.17 we illustrate this effect for the underlying in the portfolio with default probability 2.5%, exposure 300 and correlation set C. The total marginal risk is convex, although the effect is not drastic. This suggests that the risk sensitivity provides a good indication of the portfolio unexpected loss for moderate changes in the weight of each underlying.

Calculations on other, more granular, portfolios do not always show the general trends we found above. First, for small default probabilities or large exposures, the default probability-adjusted marginal capital can be quite small. The simple explanation of this is that the risk presented by such a position (a very small probability of a very large loss) is not significant at the confidence level used. Not surprisingly, in such a situation the marginal capital increases with the confidence level (the position is considered more "risky").

4.5 PORTFOLIO OPTIMISATION

The next stage in the analysis is to develop techniques to actively manage the credit risk of a portfolio of risky assets. The advent of the credit derivatives market provides the instruments necessary to accomplish this. Credit exposure to individual names or portfolios can be bought or sold through credit default swaps or structured credit derivatives products. We cover these topics in the next chapter. Optimal portfolio allocation has been a longstanding problem in portfolio management (Grinold and Kahn, 1999). The aim of this section is to develop a general framework for optimising a credit portfolio that is compatible with the models discussed in the previous chapter. The direct application of traditional Markowitz (1952) theory to credit portfolios is not appropriate because the standard deviation is not a legitimate measure of risk when the distribution of portfolio returns is highly skewed and fat-tailed (Arvanitis *et al* 1998). We could, therefore, propose replacing the standard deviation of the portfolio return with the unexpected loss at a given confidence level. The obvious disadvantage of this is that the computation of the unexpected loss would require time-consuming simulations. Furthermore, if we propose that an optimal portfolio should be defined in terms of risk and return, we will have to digress somewhat and consider whether or not our definition of risk is appropriate. If it is not, we would expect to get some strange results from the optimisation procedure. Our next task, therefore, is to consider what constitutes a coherent measure of risk that can be used to optimise the risk/return characteristics of a credit portfolio.

4.5.1 A coherent measure of risk

The concept of a "coherent risk measure" has been developed by Artzner *et al*, 1999). For two random variables X and Y (representing in this context losses), a coherent risk measure ρ is a function that satisfies the following requirements.

1. Monotonicity	For $X \geq Y$, $\rho(X) \geq \rho(Y)$.
2. Positive homogeneity	$\rho(\lambda X) = \lambda \rho(X)$, where λ is a positive real number.
3. Translation invariance	$\rho(X + a) = \rho(X)$, where a is a real number.
4. Sub-additivity	$\rho(X + Y) \leq \rho(X) + \rho(Y)$.

These are reasonable intuitive requirements of a risk measure. The sub-additivity requirement – which stipulates that adding two risks together should never create more risk than the sum of the individual risks – is most important. This is a diversification condition. Note that neither the standard deviation nor the unexpected loss measure satisfy the sub-additivity condition.[2] As a simple example, consider two equal but independent losses, each with a probability of occurrence of 0.75%. Based on the 99th percentile, the risk of each is zero since the probability of incurring a loss is less than 1%. Now, however, suppose that we add these risks together, in which case the probability that either one of the losses occurs is almost 1.5%, which is within this confidence interval. Therefore, the VAR of the aggregate portfolio is greater than zero. We have created risk by adding two individual risks together and have violated the fundamental rule of diversification.

Another more realistic example of the violation of sub-additivity through use of a percentile-based risk measure can be constructed by considering a large and inhomogeneous portfolio, as would be encountered in practice. Let us denote the capital at the $(100 - \alpha)$th percentile by K. Now suppose we add a large exposure to the portfolio that is greater than K but has a probability of default approximately equal to α. If the probability of default is less than α, the capital will not increase because the new large loss has a probability of occurring outside the confidence level. Conversely, if the probability of default is greater than α, the capital will increase considerably since the default of the new exposure now represents the "worst case". In the latter case, the new exposure would have a large risk contribution, whereas in the former the risk contribution would be zero. So, for a small change in the default probability there is a huge change in the portfolio capital.

These two simple examples show that a percentile is not a feasible measure of risk. This is probably is not such an issue in calculations of portfolio risk, or even of risk sensitivities, but it may give erroneous results in portfolio optimisation. This is because an optimisation algorithm may "reduce" the risk falsely – for example, by putting all the weight into a single exposure. We should therefore consider other measures of risk that still capture the potential skewness and fat tails of the underlying distribution but which also meet all the requirements of a coherent measure of risk, as outlined above. However, since the concept of unexpected loss as measured by a certain percentile is well understood and commonly used, we would like the new risk measure to have a similar simple interpretation as well. It turns out that there is a measure that meets all these requirements and is, furthermore, closely related to the unexpected loss.

4.5.2 Expected shortfall
Recall that the unexpected loss is defined by

$$\Pr\left[UL_{\alpha,n} > L_p \right] = \alpha \qquad (27)$$

The unexpected loss is the maximum loss that will be incurred over a given time horizon at a confidence level of α. However, it provides no information on the distribution of the $\alpha\%$ of losses above this value. With this in mind, consider a similar quantity:

$$E\left[L_p \,\middle|\, UL_{\alpha,n} > L_p \right] \qquad (28)$$

which is the expected loss on the portfolio. Clearly, this quantity will always be greater than the unexpected loss. We will refer it as the "expected shortfall", although it is also known as the mean excess loss, mean shortfall or tail VAR. The unexpected loss and expected shortfall are obviously quite similar and will differ depending on the shape of the tail of the distribution. The unexpected loss is the actual worst-case loss at a given confidence level, while the expected shortfall is the average of all losses above this worst-case loss. If two distributions have the same unexpected loss, the one with the fatter tail will have a higher expected shortfall. The expected shortfall is generally sub-additive (see Artzner *et al*, 1999, for more details) and is a more "continuous" measure of risk than the unexpected loss. It is, therefore, a more appropriate risk measure for optimising a portfolio.

4.5.3 Marginal risks – expected shortfall versus unexpected loss

Before applying the expected shortfall to portfolio optimisation, we will consider the similarities and differences between the expected shortfall and the unexpected loss as risk measures. We argued above that the two measures give similar results for "reasonable" portfolios. We will now test this assertion by comparing the marginal capital in the previous examples. They should exhibit similar patterns if we replace the unexpected loss with the expected shortfall, although the latter will be systematically larger. The sensitivity of the expected shortfall with respect to each exposure is (Scaillet, 2000):

$$\frac{\partial ES_{\alpha,n}}{\partial w_i} = E\left[L_i \,\middle|\, L_p > UL_{\alpha,n} \right] = \frac{E\left[L_i \, 1_{\left\{ L_p > UL_{\alpha,n} \right\}} \right]}{E\left[1_{\left\{ L_p > UL_{\alpha,n} \right\}} \right]} \qquad (29)$$

which is similar in form to Equation (23). This expression can be estimated directly via simulation by simply taking the mean of all losses above $UL_{\alpha,n}$, but we have found the following kernel estimator to be more efficient:

$$\frac{\partial ES_{\alpha,n}}{\partial w_i} = \frac{\dfrac{1}{ns} \sum_{j=1}^{s} L_{i,j} \displaystyle\int_{UL_{\alpha,n}}^{\infty} K\left(\dfrac{\sum_{k=1}^{n} L_p^s - u}{h} \right) du}{\alpha} \qquad (30)$$

where the expression represents the cumulative normal distribution function since we are using a Gaussian kernel. Figure 4.18 shows the marginal capital contributions based on the expected shortfall for the 99th and 99.9th percentiles, respectively. The portfolio is the one we used in section 4.4.3.

The marginal capital contributions based on the expected shortfall are very similar to those computed previously using the unexpected loss, although they are systematically higher. The only noticeable difference between the results shown in Figures 4.16 and 4.18 is that the relative marginal capital increases more with decreasing default probability when the expected shortfall is used. The marginal capital based on the expected shortfall is also smoother. The latter observation supports the assertion that this new risk measure has superior mathematical properties to the unexpected loss and it provides similar quantification of the portfolio risk for standard portfolios. A portfolio with a "low" expected shortfall should also have a "low" unexpected loss. Changing from the unexpected loss to the expected shortfall for analysing risk or even computing economic capital will, therefore, not create fundamental anomalies, but the mathematics will be more tractable and will not give unrealistic results for portfolios with high exposure concentrations.

4.6.4 Credit portfolio optimisation

Markowitz (1952) describes a procedure for optimal allocation of a portfolio of risky assets in a market risk context. The Markowitz mean–variance approach assumes that all individual returns are normally distributed with a certain mean and variance. Under these assumptions it is possible to define an "efficient frontier" for a given portfolio. This is a set of portfolios with a maximum ratio of return to risk, where the risk is defined in terms of the standard deviation (or, equivalently, the variance) of the portfolio returns. In Markowitz portfolio theory the fact that the standard deviation has nice differentiation properties is heavily exploited. Standard software for credit risk management allows users to optimise capital using a Markowitz-type approach.

The traditional risk measure of the standard deviation is useful in many applications, but it is inadequate for credit risk calculations because credit risk losses are characterised by a high likelihood of small profits coupled with a small chance of large losses. The loss distributions are highly skewed and standard optimisation tools developed for market risk are therefore not adequate. Expected shortfall is a convex function (Rockafellar, 1970; Shor, 1985) under quite general conditions, which allows efficient optimisation algorithms to be used. More specifically, it can be minimised (with constraints) using the well-known numerical technique of linear programming. The percentile-based unexpected loss is not convex. In practice this means that there are multiple solutions to an optimisation problem, and these are likely to be quite different. This is clearly another advantage

Figure 4.18 Risk sensitivities (based on expected shortfall) divided by the expected loss corresponding to the expected shortfall at the 99th percentile (*left*) and the 99.9th percentile (*right*) for all 75 underlyings in the hypothetical portfolio for correlation set A (*top*), B (*middle*) and C (*bottom*)

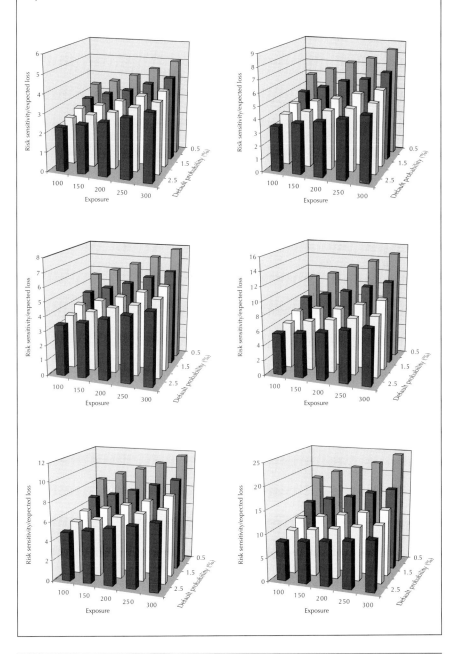

of using the expected shortfall as a risk measure. We will not go into detail on these points here; more information can be found in Andersson *et al* (2001) or Rockafellar and Uryasev (2000).

We illustrate credit portfolio optimisation using the hypothetical portfolio considered in previous sections. This will allow us to assess the accuracy of the approach as we would expect the optimal weights of each underlying to vary smoothly with exposure and default probability (as was the case with marginal capital). For the reasons described above, we will seek to optimise the expected shortfall (rather than the unexpected loss) of the portfolio for a given expected loss. The expected loss is therefore analogous to the mean in traditional Markowitz theory. This optimisation criterion can be thought of as minimising the "extreme" risk for a given level of non-extreme risk. Alternatively, it is equivalent to minimisation based on a given return if the return on each underlying is equal to some factor times the expected loss of that underlying. This is a reasonable criterion to use, especially as it simplifies interpretation of the results. Of course, it will not be true in practice, but minimisation of the expected shortfall based on a certain return is no more complex to implement.

The minimisation algorithm we use is linear programming with linear constraints. We do not give details of this approach as it is fairly standard (see, eg, Press *et al*, 1992). The linear constraints we apply are that none of the exposures may increase by more than 100% or decrease by more than 50%. This means that the portfolio weights, w_i, must be between 0.5 and 2.0. Table 4.3 gives the expected shortfalls and unexpected losses for the hypothetical portfolio when optimised under these constraints. The expected loss of the initial portfolio is 112.5. For example, A has the same expected loss as the initial portfolio but a "minimum" expected shortfall of 1145.8 – a reduction of 10%. Minimisation of the expected shortfall also reduces the unexpected loss (by 7% for portfolio A), which would be expected because the two measures are quite similar.

Table 4.3 Statistics for the example portfolio optimised under the constraints described in the text

	Expected loss	Expected shortfall*	Unexpected loss*
Initial portfolio	112.5	1278.9	951.7
A	112.5	1145.8	888.0
B	90.0	1037.1	779.7
C	100.0	1064.7	815.5
D	110.0	1125.5	867.8
E	120.0	1216.0	944.7
F	130.0	1331.2	1030.0

*$\alpha = 99\%$.

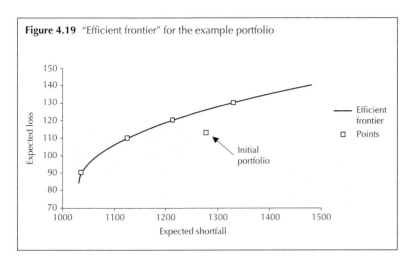

Figure 4.19 "Efficient frontier" for the example portfolio

If we perform many optimisations we can see the variation of the expected shortfall with the expected loss, as shown in Figure 4.19. A curve through the data points is concave and similar to the shape we see in traditional Markowitz mean–variance plots. It seems that the starting portfolio is actually reasonably close to the efficient frontier. This is not surprising since it does not contain underlyings that vary dramatically in their characteristics. In a real portfolio we may expect default probabilities to vary from as low as 0.02% to as high as 10–20% and exposures to vary by much more (and be stochastic). This means that there is more potential for the initial portfolio to be sub-optimal, with severe concentrations of risk.

Figure 4.20 shows the optimised weights for portfolio A in Table 4.3. The weights vary rather smoothly with default probability and exposure, although there are clearly some small errors (presumably as a result of the computations being Monte Carlo-based). The results are in line with what we saw from the risk sensitivities in that the optimal portfolio is obtained by putting more weight on the underlyings with small exposures and large default probabilities. Furthermore, the weights of the underlyings with high correlations are minimised, while for those with low correlations they are maximised.

In the example we presented in the last section we minimised the expected shortfall with respect to the expected loss, arguing that the latter quantity was similar to the return on the portfolio. In reality, we may consider maximising a risk-adjusted performance measure, such as the risk-adjusted return on capital (RAROC), the return on risk-adjusted capital (RORAC) or the risk-adjusted return on risk-adjusted capital (RARORAC). These risk-adjusted performance measures provide distinct techniques for comparing return on capital. For a discussion of these measures see Punjabi (1998) and Ong (1999).

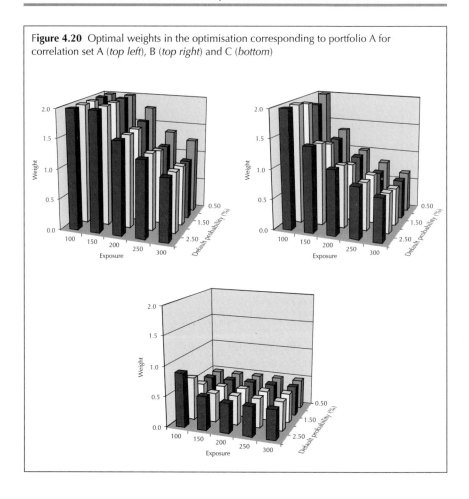

Figure 4.20 Optimal weights in the optimisation corresponding to portfolio A for correlation set A (*top left*), B (*top right*) and C (*bottom*)

4.6 CREDIT SPREAD MODEL

We have so far restricted our analysis mainly to losses from default events. For a complete model we also need to consider credit downgrades and losses arising from credit spread widening, even if this is not driven by a credit migration (downgrade) event. The credit spread represents the premium required to hold an instrument subject to credit risk and is commonly expressed as a yield differential. The migration process is defined as a simple extension to the default model, whereby further thresholds are added for each migration probability (see Chapter 3).

Credit migration has two effects: first, credit downgrades lead to a loss in the market value of assets and facilities; and, second, a downgraded counterparty is more likely to default. To calculate the loss due to credit migration, we have to be able to compute credit spread curves at future points in time for all credit classes. Jarrow, Lando and Turnbull (1997) and

Arvanitis, Gregory and Laurent (1999) present a pricing model that is consistent with this framework. We first recall the close links between credit spreads and risk-neutral default probabilities. Then we start from the simplest credit spread model and develop this in stages to achieve a realistic treatment of the dynamics of credit spreads.

4.6.1 Credit spreads and default probabilities

The price at time t of a risk-free discount bond of maturity T is

$$B(t,T) = e^{-\int_t^T f(t,\tau)d\tau}$$

where $f(t,\tau)$ is the instantaneous forward rate at time τ as seen from time t. A risky discount bond promises to pay one unit at maturity T if there is no default. We make the assumption that, in the event of default, the bond pays a constant recovery rate δ at maturity T. The prices at time t for risky discount bonds (that are not yet in default at time t) are given by:

$$v(t,T) = e^{-\int_t^T (f(t,\tau)+s(t,\tau))d\tau} = B(t,T) \times e^{-\int_t^T s(t,\tau)d\tau}$$

where $s(t,\tau)$ defines the instantaneous forward credit spread and $s(t,t)$ is the short-term credit spread. Credit spreads have a term structure in the same way that interest rates have. We denote by $q(t,T)$ the (risk-neutral) probability of default before time T as seen from time t, assuming that default has not already occurred. It is further assumed that the default event is independent of the level of interest rates. This leads to the standard equation

$$v(t,T) = B(t,T)\left[1 - q(t,T) + q(t,T)\delta\right] \tag{31}$$

Equivalently, the implied cumulative default probabilities $q(t,T)$ are given by

$$q(t,T) = \frac{1 - \dfrac{v(t,T)}{B(t,T)}}{(1-\delta)} \tag{32}$$

This relates default probabilities and forward credit spreads:

$$(1-\delta)\, q(t,T) = 1 - e^{-\int_t^T s(t,\tau)d\tau} \tag{33}$$

Thus, $(1-\delta)q(t,t+dt) \approx s(t,t)dt$ for small dt. So, short-term credit spreads $s(t,t)$ are directly related to local default probabilities $q(t,t+dt)$; by local probability of default we mean the probability of default between t and

$t + dt$ conditional on no default before t. Furthermore, we can relate the probability of default to the intensities of the default process:

$$\lambda(t) = \frac{q(t, t+dt)}{dt} \qquad (34)$$

4.6.2 Two-state model – default/no default

From Equation (33), standard computations imply that the $q(t, T)$ can be computed through the risk intensities $\lambda(t)$. That is,

$$q(t, T) = 1 - e^{\int_t^T \lambda(u)\,du} \qquad (35)$$

This corresponds to the probability of a jump occurring before time T, associated with a Poisson process with intensity $\lambda(\cdot)$. In other words, the probability of default cannot be modified by the outcome of any event, such as a change in the credit rating of the issuer of the bond. From Equation (33) we see that the forward credit spreads, $s(t, \tau)$, are also deterministic, as are the short-term credit spreads and the risk intensities of the default process, $\lambda(t)$. In discrete time this leads to the binomial model, where the probability of default does not depend on the node of the tree. In practice, where only a discrete set of prices of coupon bonds is given we need to make an additional assumption regarding the form of the default probabilities, such as a piecewise constant structure:

$$q(t, T) = 1 - e^{\int_t^T \alpha(\tau)\,d\tau}$$

where $\alpha(\tau)$ is constant and equal to $\alpha(i)$ between t_{i-1} and t_i (for example, see Chapter 5). In order to be able to estimate the forward credit spreads from bond prices, we can choose the α_i to match the ith observed bond price exactly. This stripping technique involves solving a series of non-linear equations, which can be done using a "bootstrap" technique described in standard texts (eg, Fabozzi, 1996). We should also note that this estimation of forward credit spreads makes use only of bonds in the same risky class, ie, those with equal probabilities of default and recovery rates. The forward credit spreads obtained can then be used to price instruments contingent on default events, such as default swaps.

4.6.3 Credit migration model

Instead of using a standard stripping procedure that deals with bonds in each credit class separately, we can look in greater detail at the changes in credit quality that may lead to default. This more structural modelling approach will guarantee that the different risky curves are consistently estimated; moreover, it will be possible to use information from bonds in different credit classes to build up the risky curves. Introducing some credit rating classes allows us to expand the simple default/no default model. A continuous, time-homogeneous Markov chain on a finite state space can represent the credit ratings dynamics, $S = \{1, 2, \dots, K\}$. This means that there are K possible credit ratings and that being in a given credit rating gives all the information relevant to the pricing of structures involving credit risk. The probability of movement from one credit rating to another depends only on the two credit ratings themselves and the length of the period considered (time-homogeneity). Jarrow, Lando and Turnbull (1997) first developed the model we review here. The first state represents the best credit quality and the $(K-1)$th state the worst (before default). The Kth state represents default, which is an absorbing state and provides a payment of δ times the par value at maturity. We impose the simplifying assumption that, once in this state, there is no chance of moving to a higher state – ie, there is no recovery from bankruptcy. In terms of Moody's or Standard & Poor's ratings, state one can be thought of as Aaa/AAA and state $K-1$ as C.

We can characterise the dynamics of the credit ratings by providing a set of transition matrices between ratings for any period from t to T, $Q(t, T)$. Its elements, $Q_{ij}(t, T)$, represent the probability of going from rating i at time t to rating j at time T. In particular, the last column of $Q(t, T)$ contains default probabilities, which depend on the current credit rating. Once these default probabilities are defined, it is possible (as above) to construct credit spreads that now depend on the credit rating class. In a first stage, we will consider transition matrices that can be written as

$$Q(t, T) = \exp\left(\Lambda \times (T - t)\right) \tag{36}$$

The exponent is the product of a constant matrix Λ and the length of the transition period $(T - t)$. The exponential of a matrix is defined such that

$$Q(t, T) = \sum_{n=0}^{\infty} \frac{\Lambda^n \times (T - t)^n}{n!} \tag{37}$$

Matrix Λ is called the "generator" of transition matrices $Q(t, T)$, since all of them can be deduced from a single matrix, Λ. This further simplifies the computations. Moreover, we notice that

$$\lim_{T \to t} \frac{\log Q(t, T)}{T - t} = \Lambda$$

If we (formally) think of $Q(t, T)$ as the price of some bond, Λ appears to be a short rate. Thus, the assumption of a constant generator is the analogue of the assumption of a constant short rate. It can readily be shown that the elements of the generator matrix are related to short-term default probabilities. Let us denote

$$
\Lambda = \begin{pmatrix}
\lambda_{11} & \lambda_{12} & \cdot & \lambda_{1,K-1} & \lambda_{1K} \\
\lambda_{21} & \lambda_{22} & \cdot & \lambda_{2,K-1} & \lambda_{2K} \\
\cdot & \cdot & \cdot & \cdot & \cdot \\
\lambda_{K-1,1} & \lambda_{K-1,2} & \cdot & \lambda_{K-1,K-1} & \lambda_{K-1,K} \\
0 & 0 & \cdot & 0 & 0
\end{pmatrix}
$$

For small dt, the transition matrix $Q(t, t + dt) \approx I + \Lambda dt$, where I is the $K \times K$ identity matrix. Therefore, the probability of going from rating i to rating j ($i \neq j$) between dates t and $t + dt$ is $\lambda_{ij} dt$. The probability of staying at rating i is $1 + \lambda_{ii} dt$ (λ_{ii} is always negative, as shown below). In this framework, some extra constraints are imposed on the generator matrix to ensure that the evolution of the credit spreads makes economic sense. These constraints are summarised below.

1. The transition probabilities are non-negative: $\lambda_{ij} \geq 0 \quad \forall\, i, j, i \neq j$.
2. The sum of transition probabilities from any state is unity:

$$
\left(1 + \lambda_{ii}\right) + \sum_{\substack{i=1 \\ i \neq j}}^{K} \lambda_{ij} = 1, \; j = 1, \ldots, K \quad \Rightarrow \quad \sum_{i=1}^{K} \lambda_{ij} = 0, \; j = 1, \ldots, K
$$

and

$$
\lambda_{ii} \leq 0 \quad \forall\, i
$$

3. The Kth state (default) is absorbing: $\lambda_{Kj} = 0, \; j = 1, \ldots, K$.
4. State $i + 1$ is always more risky than state i:

$$
\sum_{j \geq k} \lambda_{ij} \leq \sum_{j \geq k} \lambda_{i+1, j}, \quad \forall i, k \; \; k \neq i+1 \tag{38}
$$

Matrix Λ is further assumed to be diagonalisable – ie, $\Lambda = \Sigma D \Sigma^{-1}$, where D is a diagonal matrix. The exponential of a matrix can be calculated using the expression

$$
Q(t, T) = \Sigma \exp\left(D \times (T - t)\right) \Sigma^{-1} \tag{39}
$$

where the diagonal terms in

$$D = \begin{pmatrix} d_1 & 0 & 0 & 0 \\ 0 & . & 0 & 0 \\ 0 & 0 & d_{K-1} & 0 \\ 0 & 0 & 0 & d_k \end{pmatrix}$$

and the columns of Σ represent, respectively, the eigenvalues and the (right) eigenvectors of Λ. This expression allows for an easier computation of transition probabilities between credit ratings and default probabilities over all time horizons since $\exp(D \times (T-t))$ is simply

$$\begin{pmatrix} \exp(d_1 \times (T-t)) & 0 & 0 & 0 \\ 0 & . & 0 & 0 \\ 0 & 0 & . & 0 \\ 0 & 0 & 0 & \exp(d_K \times (T-t)) \end{pmatrix}$$

We can now provide a more explicit computation of the probabilities of default. If we denote respectively by σ_{ij} and $\tilde{\sigma}_{ij}$ the i,j elements of Σ and Σ^{-1}, and by d_j the eigenvalues of Λ, we obtain from Equation (39)

$$q_{iK}(t,T) = \sum_{j=1}^{K-1} \sigma_{ij}\,\tilde{\sigma}_{jK}\left[\exp\left(d_j(T-t)\right) - 1\right], \quad 1 \le i \le K-1 \qquad \textbf{(40)}$$

This shows the considerable importance of the eigenvalues of the generator in considering the term structure pattern of default probabilities and, hence, the term structure of credit spreads. When empirical results are presented we see that all the eigenvalues are real, which means we do not observe cyclical effects in credit ratings dynamics. It can be proved that the largest eigenvalue is equal to zero and, thus, that all eigenvalues have a negative real part.

We can now express the price of a risky zero-coupon bond, $v^i(t, t+h, \Lambda)$, of any maturity h for any credit class i according to Equation (31), which we rewrite as

$$v^i(t, t+h, \Lambda) = B(t, t+h)\left[\left(1 - q_{iK}(t, t+h)\right) + q_{iK}(t, t+h)\,\delta\right] \qquad \textbf{(41)}$$

As can be seen from this equation, the credit spread for any given risky class and maturity remains constant. The only changes in credit spreads occur when there are changes in credit ratings. From Equation (41), the credit spread for risky class i can be written as

$$-\frac{1}{T-t}\log\left[1 + (\delta-1)q_{iK}(t,T)\right] \qquad \textbf{(42)}$$

From the expression $(1-\delta)q_{iK}(t, t+dt) \approx s_i(t,t)dt$ we can obtain the short-term credit spread for credit class i, $s_i(t,t)$, as

$$s_i(t,t) = (1-\delta)\lambda_{iK} = \sum_{j=1}^{K-1} \sigma_{ij}\,\tilde{\sigma}_{jK} \qquad (43)$$

This relates almost directly the short-term credit spread and the instantaneous probabilities of default, λ_{iK}, which is the last column of the generator matrix. It can also be shown that long-term credit spreads are closely related to the recovery rate and to the second largest eigenvalue. If the recovery rate, δ, is positive, all credit spreads (whatever the initial rating) tend to zero as $1/(T-t)$. If $\delta = 0$, all credit spreads tend to $-d_{K-1}$, the second largest eigenvalue. This can be seen from

$$q_{iK}(t,T) = 1 + \sum_{j=1}^{K-1} \sigma_{ij}\,\tilde{\sigma}_{jK}\exp\left(d_j(T-t)\right) \qquad (44)$$

By including credit migration in the model, we have imposed an underlying economic structure on the evolution of the credit spreads and we do not need to specify a function arbitrarily as in the binomial model. The credit migration model can therefore be used as a powerful stripping algorithm to jointly estimate the forward credit spreads for all credit ratings using current bond prices and historical data. The model is now applicable to the pricing of instruments that are contingent on the occurrence of a credit event, such as credit protection against a downgrade. In addition, it can be used in credit portfolio management, where the portfolio is marked-to-market on the occurrence of credit events; examples of this include liquid loan portfolios and derivatives portfolios (counterparty risk). The model is extended by Lando (1998) and by Arvanitis, Gregory and Laurent (1999) to account for "memory" in changes in credit ratings and for stochastic default probabilities. It is possible to introduce a general intensity process depending on other state variables, as in Lando (1998) and Duffie and Singleton (1999).

4.6.4 Model calibration

Next, we discuss calibration of the model. The model inputs are risky bond prices of different maturities and credit ratings and a generator matrix estimated from a Moody's one-year transition matrix. For risky bond pricing, effective use of the model requires the estimation of default probabilities. We want the model to be able to match the observed market prices of risky bonds, and we also want the calibrated transition probabilities to be as close as possible to the transition probabilities provided by the ratings agencies. We will denote by Λ^{hist} a generator estimated from historical data (see Table 4.4). To perform a stable calibration we use both current bond prices and historical transition probabilities, Λ^{hist}. The price of bond n,

$n \in \{1, \ldots, N\}$, in credit class i can be expressed as

$$P^i_{n, \text{model}}(\Lambda) = \sum_{h=1}^{T} F^i_n(h) \, v^i(h, \Lambda) \qquad (45)$$

where $F^i_n(h)$ is the coupon of bond n of rating i at date h and $v^i(h, \Lambda)$ is the price of a zero-coupon bond of rating i with maturity h. A least-squares optimisation can be used to calibrate the model:

$$\min_{\tilde{\Lambda}} \left\{ \sum_{i=1}^{K} \sum_{n=1}^{N} \left(P^i_{n, \text{model}}(\Lambda) - P^i_{n, \text{market}} \right)^2 + \sum_{i,j=1}^{k} \left(\frac{\left(\lambda_{ij} - \lambda_{ij}^{\text{hist}} \right)^2}{\beta_{ij}} \right) \right\}$$

$$(46)$$

where we minimise the deviation between model and market prices while keeping the generator matrix close to the historical generator matrix. Normally, the calibrated Λ is not very different from the historical Λ^{hist}. This is a desirable property of the calibration procedure because it implies risk premia close to one. The term

$$\sum_{i,j=1}^{k} \left(\frac{\left(\lambda_{ij} - \lambda_{ij}^{\text{hist}} \right)^2}{\beta_{ij}} \right) \cdot$$

can be interpreted as the square of a norm distance between the risk-neutral measure Λ and an *a priori* measure Λ^{hist}.

This approach corresponds to Bayesian estimation. The parameters β_{ij} determine the relative accuracy required to match current bond prices and the importance of being close to historical data. The size of β_{ij} will depend on the expected use of the model. For example, if the model is to be used for pricing, market prices must be matched accurately even if this means deviating considerably from the historical generator matrix. If the number of bonds is quite large compared to the number of parameters, the bond prices will probably not be matched exactly. However, since the number of independent parameters in the generator matrix is $(K-1)^2$, it is likely that the number of bonds will be considerably smaller than this. This means that the calibration may have more than one solution. By using historical data, our procedure will give a solution that is close to the historical reality.

The model has been calibrated on a representative sample of 10 bonds from the US telecommunications industry that cover ratings from CCC to AAA. The data were obtained from Bloomberg on April 1, 1998. Tables 4.4 and 4.5 show, respectively, the historical generator matrix estimated from a Moody's one-year transition matrix (Carty and Lieberman, 1997) and the

Table 4.4 Historical generator matrix based on Moody's data

	Aaa	Aa	A	Baa	Ba	B	Caa	D
Aaa	−0.0683	0.0615	0.0066	0.0000	0.0002	0.0000	0.0000	0.0000
Aa	0.0169	−0.0993	0.0784	0.0027	0.0009	0.0001	0.0000	0.0002
A	0.0007	0.0237	−0.0786	0.0481	0.0047	0.0012	0.0001	0.0000
Baa	0.0005	0.0028	0.0585	−0.1224	0.0506	0.0075	0.0008	0.0016
Ba	0.0002	0.0005	0.0045	0.0553	−0.1403	0.0633	0.0026	0.0138
B	0.0000	0.0004	0.0014	0.0059	0.0691	−0.1717	0.0208	0.0741
Caa	0.0000	0.0000	0.0000	0.0074	0.0245	0.0488	−0.3683	0.2876
D	0.0000	0.0000	0.0000	0.0000	0.0000	0.0000	0.0000	0.0000

D: default.

Table 4.5 Calibrated generator matrix

	Aaa	Aa	A	Baa	Ba	B	Caa	D
Aaa	−0.1322	0.1265	0.0033	0.0012	0.0005	0.0004	0.0002	$\approx 10^{-5}$
Aa	0.0507	−0.1267	0.0588	0.0141	0.0002	0.0023	0.0002	0.0004
A	0.0046	0.0385	−0.0825	0.0281	0.0061	0.0033	0.0005	0.0015
Baa	0.0006	0.0103	0.0323	−0.0998	0.0437	0.0101	0.0009	0.0019
Ba	0.0006	0.0023	0.0088	0.0663	−0.2093	0.0817	0.0232	0.0264
B	0.0006	0.0020	0.0041	0.0068	0.0294	−0.2473	0.1768	0.0277
Caa	0.0005	0.0001	0.0017	0.0111	0.0294	0.0188	−0.1632	0.1016
D	0.0000	0.0000	0.0000	0.0000	0.0000	0.0000	0.0000	0.0000

D: default.

generator matrix calibrated to the market prices. We emphasise that we have been able to use all prices of bonds, including bonds with different ratings, to estimate jointly the risky term structures. We can also be certain that a riskier curve will lie above a less risky curve. It is even possible – due to the richness of the default dynamics of the model – to estimate risky curves with no or very few observations within a particular risky class (although, of course, such a result should be treated with caution). Forty-nine parameters may seem a lot, but quite a large number of bonds have been used in the estimation procedure and we are now able to derive all the default probabilities corresponding to any ratings and maturity.

The estimated credit spread curves are shown in Figure 4.21. The crosses represent the bonds used in the calibration procedure plotted according to the difference between the yield corresponding to the market price and the model price. The accuracy of the fit is indicated by the fact that all crosses lie on the actual credit spread curves.

Figure 4.22 shows model-estimated generic credit spread curves for the US industrial sector using data for 73 bonds taken from Bloomberg on September 4, 1998. Here there are too many bonds for the model to match the market prices exactly.

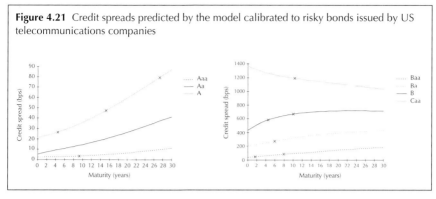

Figure 4.21 Credit spreads predicted by the model calibrated to risky bonds issued by US telecommunications companies

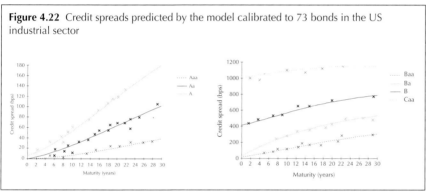

Figure 4.22 Credit spreads predicted by the model calibrated to 73 bonds in the US industrial sector

4.7 CONCLUSION

The Edgeworth expansion and the saddle-point approximation provide powerful analytical techniques for estimating the tails of the credit loss distribution under restrictive assumptions. In particular, for the approximations to be valid, the default correlation is assumed to be zero. The saddle-point approximation provides a better approximation of the tail of the loss distribution than the Edgeworth expansion or the normal approximation.

In practice, it is almost certain that the default correlation will differ from zero. In this case the analytical approximations are not directly applicable, but they can be used as powerful control variates in Monte Carlo simulations. Importance sampling and low-discrepancy sequences have been shown to outperform standard Monte Carlo in estimating tail events. Extreme value theory (EVT) has been applied successfully in credit analysis for estimating extreme events, such as multiple defaults. An important result of EVT is the Pickands–Balkema–de Haan theorem, which states that, for a large class of distributions, losses above a high threshold follow a generalised Pareto distribution. A crucial point in the successful application of EVT is estimation of the threshold above which this approximation is valid. The main tool for this purpose is the mean excess function. The marginal risk contribution of an underlying in a portfolio is defined as the increase in required economic capital for holding one more unit of the underlying. Since the economic capital is homogeneous of degree one, it can be shown, using Euler's theorem, that the unexpected loss of the portfolio can be written as the weighted sum of the risk contributions of the various underlyings. This is a very intuitive property.

Kernel estimation has proved to be a very efficient technique for estimating marginal risk contributions, which can provide the basis of a "fair" methodology for allocating economic capital among the businesses in a financial institution. A coherent measure of risk should satisfy four intuitive requirements: monotonicity, positive homogeneity, translation invariance and sub-additivity. Unfortunately, it can easily be shown that traditional VAR (unexpected loss defined by a certain percentile) does not satisfy the latter property, which is equivalent to a diversification condition. For this reason, we introduce the notion of expected shortfall. This is the expected loss on the portfolio conditional on the loss being greater than a certain percentile. The two quantities are similar for portfolios that do not have extreme exposure concentrations. Standard Markowitz mean–variance optimisation is not applicable to credit analysis because of the high skewness and kurtosis of the credit loss distribution. To take these properties into account and obtain portfolios that are truly optimised, we minimise the expected shortfall for a given expected loss.

Losses can arise not only from defaults but also from changes in the credit spread of a counterparty in a transaction. The second type of loss can sometimes be even more severe than losses due to default. To be able to incorporate credit spread changes in the simulation, we first need a model of the term structure of the credit spreads at any future point in time. Development of this model is based on the evolution of the credit migration matrix. Because there are too few market instruments and a large number of free parameters, it is efficient to estimate the model using a combination of historical and market data. Then, when we have our model, we need some means of pricing financial instruments once the term structure of the credit spreads has been determined. This is addressed in Chapter 6.

1   By bounded support we mean that the pdf vanishes outside some interval. This is the case for loss distributions, in which the loss must lie between 0 and $\sum w_i$.
2   The variance satisfies the sub-additivity condition in a degenerate way as it is additive.

BIBLIOGRAPHY

Abramowitz, M., and I. A. Stegun., 1972, *Handbook of Mathematical Functions* (New York: Dover Publications).

Anderson, W. J., 1991, *Continuous-Time Markov Chains* (New York: Springer-Verlag).

Andersson, F., H. Mausser, D. Rosen and S. Uryasev, 2001, "Credit Risk Optimization with Conditional Value-At-Risk Criterion", *Mathematical Programming* Series B 89, pp. 273–91.

Artzner, P., F. Delbaen, J.-M. Eber and D. Heath, 1997, "Thinking Coherently", *Risk* 10(11), pp. 68–71.

Artzner, P., F. Delbaen, J.-M. Eber and D. Heath, 1999, "Coherent Measures of Risk", *Mathematical Finance* 3(9), pp. 203–28.

Arvanitis, A., J. K. Gregory and J.-P. Laurent, 1999, "Building Models for Credit Spreads", *Journal of Derivatives* 6(3), pp. 27–43.

Arvanitis, A., C. Browne, J. Gregory and R. Martin, 1998, "A Credit Risk Toolbox", *Risk* 11(12), pp. 50–5.

Balkema, A., and L. de Haan, 1974, "Residual Life Time at Great Age", *Annals of Probability* 2, pp. 792–804.

Bender, C. M., and S. A. Orszag, 1978, *Advanced Mathematical Methods for Scientists and Engineers* (New York: McGraw-Hill).

Bierens, H., 1985, "Kernel Estimators of Regression Functions", in T. Bewley (ed), *Advances in Econometrics* (Cambridge: Cambridge University Press), pp. 99–144.

Carty, L. V., and D. Lieberman, 1997, *Historical Default Rates of Corporate Bond Issuers 1920–1996*, (July), Moody's Investors Service Global Credit Research.

Chekhlov, A., S. Uryasev and M. Zabarankin, "Portfolio Optimization with Drawdown Constraints", Research Report 2000-5, University of Florida.

Danielsson, J., and C. G. de Vries, 1998, "Beyond the Sample: Extreme Quantile and Probability Estimation", January. URL: http://www.RiskResearch.org/, then follow link "extreme value theory".

Davison, A. C., and D. V. Hinckley, 1988, "Saddlepoint Approximations in Resampling Methods", *Biometrika* 75(3), pp. 417–31.

Denault, M., 2000, "Coherent Allocation of Risk Capital", RiskLab Zürich. URL: http://www.risklab.ch/Papers.html.

Duffie D., and K. J. Singleton, 1998, "Ratings-Based Term Structures of Credit Spreads", Working Paper, Stanford University.

Duffie D., and K. J. Singleton, 1999, "Modelling Term Structures of Defaultable Bonds", *Review of Financial Studies* 12, pp. 687–720.

Embrechts, P., (ed), 2000, *Extremes and Integrated Risk Management* (London: Risk Books).

Embrechts, P., C. Klüppelberg and T. Mikosch (eds), 1997, *Modelling Extremal Events for Insurance and Finance* (Berlin: Springer-Verlag).

Embrechts, P., S. Resnick and G. Samorodnitsky, 1998, "Living on the Edge", *Risk* 11(1), pp. 96–100.

Fabozzi, F. J., 1996, *Bond Market Analysis and Strategies* (Englewood Cliffs, NJ: Prentice-Hall).

Falk, M., J. Hüsler and R. Reiss, 1994, *Laws of Small Numbers: Extremes and Rare Events* (Basle: Birkhäuser).

Garman, M. B., 1996, "Improving on VAR", *Risk* 9(5), pp. 61–3.

Garman, M. B., 1997, "Taking VAR to Pieces", *Risk* 10(10), pp. 70–1.

Gouriéroux, C., J. P. Laurent and O. Scaillet, 2000, "Sensitivity Analysis of Values at Risk", *Journal of Empirical Finance* 7(3–4), pp. 225–45.

Grinold, R. C., and R. N. Kahn, 1999, *Active Portfolio Management* (New York: McGraw-Hill).

Hallerbach, W. G., 1999, "Decomposing Portfolio Value-at-Risk: A General Analysis", Discussion Paper TI 99-034/2, Tinbergen Institute, Rotterdam, May. URL: http://www.fee. uva.nl/bieb/TIDPs/TIDP99nr.htm.

Jarrow, R. A., D. Lando and S. M. Turnbull, 1997, "A Markov Model for the Term Structure of Credit Risk Spreads", *Review of Financial Studies*, 10(2), pp. 481–523.

JP Morgan, 1997, CreditMetrics Technical Document (New York, NY: JP Morgan).

KMV Corporation, "Portfolio Manager, Description, Usage and Specification, Version 4.0".

Lando, D., 1998, "On Cox Processes and Credit Risky Securities", *Review of Derivatives Research* 2(2–3), pp. 99–120.

Longstaff, F., and E. Schwartz, 1995, "A Simple Approach to Valuing Risky Fixed and Floating Rate Debt", *Journal of Finance* 50(3), pp. 789–819.

Markowitz, H., 1952, "Portfolio Selection", *Journal of Finance* 7, pp. 77–91.

McNeil, A. J., 1998, "History Repeating", *Risk* 11(1), p. 99.

Morgan, B. J. T., 1984, *Elements of Simulation* (New York: Chapman & Hall).

Ong, M. K., 1999, *Internal Credit Risk Models* (London: Risk Books).

Pickands, J., 1975, "Statistical Inference Using Extreme Order Statistics", *Annals of Statistics* 3, pp. 119–31.

Press, W. H., S. Teukolsky, B. P. Flannery and W. T. Vetterling, 1992, *Numerical Recipes in C*, Second Edition (New York: Cambridge University Press).

Punjabi, S., 1998, "Many Happy Returns", *Risk* 11(6), pp. 71–6.

Reiss, R. D., and M. Thomas, 1997, *Statistical Analysis of Extreme Values* (Basle: Birkhäuser).

Rockafellar, R. T., 1970, "Convex Analysis", *Princeton Mathematics* 28.

Rockafellar, R. T., and S. Uryasev, 2000, "Optimization of Conditional Value-At-Risk", *Journal of Risk* 2(3), pp. 21–41.

Scaillet, O., 2000, "Nonparametric Estimation and Sensitivity Analysis of Expected Shortfall". URL: http://www.ires.ucl.ac.be/CSSSP/home_pa_pers/scaillet/scaill.htm.

Shor, N. Z., 1985, *Minimisation Methods for Non-Differentiable Functions* (Springer-Verlag).

Part II

Pricing and Hedging of Credit Risk

5

Credit Derivatives

5.1 INTRODUCTION

We now move on from the risk management to the pricing of credit. We begin in this chapter with a discussion of the pricing and hedging of credit derivative contracts, which largely represent pure credit risk. Chapters 6 and 7 will then move on to discuss the pricing of credit alongside interest rate and equity risk.

First, we will review the basic credit derivative products. Then we will discuss the main difference between pricing and the risk management of credit, stressing the fact that we now work with "risk-neutral" rather than "real" probabilities. This is the fundamental distinction between pricing and risk management that applies across all product classes. Next, we consider the pricing and hedging of credit derivatives using models that have been successfully applied to the credit derivative market. We present the models in three parts. The first covers basic products with values depending largely on the term structure of default probabilities (or credit spreads). Because of their importance, we also discuss asset swaps and risky bonds, which are not strictly credit derivative products. The second part covers spread option products, which depend on the volatility of the credit spread. To price these products, we need to model the evolution of the term structure of credit spreads. Finally, we consider basket default swaps, which are multiple underlying contracts with pricing and hedging highly dependent on the assumed default correlation. For a broad overview of the credit derivatives market, the reader is referred to Das (1998), Tavakoli (1998) and Nelken (1999).

Owing to the strong effort made by both practitioners and academics over the last decade, a multiplicity of different modelling approaches have been introduced. We do not cover them all here, but further reading is suggested in the bibliography at the end of this chapter. Instead, we provide an overview of the most commonly used products and present models highlighting what we believe to be the most important issues in the pricing and hedging of credit derivatives.

5.2 FUNDAMENTAL CREDIT PRODUCTS

Credit derivatives are becoming an important tool for managing credit risk, both in capital markets and in corporate banking. Below, we outline some of the most common applications:

❑ hedging default risk,
❑ freeing up credit lines to allow the continuation of transactions with a client,
❑ reducing concentration risk (country and industry),
❑ diversifying the portfolio by gaining access to otherwise unavailable credits,
❑ hedging dynamic credit risks (eg, credit exposure driven by market variables), and
❑ hedging changes in credit quality.

The main products currently traded are discussed in the following sections.

5.2.1 Credit default swap

A credit default swap (CDS) is a bilateral contract where one counterparty buys default protection or insurance with respect to a reference credit event. The contract has a given maturity, but will terminate early if the credit event occurs. Generally, this credit event will be the default of an issuer, which may be a single corporate, financial institution, government body or sovereign. The protection buyer will make periodic payments (expressed in basis points per annum on the notional amount), normally referred to as the default swap premium. In return, the protection seller will make a contingent payment to compensate the buyer if the underlying credit event does occur. The protection seller is buying credit risk while the protection buyer is selling credit risk. Since no asset is transferred, there is no need for funding the position.

Normally, the default payment on a CDS will be $(1 - \delta)$, where δ denotes the recovery rate on the reference security (eg, the value of a defaulted bond) expressed as a percentage of par. The reason for this is clear – it allows a risky asset to be (approximately) transformed into a risk-free asset. There are two settlement possibilities: physical delivery and cash settlement. For physical delivery, if a specific security is not cited, then the buyer of protection has a "cheapest-to-deliver option" since he can deliver the cheapest bond in the market in return for par.

❑ With *physical delivery*, the protection buyer delivers the defaulted asset (ie, the recovery value) in return for a payment equal to the notional value of that asset.
❑ With *cash settlement*, the protection seller pays the protection buyer an amount equal to the difference between the notional amount and the price of the (defaulted) reference asset. The value of the recovery rate is determined by a dealer survey.

In a digital (binary) default swap, the contingent payment if default occurs equals a pre-specified notional, irrespective of the value of the recovery rate.

5.2.2 Total return swap

A total return swap allows an investor to replicate an exposure to credit risk synthetically without having to buy the reference instrument. However, a total return swap is not linked solely to the occurrence of a credit event, as in a CDS (where the pure credit risk of an underlying asset is traded). In a total return swap, the interest rate risk is also sold. The total return swap buyer will pay Libor plus a spread to receive the fixed interest rate payments on the underlying asset from the seller. In addition, payments corresponding to changes in the market price of the asset will also be exchanged. This means that any depreciation in the value of the asset, including the loss in the event of default, is settled. The contract will be valued either at every coupon payment date or only at maturity. After a valuation, a payment corresponding to the price change will be made. If there is a credit event, early termination will occur and the settlement will be determined in a similar way as for a default swap.

A total return swap essentially allows all the cashflows of an underlying bond to be acquired without actually buying the bond. This may be preferable for accounting, tax or legal reasons. Also, the market in total return swaps may be more liquid than the market in the underlying bonds.

5.2.3 Asset swap

An asset swap package is a combination of an underlying bond and an interest rate swap. The fixed rate of the interest rate swap is typically chosen so that the asset swap package is bought at par. An asset swap package is therefore quite similar to a total return swap. The most significant difference between the two involves the outcome in the event of default. A total return swap terminates in the event of default, whereas in an asset swap, the interest rate swap would remain in place.[1] Later, we show how this exposure to interest rates in the event of default can be priced.

5.2.4 Credit-linked note

A credit-linked note (CLN) or credit default note is a note where the interest rate and notional payment are referenced to an underlying reference credit. The buyer of a CLN will purchase a coupon-bearing note from a special-purpose vehicle, which is collateralised with the reference securities. It is very nearly the securitisation of a credit default swap. If the underlying credit does not default, then all the coupons and principal will be paid in full. However, if default does occur, the note will pay only the recovery value of the underlying credit, δ. As compensation for taking the embedded credit risk, the note will pay a higher coupon than the corresponding Libor rate. A CLN is similar to holding a risk-free note and being short a default swap position. CLNs may also be indexed to a basket of names (see basket default swaps later). Settlement is completed in a similar way to default swaps. The defaulted underlying is either physically delivered (and the remaining payments not made) or cash-settled with a payment equal to the price of the defaulted assets determined from a dealer poll.

5.2.5 Counterparty risk on standard derivatives
An important application of credit derivatives contracts is hedging default risk on derivatives. The buyer of the hedging contract, when this counterparty defaults, will receive the risk-free mark-to-market on the underlying derivative multiplied by one minus the recovery rate, provided that this value is positive. This results in full credit protection. These insurance contracts can be used either on individual underlyings or in hedging the aggregate credit exposure of a book to take advantage of netting and reduce the cost. These issues are complex, since both the default time and exposure are random – we discuss these issues at length in Chapter 6. In this chapter, we are more concerned with contracts where the default time is random but the exposure is not.

5.2.6 Cancellable contracts
In a cancellable contract, periodic premiums are exchanged between two counterparties up to the default time of a third party. Then, the contract terminates without any further payments. For example, the holder of a cancellable swaption receives a standard swaption payout if – and only if – the third party does not default. If the seller of the cancellable swaption is default-free, the cancellable swaption is equivalent to a swaption sold by the third party, with no recovery. However, a cancellable swap differs from a risky swap. Indeed, the buyer of a cancellable swap has a negative exposure in case of default, when the present value of the swap is negative, which is not the case for the risky swap. The holder of a risky fixed-rate bond can enter into the corresponding cancellable swap to create a synthetic risky floating-rate bond. If they enter a standard swap instead, they are exposed to the uncertainty of the mark-to-market on the swap at default time.

5.2.7 Quanto default swaps
In a quanto default swap, either the premium payments or the cashflows in case of default are not in the same currency as the underlying bond. Consider a multinational that has issued a US$-denominated bond. The premium of the quanto default swap is payable in euros and, in case of default, the payment equals the recovery rate on the US$ bond payable

in euros. Expressed in US dollars, the payment equals $\delta e(\tau)$, where $e(\tau)$ is the euro/US\$ exchange rate at the default time τ and the recovery rate is δ. Let us remark that if a euro-denominated bond of the same issuer were trading, under the assumption that the recovery rate does not depend on the currency, the quanto default swap would have turned into a plain vanilla default swap on the euro bond. A quanto default swap is designed to provide protection to the holder of illiquid foreign currency bonds or non-traded loans.

5.2.8 Credit spread option
A credit spread option is an option on a particular credit spread. The protection buyer will pay a premium (normally up-front) to receive the present value at exercise of the difference between the yield on the underlying reference credit over some benchmark (eg, a Treasury bond for a fixed-rate underlying and Libor for a floating rate) and the strike of the option. If the difference between the yield of the reference credit and the benchmark (the credit spread) at an exercise date t is denoted by S_t, then the payout of a credit spread put and call are given as follows.

❏ *Credit spread put* This is the right to sell the reference asset at a pre-specified strike. Payout is proportional to $(S_t - K)^+$.
❏ *Credit spread call* This is the right to buy the reference asset at a pre-specified strike. Payout is proportional to $(K - S_t)^+$.

The call option payout increases as the credit spread tightens (S_t decreases), whereas the put option payout increases as the credit spread widens (S_t increases). Credit spread options allow hedging against credit spread volatility or ratings changes. As in the case of default swaps, they are either cash-settled or physically delivered. In the latter case, the protection buyer has the right, but not the obligation, to buy or sell the underlying to the protection seller for the strike spread. The contract can be of European, Bermudan or American type.

5.2.9 Basket default swap
A basket default swap is a default insurance contract with payments similar to that of a CDS, except that they are indexed to a basket of entities, rather than to a single reference asset. The contract will provide default protection on a number of entities in the basket and normally will not cover every single one. Consider a basket of n assets. Typical products are as follows:

❏ first to default, offering protection against the first default only;
❏ second to default, offering protection against the second to default only;
❏ first l out of n to default, offering protection against the first l defaults; and
❏ last m out of n to default, offering protection against the last m defaults.

5.2.10 Collateralised debt obligation (CDO) structures

Collateralised debt obligation (CDO) is a generic term for a collateralised loan obligation (CLO) or collateralised bond obligation (CBO). CDOs may also contain credit default swaps in addition to loans or bonds. At the simplest level, a CDO structure can be thought of as a pool of assets, which are packaged together as a portfolio and then tranched. This tranching essentially involves splitting the CDO into pieces corresponding to different portfolio losses. The tranches are usually then rated and the risk is sold on to investors via fixed or floating rate bonds. The investor has essentially gained a leveraged exposure to a relatively large diversified pool of credits. An enhanced coupon will be paid as compensation for the credit exposure to defaults in the asset pool. The tranches are effectively credit linked notes referenced to a pool (rather than a single) asset. Depending on the losses in the pool, the coupon and/or principal on the notes may be reduced, depending on the recovery value of the defaulted assets. These structures can be considered to be similar to basket default swaps (although the number of underlying assets is often far greater) where the payoff is driven by the total loss on the pool rather than simply the individual default events. The cashflows in a CDO are considerably more complex than we have described above, but we consider mainly the credit component.

5.3 FUNDAMENTAL IDEAS ON PRICING CREDIT

The basis of risk-neutral pricing for risk-free contracts is that all risk can be hedged by trading a set of fundamental instruments either statically or dynamically. As a result, investors are risk-neutral and the expected return on any asset is the risk-free rate. A consequence of this is that the value or price today (time t) of a security is given by

$$V_t = B(t, T_{t+1}) E^Q[V_{t+1}] \tag{1}$$

where E^Q represents an expectation with respect to the risk-neutral probability measure, V_{t+1} is the value of the security at time $t+1$ and $B(t, T)$ is the risk-free discount factor. In other words, the discounted price of an asset is a martingale.

Now consider a defaultable claim whose value at time $t+1$ in the event of no-default is V_{t+1} and a fraction of this, say δV_{t+1} if default occurs (δ is a fractional recovery rate). Furthermore, let p_t represent the risk-neutral probability of default during the period $[t, t+1]$, given that the asset has not defaulted up to time t. Under this condition the asset's price at time t is given by

$$\tilde{V}_t = (1 - p_t)B(t, T_{t+1}) E^Q[V_{t+1}] + p_t B(t, T_{t+1}) E^Q[\delta V_{t+1}] < V_t \tag{2}$$

ie, it is a weighted expectation of the two events (no default and default) discounted at the risk-free rate. Clearly, since p_t is greater than zero and δ is less than 1, the risky security is worth less than the corresponding risk-free security. The above analysis can be extended to show that the risky discount rate $\tilde{r}_t$ can be written in terms of the risk-free rate, r_t, the risk-neutral default probability and the recovery rate. In general, we can write $\tilde{r}_t \approx r_t + p_t(1-\delta)$, showing that the risky rate is approximately equal to the risk-free rate plus a credit spread term. A simple proof of this is given in Appendix B (for a detailed analysis, see Duffie and Singleton, 1997). In order to value using the above equation, we need as inputs the probability of a credit event occurring, the loss given that the credit event has occurred, and – as we shall see for more complex instruments – the correlation among the credit events for various reference assets. We want to stress once more that these are risk-neutral probabilities and they are extracted from market instruments rather than from historical data. Calibration of these parameters is a difficult issue, since the credit derivative market is incomplete. In particular, it is almost impossible to extract implied values for the correlation, since there are not any liquid traded instruments that depend on this parameter.

We will mainly use so-called hazard rate or reduced form models where default is a sudden and unanticipated event. This makes it possible to handle a wide variety of dynamics for credit spreads in a tractable way. Models developed by Das and Tufano (1995), Duffie and Singleton (1997), Lando (1998), and Schönbucher (2000) belong to this class. Structural models, such as Merton (1974), Longstaff and Schwartz (1995) and Black and Cox (1976), are generally harder to use in practice, largely on account of calibration issues. In these structural approaches, default is modelled as the first time the asset value hits some barrier, and this can lead to some practical difficulties. As Madan and Unal (1994) or Jarrow, Lando and Turnbull (1997) discuss, it may be cumbersome to specify the barrier endogenously, since all the claims of a firm and bankruptcy procedures have to be considered in detail. Moreover, as argued in Duffie and Lando (1997), it is difficult to handle jumps in credit spreads or non-zero short credit spreads without a lot of extra technicalities. However, these models have more structure and on certain occasions can be used to address complex pricing issues. Indeed, we will use a "structural" model for pricing basket products. We resolve some of the calibration difficulties by fitting it to the underlying default swaps. This model is a multi-period extension of that developed in Chapter 3 for computing the credit loss distribution. Another version of the same model, which follows a different calibration procedure, is used in Chapter 7 for pricing convertible bonds subject to credit risk.

5.4 PRICING FUNDAMENTAL CREDIT PRODUCTS

5.4.1 Credit default swaps

First, we present a model for the valuation of a credit default swap, which is the most fundamental credit derivative instrument. The main assumptions of the model are that:

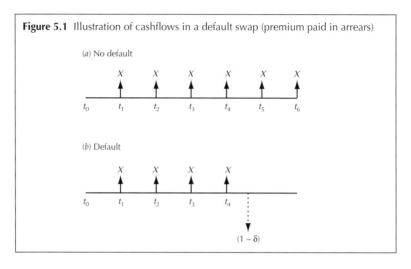

Figure 5.1 Illustration of cashflows in a default swap (premium paid in arrears)

❏ the default process is independent from the interest rate process;

❏ default can happen at a set of arbitrary, discrete dates; and
❏ the default payment is an exogenous amount that is paid immediately upon default.

In a credit default swap, the protection buyer pays a fixed premium during its term, whereas the protection seller is required to make a contingent payment if a default event occurs (Figure 5.1). Default may be defined as bankruptcy or failure to make an interest payment or a repayment of principal. A default swap, like an interest rate swap, can be considered as two legs, one corresponding to the premium payments and the other to the contingent default payment. The present value (PV) of a default swap can be viewed as the algebraic sum of the present values of its two legs. The market premium is similar to an interest rate swap in that the premium makes the current aggregate PV equal to zero. Next, we present the valuation of each leg. Since these cashflows may terminate at an unknown time during the life of the deal, we compute their value in a probabilistic sense, using the discounted expected value under the risk-neutral measure. For a greater amount of mathematical detail, see Li (1998).

The underlying variable that we will be using for the models presented in this chapter is the hazard rate of default, which is effectively the instantaneous forward default probability (see Literman and Iben, 1991). There are theoretical reasons why this is an appropriate underlying variable to use. The hazard rate at time t as seen from now (time 0) is denoted by $h(t)$. We can think of the hazard rate times the loss given default, $h(t)(1-\delta)$, as being approximately equal to the credit spread or the default swap premium (although the relationship is exact only for very small time periods). Initially, we consider that the hazard rate is deterministic over time. Later, we will show how to make the hazard rate stochastic to price more com-plex structures, whose value depends on convexity. Once the hazard rate is specified, the probability of default occurring before a certain time t is given by

$$p(0,t) = 1 - \exp\left(-\int_0^t h(u)\,du\right) \tag{3}$$

The probability of default in a small time interval is $h(t)\exp(-\int_0^t h(u)\,du)$. An analogy can be drawn between the probability of default and a Poisson process, since Equation (3) has a similar form to a non-homogeneous Poisson process.

Premium Leg
The premium payment leg is defined as a stream of fixed cashflows at times $(t_1, t_2, \ldots, t_n)$, rather like the fixed payments on a swap, that are paid either until the maturity of the deal $(T \equiv t_n)$ or until default, whichever comes first. It can be expressed as

$$PV_{0,T}^{\text{prem}} = \sum_{i=1}^{n} \Delta(t_{i-1}, t_i)\, X_T\, B(0, t_i)\, \exp\left(-\int_0^{t_i} h(u)\,du\right)$$

$$= \sum_{i=1}^{n} \Delta(t_{i-1}, t_i)\, X_T\, B(0, t_i)\,\bigl(1 - p(0, t_i)\bigr) \tag{4}$$

where $\Delta(t_{i-1}, t_i)X_T$ is the premium payment at time t_i with $\Delta(t_{i-1}, t_i)$ repre-senting the interval between payment dates (ie, approximately 0.5 for semi-annual payments, depending on the day count convention), $B(0, t_i)$ is the risk-free discount factor (ie, the price of a risk-free zero-coupon bond maturing at time t_i), and $p(0, t_i)$ is the risk-neutral probability of default in the interval $[0, t_i]$. We do not include a notional amount in the above for-mula, in which case the premium X_T will effectively be expressed as a fraction of the notional amount (eg, basis points per annum). We can express the above equation as a series of cashflows of an amount X_T, dis-counted at risk-free rate but weighted by the probability that default has *not* occurred up to the payment date.

Default leg
The default payment leg is defined as a payment of $(1 - \delta)$ which is made *only* if the underlying reference asset defaults before the maturity of the default swap. Since this payment is contingent upon default, the timing of this payment is unknown. Therefore, once again, in order to value the default payment leg of the deal, we have to calculate its value in a proba-bilistic sense. The discounted expected value under the risk-neutral measure is given by

$$PV_{0,T}^{\text{default}} = (1-\delta) \int_0^T h(s) \exp\left(-\int_0^s h(u)\,du\right) B(0,s)\,ds \qquad (5)$$

Clearly, the above represents the expectation over all possible default times. We can approximate the interval shown by assuming that default can occur at only a set of discrete (say, m) dates. Furthermore, $[p(0, t_j) - p(0, t_{j-1})]$ gives the marginal probability of default in the interval $[t_{j-1}, t_j)]$, which leads to

$$PV_{0,T}^{\text{default}} \approx (1-\delta) \sum_{j=1}^m \left[p(0, t_j) - p(0, t_{j-1})\right] B(0, t_j) \qquad (6)$$

We can render the interval $[t_{j-1}, t_j)]$ small enough to achieve convergence. We will use $(t_j - t_{j-1}) = 1$ day, so that default can effectively occur at any time. This does not slow the computations significantly. The above formulae are quite simple and intuitive, largely because we assume independence between interest rates and default events. We note that in equilibrium, the PV of each leg in Equations (4) and (5) should be equal. The market premium of a default swap $(\tilde{X}_T)$ can therefore be calculated from the following relationship:

$$\tilde{X}_T = \frac{(1-\delta) \sum_{j=1}^m \left[p(0, t_{j-1}) - p(0, t_j)\right] B(0, t_j)}{\sum_{i=1}^n \Delta(t_{i-1}, t_i) B(0, t_i)\left[1 - p(0, t_i)\right]} \qquad (7)$$

5.4.2 Accrued premium effect

In the above analysis, we did not account for the accrued premium that must be paid in the event of default. As default swap premiums are paid in arrears, an accrued premium is usually paid in the event of default as payment for the extra protected period (since the premium payment date). If the last premium payment date prior to the default event is t_k and the next premium payment date is t_{k+1}, the accrued premium due if default occurs at time τ will be approximately $(\tau - t_k)\Delta_{k,k+1}\tilde{X}_T/(t_{k+1} - t_k)$, ie, the premium due at the next date weighted by the time between the last coupon date and the default date. A simple way to approximate this is to add half a coupon period to each premium payment when valuing the premium payment leg. This is a reasonable approximation, since the average time of default is approximately half way through the period. In more exact terms, this creates an extra term that should be added to the PV of the premium leg as follows:

$$PV_{0,T}^{\text{accrued premium}} \approx \sum_{j=1}^{m} \left[p(0, t_j) - p(0, t_{j-1}) \right]$$

$$\times \left[\frac{\left(t_j - t_{j^*-1} \right) \Delta_{j^*-1, j^*} X_T}{\left(t_{j^*} - t_{j^*-1} \right)} \right] B(0, t_j) \qquad (8)$$

where t_{j^*} represents the next coupon payment date after date t_j. The effect of the accrued premium is more significant for riskier credit curves[2] (larger hazard rates) and has an insignificant effect on the pricing of default swaps on good credits, since the effect largely cancels between stripping and pricing. However, there are situations where the accrued premium can be important, eg, in pricing credit-linked notes.

5.4.3 Stripping of default probabilities

In the above expressions for default swaps, we stated that the default prob-abilities in the pricing equations were risk-neutral. Since default swaps are the fundamental products in the credit derivatives market, they will often be used to price and hedge more complex structures. This means that we should calibrate a model for pricing more complex structures by using market quotes for default swap premiums of different maturities on the same reference credit. From these market quotes, we can obtain the appro-priate risk-neutral default probabilities. We now describe a model for the cumulative default probability and show how to calibrate this model, ie, to extract the risk-neutral default probabilities from the market quotes of default swaps, assuming some exogenously determined constant recovery rate. Although this is a simple model, it creates a solid foundation frame-work within which to incorporate more complex features as required to value more complex credit derivatives, such as stochastic recovery rates, stochastic interest rates and stochastic hazard rates. The observed default swap premiums reflect both the default probability and the recovery rate in the event of default. It is not possible, therefore, to extract the value of both of these quantities only from market quotations. To resolve this, we can arbitrarily fix the recovery rate based on an educated guess relying on the historical data presented in Chapter 1. An appropriate value will therefore be in the range 10–50%. In general, the recovery rate estimate is of sec-ondary importance in pricing credit derivative structures. This is because the payout of both the instrument being priced and the hedging instrument will usually depend on the same recovery rate, which means that the effects will largely cancel. Of course, there are exceptions to this – eg, digital default swaps, which are sensitive to the assumed recovery rate.

To compute the value of the two legs of a default swap, we need to know the cumulative default probability $p(0, t)$ up to any time t. To compute the

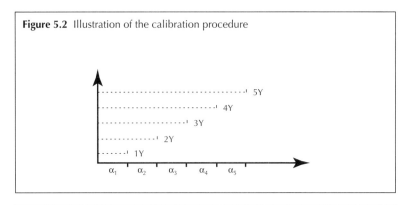

Figure 5.2 Illustration of the calibration procedure

Table 5.1 Default swaps used in the calibration example

Maturity (years)	Currency	Payment frequency	Recovery rate	Market premium
0.5	US$	Semi-annual	30%	50
1	US$	Semi-annual	30%	60
3	US$	Semi-annual	30%	80
5	US$	Semi-annual	30%	105
7	US$	Semi-annual	30%	120
10	US$	Semi-annual	30%	140

default probabilities, we first assume that the hazard rates are piecewise-constant, ie, they are constant between the maturity dates, $[T_1, T_2, ..., T_M]$, of the default swaps to which we are calibrating:

$$h(u) = \alpha_i \text{ for } i \in \left[t_{i-1}, t_i\right] \tag{9}$$

which means that the cumulative probability of default is given by

$$p(0, t_i) = 1 - \exp\left(-\sum_{i=1}^{M} \alpha_i \left(t_i - t_{i-1}\right)\right) \tag{10}$$

where the α_is are constant between the maturity dates of the default swaps we are calibrating to. The calibration procedure is performed by solving for the appropriate α_is, so that the market default swaps are re-priced correctly using Equation (7). This entails solving a set of non-linear equations in order of increasing maturity. The default swap with the shortest maturity (T_1) can be used to calibrate α_1. Consequently, as we know α_1, α_2 can be determined by the default swap with maturity T_2. This approach, known as a "bootstrap" procedure, is illustrated in Figure 5.2.

As an example of the calibration procedure, consider the default swaps shown in Table 5.1. These give a calibrated, piecewise-constant hazard rate

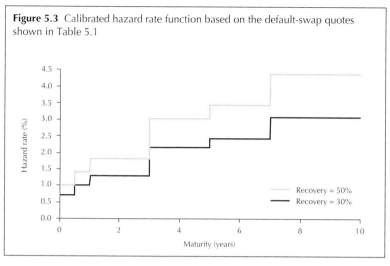

Figure 5.3 Calibrated hazard rate function based on the default-swap quotes shown in Table 5.1

Hazard rate (%) — *Maturity (years)*

Recovery = 50%
Recovery = 30%

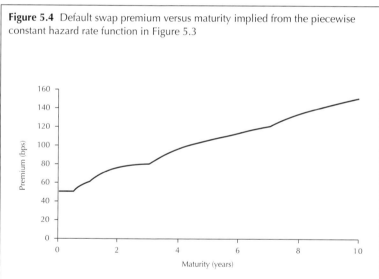

Figure 5.4 Default swap premium versus maturity implied from the piecewise constant hazard rate function in Figure 5.3

Premium (bps) — *Maturity (years)*

function (α_i), as shown in Figure 5.3 (we have included the payment of accrued premium in the event of default). A consequence of the assumption of a piecewise-constant function is that the hazard rate jumps at the maturity of each calibrating default swap. This leads to a slight discontinuity of the default swap premium with respect to maturity (Figure 5.4). The estimation of the term structure of credit spreads is discussed in Duffie (1999), whose paper is reproduced in the Appendix of this book. Chapter 4 also presents an advanced technique.

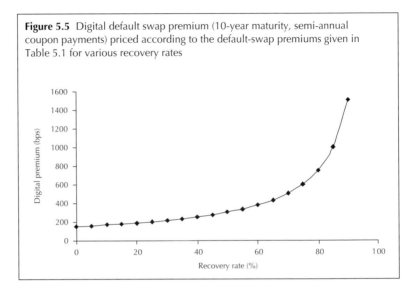

Figure 5.5 Digital default swap premium (10-year maturity, semi-annual coupon payments) priced according to the default-swap premiums given in Table 5.1 for various recovery rates

5.4.4 Digital default swaps

A digital default swap is similar to a standard default swap, but in the event of default, it pays the full notional amount independently of the recovery value of the reference asset. It can therefore be priced using Equation (7), with the recovery rate set to zero ($\delta = 0\%$). Clearly, it will demand a higher premium than a standard default swap. Its price will be sensitive to the recovery rate that has been assumed in the calibration procedure. The higher the recovery rate in the calibration, the higher the calibrated hazard rates will be. Since a digital default swap depends only on the hazard rates and not on the recovery rate, it has a price that effectively increases with the assumed recovery. Indeed, from Equation (7), since the payment of a standard and digital default swap differ only in their payments in the event of default, we would expect the premiums for the same maturity to be related through the simple expression $(1-\delta)X_{DS}^{Digital} = X_{DS}^{Standard}$. Figure 5.5 illustrates this for a 10-year digital default swap priced with the spreads used in Table 5.1. The premium increases exponentially, since, for a large recovery rate, the implied hazard rates are very high.

5.4.5 Credit-linked notes

A credit-linked note (CLN) is a structured note with an embedded credit derivative. Unlike a credit derivative, a CLN is an on-balance-sheet item requiring funding. A CLN can be thought of as being similar to a straight bond, except that in the event of default of the reference asset, an amount δ (the recovery) will be paid and the remaining coupons and principal will

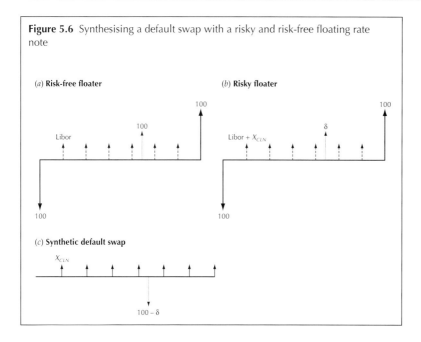

Figure 5.6 Synthesising a default swap with a risky and risk-free floating rate note

(*a*) **Risk-free floater**

(*b*) **Risky floater**

(*c*) **Synthetic default swap**

be forgone. Commonly, the coupons will be floating, but the analysis we present also encompasses a bond with fixed-rate coupons. As before, a CLN can be priced by taking the expectation over the payments in the case of default and no default, as shown in Equation (2). In the case of no default, the coupons and principal will be paid in full, whereas in the event of default the holder will receive the recovery rate δ. We will again present the analysis for a unit notional. Assuming that the maturity of the bond is $T(\equiv t_n)$ and that the coupons are paid at times $[t_1, t_2, ..., t_n]$, the present value of the n coupon and principal payments, accounting for the fact that they are paid only if default has not occurred, is given by

$$PV_{0,T}^{\text{no default}} = \sum_{i=1}^{n} \left[1 - p(0, t_i)\right] \Delta(t_{i-1}, t_i) c_{t_i} B(0, t_i)$$

$$+ \left[1 - p(0, t_n)\right] B(0, t_n) \tag{11}$$

where $p(0, t_i)$ represents the cumulative probability of default before time t_i, $\Delta(t_{i-1}, t_i) c_{t_i}$ is the expected coupon payment at time t_i and $B(0, t_i)$ is the discount factor. The second term in Equation (11) represents the payment of the principal amount at time t_n if default has not occurred previously.

The present value of the default payments can be represented in a similar way to the default leg of a default swap in Equation (6):

$$PV_{0,T}^{\text{default}} \approx \delta \sum_{j=1}^{m} \left[p(0, t_j) - p(0, t_{j-1}) \right] B(0, t_j) \tag{12}$$

Since default can occur at any time, the interval $[t_{j-1}, t_j]$ should be small enough to achieve convergence. Again, we will use $(t_j, t_{j-1}) = 1$ day in the following example.

We stated earlier that a CLN is similar to holding a risk-free bond and being short a default swap. A risky floating rate pays a coupon of Libor plus a spread as compensation for the embedded default risk. In the event of default, it pays the recovery rate δ rather than the remaining floating coupons and principal at maturity. By shorting a risk-free floating-rate note (FRN), it is possible to extract the default risk component in a floating-rate CLN. Indeed, if we consider the cashflows as shown in Figure 5.6, we can see that such a position (long a risky FRN and short a risk-free FRN) synthesises a default swap. It would, therefore, seem that the spread on a CLN should be the same as the premium on the equivalent default swap. We will now consider this point in more detail.

The arguments presented above are rather simplistic, since it is not possible to readily short bonds. We consider the arguments in more detail (see also Duffie, 1999). Consider buying a default swap for which we pay a periodic premium X_{DS}. This could be hedged by buying a floating-rate CLN referenced to the same credit. The purchase of the bond could be funded in the repo market. If the FRN is on special, then its repo rate will be $L-M$, where L is the Libor rate and M is a positive number. The risky FRN pays a spread X_{CLN} above the Libor rate. We assume that the term repo terminates when the FRN defaults. Otherwise, the arbitrage relationship is not exact. The cashflows are shown in Table 5.2. To avoid arbitrage $X_{DS} = X_{CLN} + M$, the spread on a floating-rate CLN should be lower than that on the equivalent default swap as compensation for the repo component. If we ignore the repo component, then we get $X_{DS} = X_{CLN}$, as seemed appropriate from the simple argument presented above.

If we are selling instead of buying protection, we need to sell the under-

Table 5.2 Illustration of the arbitrage relationship between a default swap and a floating-rate CLN

	Repo	Risky floating-rate note (CLN)	Default swap	Hedged position
Inception	1	−1	0	0
Coupon	−L − M	$L + X_{CLN}$	$-X_{DS}$	$X_{CLN} - M - X_{DS}$
Default	−1	δ	$(1 - \delta)$	0
No default	−1	1	0	0

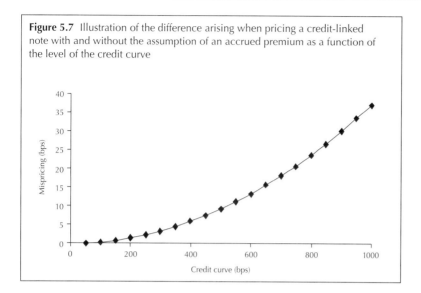

Figure 5.7 Illustration of the difference arising when pricing a credit-linked note with and without the assumption of an accrued premium as a function of the level of the credit curve

lying FRN in order to hedge. Using similar arguments, it can easily be shown that the above relationship still holds. The above argument is exact if it is assumed that default can only occur at a coupon payment date. Yet if default happens at an intermediate date, the value of the loan on the repo depends on the interest rate movements since the last fixing. The expected value at the inception of the trade will be 100 and, therefore, we should still get $X_{DS} = X_{CLN} + M$.

Furthermore, in practice, accrued interest is not normally paid on a CLN in the event of default. This means that the CLN spread should be higher than the default swap premium to compensate for this, ie, the curve is stripped assuming that the underlying default swaps have an accrued premium paid while the pricing of the CLN assumes no accrued premium. This is illustrated in Figure 5.7. Obviously, the effect is more pronounced when the credit curve is quite high, as then the probability of default is also large.

5.4.6 Asset swaps

An asset swap package is a combination of an underlying bond and an interest rate swap. In the event of default, the interest rate swap would remain in place. There is, therefore, a residual exposure to interest rate risk. Suppose we enter an asset swap, where we buy the underlying bonds, at the same time as entering the interest rate swap. We pay the bond coupon C and receive Libor plus the asset swap spread X_{AS}. However, the swap is not cancelled if the bond defaults. In case of default, the asset swap buyer, being the bondholder, receives the recovery value δ of the bond. The asset swap spread not only compensates the asset swap buyer for bearing credit

Table 5.3 Illustration of the (failed) arbitrage relationship between a default swap and an asset swap

	Bond	Swap	Repo	Default swap	Hedged position
Inception	-100	0	100	0	0
Coupon	C	$(L + X_{AS}) - C$	$M - L$	$-X_{DS}$	$M + X_{AS} - X_{DS}$
Default	δ	PV_{swap}	-100	$(100 - \delta)$	PV_{swap}
No default	100	0	-100	0	0

risk on the issuer but also repays the loan. If the bond is trading at a premium, the asset swap buyer borrows the premium from the dealer. The loan is repaid through the above market fixed payment C on the swap. It is assumed that both parties fund themselves at Libor.

To investigate the relationship between the asset swap spread and the default swap premium, we have constructed the following portfolio. Assume that we are buying protection through a default swap on the underlying bond. We then buy the asset swap package at par, which is funded in the repo market at a rate $L - M$. If the bond defaults, the asset swap holder does not suffer any losses on the bond position, since he has bought protection, but he is exposed to the interest rate swap that can have a positive or negative mark-to-market. The cashflows are shown in Table 5.3, where PV_{swap} is the mark-to-market on the swap when default occurs.

An arbitrage between asset swap spreads and default swap spreads fails, since the asset swap buyer is exposed to an interest rate swap in the event of default. We should, therefore, write that $X_{DS} = X_{AS} + M + S$, where M represents the repo component and S, which may be positive or negative, is an adjustment for the contingent interest rate swap. We discuss the computation of this term in the next section.

5.4.7 Credit contingent contracts

In a credit contingent contract, payment is dependent on the occurrence of a certain credit event. This class of financial products is very broad and provides a natural way for market participants to transfer event risk to the dealers. The protection seller can suffer substantial losses with small probability. In this section, we discuss some intuitive results, and in the next we present a more thorough mathematical analysis. The same intuition applies to more complex credit contingent contracts. (We will discuss contingent interest rate swaps when we undertake a specific case study of the pricing and hedging of a credit contingent contract.) A contingent swap in this context is defined as being like a regular interest rate swap with uncertain maturity. When a third party defaults, the swap terminates without any payment to the counterparty that has the positive mark-to-market on the swap.

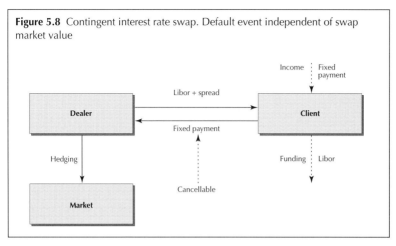

Figure 5.8 Contingent interest rate swap. Default event independent of swap market value

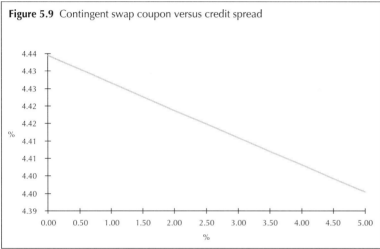

Figure 5.9 Contingent swap coupon versus credit spread

Consider a European exporter, who funds at euro Libor and has business mainly concentrated in a certain emerging market country. On the basis of business analysis, a regular income is expected, payable in euros unless the country defaults. To hedge the interest rate mismatch between assets and liabilities, the counterparty would like to enter an interest rate swap that is cancelled if the country defaults. A contingent swap is the natural hedge.

In the above example, the level of the euro interest rates, and therefore the market value of the swap, does not have any impact on the default probability. At inception, the theoretical coupon of the swap is set so that the market value of the difference between the fixed and the floating legs, accounting for the uncertain swap maturity based on the foreign country's default premium curve, equals zero. The impact of the credit spread on the equilibrium coupon (fixed rate) is shown in Figure 5.9.

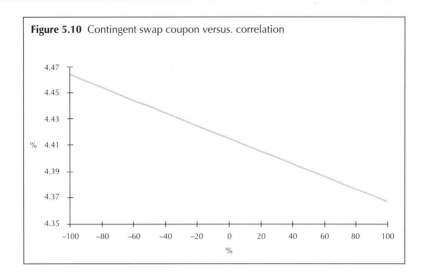

Figure 5.10 Contingent swap coupon versus. correlation

If the foreign country has issued large amounts of euro-denominated debt to be serviced by floating payments, a substantial increase in the level of the euro interest rates could trigger default. (This is what happened in the syndicated Eurodollar loan market in Mexico and Brazil in the early-1980s, when US dollar interest rates soared). Therefore, the probability of cancellation of the swap will be higher when the client has a positive mark-to-market. In order to be compensated for this adverse effect, the client would pay a lower fixed coupon than in the zero-correlation case. In Figure 5.10, we show the effect of the correlation between the Libor rate and the credit spread.

Pricing these credit contingent products can be difficult, but the biggest challenge is the risk management. The theoretical price could be a very useful benchmark, but the actual pricing should be based on the cost of the hedge and should include transaction costs and compensation for any residual variance that cannot be hedged. When the coupon is determined, as shown in Figures 5.9 and 5.10, the expected profit and loss (P&L) is zero. It can, however, have high variance, driven by the volatility of the swap rate. Therefore, for any specific trade, it is possible to realise a big gain or loss. The best way to reduce the possibility of extreme losses is to run a well-diversified book (both market and event risk) of relatively small transactions. Additional hedging could then be minimal and pricing more competitive.

A possible hedging strategy is to trade default swaps referenced to the third party. Ideally, these would be digital, so as to have no recovery rate risk. We assume that the default probability and therefore the default swap premium is independent of the level of the euro swap rate. The hedge is to buy or sell an amount of digital default swaps equal to the mark-to-market (positive or negative, respectively) of the interest rate swap. If we are using standard default swaps, then we would have to buy a larger quantity of default swaps, based on our assessment of the recovery rate in the event of default, as the payout will be the notional amount times $(1 - \delta)$. In case of default, the loss or gain on the mark-to-market on the interest rate swap will be offset by the payout on the default swap position. There is now an additional risk, due to credit spread and interest rate volatility. However, this should be substantially smaller than the default risk that has been eliminated. The variance of the P&L has been reduced drastically. The hedge has to be continuously readjusted as interest rates move. Hedging strategies of this type are covered in more detail in Chapter 6.

Securities whose payout is contingent on the occurrence of a certain event are more common than one would expect. Due to prepayments, receiving the coupons on a mortgage-backed security is contingent on the interest rate being above a certain level. If homeowners exercise their option rationally, there will be a high degree of correlation between the present value of the mortgage and the probability of contract "cancellation". This leads to substantial convexity in the pricing. A vulnerable option (the writer of the option can default) is a contingent option, where the place of the third party is taken by the option writer. Another example where the payout is contingent on a certain event is that of catastrophe and weather bonds. In a tender offer situation, the bidder enters into the hedging contract (ie, swap, option, forward, etc) only if he wins the bid. Modelling of this product is further complicated by moral hazard and adverse selection issues, which we cover in Chapter 8. In the next section, we provide a mathematical analysis of contingent interest rate swaps.

5.4.8 Contingent interest rate swaps

In this section, we consider the pricing of a contingent exposure to an interest rate swap (IRS). This applies either to an IRS that is terminated in the event of default or to one that is triggered upon default. The reference credit on which the swap is contingent is not the same as the swap counterparty. We discuss the pricing of counterparty risk in swaps in Chapter 6, where we also include more detailed derivations of the formulae given below. For pricing a contingent IRS, we need to consider the forward mark-to-market on the swap conditional upon default. We then take the expectation over all possible default times, as we did for computing the expression for the PV of the default leg of a default swap. This leads to the following equation:

$$PV_{0,T}^{IRS} = \sum_{i=1}^{n} \left[p(0, t_j) - p(0, t_{j-1}) \right] E^Q \left[Sw(t_j) \right] B(0, t_j) \qquad (13)$$

where as before, $\left[p(0, t_j) - p(0, t_{j-1}) \right]$ gives the probability of default in the

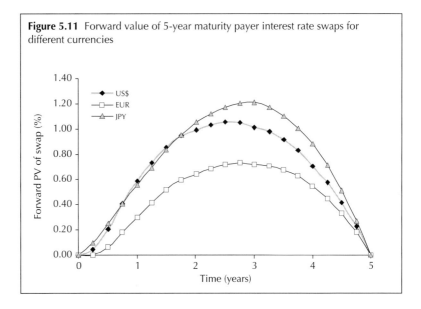

Figure 5.11 Forward value of 5-year maturity payer interest rate swaps for different currencies

interval $[t_{j-1}, t_j]$ and $B(0, t_j)$ is the risk-free discount factor. The expectation term $E^Q[Sw(t_j)]$ is the expected future value of the IRS, ie, the forward value, which we write as PVt_j:

$$E^Q\left[Sw(t_j)\right] = PV_{t_j} \tag{14}$$

This gives

$$PV_{0,T}^{\text{IRS}} = \sum_{i=1}^{n}\left[p(0, t_j) - p(0, t_{j-1})\right]PV_{t_j}\, B(0, t_j) \tag{15}$$

The resulting value of $PV_{0,T}^{\text{IRS}}$ will depend on two elements. The first is the forward value of the IRS, which is determined by the shape of the risk-free yield curve in question. If the yield curve is upward-sloping (interest rates increase with maturity), then a payer IRS (we pay a fixed rate and receive floating rate, ie, Libor) will have a positive forward value. This is illustrated in Figure 5.11 for US dollars, euro and Japanese yen swaps. The Japanese yen swap has the highest exposure, since the yen yield curve is very steep (short-term interest rates are much lower than longer-term rates). Note that the forward value of a receiver swap (we receive floating and pay fixed) is exactly opposite to the corresponding payer swap. The forward exposure of a swap increases significantly with maturity since there are many more cashflows to be exchanged and more time value. This is illustrated in Figure 5.12.

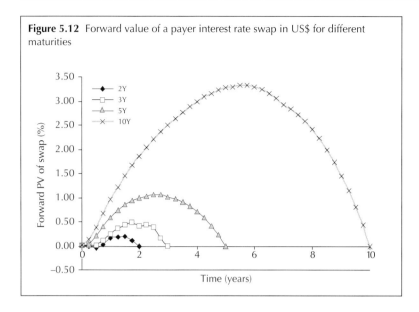

Figure 5.12 Forward value of a payer interest rate swap in US$ for different maturities

The second important factor in determining $PV_{0,T}^{IRS}$ is the probability of default. Clearly, if default is more likely, exposure to the IRS becomes more probable and, consequently, $PV_{0,T}^{IRS}$ will be higher. We now illustrate this with some pricing examples where we give the value of $PV_{0,T}^{IRS}$ in terms of basis points (bps) per annum (ie, we express $PV_{0,T}^{IRS}$ by a number of annual payments as a fraction of the notional of the swap). By doing this, we compute the value of S in the equation $X_{DS} = X_{AS} + M + S$ for the credit spread of an asset swap. Table 5.4 shows the required spreads for US dollar IRSs, and in Table 5.5 we give the spreads for Japanese yen IRSs. As expected, the figures increase with both maturity and the level of the credit curve. For Japanese yen, the adjustment is larger than for US dollars, since the forward exposure is greater, as already mentioned.

We can see that normally (aside from the repo component), an asset swap spread would be lower than the corresponding default swap premium, so that exposure to the IRS in the event of default is reflected. This value is expected to be positive, in which case we effectively make a gain on the IRS. If the yield curve is downward-sloping, the reverse is true, and the asset swap spread should be higher as compensation for the expected loss (negative exposure) on the IRS. For an asset swap on a bond with a relatively long maturity, this effect can be quite large.

We note that although we are pricing the interest rate exposure by taking the expected value of the forward swap, it is unlikely that this risk can be hedged, since trading contingent IRSs is impossible. If the volatility on the interest rate is quite high, it may be appropriate to charge for this, since it cannot be easily hedged (as discussed in the last section).

Table 5.4 Price (basis points per annum) of contingent interest rate swaps in US dollars for different maturities and levels of the credit curve

Level	Years to maturity			
(bps)	2	3	5	10
100	−0.1	−0.3	−0.9	−3.0
200	−0.2	−0.7	−1.9	−5.9
300	−0.3	−1.0	−2.8	−8.7
500	−0.5	−1.7	−4.6	−14.2

Table 5.5 Price (basis points per annum) of contingent interest rate swaps in Japanese yen for different maturities and levels of the credit curve

Level	Years to maturity			
(bps)	2	3	5	10
100	−0.0	−0.2	−1.1	−4.4
200	−0.1	−0.5	−2.1	−8.8
300	−0.1	−0.7	−3.1	−13.0
500	−0.2	−1.1	−5.2	−21.4

This would create even more disparity between asset swap and default swap spreads.

One effect we did not consider in the above model is the possible correlation between interest rates and the default event. If this correlation is positive and high interest rates are more likely to lead to default, the exposure on the IRS is likely to be higher, since we are receiving the high floating rate. The figures in the above tables would become larger, but still negative. If this correlation is negative (low interest rates are more likely to lead to default), then the numbers could be positive, in which case the asset swap could trade above the corresponding default swaps. To account for this effect, we would need a two-factor model for the evolution of the risk-free interest rate and the hazard rate. The dynamics of these two variables and their correlation will determine the exact relationship (eg, see Figure 5.10).

5.4.9 Quanto default swaps

A quanto default swap has one leg denominated in foreign currency (FC) that is not the base currency, which we assume to be the US dollar. Consider a multinational that issues bonds denominated both in US dollars and in FC. It may be desirable to make a market in FC-denominated default swaps and use the US$ default swap market as the basis for pricing and hedging. The US$ default swap market is a more appropriate reference than the underlying FC- bond market for two reasons. First, it can be more

Figure 5.13 Quanto default swap. Basic hedging strategy

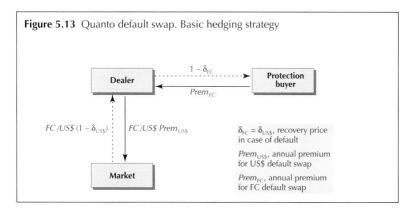

liquid, and second, and most importantly, the dealer is not exposed to the basis risk – ie, the spread between the default swap spread and the bond credit spread – which can be very volatile. Next, we present some fundamental properties of the pricing of quanto default swaps. What is crucial in the pricing and hedging of these instruments is the behaviour of the FC/US$ exchange rate – ie, the value in US dollars of one unit of the foreign currency – in case of default.

Under the above scenario, the default of the issuer does not trigger currency devaluation. This is true for small companies whose collapse will not give rise to further defaults and significantly impact the economy. The payment to the buyer of a default swap if the underlying bond defaults is $1 - \delta$, where δ is the recovery price of the bond. The buyer pays an annual premium to the seller until default occurs.

The dealer sells default protection in FC to the investor and hedges himself in the US$ default swap market. In Figure 5.13, we show the basic hedging strategy. A fundamental assumption in this analysis is that $\delta_{FC} = \delta_{US\$}$ (ie, the bond recovery price) is the same in both currencies. This is a strong assumption, since the recovery price depends not only on the issuer but also on the regulatory environment. This assumption could be relaxed easily. The major concern for the dealer is to be hedged in case of default. In order to achieve this, he buys an amount of US$ default swaps equal to the exchange rate between FC and US$. The hedge has to be dynamically adjusted in order for the dealer to be perfectly hedged. In practice, to avoid excessive transaction costs, he will follow a semi-static hedging strategy, rebalancing only if there is a major market move. The size of the two premiums $Prem_{FC}$ and $Prem_{US\$}$ will depend on the yield curves in the two currencies. If the yield curves FC and US$ are identical, then the premiums will be the same. Otherwise, they will be different, and some additional foreign exchange hedging will be required. As discussed above for credit contingent contracts, the price should also reflect the hedging cost and residual risks involved.

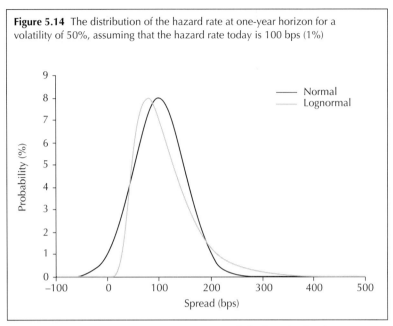

Figure 5.14 The distribution of the hazard rate at one-year horizon for a volatility of 50%, assuming that the hazard rate today is 100 bps (1%)

If a major bank or insurance company defaults, the banking system could be destabilised, triggering further defaults and leading to a currency crisis. This effect should be taken into account in determining the premium of a quanto default swap. On the other hand, it is possible for currency devaluation to trigger defaults. A local bank with assets denominated in the domestic currency (loans, credit cards, etc) and borrowings in the international markets would suffer substantial losses that could result in bankruptcy. Again, this effect would result in a reduction of the premium of the quanto default swap.

5.5 CREDIT SPREAD OPTIONS

We now show how the model discussed in section 5.4.1 can be extended to price credit spread options. We will again assume again independence between interest rates and the hazard rate. We model the latter using a one-factor model, which is realistic for pricing options on floating-rate bonds or default swaps. For options on fixed-rate bonds and asset swaps (asset swaptions), it may be appropriate to use a two-factor model for the interest rate and hazard rate, although this may not be important unless the correlation is high. So far, we have only been concerned with a deterministic hazard rate function, whereas when it comes to pricing option payouts, we must incorporate volatility in the hazard rate process. The model we describe assumes that the hazard rate of default is either normally or log-normally distributed. To appreciate the significance of either of these assumptions, we show in Figure 5.14 the difference between these two distributions. The normal model gives tractability, since it allows explicit computation of default swap prices (and European options), making the calibration faster. The lognormal model is perhaps more appropriate, since it does not permit negative hazard rates and has a reasonably fat tail, which means that large increases in the credit spread are more likely.

5.5.1 Black–Scholes approach

For a European credit spread put option of maturity t, where the maturity of the underlying is T, we can express the payout as

$$\text{Payout} = \left(\sum_{i=1}^{n} \Delta_{i-1,i} \tilde{B}(0, t_i) \right) \left(S_{t,T} - K \right)^{+} \tag{16}$$

if default has not occurred before time t. Here, $S_{t,T}$ is the forward credit spread and K is the strike credit spread. The term $\tilde{B}(0, t_i)$ represents the risky discount factor, which is simply the risk-free discount factor $B(0, t_i)$ multiplied by the probability of not defaulting in the interval $[0, t_i]$. The expression $\left(\sum_{i=1}^{n} \Delta_{i-1,i} \tilde{B}(0, t_i) \right)$ gives the PV today of receiving unit cash-flows at times $[t_1, t_2, \ldots, t_n]$, ie, the coupon payments on the underlying instrument after exercise. A simple and common approach for pricing European credit spread options is to assume that the underlying (eg, the default swap premium for an option on a default swap) is lognormally distributed over time. In this case, the value of a European credit spread option can be expressed as follows:

$$PV_{0,t,T}^{\text{Option}} = \left(\sum_{i=1}^{n} \Delta_{i-1,i} \tilde{B}(0, t_i) \right) \left[S_{t,T} N(d_1) - KN(d_2) \right]$$

$$d_1 = \frac{\ln\left(\dfrac{S_{t,T}}{K} \right) - \dfrac{1}{2}\sigma t}{\sigma \sqrt{t}}$$

$$d_2 = \frac{\ln\left(\dfrac{S_{t,T}}{K} \right) + \dfrac{1}{2}\sigma t}{\sigma \sqrt{t}} = d_1 - \sigma \sqrt{t} \tag{17}$$

Here, σ is the volatility of the default swap premiums, which can be estimated from analysing historical credit spread data; or it can be implied from market instruments if they are available. The above is very similar to the Black–Scholes (1973) option pricing formula (see, for example, Hull, 1997). However, this model cannot be used for more complex structures, such as those with more than one exercise date.

The more general model we will now describe is an extension of the above framework used for pricing default swaps and other basic credit derivatives structures. The calibration instruments are default swaps of different maturities.

5.5.2 Normal model

A fairly well-known model for interest rates is the Hull and White one-factor model (Hull and White, 1994). Indeed, we will use this for modelling the interest rate in Chapters 6 and 7. The Hull and White model assumes that the short-term interest rate follows a normal distribution with mean reversion. The mean reversion dictates that the interest rate reverts back to some particular level. This level is time-dependent, and this allows the model to fit exactly the yield curve observed today (ie, it is an arbitrage rather than an equilibrium model). A disadvantage of the model is that it permits negative interest rates due to the assumption of normality (although the probability of the rate becoming negative is generally quite small). However, an advantage of the Hull and White model is that it allows a great deal of tractability and the derivation of closed-form formulae for pricing swaps, caps and floors, and swaptions. This is even an advantage for more complex structures, since it facilitates curve fitting when using numerical schemes such as trees. Indeed, Hull and White (1994) have described a simple procedure for constructing a tree that matches the initial yield curve exactly.

Our first approach in modelling a stochastic hazard rate will be to follow an approach with similarities to Hull and White for the underlying dynamics. This approach has been suggested by Schönbucher (1999), whose work should be consulted for the technical details. The hazard rate $h(t)$ is assumed to follow the mean-reverting normal process below:

$$dh(t) = a\left(\frac{\theta(t)}{a} - h(t)\right)dt + \sigma_N dW_t \tag{18}$$

where a is the mean-reversion speed, σ_N is the volatility of the hazard rate, and $\theta(t)/a$ is the level to which the hazard rate reverts at the rate a. The parameter $\theta(t)$ can be chosen to price all the calibration instruments (default swaps) correctly by matching the forward credit spread curve (Schönbucher, 1999). As before, we assume that the expected hazard rate is constant between tenor dates of the underlying default swaps. We will assume for simplicity that the volatility of the hazard is constant, but this assumption can readily be lifted.

5.5.3 Lognormal model

An obvious criticism of the normal model is that it allows the hazard rate to become negative, in which case the probability of default will also

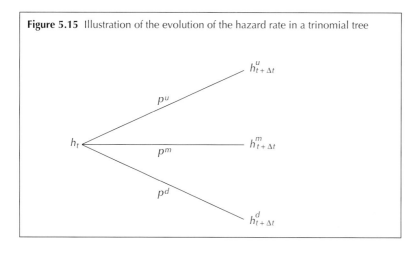

Figure 5.15 Illustration of the evolution of the hazard rate in a trinomial tree

become negative. Indeed, the probability of negative hazard rates can be quite large, since typical hazard rates, as opposed to interest rates, may be quite small but fairly volatile. For this reason, we propose an alternative specification of the model:

$$\frac{\mathrm{d}h(t)}{h(t)} = \theta(t)\mathrm{d}t + \sigma_{LN}\mathrm{d}W_t \tag{19}$$

In this model, the hazard rate is lognormally distributed (but with no mean-reversion) and is therefore guaranteed to be positive. However, this specification does not permit closed-form formulae as in the normal case, and therefore the calibration procedure will be more difficult.

5.5.4 Implementation of models
The most common credit spread option products have Bermudan[3] or American features, but no path dependency. For this reason, we will illustrate the implementation of the two proposed models on a tree.

In a trinomial tree, the underlying variable (ie, the hazard rate) evolves as shown in Figure 5.15.:

In the normal model,

$$h^d_{t+\Delta t} = h_t - \sigma_N \sqrt{3\Delta t} ,$$

$$h^m_{t+\Delta t} = h_t \text{ and}$$

$$h^u_{t+\Delta t} = h_t + \sigma_N \sqrt{3\Delta t}$$

while in the lognormal model

$$h^d_{t+\Delta t} = \frac{h_t}{\exp\left(\sigma_{LN}\sqrt{3\Delta t}\right)},$$

$$h^m_{t+\Delta t} = h_t \quad \text{and}$$

$$h^u_{t+\Delta t} = h_t \times \exp\left(\sigma_{LN}\sqrt{3\Delta t}\right)$$

The probabilities are chosen so as to match the mean and variance and to ensure that they sum to one. The relationship between the normal and log-normal volatilities is $\sigma_N = h_0\sigma_{LN}$, where h_0 represents the initial (spot) hazard rate. To incorporate default, we build the tree in the usual way and then add a default branch to each node in the tree and modify the transition probabilities accordingly (Figure 5.16).

The default probability between t_{i-1} and t_i can be calculated from the realised hazard rate on the tree according to

$$p^{\text{def}}_t = 1 - \exp\left(-h_t\Delta t\right) \tag{20}$$

As mentioned above, both models can be fitted to effectively determine the appropriate hazard rate function. This involves shifting each portion of the tree, as illustrated in Figure 5.17. As before, we assume that the calibration instruments will be default swaps of various maturities. If the default swaps have ordered maturities given by $[t_1, t_2, ..., t_M]$, then the entire tree between times T_j and T_{j-1} is shifted so as to match the price of the default swap with maturity $T_j (T_0 = 0)$.

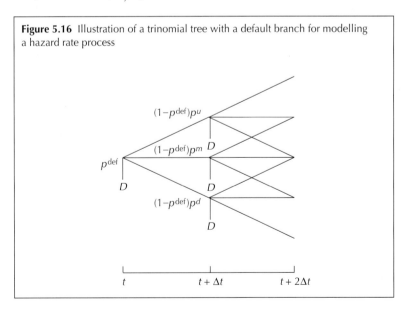

Figure 5.16 Illustration of a trinomial tree with a default branch for modelling a hazard rate process

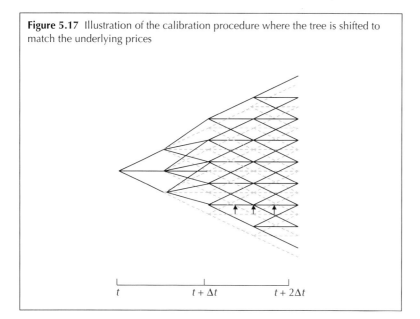

Figure 5.17 Illustration of the calibration procedure where the tree is shifted to match the underlying prices

For the normal model, the required shifts can be calculated analytically, as described by Schönbucher (1999), once the hazard rate function has been determined from the underlying default swap market (as described in section 5.4.3). For the lognormal model, the parameters should be computed numerically by pricing each default swap sequentially in order of increasing maturity. At the jth stage, the tree in the region $[T_{j-1}, T_j]$ is shifted so that the PV of the jth default swap is zero.

Next, we discuss how to price an option to enter into a default swap. This contract is very similar to a credit spread option on a floating-rate bond with the same maturity (apart from the accrued interest effect discussed earlier) – ie, an option to buy default protection is equivalent to an option to sell the floating-rate bond at the same strike credit spread.

To price a default swap in the tree, we have to account for the premium leg and the default leg. Given the values at time $t + \Delta t$, the value of the contract (we buy protection, ie, pay the premium leg) at time t will be given by

$$DS_t = \left[\left(1 - p^{\,\mathrm{def}}\right) \left(p^{\,d} DS_{t+\Delta t}^{\,d} + p^{\,m} DS_{t+\Delta t}^{\,m} + p^{\,u} DS_{t+\Delta t}^{\,u} \right) + p^{\,\mathrm{def}}\left(1 - \delta\right) \right]$$

$$\times B(t, t + \Delta t) - 1_{t \in [d_1, d_2, \dots, d_n]} \Delta_{t-1, t} C_t \tag{21}$$

The first term is the discounted expectation of the four possible scenarios, assuming that in default the default swap pays $(1 - \delta)$, where δ is the recovery rate. The second term accounts for coupon payments in the default swap, assuming that they are made at times $[d_1, d_2, \dots, d_n]$. $\Delta_{t-1, t} C_t$ denotes

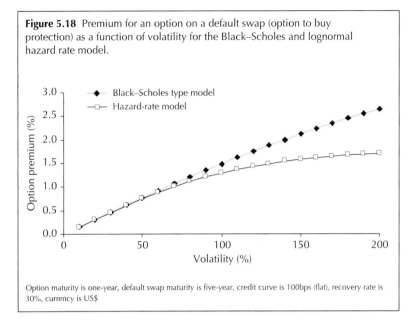

Figure 5.18 Premium for an option on a default swap (option to buy protection) as a function of volatility for the Black–Scholes and lognormal hazard rate model.

Option maturity is one-year, default swap maturity is five-year, credit curve is 100bps (flat), recovery rate is 30%, currency is US$

the premium paid on the default swap at time t and $B(t, t + \Delta t)$ is the discount factor.

To price an option to enter into a default swap, we first calculate the discounted expected value of the option (at the end of the tree the option is worth zero) according to

$$ODS'_t = \left(1 - p^{\text{def}}\right)\left(p^d ODS^d_{t+\Delta t} + p^m ODS^m_{t+\Delta t} + p^u ODS^u_{t+\Delta t}\right) B(t, t + \Delta t)$$

(22)

which assumes that, in the event of default, the option cannot be exercised (the payout is zero). Other specifications can be incorporated. We should then, for early exercise, apply the test at every exercise date (boundary condition), $ODS_t = \max(ODS'_t, DS_t)$. In the above analysis, we have described the pricing of an option to buy default protection, but, of course, this can readily be extended to the opposite contract. Furthermore, a cancellable default swap can be decomposed into a standard default swap plus an option to enter into the reserve default swap.

5.5.5 Examples
Next, we give some pricing examples. We analyse the sensitivity of the prices to both the input parameters and the process followed by the hazard rate. First, we consider the difference between the simple Black–Scholes type formula and the lognormal hazard rate model. Both assume a lognormal distribution for the underlying variable, but this variable is different.

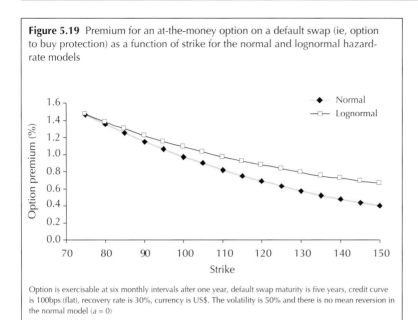

Figure 5.19 Premium for an at-the-money option on a default swap (ie, option to buy protection) as a function of strike for the normal and lognormal hazard-rate models

Option is exercisable at six monthly intervals after one year, default swap maturity is five years, credit curve is 100bps (flat), recovery rate is 30%, currency is US$. The volatility is 50% and there is no mean reversion in the normal model ($a = 0$)

In the Black–Scholes type model, it is the default swap premium, whereas in the hazard rate model, it is the actual hazard rate of default.

We consider a European "default and out" credit spread put option of maturity one-year, which gives the right to buy five-year protection on a US$-denominated reference asset with a flat credit curve of 100bps. The premium is shown in Figure 5.18 for both models as a function of volatility. When the volatility is reasonably low, the models give almost identical results, whereas for high volatility there can be a large difference. This highlights an important feature of credit spread put options compared with other options, which is the effect of default. If the credit spread is very high, then the option is very in-the-money, but default is also more likely. If default occurs before we can exercise the option, then the contract is worth nothing. For a credit spread put option, these effects act in opposite directions, whereas for a call option, they act in the same direction.

We now compare the normal and lognormal hazard rate models by considering the pricing of an option that is similar to the one above, yet of Bermudan style, exercisable every six months from year 1 to year to year 6, with exercise dates coinciding with coupon payment dates). Figure 5.19 shows the premium as a function of the option strike spread for both models with a volatility of 50% ($\sigma_{LN} = \sigma_N/h_0 = 0.5$). When the option is very in-the-money, the models are fairly close, but there is quite a large discrepancy for out-of-the-money options. This difference is easy to understand, since the lognormal model has a much fatter tail and, therefore, attaches

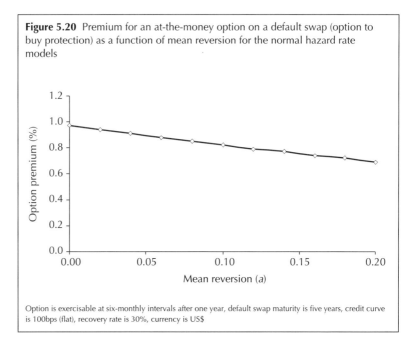

Figure 5.20 Premium for an at-the-money option on a default swap (option to buy protection) as a function of mean reversion for the normal hazard rate models

Option is exercisable at six-monthly intervals after one year, default swap maturity is five years, credit curve is 100bps (flat), recovery rate is 30%, currency is US$

greater probability to large increases in the hazard rate. Furthermore, if we incorporate mean reversion in the normal model, the premium decreases still further (Figure 5.20).

5.5.6 Hedging
In the well-known Black–Scholes model, an implicit assumption in the derivation of the pricing formula is that the option can be dynamically hedged by trading the underlying stock. This is known as delta hedging. It is possible to delta hedge credit spread options by trading the underlying contract, ie, a default swap. For example, consider the option on the default swap example above (Figure 5.19). The delta of this option is shown as a function of volatility in Figure 5.21. This shows similar behaviour to, for example, an equity option. Ignoring transaction costs, the cost of such a hedging strategy should be equal to the price of the option computed by the model. This assumes that the hedge will be adjusted continuously (in practice, say, once a day).

Therefore, it seems reasonable that the credit spread option can be hedged by holding a position in the underlying default swap according to its delta. In a delta-hedged position, at the exercise date, we will have either a delta of 100% (full position in default swap so that the payout matches that of the exercised option exactly) or a delta equal to 0% (if the option is out-of-the-money). However, there is one issue here that is not encountered

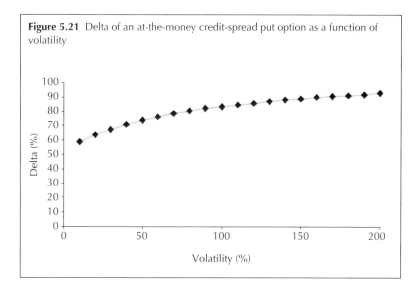

Figure 5.21 Delta of an at-the-money credit-spread put option as a function of volatility

in the hedging of other options: the possibility of default. In the event of default, the spread option will be worth nothing,[4] whereas the default swap position will be worth $(1-\delta)$. A way to avoid this mismatch is to hedge the option with the same underlying, ie, a forward-starting default swap starting at the first exercise of the option. Although such a contract cannot normally be readily traded, it can be synthetically created by holding long and short default swap positions. For example, a long position in a five-year default swap forward starting in one year can be constructed by going long six-year protection and short one-year protection. However, as with interest rate swaps, we cannot directly synthesise a forward-starting default swap from long and short positions unless the default swap curve is flat (ie, the premium is the same for all maturities).

5.5.7 Jumps in the credit spread

An extension to the models presented for pricing credit spread options is the incorporation of jumps in the credit spread. Jumps may be firm-specific, occurring as a result of an upgrade or downgrade in a particular firm or because some information is being made available to the market, or they may be non-firm specific, occurring, for example, when the credit spreads for a particular sector or region widen or tighten. The jumps may even be more general; for instance, a "flight-to-quality" jump occurs when spreads with the same rating move together. Normally, credit spread jumps will be positive – and will worsen credit quality – as a result of negative market information rather than vice versa. This could have a significant impact on the pricing of options on default swaps, particularly if they are out-of-the-money puts. Models based on such a framework, often known as jump-diffusion models, have been proposed (Duffie, Pan and Singleton, 2000; Zhou, 1997). However, a problem here is the calibration of both size and frequency of the jumps. Because the size of the jumps is invariable to a change of measure, it can be estimated from historical data. For a reliable estimation, a very long time series of credit spread data would be needed. It may not be possible to distinguish between large, infrequent jumps and more regular, but smaller, jumps. For estimating the frequency of the jumps, we need traded instruments that are sensitive to the jump frequency; these are not usually available. The jump frequency is not invariable to a change of measure from historical to risk-neutral and, therefore, historical data cannot be used to perform this estimation. It is very likely that the calibration of the model would be unstable – consequently, we would have little confidence in the prices of the credit spread options. On the other hand, ignoring the jumps can introduce substantial model error, especially for long-dated options. Increasing the volatility as a proxy for the jumps will not always work.

5.6 MULTIPLE UNDERLYING PRODUCTS

We now move on to multiple underlying credit derivatives, with an emphasis on baskets. These are probably the most complex products to price and hedge. We explore how Merton's firm value model can be extended for modelling basket default swaps. Typical products in this class are the "worst of" and the first l or the last m to default in a basket of n assets. One can, in theory, structure products that provide protection against any designated default events. The analysis we present is applicable both to baskets of a few assets, typically between five and 10, which are actively managed, and to traditional CDOs with a large number of assets. The model incorporates the "clustering" of defaults over time due to default correlation – this is crucial to the pricing of these products, since we are dealing with extreme events far into the tail of the loss distribution. The required parameters for calibrating the model are the underlying credit curves, the recovery rates (even though they have a second-order effect), and the correlation matrix among the stock returns (or "asset returns") of each underlying. We will see that the lack of market-implied parameters for the correlation substantially complicates the risk management of the product and introduces uncertainty into the price. This is not specific to the model at hand, but it is inherent to the product and the market.

First, we define various basket contracts and derive simple arbitrage bounds for their premiums. We proceed with the development of a formal pricing framework, based on the standard firm value model. We generalise the one-period model into a multi-period framework, where the value of the firm follows a random walk. The credit spread follows a stochastic process – centred at its forward – which is driven by the firm value process. Within the assumptions of the model, delta hedging provides perfect protection against default and changes in the credit spread. This is a consequence of the fact that defaults in this framework are anticipated – ie, the credit quality of the firm deteriorates progressively without sudden changes. The above statement is strictly true only in the continuous-time version of the model. In real markets, default events are not anticipated.

We then discuss hedging strategies, showing that delta hedging is probably not totally effective (no matter how good the model with which the deltas are computed), since substantial losses can be incurred when defaults occur. Finally, we introduce hedging strategies that can provide protection against defaults and credit spread volatility. However, the hedge is still not perfect, since it involves a subjective judgement regarding the unwind cost of the hedge in the event of default.

5.6.1 Product definitions
In this section we cover two broad classes of basket products: basket default swaps and CDOs.

Basket default swap
Consider a basket consisting of n underlyings, each with a recovery rate given by δ_i. The contract will pay an amount $(1-\delta_i)$ when an underlying defaults at time τ as long as $k^{\min} \le k_{\tau-} < k^{\max}$, where $k_{\tau-}$ denotes the number of defaults immediately before time τ. The choice of $k^{\min}$ and $k^{\max}$ then defines the precise structure of the contract, as shown below.

$k^{\min} = 0, k^{\max} = 1$	"First to default" or "Worst of"
$k^{\min} = 1, k^{\max} = 2$	"Second to default"
$k^{\min} = 0, k^{\max} > 1$	"First $l\,(= k^{\max})$ out of n to default"
$k^{\min} = n - m$ and $k^{\max} = n$	"Last m out of n to default"

The number of defaults covered by a basket default swap is $(k^{\max} - k^{\min})$ and the premium paid will effectively be the quoted premium times $(k^{\max} - k^{\min})$. In other words, the premium paid is consistent with the number of defaults on which protection is being bought, and will effectively amortise by the notional of the defaulted asset after a default event has occurred. This can lead to some interesting results in terms of managing the premiums, which we describe later on. When no more default events are covered, then the contract will terminate as in a standard default swap.

CDO-type structures
As described earlier, a CDO structure is essentially a securitisation of the credit risk of a pool of assets (loans or bonds) that are packaged together as a portfolio and then tranched. The payout is similar to a basket default swap but is defined in terms of actual losses rather than number of

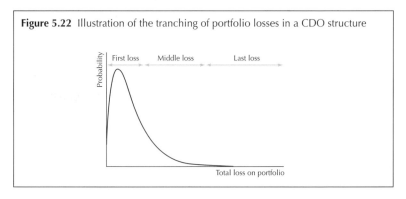

Figure 5.22 Illustration of the tranching of portfolio losses in a CDO structure

defaults. This tranching essentially involves splitting the CDO into pieces corresponding to different portfolio losses (Figure 5.22). The pricing of a CDO tranche effectively amounts to pricing a CLN referenced to a pool of assets (rather than a single asset).

We define the CDO as consisting of m underlyings each with a recovery rate given by δ_i. A tranche is defined by lower and upper loss limits which we denote L^{min} and L^{max}. When any asset in the pool defaults, the total loss increases by $(1-\delta_i)$, where δ_i denotes the recovery rate of the defaulted asset. The total loss will be divided among the tranches according to the way in which the tranching is performed (ie, how L^{min} and L^{max} are defined for each tranche). A possible structure could be as follows:

$L^{min} = 0, L^{max} = X$ This is often called the "first loss" piece, since it absorbs the first losses and is therefore very risky. It probably would not be rated. Similar to a first-to-default basket default swap.

$L^{min} = X, L^{max} = Y$ We will call this the "second loss" or mezzanine piece. There may be one or more pieces in the middle of the tranche.

$L^{min} = Y, L^{max} = N$ This covers the "last loss" on the portfolio, where N is the total notional of the pool of assets. Generally, the probability that a loss will be incurred is very small. This is similar to a last a out of n to default basket default swap.

5.6.2 Model
Several different approaches can be used to price basket products (eg, Finger, 2000). We will show how the model presented in Chapter 3 for computing the credit loss distribution can be extended to multiple time horizons and how it can be applied in the pricing of price basket structures. (Hull and White, 2001, have independently proposed a similar model to the one we describe here.) A main advantage of this model is that it can generate correlated default events. Therefore, if a single default occurs, the rest of the underlyings are more likely to default in the future (or, equiva-

lently, the other credit spreads will have widened at the default time). This means that the probability of multiple defaults increases. This in turn increases the "tail" of the distribution of the number of defaults, with a significant impact on the premium of a basket – eg, it leads to a reduction in the premium for a "first to default". Again, the most important issue to tackle here is the estimation of default correlation. For example, consider the "last loss" piece of the portfolio shown in Figure 5.22. Clearly, if the assets in the basket are highly correlated, there will be a greater chance of multiple defaults occurring, taking the total loss into the tail region. Therefore, the price of the "last loss" tranche will be high. This is similar to the issue discussed in Chapter 3, where we saw that high default correlation causes a significant increase in the economic capital of a portfolio. The model is calibrated using default swap premiums, since default swaps are the assumed hedging instruments.

We want to stress that default correlation is fundamentally different from credit spread correlation. We have found credit spread-based models not to be capable of providing reasonable premiums for the basket products. The main drawback has been that even for high credit spread correlation, the corresponding default correlation is too low. A possible way to correct that this would be to add common jumps, but the model then becomes unstable and difficult, if not impossible, to calibrate.

In Chapter 3, we showed how to generate correlated default events by first drawing from a multivariate normal distribution with correlation matrix Λ. The binary default variables can then be generated from the normal variables using the indicator function, $d_i = 1_{\tilde{Y}_i \leq k_i}$, where k_i is chosen to match the required default probability (see Chapter 3 for more details). We also highlighted that the financial interpretation of the normal variables is that they represented the "asset return" of the company in question. This is similar to the famous Merton (1974) model, which treats the firm value as a stochastic quantity that triggers default when it hits a certain lower boundary. We could, therefore, write down processes for the firm value, $V_t^{(i)}$, of each underlying in the basket as

$$\frac{dV_t^{(1)}}{V_t^{(1)}} = \mu^{(1)} dt + \sigma^{(1)} dW_t^{(1)}$$

$$\frac{dV_t^{(2)}}{V_t^{(2)}} = \mu^{(2)} dt + \sigma^{(2)} dW_t^{(2)}$$

$$\dots$$

$$\frac{dV_t^{(n)}}{V_t^{(n)}} = \mu^{(n)} dt + \sigma^{(n)} dW_t^{(n)} \tag{23}$$

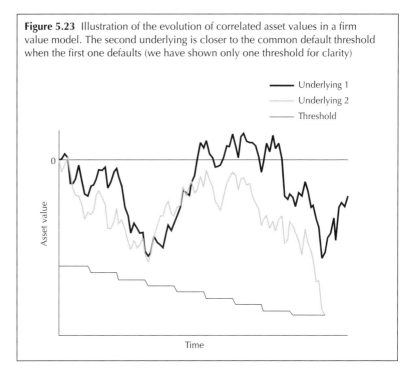

Figure 5.23 Illustration of the evolution of correlated asset values in a firm value model. The second underlying is closer to the common default threshold when the first one defaults (we have shown only one threshold for clarity)

where $\mu^{(i)}$ and $\sigma^{(i)}$ represent the return and volatility of the ith firm value, and the $dW^{(i)}$s are correlated normal variables as before. We assume that the correlation is constant with respect to time and firm value.

Now, if we introduce a series of S thresholds, which change over time (as discussed below) and represent the default point of each asset, then we can again introduce correlated defaults as illustrated in Figure 5.23. This not only makes it more likely that the underlyings will default together but also means that when there is one default, the other assets are likely to be in a worse state. The financial interpretation of this is that, in general, when there is default, in general other credit spreads will widen. This effect will be sensitive to the underlying correlation matrix.

A firm value model can be used to calculate default probabilities based on a firm's capital structure and asset volatility. This was the original idea presented by Merton (1974). This can be done by assuming that a firm defaults when the value of its liabilities exceeds the value of its assets. However, we will use the model in a different way by assuming that we will actually input the default probabilities to calibrate it, rather than making assumptions about the firm's volatility or capital structure. This is more in the spirit of Black and Cox (1976) or Longstaff and Schwartz (1995). The default probabilities are stripped from default swap quotes for each underlying in the basket, as described earlier in this chapter. This also means that we no longer need to consider the firm's capital structure and its evolution as dictated by Equation (23). A change in either the mean or the variance of the return in Equation (23) will change the position of each calibrated threshold, but will not affect the default structure.[5] We will, therefore, take the mean return to be zero and the volatility to be one, so that the return on the firm value or its assets is again represented by a standard normal variable.

We work in discrete time, using a total of S time-steps $[t_0, t_1, \ldots, t_s]$ up to the maturity of the deal at t_s. At each time, each firm value changes by an amount $dW^{(i)}$, which is a random variable drawn from a normal distribution, adhering to the relevant correlation matrix for the $dW^{(i)}$s. We can arbitrarily fix each starting value, V_0^a. Note that this actually corresponds to a normal model rather than the lognormal model represented by Equation (23). Assume that for each underlying we have the default probability in each sub-interval, derived either from historical data or by stripping these probabilities from default swap quotes, as described above. The default probability in the sub-period $[t_{j-1}, t_j]$ at time j for the underlying a in the basket is denoted by $p_{j-1,j}^a$. We then define a series of thresholds which are piecewise-constant, so that the threshold in $[t_{j-1}, t_j]$ for the underlying a in the basket is $k_{j-1,j}^a$. Clearly, the position of the first threshold can be determined, as before, by $k_{0,1}^a = \Phi^{-1}(p_{0,1}^a)$, where $\Phi^{-1}(\cdot)$ represents the inverse, cumulative normal distribution function. This ensures that $E\left[1_{V_1^a < k_{0,1}^a}\right] = p_{0,1}^a$, ie, the probability that the firm value goes below the threshold is equal to the default probability.

However, the next thresholds are not so easy to find, since we must always condition on being alive until the beginning of the period. For example, the second threshold should be determined such that

$$\text{Prob}\left[V_1^a > k_{0,1}^a \cap V_2^a < k_{0,2}^a\right] = E\left[1_{V_1^a > k_{0,1}^a} 1_{V_2^a < k_{1,2}^a}\right] = p_{1,2}^a \quad (24)$$

Equation (24) can be interpreted as "the probability that the firm value is below the threshold at the end of period 2, given that it was above the threshold at the end of period 1, and is equal to the default probability in the interval". In general, to find any threshold k_j^x, we apply the following formula:

$$E\left[\left(\prod_{l=1}^{j-1} 1_{\left\{k_l^x \geq T_l^x\right\}}\right) 1_{\left\{k_j^x < T_j^x\right\}}\right] = p_{t_{j-1}, t_j}^a \quad (25)$$

where the term on the left-hand side gives the probability that the asset value is above the threshold at times t_1 through to t_{j-1}, and then below the threshold at time t_j. For sufficiently small time intervals, this should be equal to p_{t_{j-1}, t_j}^a, the default probability for the ath underlying in $[t_{j-1}, t_j]$. We can now calibrate the model first to price the underlying default swaps and, second, to price basket default swaps and CDO structures.

In Equation (25) the calculation of the thresholds can be done numerically via the same Monte Carlo simulation as is used for the pricing. Alternatively, an analytical approach can be used, such as that described by Hull and White (2001). We have found that the numerical calibration of the thresholds is slower but gives superior accuracy.

Having calibrated the model, it is possible to price basket products by generating many simulations of the firm value, calculating any defaults and then valuing the premium and default legs accordingly. Like a default swap, a basket structure can be priced as two separate legs: one for the premium payments and one for the default payments. The total expected payout for the basket can be approximated by the sum of the expected payout in each interval $[t_{j-1}, t_j]$. The time-step should be small enough for the likelihood of having more than one default in any interval to be negligible. We can compute the fair premium of the basket by equating the PV of the two legs as before.

5.6.3 Estimation of correlation

The most difficult factor to incorporate in the model for pricing basket products is the estimation of the underlying correlations. As default is a rare event, estimating the correlation between two default events cannot be achieved by standard statistical methods. Instead, some proxy for default or credit behaviour must be used. One advantage of using a firm value model is that the correlation can be estimated directly from market data. The simplest way to do this is to use the equity return of each component of the basket as a proxy for the true firm value return (ie, the asset return). Alternatively, we can try to estimate the firm value correlations more accurately by also including also the firm's debt of the firm in the analysis. However, this parameter is not easy to observe, as there may be many bonds, or even warrants or convertibles, issued. However, it is possible to use a simplified approach (see our discussion of the KMV "Asset Value model" in Chapters 1 and 3). A preferable way to estimate the correlations would be to use implied numbers from traded instruments. The credit derivatives market is still far too immature for this to be possible. However, if products are traded where the payout is based on the default of two underlyings, their default correlation can be estimated directly. One simple example of such a structure is a default swap traded with a credit-risky counterparty, so that the correlation between the protection seller and underlying credit is important. This makes it possible (in theory) to hedge the correlation between these two underlyings in a larger basket. The hedges would, of course, be dynamic and model-dependent.

5.6.4 Basic relationships

We first consider three different basket contracts and derive some upper and lower bounds for the different premiums. We consider that the size of

Table 5.6 Premiums of various basket products according to the realised number of defaults

	No defaults	One default	Two defaults
First two to default	$2X^{0,2}$	$X^{0,2}$	0
First to default	$X^{0,1}$	0	0
Second to default	$X^{1,2}$	$X^{1,2}$	0

the basket is N, the individual default swap premiums are given by $[X_1, X_2, ..., X_N]$ and that the credit curves are flat (ie, the default swap premiums are the same for all maturities). We consider that only positive correlation is possible, as is likely to be the case in practice.

First to default
The protection buyer is protected against only the first default and pays a premium – say, $X^{0,1}$ (the superscripts 0 and 1 refer to $k^{\min}$ and $k^{\max}$, as defined earlier) – until any default occurs. Since this contract only offers partial protection, we would expect an upper bound to the premium to be the sum of the individual default swap premiums, $\sum_{i=1}^{N} X_i$. A lower bound for the premium would be the maximum of the individual default swap premiums, $\max(X_1, X_2, ..., X_N)$, which corresponds to the case when the correlation is a maximum (since here the riskiest credit will always be the first to default): $\max(X_1, X_2, ..., X_N) \leq X^{0,1} \leq \sum_{i=1}^{N} X_i$.

Second to default
The protection buyer is protected only against the second default, and pays a premium, $X^{1,2}$, until the occurrence of this event. The premium will be less than for a first to default, $X^{1,2} < X^{0,1}$, since two defaults are always less likely than one (assuming that the credits are not perfectly correlated).

First two to default
The protection buyer is protected against the first two defaults, paying a premium of $2X^{0,2}$ until the first default and then $X^{0,2}$ until the second. The total premium for this contract should be greater than for a first to default. Furthermore, consider hedging this contract with a first to default and second to default. The default payments match exactly, but the structure of the premiums are different, as shown in Table 5.6. It is clear that $X^{0,2} < X^{1,2}$, in which case we must have $2X^{0,2} < (X^{0,1} + X^{1,2})$, to balance the expected premium payments. We can therefore see that $X^{0,1} < 2X^{0,2} < (X^{0,1} + X^{1,2})$ provides a reasonably tight bound on the value of $X^{0,2}$, since $X^{1,2}$ should normally be quite small.

5.6.5 Basket default swap pricing
We now consider pricing a five-year maturity, euro-denominated basket

Table 5.7 Premiums (bps) for a five-year maturity, euro-denominated basket of five names, all underlyings at 100bps with recovery rates of 30%, semi-annual premiums

| | Correlation (λ) | | |
	0%	25%	50%
First to default	500	436	357
Second to default	57	88	112
Third to default	4	19	42
Fourth to default	0	3	14
Fifth to default	0	0	3
Total	561	546	528
First two to default	259	249	228
Last three to default	0	2	9

with five underlyings, each of which has a flat credit curve of 100bps and a recovery rate of 30%. We assume that the elements of the correlation matrix representing the correlation between the firm values (the asset return correlations) are all equal to λ. We choose a homogeneous basket to simplify the interpretation of the results. In Table 5.7 we show the premiums for different contract specifications and values of λ. To aid the interpretation of the results, we also show in Figure 5.24 the probabilities for each number of defaults occurring as a function of correlation. (Note that since these probabilities are, in a sense, risk-neutral, they are extracted from the market default swap quotes, although they also depend on the correlation, which is historical). We note that, as discussed in Chapter 3, the impact of (positive) default correlation is to increase the probability of no defaults or multiple (in this case, two to five) defaults, and decrease the probability of few defaults (in this case, one).

We will now go through the different contracts and explain the results, referring to the comments made previously.

First to default
When the correlation is zero, the premium for the first to default is 500bps (when accounting for accrued premium at default time), which, as stated before, is the sum of the individual default swap premiums. One explanation is that it is possible to hedge this contract with 100% (ie, the same notional) of each default swap. At default time, the cashflows of the first to default and the corresponding default swap cancel (ie, opposite payments of $(1-\delta)$). Since there is no correlation, the occurrence of default implies nothing about the credit spreads of the other underlyings in the basket. This means that in expectation, the rest of the default swaps will be unwound at zero cost. This point is true only when the correlation is zero and the credit spread curves are flat. As the default correlation increases,

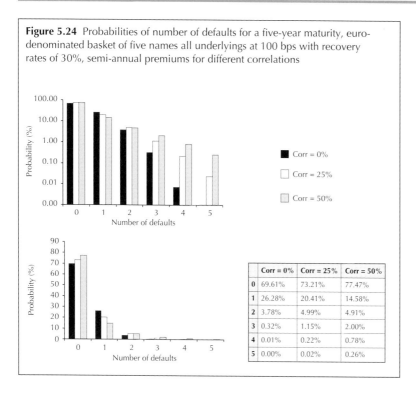

Figure 5.24 Probabilities of number of defaults for a five-year maturity, euro-denominated basket of five names all underlyings at 100 bps with recovery rates of 30%, semi-annual premiums for different correlations

	Corr = 0%	Corr = 25%	Corr = 50%
0	69.61%	73.21%	77.47%
1	26.28%	20.41%	14.58%
2	3.78%	4.99%	4.91%
3	0.32%	1.15%	2.00%
4	0.01%	0.22%	0.78%
5	0.00%	0.02%	0.26%

the premium decreases in relation to the sum of the individual default swap premiums. High default correlation means that multiple defaults are more likely and, therefore, that the degree of protection provided by the first-to-default swap (compared with holding each one of the underlying default swaps) is diminished.

Second, third, fourth or fifth to default
The premium for an nth to default decreases as n increases, since the probability of n defaults becomes more unlikely. The effect of correlation is to increase the premium, since this increases the probability of multiple defaults. Relatively speaking, this effect is more dramatic for larger n.

Sum of first, second, third, fourth and fifth to default
The total premium for these five contracts is always greater than the sum of the individual default swap premiums. This can be seen by using a similar argument as presented in Table 5.7.

First two to default
The relationship we discussed above, $X^{0,1} < 2X^{0,2} < (X^{0,1} + X^{1,2})$, is satisfied by the computed premiums. The premium increases with correlation,

Table 5.8 Deltas (%) for a five-year maturity, euro-denominated basket of five names, all underlyings at 100bps with recovery rates of 30%, semi-annual premiums for different correlations

	Correlation (ρ)		
	0%	**25%**	**50%**
First to default	88.1	72.3	61.8
Second to default	21.3	26.5	25.9
Third to default	2.0	7.9	12.5
Fourth to default	0.0	1.6	4.7
Fifth to default	0.0	0.1	1.2
Total	111.4	108.4	106.1
First two to default	102.2	96.2	86.0
Last three to default	0	1.7	5.9

Note that since the underlying credits are the same, so are the deltas.

although this effect is not as dramatic as for some of the other contracts. This is because the probability of two defaults increases with correlation, whereas the probability of a single default decreases. There are examples where the premium of such a contract (eg, a larger basket or different underlying credit spreads) would decrease with correlation.

Last three to default
For this structure, the premium is small, since it is driven by the probability of three or more defaults. The premium increases with correlation as the probability of three or more defaults increases.

5.6.6 Basket default swap hedging
We now consider the hedging of basket default swaps with the underlying default swaps.

Delta hedging
We define the delta with respect to the ith underlying in the basket, as the sensitivity of the basket with respect to a 1bp shift in the underlying default swap premium curve divided by the sensitivity of the underlying default swap to the same move. The deltas for the examples are shown in Table 5.8. We assume that the maturities are the same. Consequently, a delta of 100% means that the hedge should consist of the underlying default swap with the same notional amount and same maturity as the basket. The fact that the maturities are equal is not important in practice, but serves to make the analysis more transparent.

We first show how the delta changes for different levels of the underlying credit curve and correlations (Figure 5.25). Clearly, since we consider baskets where the underlying credit curves are the same, the deltas will be

Figure 5.25 Deltas as a function of the credit curve level and correlation for a five-year maturity, euro-denominated, homogeneous basket of five names with recovery rates of 30%, semi-annual premiums

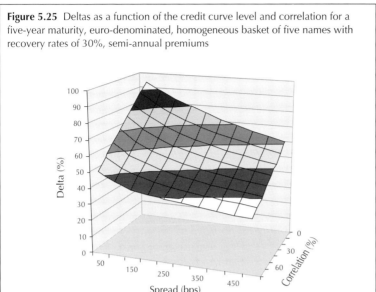

Figure 5.26 Deltas as a function of the size of basket for different correlation for a five-year maturity, euro-denominated, homogeneous basket with recovery rates of 30%, semi-annual premiums

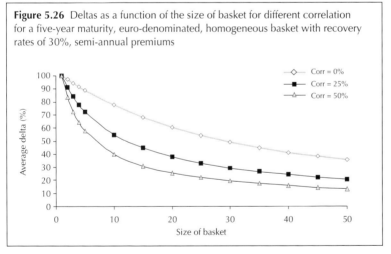

equal. What is interesting is that even for zero correlation, the delta is not 100%. The significance of this will be discussed below. The delta decreases with increasing credit curves and increasing correlation. We also show that the delta decreases as the size of the basket increases (Figure 5.26).

Delta–gamma hedging
Let us consider the delta hedging of a first-to-default basket with the underlying default swaps of the same maturity. If we consider the basket

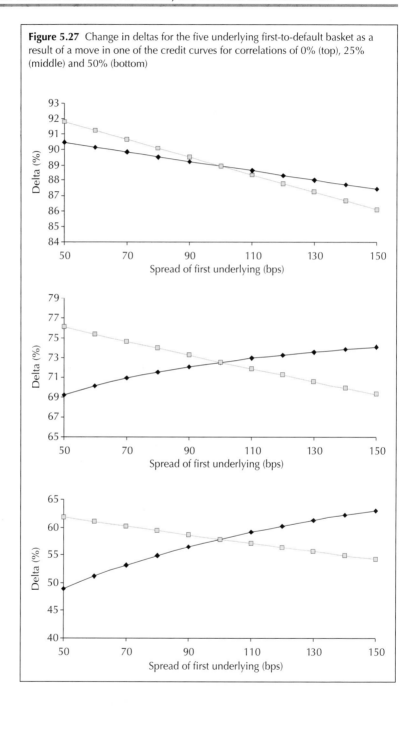

Figure 5.27 Change in deltas for the five underlying first-to-default basket as a result of a move in one of the credit curves for correlations of 0% (top), 25% (middle) and 50% (bottom)

with all underlying credit curves at 100bps, the initial delta will be 72.3% if the correlation is 25%. This means that if we are buying protection on the basket, we would sell protection on all the underlyings, but with each on a smaller notional. However, it is unlikely that such a position could be rebalanced frequently on account of high transaction costs. For this reason, we will now consider the effects on the deltas of credit spread movements of the underlyings in the basket. In Figure 5.27, we show the change in the basket delta caused by a change in the credit spread of one of the under-lying default swaps for correlations of 0%, 25% and 50%. If this credit spread widens (or, conversely, tightens) then the corresponding delta would increase (or decrease) while the deltas corresponding to the rest of the default swaps would decrease (or increase). This is true only for corre-lations of 25% and 50%. This effect is intuitive. When a credit spread widens, this underlying is closer to default and we should expect to sell a higher amount of this default swap in order to offset the potential payout at default, which has become more likely.

Next, we consider a more complex scenario in which two, rather than one, underlying credit spreads move. In Figure 5.28, we show the hedging error arising from the delta hedge discussed above – ie, buying protection on the first-to-default basket and delta hedge by selling protection on all the underlying default swaps – as two of the underlying credit spreads move. Clearly, it is possible to be very exposed even to modest changes in the credit spreads. This would be the case either if continuous rebalancing were impossible or if there were jumps in the credit spreads. Another way to describe this is that this basket position has a large gamma. The gamma has opposite signs depending on whether the credit spreads move together or in opposite directions (this is not true when the correlation is low). Also, it is very dependent on the level of the correlation. With these points in mind, it may be advisable to hedge with respect to the delta and gamma for each underlying in the basket. To be gamma-neutral as well as delta-neutral, we need another hedging instrument. A possible way to improve the hedge would be to hold two default swaps of different maturities for each underlying in the basket. This may seem to be a fairly complex strat-egy, but nevertheless, it is more robust, which means that the hedge will need to be rebalanced less frequently.

Delta versus default hedging
So far, we have discussed the hedging of baskets with respect to changes in the underlying spreads. The major issue we have ignored is the possibility of default. To illustrate the danger of mis-hedging, consider selling protec-tion on a first-to-default basket and hedging it dynamically by buying protection on all the underlying default swaps (according to the deltas given by the model). If the kth underlying defaults, then the P&L of the hedged position will be determined as follows:

Figure 5.28 Illustration of the change in P&L for a portfolio consisting of the first-to-default basket, delta-hedged with short positions in all the underlying default swaps due to movements in two of the underlying credit spreads. Correlation = 0% (top), 25% (middle) and 50% (bottom)

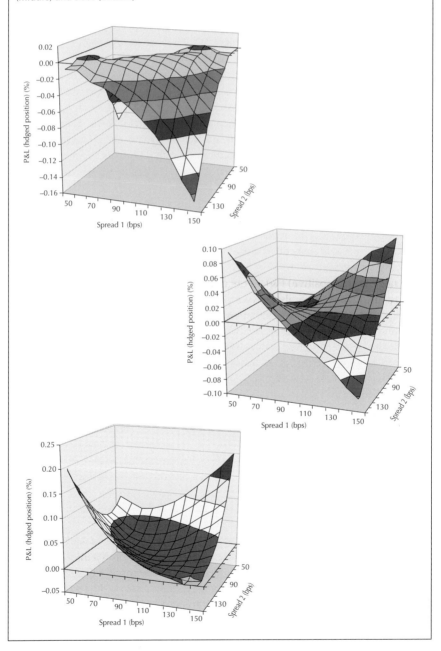

First to default $-(1-\delta_k)$

Default swaps $+\Delta_k(1-\delta_k)+\sum_{\substack{i=1 \\ i\neq k}}^{N} PV^{DS_i}$

where δ_k is the recovery rate on the defaulted underlying, Δ_i is the delta at the last rebalancing date and PV^{DS_i} is the PV of the default swap on underlying i immediately after default. Now consider the case where the correlation is zero. As mentioned above, this implies that the underlying credits are completely independent;[6] consequently, we would expect the unwind cost of the other default swaps to be approximately zero. This is true only in expectation and ignores transactions costs. We can, therefore, see that in the case of zero correlation, we would expect to make a loss of approximately $(1-\Delta_k)(1-\delta_k)$ when the kth underlying defaults. This can clearly cause a large hedging error, especially when the size of the basket is high and/or the credit spreads are quite large.

A drawback of delta (or delta–gamma) hedging of a basket default swap is that we are hedged against small changes in the credit spreads, but we may be very exposed in the event of default. We could express this by saying that we are "delta-neutral" but not "default-neutral". If we are selling (or buying) protection on the basket, then the hedged position is likely to have a negative (or positive) P&L at default time. However, since the delta is less than 100%, we will also have a positive (or negative) carry on the hedged basket position – from the difference between the premiums on the basket and the hedging- default swaps – when we are selling (or buying) protection. For example, in the case with zero correlation, the delta from Table 5.8 can be seen to be 88.1%. If we sell protection on the basket, then we are receiving 500bps, whereas buying protection on the five underlyings costs only 88.1% × 500 = 441bps, given a positive carry of 59bps per annum (of course, this will change as the deltas change, but will always be positive). We can, therefore, consider this income to be compensation for the loss that is likely to be suffered when the first default occurs. These arguments are exactly the reverse if we are buying protection on the first to default, ie, we pay a higher premium on the basket than we receive on the hedge, but we stand to make a large gain if any single underlying defaults.

Ideally, when hedging a basket, we would like to be "delta-neutral" and "default-neutral". This can be achieved in two ways. The first is to hold 100% of each underlying default swap, but to adjust the maturity of each to match the delta (ie, we use a shorter maturity on the default swap than on the basket). A disadvantage of this strategy is that we cannot adjust our delta by buying or selling protection but instead have to vary the underlying maturity in the hedge, which is much harder. A second solution is to delta-hedge as described above, but then also to trade short-term default swaps (ie, the maturity is so short that the delta is close to zero) so as to be

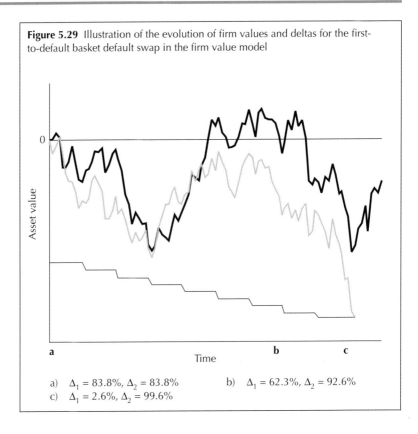

Figure 5.29 Illustration of the evolution of firm values and deltas for the first-to-default basket default swap in the firm value model

a) $\Delta_1 = 83.8\%$, $\Delta_2 = 83.8\%$ b) $\Delta_1 = 62.3\%$, $\Delta_2 = 92.6\%$
c) $\Delta_1 = 2.6\%$, $\Delta_2 = 99.6\%$

default-neutral too. For example, in the above case, we would hold 88.1% of each default swap with the same maturity as the basket and then 11.9% of short-term (eg, three-month maturity) default swaps. A similar idea is discussed in Arvanitis and Laurent (1999). We note that, even in this case, we are still not completely hedged in the event of default, since the unwind cost of the default swaps is not even known (although it is approximately zero in expectation if the correlation is zero, as discussed above).

When the correlation is positive, the above hedging strategy needs to be modified, because we now expect that, in the event of default, the other credit spreads in the basket will have widened. This means that we should not hold the full notional of each default swap. We probably need to make a subjective judgement about how much the rest of the credit spreads will widen if a particular default occurs or compute this using the model.

Anticipated defaults
The above analysis assumes (implicitly) that default is a sudden, unanticipated event. This represents the worst possible scenario in terms of hedging. If default is anticipated, the delta-hedging strategy is more effi-

cient, since the credit spread of the underlying will widen before default. If the transition into default is completely smooth, the default time is anticipated, and we end up with one delta of 100% and all others of zero. This is, indeed, an underlying assumption in the model we have described for pricing baskets. We illustrate this by showing the possible evolutions of the firm value and the associated deltas for two of the underlyings in Figure 5.29. We see that as the second underlying moves towards default, its delta with respect to this underlying approaches 100% while the delta of the other underlying approaches zero.

Finally, we emphasise again that the hedging strategies described above are all dynamic and that the optimal hedge should also take the potentially large transaction costs into consideration.

5.6.7 CDO pricing and hedging

The majority of the points addressed in the previous sections also apply to the pricing and hedging of CDO structures. We will not, therefore, go over the same points again, but will instead focus on a particular example of the pricing of a CDO-type structure. We follow two different approaches. In the first approach we think of the CDO as a small portfolio and apply the model described in Chapter 3. In the second approach we think of it as a large basket, and so apply the model described in the previous section. The "right" way to price the transaction depends on how we intend to manage the risk. We note that, theoretically, the two models are very similar; only the calibration is drastically different.

Our example is a five-year CDO denominated in US dollars with 50 underlyings. Their Moody's ratings, corresponding credit spreads and notionals are shown in Table 5.9. To emphasise the differences in these two approaches, we have deliberately chosen the widest spreads for given ratings. Throughout, we will use a recovery rate of 30%. We also show the "historical spreads" computed using the historical default probabilities with a simple calculation (presented in Appendix B).

The portfolio is split into four tranches (Tranches 1–4), covering losses 0–25, 25–75, 75–150, and 150–400, respectively.

First, we apply to the pricing of the CDO the credit portfolio management model presented in Chapter 3. This only takes the rating (rather than the spread) into account and uses historical data to determine the default probabilities via a transition matrix. We use Moody's one-year 18-state transition matrix, as reproduced in Appendix A. We include the effect of credit migrations in the generation of losses. We will refer to this as the "ratings-based" approach. The second approach is to apply the model for basket default swaps described in this chapter, using the spread of each underlying as input. As indicated above, the only difference in pricing CDO-type structures is that the loss is defined in terms of the minimum and maximum losses rather than the number of defaults. We will refer to

Table 5.9 Details of the underlyings in the CDO structure used for the example

	Notional	Rating	Spread (bps)	Historical spread (bps)		Notional	Rating	Spread (bps)	Historical spread (bps)
1	15	Aa3	40	6	26	5	Baa1	130	16
2	15	Aa3	50	6	27	10	Baa1	220	16
3	15	A1	50	4	28	5	Baa1	300	16
4	15	A1	50	4	29	5	Baa1	160	16
5	10	A1	60	4	30	10	Baa1	100	16
6	10	A1	60	4	31	5	Baa1	80	16
7	10	A2	80	4	32	10	Baa1	130	16
8	10	A2	70	4	33	5	Baa2	120	27
9	10	A2	90	4	34	10	Baa2	190	27
10	10	A2	100	4	35	5	Baa2	120	27
11	10	A2	90	4	36	5	Baa2	125	27
12	10	A2	80	4	37	5	Baa2	80	27
13	5	A3	60	8	38	5	Baa2	250	27
14	5	A3	50	8	39	5	Baa2	100	27
15	5	A3	80	8	40	10	Baa3	250	57
16	5	A3	60	8	41	5	Baa3	165	57
17	10	A3	100	8	42	5	Baa3	250	57
18	10	A3	60	8	43	10	Baa3	190	57
19	5	A3	80	8	44	10	Baa3	150	57
20	5	A3	60	8	45	10	Baa3	180	57
21	5	A3	70	8	46	5	Baa3	155	57
22	10	Baa1	150	16	47	10	Baa3	190	57
23	5	Baa1	110	16	48	5	Ba1	250	102
24	10	Baa1	200	16	49	5	Ba1	375	102
25	10	Baa1	170	16	50	5	Ba2	550	144

this second approach as the "spread-based" approach. The two models are quite similar, since they assume the same dynamics for the evolution of the underlying variables.

The rating-based model presented in Chapter 3 and the spread-based model presented here are also quite similar. The main difference is that the former uses historical default data, whereas the latter is calibrated to market default swaps and therefore extracts the default probability directly from the given credit spread. Both models incorporate correlation in the same way. To allow comparison of the results, we use a correlation of 50% in each. The pricing of each tranche within the two models is shown in Table 5.10, and the loss distributions are shown in Figure 5.30. We give both the expected loss and price of each tranche. The spread represents the fair premium that should be paid on a default swap covering the losses in question, taking into account the amortisation effects. In the ratings-based model, the expected loss is as defined in Chapter 3, whereas in the spread-based model, it is computed by taking only the default leg. Clearly, the

Table 5.10 Pricing of each tranche in the CDO structure given in Table 5.9

Tranche	Losses covered	Spread-based approach		Ratings-based approach	
		Expected loss	Price (per annum)	Expected loss	Price (per annum)
1	0–25	2.69%	1,281bps	0.98%	468bps
2	25–75	1.85%	355bps	0.18%	35bps
3	75–150	0.70%	86bps	0.02%	2bps
4	150–400	0.12%	5bps	0.00%	0bps

Figure 5.30 Loss distributions for the CDO structure in Table 5.9 using both approaches

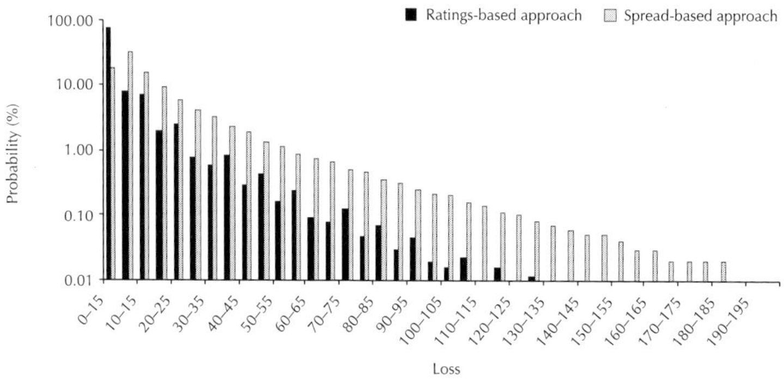

ratings-based approach gives much lower prices for the structure than the spread-based approach. This is not surprising, since the default probabilities extracted from the spreads will be much higher than those obtained from historical data. This reflects the fact that the credit spreads not only compensate for the "real" (ie, historical) probability of default but also contain a premium for effects such as liquidity.

We deliberately chose high spreads for each rating in the above CDO, which means that the discrepancy between the ratings-based and spread-based approaches is amplified. Ratings agencies use historical data to assess the riskiness of a particular CDO tranche.[7] For example, this would imply that Tranche 3 should be very highly rated (for example, Aaa or Aa) because it has an expected loss of only 0.02%. However, the spread-based model suggests a very different result: this tranche is considerably more "risky".

The difference between the two approaches rests largely in the use of historical or risk-neutral default probabilities. The latter approach is

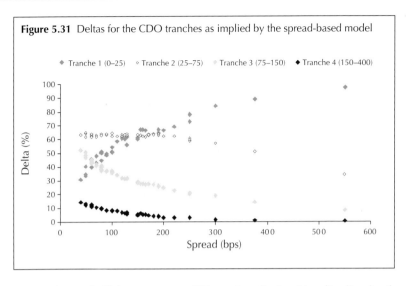

Figure 5.31 Deltas for the CDO tranches as implied by the spread-based model

appropriate only if the structure will be put on the banking/trading book and marked-to-market. If so, we may be hedging the structure and, consequently, the cost of this hedge will be driven by the market spreads. If this is not the case, we should care about the real (historical) probabilities and use the former approach.

In the delta hedging of such a large structure as this, all of the complex hedging issues for basket default swaps (eg, liquidity, correlation, gamma-neutrality and default-neutrality) that we discussed above also apply here. Indeed, the situation is even more complex, since there are many more underlyings to trade. Not only will this increase the transaction costs associated with dynamic hedging but it also means that defaults are more likely to occur in the structure. In the event of a default, the other deltas will jump, which will necessitate a rebalancing all of the other positions. We have computed the deltas of all the underlyings for each tranche of the CDO against the spread. These are shown in Figure 5.31 (the randomness arises from the different notionals and Monte-Carlo error).

The behaviour of the deltas with respect to the spreads provides some clues as to the hedging of each tranche. For the first loss piece (Tranche 1), the deltas are larger for the worse credits, since these are more likely to default first. The reverse is true for the last loss tranches (3 and 4). An intuitive understanding of this is that by the time the total loss reaches this region, the worse credits will already have defaulted. This effect is most severe for the underlying with the highest spread. It has a delta close to 100% for Tranche 1 (since it is most likely to default first) and close to zero for Tranche 4 (since it is very unlikely to be still alive when the total loss has reached 150). These observations for Tranches 1 and 4 imply that they will be quite difficult to hedge, since small movements in each spread will bring about significant changes in the deltas. For Tranche 2, we see that the delta is much flatter with respect to spreads, so the hedge may not need to be adjusted so frequently.

5.7 CONCLUSIONS

We have presented models for pricing and hedging the credit spread volatility and the default events in various credit derivative contracts. To implement the proposed strategies, we should be able to trade standard or digital (binary) default swaps, which tend to be very illiquid. Therefore, it is likely that the hedge will be implemented using standard default swaps and so would not provide perfect protection if default occurs. Even if we use standard default swaps, it is possible that disruption in the default swap market may prevent us from adjusting the hedge ratios or rolling over the hedging portfolio.

Of critical importance for hedging effectively is also the ability to compute the correct hedge ratio. When the ratio of the promised payout to the actual payout of the underlying hedging default swap contract is predetermined at default time, computing the hedge ratio is straightforward. However, there might be a number of discontinuities at default time. For example, if we hedge a credit contingent contract, whose payout is not linear to the recovery rate, with standard default swaps, we are exposed to significant recovery rate risk. Another example is a quanto default swap, where default of a major local issuer could destabilise the economy and trigger currency devaluation. In implementing the hedging strategy, we must take into account the jump in the exchange rate at default time. More precisely, we should have in our portfolio short-term default swaps, equal to the exchange rate after default. Since this is, in general, unknown, we can only hope to be correct on the average. Consequently, the accuracy of the hedge deteriorates. The hedge would have to be constructed using local currency default swaps, which is different from a hedge that assumes that default does not affect the foreign exchange rate.

The hedge also breaks down when there are simultaneous default events. In a stock market crash several brokerage firms may default simultaneously. Systemic risk is a similar case: the failure of a major bank may cause a disruption in the payment system. In the extreme case of two default events occurring together, we need only one of the two underlying default swaps to hedge the first-to-default swap. In the intermediate case, where there is both a common default event and an issuer-specific default event, it is not possible to get a perfect hedge at default time, since we do not know in advance if default is due to systemic or specific risk. The joint distribution of default times degenerates, and the holding of two default swaps is now a super-replicating hedge at default time.

We have extended the standard one-period firm value model into a multi-period framework for pricing basket default swap products. The model has the advantage of simplicity and provides a natural way to incorporate default correlation. It is calibrated on default swap premiums. The lack of market-implied parameters for the correlation complicates the risk management of the product substantially and introduces uncertainty into the price. This is not specific to the model at hand, but it is inherent to the product and the market.

Because the delta can be very volatile and because it is unlikely that it could be rebalanced frequently on account of high transaction costs, it is possible to be very exposed to even modest changes in the credit spreads. Another way to describe this is that the basket position has a large gamma, which is very dependent on the level of the correlation. With these points in mind, it may be advisable to hedge with respect to the delta and gamma for each underlying in the basket. In order to be gamma-neutral as well as delta-neutral, we need another hedging instrument. One possible way to implement the improved hedge would be to hold two default swaps of different maturities for each underlying in the basket. This strategy may seem complex, but it is more robust and requires less frequent rebalancing of the hedge.

A drawback of delta-hedging (or gamma-hedging) of a basket default swap is that we are hedged against small changes in the credit spreads, but we may be very exposed in the event of default. We could express this by saying that we are "delta-neutral" (or gamma-neutral) but not "default-neutral". Ideally, when hedging a basket, we would like to be hedged both against credit-spread volatility and default events. This can be achieved in two different ways. The first is to hold 100% of each underlying default swap and to adjust the maturity of each in order to match the delta (ie, we use a shorter maturity on the default swap than on the basket). A disadvantage of this strategy is that we cannot adjust our delta by buying or selling default swaps, but instead have to vary the underlying maturity in the hedge, which is much harder. A second solution is to delta-hedge, but also to trade short-term default swaps so as to be default-neutral, too. We note that, even in this case, we are still not completely hedged in the event of default, since the unwind cost of the default swaps is unknown.

When the correlation is positive, the above hedging strategy needs to be modified because we now expect that, in the event of default, the other credit spreads in the basket will have widened. Therefore, we should not hold the full notional of each default swap. We need to make a subjective judgement about how much the rest of the credit spreads will widen if a particular default occurs.

In the next chapter, we will apply the same fundamental principles for pricing and hedging interest rate derivatives with risky counterparties.

APPENDIX A

Table A1 Moody's one-year 18-state transition matrix (%)

	Aaa	Aa1	Aa2	Aa3	A1	A2	A3	Baa1	Baa2	Baa3	Ba1	Ba2	Ba3	B1	B2	B3	Caa	Default
Aaa	90.23	5.60	2.59	0.55	0.61	0.27	0.11	0.00	0.00	0.00	0.04	0.00	0.00	0.00	0.00	0.00	0.00	0.00
Aa1	3.30	78.24	8.38	6.93	2.59	0.20	0.00	0.24	0.00	0.00	0.12	0.00	0.00	0.00	0.00	0.00	0.00	0.00
Aa2	0.83	2.45	81.23	8.82	4.28	1.12	0.87	0.20	0.06	0.00	0.00	0.00	0.07	0.07	0.00	0.00	0.00	0.00
Aa3	0.13	0.44	3.03	80.03	10.55	3.95	0.94	0.17	0.26	0.22	0.00	0.05	0.13	0.00	0.00	0.00	0.00	0.10
A1	0.08	0.13	0.64	4.69	81.94	7.49	2.90	0.74	0.22	0.18	0.38	0.37	0.07	0.17	0.00	0.00	0.00	0.00
A2	0.04	0.04	0.23	0.70	5.77	81.00	7.37	3.08	0.89	0.29	0.20	0.13	0.13	0.04	0.07	0.00	0.03	0.00
A3	0.04	0.11	0.00	0.21	1.53	9.07	75.40	6.93	3.85	1.48	0.46	0.19	0.27	0.43	0.05	0.00	0.00	0.00
Baa1	0.06	0.00	0.09	0.12	0.15	3.29	9.00	73.47	7.87	3.16	0.97	0.48	0.46	0.64	0.12	0.00	0.05	0.05
Baa2	0.00	0.13	0.17	0.17	0.19	0.98	3.80	8.12	74.07	7.86	2.03	0.43	0.73	0.49	0.50	0.31	0.00	0.06
Baa3	0.04	0.00	0.00	0.07	0.21	0.61	0.45	4.45	10.70	69.14	7.13	3.09	2.08	0.90	0.33	0.13	0.14	0.53
Ba1	0.12	0.00	0.00	0.00	0.16	0.11	0.67	0.92	3.06	6.73	74.99	4.91	4.06	0.83	1.38	1.12	0.12	0.83
Ba2	0.00	0.00	0.00	0.00	0.00	0.13	0.14	0.38	0.50	2.62	7.76	74.03	6.13	1.34	4.22	1.74	0.27	0.75
Ba3	0.00	0.03	0.03	0.00	0.15	0.23	0.14	0.14	0.22	0.83	2.58	5.10	75.63	2.68	6.33	2.63	0.58	2.86
B1	0.00	0.05	0.04	0.00	0.15	0.06	0.19	0.08	0.32	0.45	0.37	2.72	6.65	76.55	1.67	5.29	1.01	4.40
B2	0.00	0.00	0.10	0.00	0.16	0.00	0.07	0.16	0.12	0.00	0.26	2.10	3.69	5.72	67.50	7.97	2.92	9.23
B3	0.00	0.00	0.00	0.00	0.00	0.00	0.00	0.11	0.18	0.20	0.21	0.33	1.48	4.76	2.53	71.26	4.59	14.36
Caa	0.00	0.00	0.00	0.00	0.00	0.00	0.00	0.00	0.60	0.60	0.81	0.00	2.49	2.81	1.32	3.09	58.42	29.87

APPENDIX B – ILLUSTRATION OF THE APPROXIMATE COMPUTATION OF THE HISTORICAL SPREAD BASED ON THE RATINGS TRANSITION MATRIX IN APPENDIX A

Consider that the price today of a risk-free zero-coupon bond with maturity T is $B(0, T)$. In terms of a continuously compounded interest rate r, we can express this as

$$B(0, T) = \exp(-rT) \qquad \text{(A1)}$$

On the other hand, we assume that the return on a risky zero-coupon bond of the same maturity will be $r + c$, where c represents a credit spread which is compensation for the default risk. This means that the price of this bond can be written as

$$\tilde{B}(0, T) = \exp\left[-(r+c)T\right] \qquad \text{(A2)}$$

From Equation (A2), we can write the fair price of this bond in terms of the risk-free bond, $\tilde{B}(0, T)$, the recovery rate, δ, and the default probability in the interval $[0, T]$, $p(0, T)$:

$$\tilde{B}(0, T) = \left[1 - p(0, T)\right] B(0, T) + p(0, T) \delta B(0, T)$$

$$= B(0, T) \left[1 - (1 - \delta) p(0, T)\right] \qquad \text{(A3)}$$

From the above, we can solve for the credit spread on the risky bond, in terms of the historical default probability, $p(0, T)$.

$$\frac{\tilde{B}(0, T)}{B(0, T)} = \frac{\exp\left[-(r+c)T\right]}{\exp\left[-rT\right]}$$

$$= \exp\left[-cT\right] = \left[1 - (1 - \delta) p(0, T)\right] \qquad \text{(A4)}$$

In the case we are interested in, the value of $p(0, T)$ can been found by raising the one-year transition matrix to the appropriate power. Note that this is a simple way to extract an approximate spread based on historical data but is not an appropriate way to price a risky bond, since the probability is not risk-neutral.

Since for small x, we can write $\exp(x) \approx 1 + x$, Equation (A4) can be simplified to give $c \approx (1 - \delta) p(0, T) / T$.

1   This is partly why asset swap spreads and default swap spreads are not equivalent.
2   We will use the term "credit curve" to signify the default swap quotes for different maturities on the same underlying reference credit.
3   By Bermudan, we mean options that can be exercised at a number of pre-specified dates in the future.
4   This is the assumption we are making for the purposes of the example. It is also possible to structure the contract so that the option can be exercised in the event of default. The model

can easily be modified to incorporate this feature, although this may result in a substantially higher price.

5   This point may seem unusual. However, it can be readily checked in a one-period model that the parameters for the two Brownian motions do not change the joint default probability when the model is calibrated to each individual default probability.

6   We note that the independence arises from the choice of zero correlation *and* the multivariate normal structure of the model. There are cases of multivariate distributions where zero correlation does not imply independence. See Li (1999).

7   Although the rating-based model we propose is not the same as those used by the rating agencies, the main point here is that we compare an approach based on historical data to one based solely on market data.

BIBLIOGRAPHY

Arvanitis, A., and J. Gregory, 1999, "A Credit Risk Toolbox", ed. David Shimko, *Credit Risk Models and Management* (London: Risk Books), pp. 283–9.

Arvanitis, A., and Laurent, J-P., 1999, "On the Edge of Completeness", *Risk* 12(10), pp. 61–5.

Bielecki, T., and M. Rutkowski, 2000, "HJM with Multiples", *Risk* 13(4).

Black, F., and J. C. Cox, 1976, "Valuing Corporate Securities: Some Effects of Bond Indenture Provisions", *Journal of Finance* 31(2), pp. 351–67.

Black, F., and M. Scholes, 1973, "The Pricing of Options and Corporate Liabilities", *Journal of Political Economy* 81(3), pp. 637–54.

Das, S., ed., 1998, *Credit Derivatives: Trading and Management of Credit and Default Risk* (Singapore: John Wiley).

Das, S., and P. Tufano, 1996, "Pricing Credit Sensitive Debt When Interest Rates, Credit Rating and Credit Spreads are Stochastic", *Journal of Financial Engineering* 5(2), pp. 161–98.

Duffie, D., 1998, "First-to-default valuation", Working paper, Graduate School of Business, Stanford University. [http://www.stanford.edu/~duffie/working.htm]

Duffie, D., 1999, "Credit Swap Valuation", *Financial Analysts Journal* 55(1), 1999, pp. 73–87.

Duffie, D., and N. Garleanu, 1998, "Risk and Valuation of Collateralized Debt Obligations", *Financial Analysts Journal* 57(1), pp. 41–59.

Duffie, D., and D. Lando, 1997, "The Term Structure of Credit Spread with Incomplete Accounting Information", Working paper, Graduate School of Business, Stanford University, forthcoming, *Econometrica.*

Duffie, D., and J. Liu, 1997, "Floating-Fixed Credit Spreads", Working paper, Graduate School of Business, Stanford University, forthcoming, *Financial Analysts Journal.*

Duffie, D., J. Pan and K. Singleton, 2000, "Transform Analysis and Asset Pricing for Affine Jump Diffusions", *Econometrica* 68, pp. 1343–76.

Duffie, D., and K. Singleton, 1999, "Modeling Term Structures of Defaultable Bonds", *Review of Financial Studies*, 12(4), pp. 687–720.

Finger, C. C., 2000, "A Comparison of Stochastic Default Rate Models", *CreditMetrics Monitor* (April), pp. 49–76. [http://www.riskmetrics.com/research/journals]

Gupton, G., C. Finger and M. Bhantin, 1997, CreditMetrics Technical Documentation (New York: JP Morgan and Co).

Hull, J. C. 1997, *Options, Futures, and Other Derivatives*, Third edition (Prentice-Hall International Inc).

Hull, J., and A. White, 1990, "Pricing Interest Rate Derivative Securities", *Review of Financial Studies* 3(4), pp. 573–92.

Hull, J., and A. White, 1994, "Numerical Procedures for Implementing Term Structure Models I: Single-Factor Models", *Journal of Derivatives* 2(1), pp. 7–16.

Hull, J., and A. White, 2001, "Valuing Credit Default Swaps II: Modeling Default Correlations", *Journal of Derivatives* 8(3), pp. 12–22.

Jarrow, R., and S. Turnbull, 1995, "Pricing Derivatives on Financial Securities Subject to Credit Risk", *Journal of Finance* 50(5), pp. 53–85.

Jarrow, R., D. Lando and S. Turnbull, 1997, "A Markov Model for the Term Structure of Credit Risk Spreads", *The Review of Financial Studies* 10(2), pp. 481–523.

Lando, D., 1998, "On Cox Processes and Credit Risk Securities", *Review of Derivatives Research* 2(2/3), pp. 99–120.

Li, D., 1998, "Constructing a Credit Curve", in *Credit Risk*, A RISK Special Report (November), pp. 40–4.

Li, D, 1999, "The Valuation of Basket Credit Derivatives", *CreditMetrics Monitor* (April), pp. 34–50. [http://www.riskmetrics.com/research/journals]

Li, D, 2000, "On Default Correlation: A Copula Approach", *Journal of Fixed Income* 9(?), (March), pp. 43–54.

Litterman, R., and T. Iben, 1991, "Corporate bond valuation and the term structure of credit spreads", *Journal of Portfolio Management*, 17, pp. 52–65.

Longstaff, F., and E. Schwartz, 1995, "A Simple Approach to Valuing Risky Fixed and Floating Rate Debt", *Journal of Finance* 50(3), pp. 789–819.

Madan, D., and H. Unal, 1994, "Pricing the Risks of Default", Working paper 94-16, The Wharton Institutions Centre.

Merton, R., 1974, "On the Pricing of Corporate Debt: The Risk Structure of Interest Rates", *Journal of Finance* 29(2), pp. 449–70.

Nelken, I., 1999, *Implementing Credit Derivatives*, Irwin Library of Investment and Finance (New York: McGraw-Hill).

Bielecki., T, and M. Rutkowski., 2000, "HJM with multiples", *Risk* 13(4), pp. 95–7.

Schmidt, W. M., "Modelling correlated defaults", Working paper, Deutsche Bank AG, Germany.

Schönbucher, P. J., 1999, "A Tree Implementation of a Credit Spread Model for Credit Derivatives". Working paper [http://www.finasto.uni-bonn.de/~schonbuc/index.html].

Schönbucher, P. J., 2000, "A Libor Market Model With Default Risk", Working paper, University of Bonn.

Tavakoli, J. M., 1998, *Credit Derivatives: A Guide to Instruments and Applications*, Wiley Series in Financial Engineering (New York: John Wiley & Sons).

Zhou, C., 1997, "A Jump–Diffusion Approach to Modelling Credit Risk and Valuing Defaultable Securities", *Finance and Economic Discussion Paper Series* 15 (Board of Governors of the Federal Reserve System), March.

6

Pricing Counterparty Risk in Interest Rate Derivatives

This chapter describes a general procedure for pricing and hedging counterparty risk in interest rate derivatives. The method takes into account variable exposures and random default times. We consider pricing of contracts on a stand-alone and on a portfolio basis. In this context, by "portfolio" we mean all deals under a single master agreement. When we price a deal on a portfolio basis, existing deals under the same master agreement are taken into account in pricing new transactions, due to the netting of exposures in the event of default. We also discuss briefly collateral and wrong-way exposures. In the Appendices we provide derivations of the main results.

6.1 INTRODUCTION

We focus on standard derivatives, ie, interest rate and cross-currency swaps, caps, floors and swaptions. We demonstrate how the cancellation feature affects the credit risk of a European cancellable swap. For each one of the above products, we compute the expected loss and the required credit spread in order to compensate for the potential losses if default occurs. The credit risk of exotic products can be computed by approximating their cashflows with the above standard instruments. We decided not to present this work here, since these approximations are covered in texts that focus on interest rate derivatives. Direct computation of the credit risk of exotics is possible, but we have found the computations too complex to be of practical interest. Products with American features, such as Bermudan swaps (ie, cancellable swaps with many cancellation dates) have been approximated with Europeans. An accurate computation on a stand-alone basis is tractable using a tree or a partial differential equation (PDE) solver, but this would not be particularly useful, since for the portfolio approach, the above method would have to be coupled with Monte Carlo, and this is not a particularly easy task. The inputs into the model are the counterparty default swap premiums of various maturities. We rationalise this choice later in the text. The last part of this chapter focuses on a general, dynamic hedging technique using standard default swaps. We discuss the hedging of both default and credit-spread risk (the latter arising from stochastic default swap premiums).

Since we will consider potential defaults until the maturity of the contract or portfolio in question, it is not necessary for pricing to consider changes in the default swap premiums over the life of the contract. If we were to compute the expected loss over shorter periods, stochastic default swap premia should be included in the analysis. The portfolio value at the end of the period in question would depend on the default swap premiums at the time, and this should be taken into account when the portfolio is marked-to-market (see Jarrow, Lando and Turnbull, 1997, or Arvanitis, Gregory and Laurent, 1999).

6.2 OVERVIEW

Consider a "bank" that enters into an interest rate swap with a risky counterparty "ABC". The bank bears the risk that ABC will default; therefore, it should be compensated by receiving a credit spread x above Libor, as shown below.

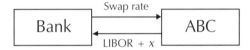

The credit spread x is determined by the probability that ABC will default and the estimated loss to the bank in this scenario. It will be shown later in the text that the determining factors are the shape of the yield curve, the volatility of the interest rates, the swap maturity and ABC's default probability (derived from the ABC credit default swap premiums traded in the market, which, as we shall see later, will be the hedging instruments). Here, we will assume that only ABC can default, since we are developing the pricing from the perspective of a financial institution of high credit quality. The theory can be extended to the general case where both counterparties are risky (see Duffie and Huang, 1996).

We assume that the value of x should be fixed so that at inception the swap has zero present value (PV) (when counterparty risk has been properly taken into account). The reasons for doing this are explained in detail below. We assume that, in the event of default of ABC when the bank is owed money, it will receive δ times the risk-free PV, where $0 \leq \delta \leq 1$ is a fixed recovery rate. If the bank owes ABC money, it will have to pay the total risk-free PV to ABC. These two scenarios are illustrated in Figure 6.1. This is the loss suffered relative to the risk-free swap, and it should not be confused with what is presented in the hedging section.

The expected loss (EL) is defined as the expected value today of all possible losses from default during the lifetime of the deal. An equivalent way of expressing this is to say that the expected loss is the difference between

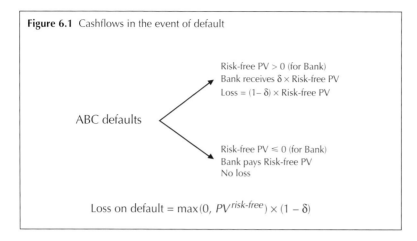

Figure 6.1 Cashflows in the event of default

ABC defaults

Risk-free PV > 0 (for Bank)
Bank receives δ × Risk-free PV
Loss = (1− δ) × Risk-free PV

Risk-free PV ⩽ 0 (for Bank)
Bank pays Risk-free PV
No loss

Loss on default = max(0, $PV^{risk\text{-}free}$) × (1 − δ)

the risky and the risk-free PV (we discuss this in more detail in Appendix A), hence:

$$EL(swap) = PV^{risk\text{-}free}(swap) - PV^{risky}(swap) \qquad (1)$$

Note that this is actually a general expression for any deal or portfolio of deals. The key point in the analysis is the computation of the expected loss, either on a stand-alone or on a portfolio basis. For the swap we are considering, the bank would require the spread to compensate for the expected loss, ie,

$$PV^{risky}(swap + x) = PV^{risk\text{-}free}(swap) \qquad (2)$$

Since the risk-free PV is sub-additive, expression (1) for the expected loss can be simplified to give:

$$PV^{risk\text{-}free}(x) = EL(swap + x) \qquad (3)$$

which shows clearly that the spread x is compensation for the expected loss. Note that the above equation is non-linear and it must therefore be solved iteratively.

If we let h_s represent the hazard rate of default (the default probability within a very short time period) and denote the time of default by τ, the default density is given by:

$$\frac{dP\,(\tau < s)}{ds} = \exp\left(-\int_t^s h_u\,du\right)h_s \qquad (4)$$

where $\exp\left(-\int_t^s h_u\,du\right)$ is the probability of no default in the time interval $[t, s]$.

Therefore, $\exp\left(-\int_t^s h_u du\right)h_s ds$ is the probability of default between s and $s+ds$, given that no default has occurred before.

Therefore, the expected loss (EL_t) at time t over the life of the contract $[t, T]$ can be computed using the following equation:

$$EL_t = (1-\delta)E_t\left[\int_t^T \exp\left(-\int_t^s h_u du\right)h_s B(t,s)\max\left(PV_s, 0\right)ds\right] \quad (5)$$

where $B(t, s)$ is the risk-free discount factor and PV_s is the risk-free present value of the contract at time s. This equation is generally, but not always, valid. This is not surprising since this expression simply states that the expected loss is the discounted expected value of the positive exposure multiplied by the probability of default, summed over all default times and adjusted for the recovery rate. For an interest rate swap the bank is short a series of European swaptions. For other products the bank is short a series of options that are different from swaptions. However, for more complex products, such as swaptions, where we need to include the exercise condition, the basic expression for the expected loss is more complex than Equation (5).

Consider now a swap that has maturity T. It can be shown from Equation (5) (see Appendix A) that the expected loss at time t is given by:

$$EL_t = (1-\delta)\sum_{i=1}^n E_t\left[\int_{T_{i-1}}^{T_i} h_s \exp\left(-\int_t^s h_u du\right)B(t,s)Sw(s,T_1,T_n)^+ ds\right] \quad (6)$$

where the cashflows of the swap occur at dates T_i ($i = 1, \dots n$) and $Sw(s, T_1, T_n)$ is the value of the swap at time s, ie, $Sw(s, T_1, T_n)^+ = \max(Sw(s, T_1, T_n), 0)$.

In order to simplify matters, we assume that the default probability is independent of the risk-free interest rates. Without making this assumption, the computations would become very intractable (although applying numerical techniques, such as Monte Carlo simulation, would still, in principle, be possible). Another major difficulty would be the estimation of correlations between market and credit variables. Under the zero correlation assumption, the above expression can be simplified as follows:

$$EL_t =$$

$$(1-\delta)\sum_{i=1}^n E_t\left[\int_{T_{i-1}}^{T_i} h_s \exp\left(-\int_t^s h_u \delta u\right)\delta s\right]E_t\left[\int_{T_{i-1}}^{T_i} B(t,s)Sw(s,T_1,T_n)^+ \delta s\right]$$

$$(7)$$

This simplified expression is substantially easier to compute, since there are no correlation terms. In most scenarios, the independence assumption would be adequate. We can think of two circumstances where the cross-correlation terms could be important. The first occasion is when ABC's business is greatly affected by the business cycle and its credit quality therefore becomes correlated with the interest rates. Second, it is possible that when certain exposures increase beyond a certain level, they may trigger default. But even in these scenarios, the correlation terms would be very arbitrary, since it would be almost impossible to estimate the correlation to input into the model. This, of course, does not mean that the expressions would not be useful, since they can provide the basis for some interesting sensitivity analysis to help us understand our risk better. There is a tractable way to incorporate correlation and it is discussed later on in this chapter.

We further simplify the above expression by assuming that the hazard rate is deterministic. As discussed earlier, for pricing this simplification is of no consequence. We relax this assumption in the hedging section. The consequence will be that the cost of the hedge will be stochastic and it will not be known in advance. Equation (7) can be rewritten as follows:

$$EL_t = (1-\delta) \sum_{i=1}^{n} E_t \left[\int_{T_{i-1}}^{T_i} p_s \, ds \right] E_t \left[\int_{T_{i-1}}^{T_i} B(t,s) Sw(s,T_1,T_n)^+ \, ds \right] \quad (8)$$

where $p_s ds$ is the marginal risk-neutral default probability between s and $s+ds$. In order to implement the model, we next consider a discrete time version of Equation (5). We discretise the interval $[t, T]$ into N smaller sub-intervals. A suitable discretisation interval could be the period between swap payment dates (eg, three months), which is accurate, while allowing the computations to be done quickly. Under the independence assumption, we get a simple expression for the expected loss:

$$EL_t = (1-\delta) \sum_{i=1}^{N} p(t_i) \times E_t \left[Df(t_i) \max\left(0, PV_{t_i}\right) \right] \quad (9)$$

where PV_{t_i} and $Df(t_i)$ represent the risk-free present value of the contract and the risk-free discount factor respectively at t_i. $p(t_i)$ is the marginal risk-neutral default probability of ABC in the interval $[t_{i-1}, t_i]$. If $A(t)$ is the ABC survival probability at time t, then $p(t_i) = A(t_{i-1}) - A(t_i)$. The expected loss for the swap is thus equivalent to a weighted sum of European swaptions with maturities up to the maturities of the underlying swap. This leads to analytical expressions for a single swap, which, of course, depend on the interest rate model used.

Using the decomposition in Equation (7), closed-form formulae can be derived for interest rate swaps, caps/floors and interest rate swaptions, resulting in fast computations. Such computations, using the Hull and White interest rate model (other yield curve models could be used), are described in the appendices. More complex products, such as cross-currency swaps and portfolios of deals, are priced via Monte Carlo simulation, since analytical expressions cannot be derived. Later in this chapter, we provide examples of the computation of the credit spread for various deals and investigate the parameters that affect the credit spread.

6.3 EXPECTED LOSS VERSUS ECONOMIC CAPITAL

We shall show later how it is possible to dynamically hedge the credit risk of an interest rate derivative if there is a sufficiently liquid market in the underlying default swaps. If this is the case, then by arbitrage arguments, the spread x for the deal should represent the cost of the hedging strategy (ie, the cost of transforming the risky deal into a risk-free deal). The expected loss on the contract equals the expected cost of the hedge. In other words, transactions should be priced to cover at least the expected loss from adverse credit events. In most financial institutions, an amount equal to the expected loss is commonly kept in a credit reserve account against possible future losses and it is not realised P&L. As we will show in the last section, the hedge has to be dynamically rebalanced; because of stochastic default swap premia, its cost is not fixed in advance. Since we are performing the analysis in a complete market framework, historical default probabilities are not relevant.

However, if the market for default swaps is not sufficiently liquid, then the bank must take on the additional credit risk. Economic capital needs to be held against a credit portfolio to cushion against possible adverse credit events, such as multiple defaults (see Chapter 3). A certain percentile of the credit loss distribution – eg, 99.9% (depending on the bank's policy) – defines the economic capital. A possible way to calculate x is to require that it covers the marginal increase in economic capital (the additional capital required to support the new deal). In this case, we do not use risk-neutral parameters, as capital is computed using historical parameters, both for the interest rate and the default processes. It is the actual default probability of ABC which is appropriate (this may be estimated according to its rating). Since a credit loss distribution (Figure 6.2) is typically highly skewed – the economic capital could be much higher than the expected loss, even though we cannot be conclusive. In general it is not possible to conclude which method will give a higher x. The relative magnitude of the two prices will depend on the relationship between the risk-neutral and the historical default probabilities, which is driven by the risk premiums. On one hand, real default probabilities tend to be smaller than the risk-neutral ones, particularly for good credits. On the other hand, for the same inputs, because the credit loss distribution is highly skewed, the economic capital is much higher than the expected loss. These two factors have opposite

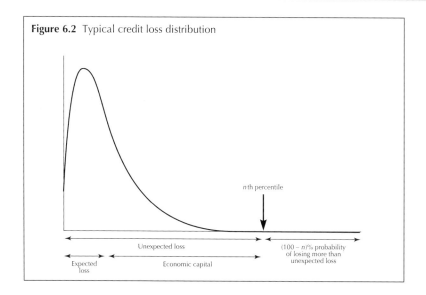

Figure 6.2 Typical credit loss distribution

effects. For Aaa-rated assets, the risk-neutral default probabilities tend to be substantially higher than the historical ones. In this case, it would be expected that the risk-neutral price be higher than the capital-based price.

For the purposes of this chapter, we will assume that a reasonably liquid market for default swaps does exist and that we can price using risk-neutral expectations without any need to consider capital.

6.4 PORTFOLIO EFFECT

In this context, the portfolio effect is the impact of existing deals under a single master agreement on the risk profile of a new transaction. Normally, such deals will be with a single counterparty or possibly a counterparty or its subsidiaries. Under a master agreement, it is possible to net deals in the event of default. This means that for m different deals under the same master agreement, the exposure is:

$$\text{Netted exposure} = \max\left(\sum_{k=1}^{m} PV_k^{risk\text{-}free}, 0\right) \tag{10}$$

This is, of course, less than the un-netted exposure, if there is no master agreement:

$$\text{Gross exposure} = \sum_{k=1}^{m} \max\left(PV_k^{risk\text{-}free}, 0\right) \geq \max\left(\sum_{k=1}^{m} PV_k^{risk\text{-}free}, 0\right) \tag{11}$$

To compute the spread of a new deal with a counterparty with whom there is at least one master agreement, existing deals should be taken into account, since the risks will cancel out to some degree. This will lead to a reduction in the spread x required for the new deal compared to the stand-alone deal. The credit spread x is computed so that the total risky PV is the same as if a risk-free deal without a spread had been added to the portfolio.

$$PV^{risky}(\text{portfolio} + \text{deal} + x) = PV^{risk\text{-}free}(\text{deal}) + PV^{risky}(\text{portfolio}) \quad (12)$$

Similar to the stand-alone case (Equation (3)), it can be shown that this leads to:

$$PV^{risk\text{-}free}(\text{portfolio}) + PV^{risk\text{-}free}(\text{deal}) + PV^{risk\text{-}free}(x) - EL(\text{portfolio} + \text{deal} + x)$$
$$= PV^{risk\text{-}free}(\text{deal}) + PV^{risk\text{-}free}(\text{portfolio}) - EL(\text{portfolio})$$

$$PV^{risk\text{-}free}(x) = EL(\text{portfolio} + \text{deal} + x) - EL(\text{portfolio}) \quad (13)$$

The interpretation of the above equation is that the spread is compensation for the marginal increase in the expected loss, which will be less than or equal to the stand-alone expected loss. Taking into account the other deals always reduces the spread, unless the new deal is perfectly correlated with the rest of the portfolio; this is never going to be the case in a real portfolio. To account for the portfolio effect, we need to simulate all the underlying parameters (interest rates and FX rates) and price every existing deal under all possible scenarios in order to correctly quantify the effect of adding the new deal to the portfolio.

We will now go through the basic products and show tables with the expected loss and spread for each one. We will also demonstrate the dependence of the spread on the model parameters (volatility and mean reversion). We discussed the exposure profiles of these products earlier, in Chapter 2.

6.5 THE MODEL

6.5.1 Interest rates

For the risk-free interest rates, we use a one-factor Hull and White (1990) model with constant volatility and mean reversion. This choice gives some analytical tractability and is fairly easy to implement. The dynamics of the short term rate are described by:

$$dr = (\theta(t) - ar)\,dt + \sigma\,dz \quad (14)$$

where the volatility σ and the mean reversion rate a are constant. In this model, the short rate reverts to $\theta(t)/a$ at a rate given by a. The volatility and mean reversion rate are calibrated to the market prices of swaptions (we use least-squares optimisation). The mean reversion level, $\theta(t)$, is chosen to match the initial term structure of the risk-free interest rates. For European products, the assumption of constant parameters has proved adequate. Later on, we investigate their impact on the credit spreads.

6.5.2 FX rates
The foreign exchange (FX) rates are modelled as lognormal processes according to the following equation:

$$dX_t = \mu_{FX}(t)dt + \sigma_{FX}dz \qquad (15)$$

The drift is determined by the standard arbitrage-free relationship and it depends on the two yield curves. The volatility is calibrated using the market prices of FX options.

Next, we present numerical examples using market parameters (ie, yield curves, FX rates, volatility and mean reversion of the short-rates and the FX volatilities) as of June 13, 2000.

6.6 INTEREST RATE SWAPS
6.6.1 Standard swap – same payment dates
In Table 6.1, we show the expected loss and the credit spread for interest rate swaps of various maturities for the US dollar, euro, UK pound and Japanese yen. All swaps shown have quarterly payments (the swap rate versus the corresponding three-month Libor reference rate, with the appropriate forward basis spread added). The default swap curve is assumed to be flat. The spread is calculated on the floating leg, eg, for a payer swap the bank pays the fixed rate and receives Libor + x. Note, therefore, that the spread is an annual charge, whereas the expected loss is over the life of the deal.

We can make the following observations about the magnitude of the computed numbers.

1. The spreads increase with maturity, since the variance of the interest rates will be greater over a longer period. As we have already discussed, the bank is short a series of European swaptions. As the maturity of the swap increases, the value of the swaptions and consequently the expected loss increases.
2. For the specific examples, the expected loss and the credit spread are generally higher for a payer swap than for a receiver swap. This is due to the positive slope of the yield curves and it is most pronounced for the yen, since this is the yield curve with the greatest slope. An intuitive interpretation is that if the yield curve is upward-sloping, then in a payer swap the bank tends to be a net payer at the beginning of the transaction and a net receiver closer to maturity, resulting in high exposure. A more formal interpretation is that in a payer swap, when the yield curve is upward sloping the bank is short a series of European

Table 6.1 Expected losses and spreads (bps) for interest rate swaps of different currencies with quarterly payments for varying maturities and default swap premiums (DS prem)

a) US$ payer swaps

DS prem	Expected loss (bps)				Required spread (bps)			
	2Y	3Y	5Y	10Y	2Y	3Y	5Y	10Y
100 bps	0.9	2.0	6.0	23.3	0.4	0.7	1.4	3.2
200 bps	1.6	3.8	11.4	42.8	0.9	1.4	2.7	6.1
300 bps	2.4	5.7	16.7	61.9	1.3	2.1	4.0	8.8
500 bps	4.0	9.2	26.5	93.9	2.1	3.4	6.4	13.6

b) US$ receiver swaps

DS prem	Expected loss (bps)				Required spread (bps)			
	2Y	3Y	5Y	10Y	2Y	3Y	5Y	10Y
100 bps	0.6	1.7	5.3	17.9	0.4	0.6	1.2	2.4
200 bps	1.3	3.4	10.1	33.1	0.7	1.3	2.4	4.7
300 bps	2.0	5.0	14.9	47.9	1.1	1.9	3.6	6.8
500 bps	3.2	8.1	23.6	73.3	1.7	3.0	5.7	10.6

c) euro payer swaps

DS prem	Expected loss (bps)				Required spread (bps)			
	2Y	3Y	5Y	10Y	2Y	3Y	5Y	10Y
100 bps	0.7	1.9	5.8	23.0	0.4	0.7	1.3	2.9
200 bps	1.5	3.7	11.0	42.3	0.8	1.3	2.5	5.6
300 bps	2.3	5.4	16.2	61.2	1.2	2.0	3.7	8.0
500 bps	3.7	8.8	25.6	93.0	1.9	3.2	5.9	12.4

d) euro receiver swaps

DS prem	Expected loss (bps)				Required spread (bps)			
	2Y	3Y	5Y	10Y	2Y	3Y	5Y	10Y
100 bps	0.4	1.2	3.8	12.8	0.3	0.4	0.8	1.6
200 bps	1.0	2.4	7.3	23.7	0.5	0.9	1.7	3.1
300 bps	1.4	3.6	10.7	34.2	0.8	1.3	2.4	4.5
500 bps	2.4	5.8	17.0	52.2	1.2	2.1	3.9	6.9

swaptions that are in the money. In the case of a receiver swap, it is short a series of European swaptions that are out of the money. We would expect, in the latter case, the credit spread of the swap to be more sensitive to the volatility.

3. The expected loss and the spread increase with increasing default swap curve, but they are only linear in the default swap premiums to first order. This can be demonstrated with a simple example. Consider a two period model where the probability of default is 1% in each period. The total probability of default is $1\% + 99\% \times 1\% = 1.99\%$. If the probability of default were 5%, the total probability would be $5\% + 95\% \times 5\% =$

Table 6.1 (continued)

e) UK£ payer swaps

DS prem	Expected loss (bps)				Required spread (bps)			
	2Y	3Y	5Y	10Y	2Y	3Y	5Y	10Y
100 bps	0.6	2.2	5.9	24.2	0.4	0.8	1.4	3.2
200 bps	1.4	4.2	11.1	44.6	0.7	1.6	2.7	6.2
300 bps	2.0	6.3	16.3	64.3	1.1	2.3	3.9	8.9
500 bps	3.3	10.1	25.9	97.3	1.8	3.8	6.2	13.7

f) UK£ receiver swaps

DS prem	Expected loss (bps)				Required spread (bps)			
	2Y	3Y	5Y	10Y	2Y	3Y	5Y	10Y
100 bps	0.4	1.8	5.7	22.6	0.3	0.7	1.3	3.0
200 bps	1.0	3.6	10.8	41.7	0.5	1.3	2.6	5.8
300 bps	1.5	5.3	15.8	60.4	0.8	2.0	3.8	8.4
500 bps	2.4	8.5	25.0	91.9	1.3	3.2	6.0	12.9

g) ¥ payer swaps

DS prem	Expected loss (bps)				Required spread (bps)			
	2Y	3Y	5Y	10Y	2Y	3Y	5Y	10Y
100 bps	0.8	2.5	9.4	47.7	0.4	0.8	1.9	4.9
200 bps	1.8	4.9	18.0	87.5	0.9	1.6	3.7	9.5
300 bps	2.6	7.2	26.5	126.8	1.3	2.4	5.4	13.7
500 bps	4.3	11.7	41.9	192.5	2.1	3.9	8.6	21.3

h) ¥ receiver swaps

DS prem	Expected loss (bps)				Required spread (bps)			
	2Y	3Y	5Y	10Y	2Y	3Y	5Y	10Y
100 bps	0.4	1.4	4.2	17.2	0.3	0.5	0.8	1.8
200 bps	1.1	2.7	8.0	31.9	0.6	0.9	1.6	3.4
300 bps	1.7	4.0	11.7	46.1	0.8	1.3	2.4	4.9
500 bps	2.7	6.4	18.6	70.4	1.4	2.1	3.8	7.6

9.75%, which is less than 5 × 1.99%. The exposure profiles of standard swaps are demonstrated in Figures 2.1 and 2.2

6.6.2 Swaps with unequal payment frequencies

In section 2.3.2, we discussed swaps where the fixed and floating legs have different frequencies and will therefore have a different risk profile to a standard interest rate swap. The exposure profiles of these swaps are depicted in Figure 2.4. The impact on the spread of the different payment frequencies is illustrated in Table 6.2, which should be compared with Table 6.1. We have assumed that the fixed payments are made semi-

Table 6.2 Expected losses and spreads (bps) for interest-rate swaps with unequal payment frequencies (DS = default swap)

a) US$ payer swap (pay fixed semi-annually and receive quarterly floating)

	Expected loss				Required spread			
DS prem	2Y	3Y	5Y	10Y	2Y	3Y	5Y	10Y
100 bps	0.6	1.2	4.5	20.1	0.3	0.4	1.1	2.8
200 bps	1.1	2.4	8.6	37.3	0.6	0.9	2.1	5.3
300 bps	1.7	3.5	12.6	53.8	0.9	1.3	3.0	7.6
500 bps	2.7	5.7	19.9	81.5	1.5	2.1	4.8	11.7

b) US$ receiver swap (receive fixed quarterly and pay semi-annual floating)

	Expected loss				Required spread			
DS prem	2Y	3Y	5Y	10Y	2Y	3Y	5Y	10Y
100 bps	1.6	3.5	7.7	21.6	0.9	1.3	1.8	2.9
200 bps	3.3	6.6	14.5	39.3	1.8	2.5	3.5	5.6
300 bps	4.9	9.8	21.4	57.0	2.6	3.7	5.1	8.1
500 bps	7.9	15.9	33.9	87.3	4.3	5.9	8.2	12.6

annually, while the floating payments are made quarterly. The first payment is assumed to be floating, followed by a fixed and a floating payment in the following quarter. As expected, the expected loss for the fixed payer has been decreased, as on average the payer owes money to the floating rate payer. The opposite is true for a receiver swap.

6.6.3 Principal amortising swaps

For an interest rate swap with amortising notional, the expected loss will decrease, since the interest rate payments will be computed on a smaller notional than in a straight swap. The impact of amortisation on the risk profile is demonstrated in Figure 2.5. However, the spread will also depend on the amortised notional and it will therefore decrease over time. It is unclear whether the required spread will be lower or higher for an amortising swap. In Table 6.3, we give an example of the expected loss and the spread of an interest rate swap with notional amortising linearly to zero. The expected loss is smaller than the standard swap (compare Table 6.3 with Table 6.1a) as would be expected. The spread is also smaller. The change in the credit spread relative to that of the corresponding standard swap depends on the default swap curve, the yield curve and the volatility curves, as well as the amortisation rate. However, we have found as a general rule (even though it is not always true for all such swaps) that the spread is smaller than the corresponding swap with constant notional.

6.6.4 Cancellable swaps

Next, we analyse a cancellable swap, where we assume that the bank has the right to cancel the swap. As we discussed earlier, we consider only

Table 6.3 Expected losses and spreads (bps) for interest-rate swaps with amortising notional (DS = default swap)

a) US$ payer swap

	Expected loss				Required spread			
DS prem	2Y	3Y	5Y	10Y	2Y	3Y	5Y	10Y
100 bps	0.3	0.6	1.9	7.9	0.3	0.4	0.9	2.0
200 bps	0.5	1.2	3.7	14.9	0.5	0.9	1.7	3.8
300 bps	0.7	1.8	5.5	21.7	0.8	1.3	2.5	5.5
500 bps	1.2	3.0	8.8	33.6	1.2	2.1	4.0	8.6

European cancellable swaps with just one cancellation date. In the risk-free case, the right to cancel is equivalent to being long a European swaption to enter into the opposite swap. The present value of the difference between the fixed leg of the cancellable and the corresponding standard swap equals the premium of the swaption. Clearly, the latter is smaller than the former. This product can be priced using Monte Carlo simulation.

Next, we introduce credit risk. An analytical expression for the expected loss on a European risky cancellable swap is derived in Appendix D. We assume that the bank is the fixed rate payer and that it has the right to cancel. In most cases, the fixed rate payment will be higher than that in the corresponding standard risky payer swap. Under this scenario, we have the following stylised facts:

Almost always, the expected loss will be smaller for a cancellable swap compared to the standard swap, although it cannot be proved mathematically. It is actually possible to construct a rather contrived example where the opposite holds. One might expect the expected loss to increase, since the bank has bought a swaption from ABC, increasing its overall exposure to ABC. For most scenarios, this is not the case as rationalised by the following two points:

1. The premiums for the options in the cancellable contract are not paid up front, but over the whole term of the contract (as part of an increased rate compared to the swap rate). So, in case of default before maturity of the swap, the entire premium for the option has not yet been paid.
2. The decision whether to cancel the risky cancellable contract is based on the PV of the risky contract, hence, the default risk is taken into account in the cancellation decision. One could imagine a situation where the reason for cancelling the risky contract would be to avoid future default losses. Having the right to cancel the swap reduces counterparty risk.

It is not possible to say if the spread is smaller for the standard swap than the cancellable swap. It can go either way. This can be easily appreciated by observing that even though the expected loss for the cancellable swap is smaller, its delta is smaller too. These two effects have opposite impact on

Table 6.4 Five-year US$ cancellable payer swap with quarterly payments. The default swap curve is flat at 200 bps

Cancel date	None	at two years	at three years	at four years
Fixed rate	7.23%	7.56%	7.43%	7.27%
Spread	2.8 bps	3.1 bps	3.1 bps	3.0 bps
Expected loss	12.0 bps	10.3 bps	11.5 bps	12.0 bps

Table 6.5 Sensitivity of expected loss and credit spread (bps) to short rate volatility

US$ payer swap

	Expected loss				Required spread			
	2Y	3Y	5Y	10Y	2Y	3Y	5Y	10Y
σ = 1%	1.0	2.5	7.1	25.5	0.6	0.9	1.7	3.7
σ = 2%	2.0	4.9	14.6	54.6	1.1	1.8	3.5	8.0
σ = 3%	2.9	7.4	22.5	87.6	1.6	2.8	5.5	12.8
σ = 5%	4.9	12.6	39.5	164.1	2.6	4.7	9.7	24.0

the credit spread. In Table 6.4, we show the expected loss and spread for a European cancellable interest rate swap for different cancellation dates.

We see from Table 6.4 that the expected loss on the cancellable increases as we move the cancellation date forward, but it remains less than the standard swap. The spread is higher for the cancellable than for the standard swap.

The example where the expected loss is larger for the cancellable swap compared to the standard swap corresponds to a downward-sloping default swap curve, so that there is very little default risk after the maturity of the option. Also, the volatility curve is very upward sloping (ie, the volatility increases rapidly with the underlying maturity). This would seem very unlikely to occur in practice.

6.6.5 Effect of volatility and mean-reversion

We have already demonstrated the effect of the shape of the yield curve, the level of the default swap curve and the maturity in determining the credit spread of an interest rate swap. We now consider the effect of the parameters controlling the variance, ie, the volatility and the mean reversion rate (σ and a in Equation (14)). In the previous examples, these parameters were calibrated using the market prices of long-dated swaptions. In Table 6.5, we demonstrate the impact of the short rate volatility. The default swap curve has been fixed at 200 bps and the mean reversion parameter is $a = 0.1$. As mentioned earlier, the credit spread is very sensitive to the volatility, since the bank is short a series of European swaptions.

Table 6.6 Sensitivity of expected loss and credit spread (bps) to short rate mean reversion rate

US$ payer swap

	Expected loss				Required spread			
	2Y	3Y	5Y	10Y	2Y	3Y	5Y	10Y
a = 0.200	1.8	4.3	11.7	36.3	1.0	1.6	2.8	5.3
a = 0.100	2.0	4.9	14.6	54.6	1.1	1.8	3.5	8.0
a = 0.067	2.0	5.1	15.8	63.6	1.1	1.9	3.8	9.3
a = 0.050	2.1	5.3	16.4	68.9	1.1	2.0	4.0	10.1

In Table 6.6 we show the impact of the mean reversion period, where the default swap curve has been fixed at 200 bps and the volatility at 2%. As a decreases, the expected loss and the credit spread increase. This is particularly true for long-dated swaps. This can be easily seen from the fact that the variance of the short rate over time t is $\sigma^2(1 - \exp(-2at))/2a$ and is therefore decreasing with increasing a. From the Black–Scholes formula, it is clear that the price of European options increases with the variance of the short rate over a certain period (ie, the credit risk of the bank is decreasing with increasing a, as it is short a series of European options).

The expected loss and spread increase significantly with increasing volatility. However, the relative magnitude of this effect seems fairly independent of maturity. As a increases, the impact of mean reversion is smaller, which also causes an increase in the expected loss and credit spread. This is due to the fact that the short rate has a larger variance and the impact is more pronounced for long-dated instruments.

6.7 CROSS-CURRENCY SWAPS

6.7.1 Standard swap with exchange of notionals

For cross-currency swaps, the most important risk is the FX risk on exchange of notionals at the maturity of the deal. This effect is even more pronounced if the forward FX rate is far from the spot rate, ie, for deals where interest rates in one currency are significantly lower than in the other. Because of interest rate parity, we would expect the currency with higher interest rates (the discount currency) to depreciate relative to the currency with lower rates (the premium currency) – see Hull (2000) for a detailed explanation of this effect. Therefore, if the bank pays the former and receives the latter, it would have significant credit exposure driven by the exchange of principal at maturity. The spread of that swap would be substantially higher than that of the opposite swap. This is illustrated in Table 6.7.

We see a big asymmetry in the numbers in Table 6.7, as expected. This is most pronounced for US$/Japanese ¥, since yen interest rates are much lower than US rates.

Table 6.7 Expected losses and spreads (bps) for cross-currency swaps with fixed semi-annual payments (DS = default swap)

a) Pay fixed US$/Receive fixed euro

	Expected loss				Required spread			
DS prem	2Y	3Y	5Y	10Y	2Y	3Y	5Y	10Y
100 bps	8.8	17.5	38.9	101.2	4.6	6.3	8.9	13.4
200 bps	17.3	34.3	74.9	187.4	9.2	12.5	17.4	25.5
300 bps	25.6	50.2	108.0	260.9	13.6	18.4	25.4	36.3
500 bps	41.3	79.9	166.6	376.3	22.2	29.7	40.1	54.8

b) Pay fixed euro/Receive fixed US$

	Expected loss				Required spread			
DS prem	2Y	3Y	5Y	10Y	2Y	3Y	5Y	10Y
100 bps	5.7	10.6	21.6	48.8	3.0	3.8	4.9	6.4
200 bps	11.3	20.7	41.6	91.2	6.0	7.5	9.6	12.1
300 bps	16.6	30.4	60.1	127.9	8.8	11.1	14.0	17.3
500 bps	26.9	48.5	93.4	187.7	14.4	17.8	22.0	26.0

c) Pay fixed US$/Receive fixed UK£

	Expected loss				Required spread			
DS prem	2Y	3Y	5Y	10Y	2Y	3Y	5Y	10Y
100 bps	5.7	11.3	26.2	78.0	3.0	4.2	6.2	10.8
200 bps	11.1	22.1	50.5	144.9	6.0	8.2	12.1	20.5
300 bps	16.5	32.4	72.9	202.3	8.9	12.1	17.7	29.3
500 bps	26.6	51.5	112.9	293.5	14.6	19.6	28.0	44.3

d) Pay fixed UK£/Receive Fixed US$

	Expected loss				Required spread			
DS prem	2Y	3Y	5Y	10Y	2Y	3Y	5Y	10Y
100 bps	4.6	8.8	18.4	42.1	2.5	3.3	4.3	5.8
200 bps	9.1	17.2	35.4	79.0	4.9	6.4	8.4	11.0
300 bps	13.4	25.3	51.2	111.2	7.3	9.4	12.3	15.7
500 bps	21.8	40.3	79.6	164.4	11.8	15.2	19.5	23.9

e) Pay fixed US$/Receive fixed Japanese ¥

	Expected loss				Required spread			
DS prem	2Y	3Y	5Y	10Y	2Y	3Y	5Y	10Y
100 bps	14.1	30.1	73.1	214.5	7.1	10.1	15.0	23.4
200 bps	27.8	58.8	140.2	395.0	14.0	19.8	29.1	44.6
300 bps	41.1	86.1	201.8	546.8	20.7	29.3	42.6	63.7
500 bps	66.4	136.8	310.3	780.1	33.8	47.3	67.5	96.2

f) Pay fixed Japanese ¥/Receive fixed US$

	Expected loss				Required spread			
DS prem	2Y	3Y	5Y	10Y	2Y	3Y	5Y	10Y
100 bps	4.5	7.8	14.8	32.2	2.2	2.6	3.0	3.4
200 bps	8.9	15.3	28.6	60.9	4.4	5.1	5.8	6.6
300 bps	13.1	22.4	41.5	86.3	6.6	7.5	8.5	9.4
500 bps	21.3	35.9	64.9	129.2	10.7	12.1	13.5	14.4

Table 6.8 Expected losses and spreads (bps) for cross-currency swaps with fixed semi-annual payments and amortising notional (DS = default swap)

Pay fixed US$/Receive fixed euro

	Expected loss				Required spread			
DS prem	2Y	3Y	5Y	10Y	2Y	3Y	5Y	10Y
100 bps	5.2	9.1	18.7	47.1	4.9	6.4	8.1	11.2
200 bps	10.3	17.8	36.1	87.3	9.8	12.7	15.9	21.4
300 bps	15.2	26.1	52.1	121.5	14.5	18.7	23.2	30.5
500 bps	24.6	41.5	80.3	175.3	23.6	30.2	36.6	46.0

Table 6.9 Sensitivity of expected loss and credit spread (bps) to FX volatility

Pay fixed US$/Receive fixed euro

	Expected loss				Required spread			
	2Y	3Y	5Y	10Y	2Y	3Y	5Y	10Y
$\sigma = 10\%$	14.1	28.3	62.9	162.1	7.5	10.3	14.6	22.1
$\sigma = 15\%$	19.3	38.0	82.5	204.0	10.2	13.8	19.2	27.7
$\sigma = 20\%$	24.6	47.9	102.7	248.0	13.0	17.4	23.9	33.7

6.7.2 Effect of principal amortisation

Amortising cross-currency swaps is similar to amortising interest rate swaps (see section 6.6.3). In an amortising cross-currency swap, as the swap principal amortises there is an exchange of principal corresponding to the amortised amount. This means that the FX risk is reduced, since the principal is exchanged earlier in the life of the transaction, as illustrated in Table 6.8. This explains the decrease in the expected loss compared to a regular cross-currency swap.

6.7.3 Effect of FX volatility

In Table 6.9, we demonstrate the impact of FX volatility on the expected loss and the level of the credit spread of the cross-currency swap. The default swap curve is flat at 200 bps. The bank is short a series of European cross-currency swaptions, whose prices are substantially affected by the FX volatility.

Not surprisingly, the expected loss and spread is very sensitive to the FX volatility (Table 6.9), as this drives the risk from the exchange of notionals at maturity. Cross-currency swaps, where the yield curves are at similar levels, are almost at parity and will be most sensitive to volatility, since the embedded swaptions are at the money.

Table 6.10 Expected losses for caps and floors (bps). The default swap curve is fixed at 200 bps

Long cap (strike 5.5%) and floor (strike 4.75%) on three-month euro, maturity five years

	Cap				Floor			
	2Y	3Y	5Y	10Y	2Y	3Y	5Y	10Y
strike = 4.5%	2.6	7.0	22.7	97.1	1.1	2.9	8.5	29.2
strike = 5.0%	1.8	4.9	17.0	77.2	1.8	4.4	12.3	40.1
strike = 5.5%	1.1	3.3	12.3	60.0	2.8	6.4	17.0	53.6
strike = 6.0%	0.6	2.1	8.6	45.5	3.9	8.8	22.7	69.9

6.8 CAPS AND FLOORS

For caps and floors, the premium is normally paid up-front, which means that there is only credit risk on a long position (Table 6.10). The computation of the expected loss is easier compared with interest rate and cross-currency swaps, as the PV can only be positive and all that needs to be computed is the forward value of the contract in question: in other words, the "max" operator in Equation (5) is cancelled. This allows analytical expressions to be derived (see Appendix B).

6.9 SWAPTIONS

6.9.1 Cash-settled versus physical delivery

The expected loss for a cash-settled swaption is easy to derive, since its PV can only be positive. For physical delivery (swap settled) swaptions, there is an additional risk as, upon exercise the bank will enter into a risky swap rather than receiving a cash payment. It is still possible to derive an analytical expression for a physical delivery swaption, at least in the Hull and White interest rate model. The derivation is shown in Appendix C. This involves a 2D integral that represents the joint probability of exercise of the swaption and a positive swap exposure. In Table 6.11, we give examples of the expected loss for different swaptions. The default swap curve is fixed at 200 bps. Consider a one-year maturity physical delivery swaption on a swap with strike 7.5% and maturity five years. The expected loss for the swaption is 2.0 bps (from now until the exercise date) and 7.3 bps for the swap (exercise date until swap maturity). The latter figure takes into account the fact that the swaption may not be exercised. There are two possible ways the deal could be structured:

1. As an up-front charge of 9.3 bps to cover the total expected loss. However, given that the swaption is out-of-the-money, this may seem quite large, and it would deter potential clients.
2. A second possible structure is to add a spread on the swap rate, which will be paid only if the swaption is exercised. The expected loss would

Table 6.11 Expected loss and spreads (bps) for US$-denominated cash settled two-year swaption, based on a five-year payer swap

Strike	Cash settled				Physical delivery (unconditional expected loss)				Physical delivery (conditional spread)			
	1Y/5Y	2Y/5Y	1Y/10Y	2Y/10Y	1Y/5Y	2Y/5Y	1Y/10Y	2Y/10Y	1Y/5Y	2Y/5Y	1Y/10Y	2Y/10Y
6.5%	6.7	13.2	10.9	21.4	17.2	17.4	51.8	50.6	6.4	7.5	10.8	12.8
7.0%	4.0	8.4	6.1	12.9	11.7	12.7	32.7	34.9	4.9	6.5	8.6	11.1
7.5%	2.0	4.9	2.8	6.8	7.3	9.0	19.1	23.4	4.0	5.8	7.2	10.1
8.0%	0.9	2.6	1.1	3.2	4.2	6.1	9.5	14.3	3.3	5.2	6.0	9.3

be added to the swap structure, in which case, conditional upon exercise of the swaption, there should be a spread of 6.4bps on the swap.

The conditional spread is still quite large for an out-of-the-money swaption, as it will only be exercised if the PV of the swap is positive.

6.9.2 Effect of exercise based on risky PV

In the case of physical delivery, the bank enters into a risky swap when the swaption is exercised. The exercise decision should therefore be based on the risky and not the risk-free PV. We show an example of this effect in Table 6.12. There is a small increase in the expected loss and spread for sub-optimal exercise based on the risk-free PV. This effect is more significant when the default swap premium is larger, as the difference between risk-free and risky PV at exercise is more pronounced.

Table 6.12 Same as Table 6.11, showing the impact of exercise based on the risky PV for physical delivery swaptions with strike at 7.0% for default swap curves of 200bps and 500bps

	Physical delivery (unconditional expected loss)				Physical delivery (conditional spread)			
	1Y/5Y	2Y/5Y	1Y/10Y	2Y/10Y	1Y/5Y	2Y/5Y	1Y/10Y	2Y/10Y
Exercise risk-free PV (200bps)	11.7	12.8	33.4	35.5	4.9	6.6	8.8	11.3
Exercise on risky PV (200bps)	11.6	12.7	32.7	34.9	4.9	6.5	8.6	11.1
Exercise risk-free PV (500bps)	25.2	26.8	69.0	70.0	11.7	14.9	20.9	24.8
Exercise on risky PV (500bps)	24.5	26.4	65.4	67.9	11.5	14.7	19.9	24.1

Table 6.13 Hypothetical portfolio of five interest rate swaps and a new transaction

	Maturity (years)	Pay/rec	Notional (US$ millions)	Swap rate (%)
Deal one	1.5	Rec	100	6.80
Deal two	1.0	Rec	100	6.65
Deal three	1.0	Rec	100	6.75
Deal four	1.5	Rec	100	6.80
Deal five	5.5	Pay	400	6.50
New deal	8.0	Pay/Rec	250	7.15

Table 6.14 Expected loss and credit spread, basis points (bps), for an eight-year interest rate swap (pay/rec) added to the hypothetical portfolio

	(Marginal) expected loss		Required spread	
	Pay	Rec	Pay	Rec
Stand-alone	29.2	24.1	5.1	3.9
Portfolio	27.4	−12.0	4.8	−2.2

6.10 PORTFOLIO PRICING

We now show the importance of taking into account the existing deals covered by a single master agreement, when pricing a new transaction.

6.10.1 Interest rate swap

Consider a hypothetical portfolio of four US$ interest rate swaps under the same master agreement. Consider the effect of adding a new US$250 million notional interest rate swap of eight-year maturity. The deals are shown in Table 6.13.

In Table 6.14, we show the expected loss and credit spread for the new swap, both on a stand-alone and on a portfolio basis (see Equation (13) for the computation of the portfolio credit spread). The portfolio effect is small for a payer swap, but it is significant for a receiver swap. Indeed, the portfolio credit spread and the expected loss (marginal) are negative in the latter case, indicating that the overall credit risk is reduced even though a new deal is added.

Figure 6.3 shows the impact of the new payer and receiver swaps on the portfolio exposure profile (see Chapter 2 for further explanation of the definition of the exposure profile). This figure supports the spreads in Table 6.14. The payer interest rate swap increases all exposures, which explains why the portfolio effect is so small for this deal (the reduction is probably due to an offset of cashflows in the short term from deals one to four). The receiver interest rate swap decreases all the exposures, presumably because

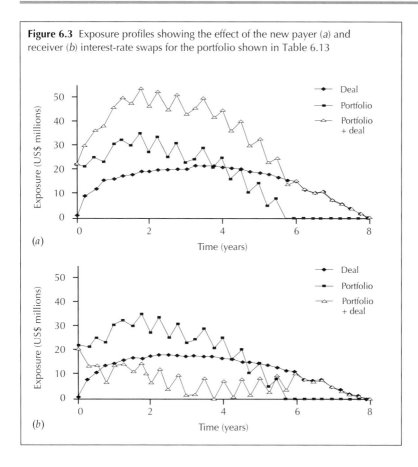

Figure 6.3 Exposure profiles showing the effect of the new payer (*a*) and receiver (*b*) interest-rate swaps for the portfolio shown in Table 6.13

it offsets the existing cashflows of deal five. This explains why the portfolio expected loss and credit spread are negative for this deal. The bank would be willing to pay a premium, since the deal reduces the overall expected loss of the portfolio.

6.10.2 Cross-currency swap

Suppose that the portfolio in Table 6.13 also contains a cross-currency swap of maturity eight years and notional US$50 million, where the bank pays floating US$ and receives floating euro (quarterly payments). We now consider adding a new US$/euro cross-currency swap to this portfolio of five interest rate swaps and one cross-currency swap. The expected loss and spread on a stand-alone and on a portfolio basis are shown in Table 6.15.

Clearly, a new deal where the bank pays euro and receives US$ creates much better diversification in the portfolio than the opposite one. This is because such a deal has an opposite FX exposure to the existing deal. As a result, the bank would be willing to charge a negative spread to cancel out

Figure 6.4 Exposure profiles showing the effect of the new pay US$, receive euro (a) and receive US$, pay euro (b) cross-currency swaps on the portfolio shown in Table 6.15

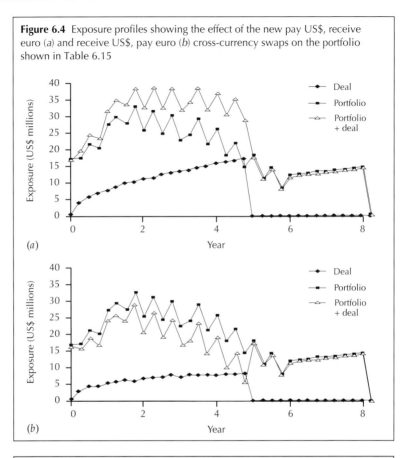

(a)

(b)

Table 6.15 Cross-currency swap added to hypothetical portfolio in Table 6.13 and the new deal

	Maturity (years)	Pay currency	Receive currency	Notional (US$ millions)
Deal six	8.0	Floating US$	Floating euro	50
New deal	5.0	Fixed US$/euro	Fixed euro/US$	50

some of the FX exposure in the portfolio, even though the maturities of the deals are three years apart. The impact on the exposure of the two possible new deals is shown in Figure 6.4.

6.10.3 Cap/floor

Suppose that the portfolio in Table 6.13 also contains an ATM cap or floor on three-month Libor of maturity five years, notional 100 million and strike 7%. We now consider adding these deals to the portfolio of five interest

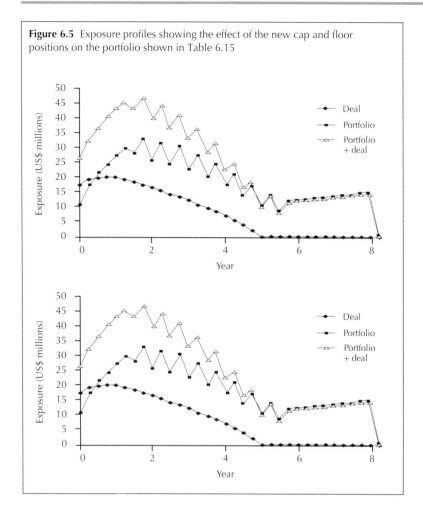

Figure 6.5 Exposure profiles showing the effect of the new cap and floor positions on the portfolio shown in Table 6.15

rate swaps. The expected loss and spread on a stand-alone and portfolio basis are shown in Table 6.17.

Clearly, adding a floor to the portfolio is better than adding a cap. This can be understood, since there is a large notional interest rate swap (deal five) of the same maturity where the bank pays fixed and will therefore have high exposure on this position if interest rates rise. There is little diversification benefit from adding a cap, which has the same exposure for high interest rates. However, the floor position will have high exposure when interest rates are low, which will be partly offset by the interest rate swap. We can see this clearly in the exposure profiles shown in Figure 6.5. For the new floor position, there is no additional risk, except for short maturities. The increase in the exposure for short maturities is due to deals one to four.

Table 6.16 Expected loss and credit spread (bps) for the five-year cross-currency swap (pay US$/rec US$), added to the hypothetical portfolio

| | Expected (incremental) loss | | Required spread | |
	Pay US$	Rec US$	Pay US$	Rec US$
Stand-alone	78.9	47.5	18.3	10.9
Portfolio	52.6	31.4	12.2	–7.2

Table 6.17 Expected loss and credit spread (bps) for five-year cap and floor on three-month Libor, added to the hypothetical portfolio

| | (Incremental) expected loss | | Required spread | |
	Cap	Floor	Cap	Floor
Stand-alone	9.9	7.5	2.4	1.8
Portfolio	8.8	3.1	2.2	0.7

6.10.4 Effect of increasing notional

The portfolio effect seen in Figure 6.5 decreases with increasing notional of the new deal. As the notional of the new deal becomes large with respect to the other deals, the expected loss and spread increase towards their stand-alone values. An example of this is shown in Figure 6.6 for the cross-currency swap, where the bank pays euro and receives US$ in the example in Table 6.16.

Clearly the portfolio effect diminishes as the notional increases and the deal dominates the portfolio, behaving more like a stand-alone deal.

6.10.5 General comments regarding the portfolio effect

There are numerous examples that could help us to explore the portfolio effect for different combinations of new deals and portfolios. However, rather than doing this, we will instead restrict ourselves to a brief review of some of the important factors we have come across when pricing new deals in portfolios. Whilst some effects (eg, regarding offsetting cashflows in swaps) can be predicted, there can also be some subtleties in portfolio pricing, in particular when analysing products with optionality features.

1. Regardless of the existing deals in the portfolio, if the PV (current or expected future PV) is very negative, then a new deal will have a small expected loss, as the bank only loses in default when the PV is positive. Therefore, any deal will have a small or negative credit spread.
2. For an interest rate swap, the most important factor is the total notional of the existing payer and receiver swaps denominated in the same currency. A new payer swap added to a portfolio largely consisting of receiver swaps of that currency will clearly be a good trade.

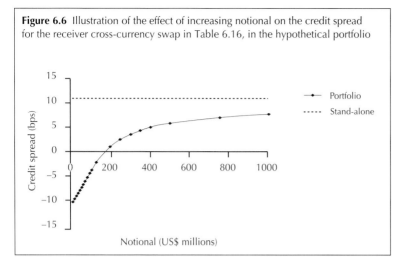

Figure 6.6 Illustration of the effect of increasing notional on the credit spread for the receiver cross-currency swap in Table 6.16, in the hypothetical portfolio

3. When we consider a cross-currency swap in a portfolio, the most impor-tant factor is the exchange of notionals. For example, if another cross-currency swap that has an opposite exposure to the relevant FX rate is added, the risk may be dramatically reduced.
4. The risk of high interest rates for a receiver swap will be reduced if there is a short cap position in the portfolio, whereas a receiver swap and a long cap position create a large credit exposure due to a potential interest rate rise.
5. As mentioned above, for deals with optionality, the portfolio effect can be difficult to predict. Consider being long a payer and a receiver swap-tion. If only one is exercised, there is more credit risk than if both or neither are exercised. Credit risk should play a role in the exercise deci-sion, which should therefore be based on the overall risky PV of the portfolio.

6.11 EXTENSIONS OF THE MODEL

6.11.1 Collateral

Common practice for reducing the credit exposure is to take collateral, as this can be liquidated in the event of default. Commonly, there will be a threshold exposure below which collateral is not required. Above this threshold, the collateral will be called in blocks – therefore the minimum margin call amount is important. We give an example in Figure 6.7 for a single interest rate swap, showing the exposure to be almost capped by the threshold with some additional risk caused by the minimum margin call amount.

The analysis given is only a simplified treatment. We should also con-sider the correlation between the exposure and the collateral value. If it is

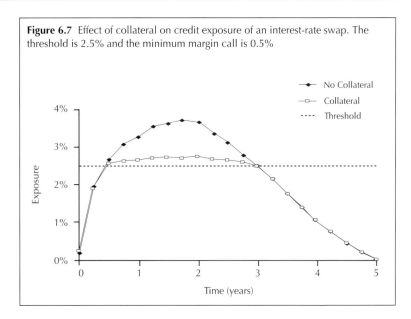

Figure 6.7 Effect of collateral on credit exposure of an interest-rate swap. The threshold is 2.5% and the minimum margin call is 0.5%

positive, then the credit risk will be further decreased, since the value of the collateral is likely to increase with the exposure. For example, if the collateral for a cross-currency swap position is denominated in the currency the bank receives, then it is more effectively protected against increased exposure, which is caused by the strengthening of that currency. Collateral liquidation is discussed in Chapter 8.

6.11.2 Wrong-way exposure

A so-called "wrong-way" exposure arises when there is an unfavourable correlation between the value of a derivative and the default probability of the counterparty. This correlation means that the expected exposure conditional on default is considerably larger than the unconditional expected exposure. Wrong-way exposure can apply to all types of deals, but is best illustrated using a cross-currency swap. For example, suppose that conditional on default, the expected value of a FX rate FX_t^d will be given by a factor η times the unconditional forward FX rate FX_t.

$$E[FX_t^d/\text{default}] = \eta FX_t \qquad (16)$$

Such an effect is easy to incorporate into our model and is much simpler than trying to directly incorporate correlation in the computation of expression (5). Consider a 10-year cross-currency swap with counterparty ABC, where the bank receives floating US dollars and pays floating Thai baht. The default swap premium is 250 bps and the recovery rate is 30%. We

Table 6.18 Impact of wrong-way exposure on the credit risk for a cross-currency swap

	Expected loss	Spread
$\eta = 1.0$	142.3bps	21.4bps
$\eta = 0.9$	239.3bps	36.0bps
$\eta = 0.8$	366.5bps	55.4bps
$\eta = 0.7$	509.3bps	76.8bps

show in Table 6.18 that the expected loss and the credit spread on the swap increase substantially as η decreases. The reason for this is that if the bank is paying in Thai baht, then at default the exposure on the swap will be large and positive when $\eta < 1$. This corresponds to the assumption that the baht has depreciated against the dollar.

The above analysis is a simple and tractable way in which to incorporate correlation between the exposure and the default probability. Of course, the method suffers from the estimation problems we discussed earlier, since it is difficult to obtain a good estimate of η. Of course, even having a rough estimate of η can be valuable information. A more comprehensive discussion of wrong-way exposure is given in JP Morgan (1999).

6.12 HEDGING
In this section, we consider hedging the credit risk in interest rate derivatives, both stand-alone and for portfolios. We initially consider hedging against defaults. This means that the requirement of an effective hedge is that the P&L of the hedged position should not change at default time. We then show that it is also possible to simultaneously hedge against changes in the credit spread. This is important if, for instance, the bank wants to be hedged against the possible decrease in the risky PV of an interest rate swap, if the credit spread of its counterparty widens.

We will demonstrate the general principles for hedging against defaults and stochastic default swap premia by applying them to an interest rate swap. However, the analysis is valid for any variable exposure, ie, for any of the contracts described in this chapter and for portfolios.

6.12.1 Hedging the default risk
Immediately prior to default, we assume a swap is marked-to-market at its risky PV. Denote the recovery rate by δ_{swap}. In the event of default at time τ, the bank receives from the counterparty a fraction of the risk-free PV if positive, while it must pay the risk-free PV if negative (technically we should write $PV_{\tau-}^{risky}$ to denote the PV just prior to default, but this is omitted for clarity), ie,

Before default: PV_τ^{risky}

After default: $\delta_{swap}(PV_\tau^{risk\text{-}free})^+ + (PV_\tau^{risk\text{-}free})^-$

The change in the P&L at the default time or loss on default (LOD_τ) is therefore given by:

$$LOD_\tau = \delta_{swap}(PV_\tau^{risk\text{-}free})^+ + (PV_\tau^{risk\text{-}free})^- - PV_\tau^{risky} \tag{17}$$

The bank should hold a default swap position so as to incur no loss in the aggregate position in the event of default. The payoff of a default swap is $(1-\delta_{ref})N_{ds}$ where N_{ds} is the notional and δ_{ref} is the recovery rate on some reference asset, eg, a bond. The analysis is also applicable to a digital default swap, where we simply need to set $\delta_{ref} = 0$. The required notional of default swap is given by setting the PV of the portfolio at default to zero:

$$(1-\delta_{ref})N_{ds} + LOD_\tau = 0 \tag{18}$$

$$N_{ds} = \frac{PV_\tau^{risky} - \delta_{swap}\left(PV_\tau^{risk\text{-}free}\right)^+ - \left(PV_\tau^{risk\text{-}free}\right)^-}{\left(1-\delta_{ref}\right)} \tag{19}$$

Note that the default swap position should be continuously rebalanced as the PV of the swap changes.

We can gain a greater insight into the above equation by considering the following two situations.

1. $PV_\tau^{risk\text{-}free} > 0$

In this case $N_{ds} = \dfrac{PV_\tau^{risky} - \delta_{swap} PV_\tau^{risk\text{-}free}}{\left(1-\delta_{ref}\right)}$ (20)

When this is positive, which is most likely, the bank should be long default swaps. The position in default swaps should be sufficient for the bank to offset the loss of the risky PV, less the recovered amount in the event of default. This quantity may be negative, even though unlikely, if the risky PV is small or the recovery rate is high, in which case the bank should hold a short default swap position. The short default swap position would offset the gain, $\delta_{swap} PV_\tau^{risk\text{-}free} - PV_\tau^{risky}$, made at default.

2. $PV_\tau^{risk\text{-}free} \leq 0$

Hedge with $N_{ds} = \dfrac{-PV_\tau^{risk\text{-}free} + PV_\tau^{risky}}{\left(1-\delta_{ref}\right)}$ (21)

In this case, the bank should take a short position in default swaps so as to hedge the positive jump in the P&L at the default time. This occurs because the bank marks the deal at the risky PV, but only pays the risk-free PV in the event of default.

We note as an aside that if $PV_\tau^{risky} \geq 0$ (in which case $PV_\tau^{risk-free} > 0$) and the recovery rates are equal, $\delta = \delta_{swap} = \delta_{ref}$,

$$N_{ds} = PV_\tau^{risky} - \frac{\delta}{(1-\delta)}\left(PV_\tau^{risk-free} - PV_\tau^{risky}\right) = PV_\tau^{risky} - \frac{\delta}{(1-\delta)}EL_\tau$$

(22)

In this case, the notional of the default swap is equal to the risky PV of the swap less a correction term that is determined by the recovery rate and the expected loss. This term is likely to be small in practice. The result that we might have intuitively expected would be to hold a position equal to the risky PV of the swap. However, the correction term above arises, since the bank asks for the risk-free PV in the event of default.

We illustrate the hedging of default risk with the example below.

Interest rate swap
The bank pays 6.5% semi-annually and receives six-month Libor on US$1 million from February 4, 2000 until February 4, 2008. Default swap curve = 250 bps, $\delta_{swap} = \delta_{ref} = 30\%$.

Risk-free PV	= US$44,223
Risky PV	= US$38,326

$$N_{ds} = \frac{PV_\tau^{risky} - \delta_{swap} PV_\tau^{risk-free}}{\left(1 - \delta_{ref}\right)} = US\$35,799$$

In the event of default:

P&L (swap)	= −US$38,326
Recovery (swap)	= 30% × US$44,223 = US$13,267
P&L (default swap)	= (1 − 30%) × US$35,799 = US$25,059
Aggregate P&L	= US$0

The maturity of the default swap is not important for hedging default risk as long as the notional is correct and the hedging portfolio is continually rebalanced.

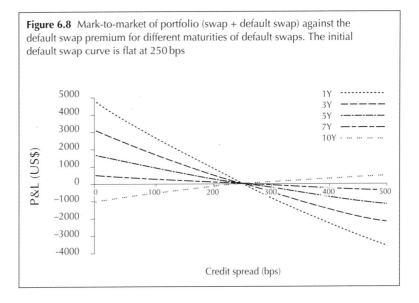

Figure 6.8 Mark-to-market of portfolio (swap + default swap) against the default swap premium for different maturities of default swaps. The initial default swap curve is flat at 250 bps

6.12.2 Hedging credit spread risk

Using the above strategy, there is still an exposure to changes in the credit spread, since the risky swap rate is fixed at the start of the contract. We illustrate this using the above example.

If the default swap curve widens, the P&L on the swap will be negative (since the risky PV will decrease), while the long default swap position will increase in PV. However, it is only by chance that these will cancel. Figure 6.8 shows the change in value of the portfolio for various parallel shifts in the default swap curve using the different hedging instruments.

From Figure 6.8, it is clear that the maturity of the hedging instrument is important. An obvious strategy is therefore to choose the default swap so as to delta hedge, ie, the deltas of the swap and the default swaps are equal (we define the delta here as the change with respect to a 1bp change in the default swap spread). The delta of the swap is –0.1968 bps (this is negative, as an increase in the spread will decrease the value of the swap). Choosing a default swap to match this delta, gives a required maturity of 8.1 years. Figure 6.9 shows the performance of this hedge with changes in the default swap premium.

Note that the required maturity of the default swap depends not only on the swap maturity but also on the PV of the swap. This means that over time, the bank should rebalance both the number of default swaps and their maturity. In Table 6.19, we illustrate this by showing the number of default swaps required to hedge various payer interest rate swaps of different PVs.

There are two factors that determine the required maturity:

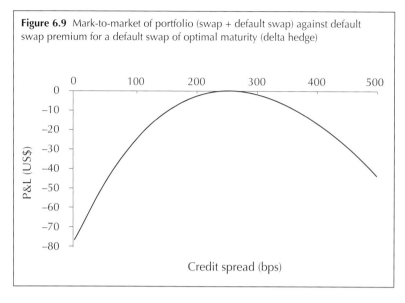

Figure 6.9 Mark-to-market of portfolio (swap + default swap) against default swap premium for a default swap of optimal maturity (delta hedge)

1. As the PV of the swap decreases, the sensitivity to changes in the credit spread also decreases. The delta of the default swap is increasing with maturity. This means that the required maturity would decrease with decreasing PV.
2. As the PV of the swap decreases, the notional of the default swap held also decreases. This means that the required maturity would increase to offset the decreasing default swap position.

Clearly, the latter effect is dominant in the example presented here. It seems likely that for reasonably small PVs, the required default swap maturity will be too large. A solution to this problem is described later.

The above example shows that by choosing the notional and maturity of the default swap to match the PV and delta of the risky swap, it is possible to hedge against default and default swap premium volatility very well. However, it is clear that there are still some potential losses for large changes in the default swap curve which could occur, for example, as a result of a credit crash.

Table 6.19 The notional and maturity of default swaps required to hedge default and spread risk in various interest rate swaps

Fixed rate	Delta	Risk-free PV	Required notional	Required maturity
6.00%	−0.2740	US$67,353	US$55,864	5.42 years
6.25%	−0.2342	US$52,078	US$42,417	6.45 years
6.50%	−0.1966	US$36,817	US$28,916	8.20 years
6.75%	−0.1618	US$21,529	US$15,286	15.86 years

6.12.3 Hedging jumps in the credit spread

One way to better hedge against large jumps in the credit spread is to match not only the delta of the swap but also the gamma. To do this, a second default swap is required. The conditions will be:

$$N_{ds\,1} + N_{ds\,2} = \frac{PV_\tau^{risky} - \delta_{swap}\left(PV_\tau^{risk\text{-}free}\right)^+ - \left(PV_\tau^{risk\text{-}free}\right)^-}{\left(1 - \delta_{ref}\right)}$$

$$N_{ds\,1}\,\Delta_{ds\,1} + N_{ds\,2}\,\Delta_{ds\,2} = \Delta_{swap}$$

$$N_{ds\,1}\,\gamma_{ds\,1} + N_{ds\,2}\,\gamma_{ds\,2} = \gamma_{swap} \tag{23}$$

Since we have four quantities to determine and only three conditions, we arbitrarily fix the maturity of one default swap to be $T_{ds1} = 3Y$ (we show an alternative strategy in the next section). Solving for the above, we obtain:

$$N_{ds1}(0) = -US\$12{,}036,\ N_{ds2}(0) = US\$48{,}853,\ T_{ds2} = 6.55Y$$

We show the effectiveness of this strategy in Figure 6.10. Using two default swaps clearly gives a much better hedge against large moves in the credit spread.

Figure 6.10 Hedged swap vs default swap curve level. The hedge consists of a dynamically adjusted default swap position with optimal maturity (delta hedge) and two default swaps with optimal notionals and maturities (delta-gamma hedge)

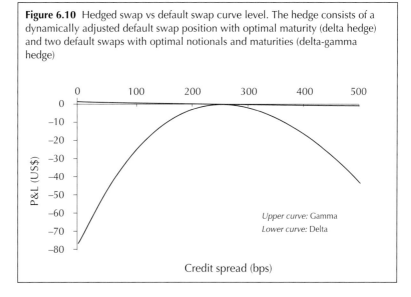

Upper curve: Gamma
Lower curve: Delta

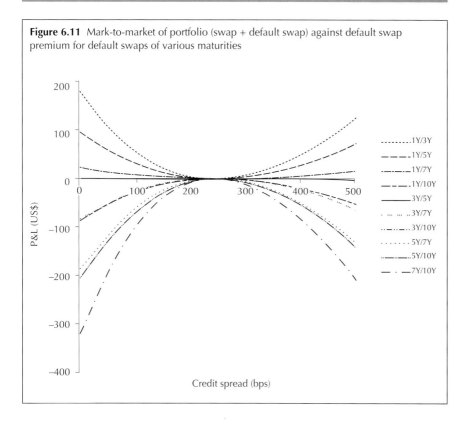

Figure 6.11 Mark-to-market of portfolio (swap + default swap) against default swap premium for default swaps of various maturities

6.12.4 Hedging when the PV is negative

Consider a swap with a negative or small positive PV. The bank needs a small default swap position to hedge the jump in the PV in the event of default, but also wishes to hedge the default swap premium volatility. However, since the notional of default swaps is likely to be small, it may not be possible to hedge the default swap premium volatility, since the required default swap maturity would be too large (for example, see Table 6.19). To overcome this, the bank can trade long and short positions in default swaps with almost equal notionals.

$$N_{ds1} + N_{ds2} = \frac{PV_{\tau}^{risky} - \left(PV_{\tau}^{risk\text{-}free}\right)^{-}}{\left(1 - \delta_{ref}\right)}$$

$$N_{ds1}\Delta_{ds1} + N_{ds2}\Delta_{ds2}\,(t) = N_{swap}\,\Delta_{swap} \tag{24}$$

We have only two equations, but we need to find four unknowns. In the previous section, we arbitrarily fixed the maturity of one of the default swaps, but here we use a different approach. Since, in practice, the market for default swaps will be quite limited, we assume that the bank can trade only default swaps of maturities 1Y, 3Y, 5Y, 7Y and 10Y. We solve for each pair of maturities. Figure 6.11 shows the effectiveness of each strategy.

From the above, it is clear that best hedge was the 3Y/5Y combination, which had a loss of only US$5 (0.0005%) for the spread jumping from 250bps to 500bps. Not surprisingly, it was found that the gamma of this combination matched that of the swap very closely. This strategy works just as well as the last one, and given that the default swap market is likely to be quite limited, it is probably more practical, as it can be dynamically adjusted without requiring continuous changes of the maturity of the default swaps.

6.12.5 Non-parallel shifts

The hedging strategies described above are valid for any default swap term structure (upwards-sloping, downwards-sloping, flat) but only for parallel shifts of the curve. We now use the default swap term structure as shown in Table 6.20, and consider the impact of non-parallel shifts.

We consider employing the basic delta hedging strategy and show the effect of non-parallel and parallel shifts in the default swap term structure in Figure 6.12. The non-parallel shifts involve steepenings, flattenings and inversions. The figures on the x-axis represent the average shift in the default swap premium. For parallel shifts, this simple hedging strategy is still effective, even when the default curve is not flat. However, for non-parallel shifts it is clearly not appropriate.

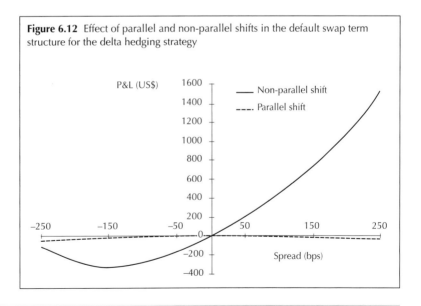

Figure 6.12 Effect of parallel and non-parallel shifts in the default swap term structure for the delta hedging strategy

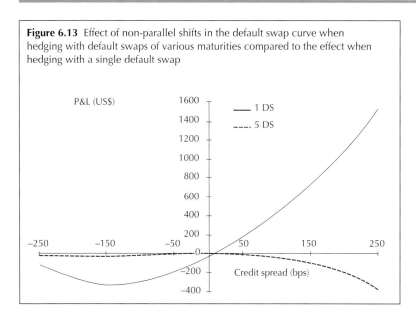

Figure 6.13 Effect of non-parallel shifts in the default swap curve when hedging with default swaps of various maturities compared to the effect when hedging with a single default swap

To hedge the swap against changes in shape of the default swap term structure, it is necessary to trade default swaps of different maturities. The notional of each default swap is determined according to the sensitivity of the price of the swap with respect to the default swap premium at that maturity. The notionals of the default swaps are shown in Table 6.21.

Table 6.20 Default swap term structure used for hedging

Maturity	Default swap premium
1Y	250bps
3Y	260bps
5Y	270bps
7Y	285bps
10Y	300bps

Table 6.21 Notionals of default swaps (DS) required to hedge against non-parallel shifts in the default swap curve

DS maturity	DS Notional (US$)
1Y	−11,510
3Y	454
5Y	12,470
7Y	25,767
10Y	4,891

6.13 CONCLUSION

We have presented an integrated practical approach for pricing and managing counterparty risk across fixed-income instruments. The traditional approach in derivatives has been to consider credit as a non-traded risk that can only be managed with credit limits and collateral. This approach, even though valuable and intuitive, can lead to inefficient practices and divergence from the pricing of credit derivatives, where credit is actually traded. In the method presented, credit is treated as just another source of risk (along with interest rates, foreign exchange, etc). Although more illiquid than the other sources of risk, the proposed method still allows credit to be actively managed if there is a relatively liquid secondary market for default swaps. We have applied this methodology to stand-alone interest rate and cross-currency swaps, caps/floors, swaptions and cancellable swaps. The advantage of the proposed methodology is that the credit spread is based on the current conditions of the default swap market, rather than using historical data. This chapter complements the work presented in Chapters 3 and 4, where we assumed that credit risk is not hedgeable and that a sufficient amount of economic capital should therefore be held by the financial institutions to guard against future credit events. It presents one step towards pricing credit consistently across a financial institution, therefore avoiding inconsistent pricing among divisions.

We have also discussed the pricing of new transactions when there are existing deals covered by the same master agreement. Since deals priced on a portfolio basis can never require a higher spread than stand-alone deals, this can give incentives to marketers, and provide a competitive edge by giving aggressive prices, while at the same time improving the risk profile of the bank's portfolio. We have described a dynamic strategy for hedging an uncertain credit exposure against default, default swap premium volatility and jumps in the default swap premiums. The hedge is effective both against parallel shifts and changes in the shape of the default swap curve. It is necessary to use varying amounts of default swaps over a whole range of maturities. The hedge ratios have to be rebalanced over time.

Here, we assumed that only one of the two counterparties incurred default risk. It is possible to incorporate bilateral default risk in the model. Furthermore, we assumed independence between the probability of default and interest rates/FX rates. The model can be extended to incorporate this correlation, as it can be important in certain circumstances. The computations then become substantially more difficult and computational problems arise. We described a simple way of doing this for which the computations do not become any more difficult.

BIBLIOGRAPHY

Arvanitis, A., 2000, "Getting the Pricing Right", *Risk* 13(9), September, pp. 115–9.

Arvanitis, A., J. Gregory and J-P. Laurent, 1999, "Building Models for Credit Spreads", *Journal of Derivatives* 6(3), pp. 27–43.

Arvanitis, A., and J-P. Laurent, 1999, "On the Edge of Completeness", *Risk* 12(10), October, pp. 61–5.

Duffie, D. and M. Huang, 1996, "Swap Rates and Credit Quality", *Journal of Finance*, 51(3), pp. 921–50.

Giberti, D., M. Mentini and P. Scabellone, 1993, "The Valuation of Credit Risk in Swaps: Methodological Issues and Empirical Results", *The Journal of Fixed Income*, March, pp. 24–36.

Hull, J. C., 2000, *Options, Futures and Other Derivatives,* Fourth Edition (Prentice-Hall International).

Hull, J. C., and A. White, 1990, "Pricing Interest Rate Derivative Securities", *Review of Financial Studies* 3(4), pp. 573–92.

Hull, J. C., and A. White, 1995, "The Impact of Default Risk on the Prices of Options and Other Derivative Securities", *Journal of Banking and Finance* 19, pp. 299–322.

Jarrow, R., D. Lando and S. Turnbull, 1997, "A Markov Model for the Term Structure of Credit Risk Spreads", *Review of Financial Studies*, 10(2), pp. 481–23.

Jarrow, R., and S. Turnbull, 1995, "Pricing Derivatives on Financial Securities Subject to Credit Risk", *Journal of Finance*, March, pp. 53–85.

Jarrow, R., and S. Turnbull, 1997, "When Swaps Are Dropped", *Risk* 10(5), May, pp. 70–5.

JP Morgan, 1999, "Wrong-Way Exposure", *Risk* 12(7), July, pp. 52–5.

JP Morgan, 2000, "Modelling Derivative Risk in the Presence of Collateral and Netting", *Risk*, January.

Merton, R. C., 1974, "On the Pricing of Corporate Debt: The Risk Structure of Interest Rates", *Journal of Finance* 29, pp. 449–70.

Sorensen, E. H. and T. F. Bollier, 1994, "Pricing Swap Default Risk", *Financial Analysts Journal*, May–June, pp. 23–33.

APPENDIX A – DERIVATION OF THE FORMULA FOR THE EXPECTED LOSS ON AN INTEREST RATE SWAP

We derive a general expression for the risky PV of an interest rate swap and we show that it is equal to the risk-free PV less the expected loss.

Consider the valuation at time t of an interest rate swap with fixed rate κ and maturity T with cashflows occurring at dates T_i $(i = 1,\ldots, n)$. The PV of this swap is equal to the sum of the following contingent payments:

1) Payment at default time τ, $(P_{1,t})$
2) Payments at dates T_i, conditional on default having not occurred, $(P_{2,t})$

We will assume independence between the interest rates and hazard rates, which is crucial in simplifying the resulting expressions.

Consider a receiver swap (the bank pays floating and receives fixed payments). The default payments can be written as:

$$P_{1,t} = E_t \left[\int_t^{T_1} h_s \exp\left(-\int_t^s (r_u + h_u)\,du \right) D_s\,ds \right]$$

$$+ \sum_{i=1}^{n-1} E_t \left[\int_{T_i}^{T_{i+1}} h_s \exp\left(-\int_t^s (r_u + h_u)\,du \right) D_s\,ds \right]$$

$$= E_t \left[\int_t^{T_1} h_s \exp\left(-\int_t^s h_u\,du \right) B(t,s) D_s\,ds \right]$$

$$+ \sum_{i=1}^{n-1} E_t \left[\int_{T_i}^{T_{i+1}} h_s \exp\left(-\int_t^s h_u\,du \right) B(t,s) D_s\,ds \right] \qquad \text{(A1)}$$

where E_t is the conditional expectation under the risk neutral probability measure with respect to information available at date t, r_t is the spot interest rate at time t and h_t is the hazard rate which gives the instantaneous probability of default, D_s is the payment that is made when default occurs at time s and $B(t,s)$ is the risk-free discount factor. In Equation (A1), $\exp\left(-\int_t^s r_u du\right)$ is the discount factor from time t to s, $\exp\left(-\int_t^s h_u du\right)$ gives the probability of no default from time t to s and $h_s ds$ gives the probability of default in an infinitesimal period ds.

We assume that at default time the bank receives a fraction of the risk-free PV if it is positive and pays the whole risk-free PV if it is negative (as shown in Figure 6.1). We can therefore write D_s more explicitly as:

$$D_s = \delta Sw(s, T_1, T_n)^+ + Sw(s, T_1, T_n)^- \qquad \text{(A2)}$$

where $Sw(s, T_1, T_n)$ is the value of the forward swap at time s. Since $x^- = x - x^+$, the above expression can be written as:

$$D_s = Sw(s, T_1, T_n) - (1 - \delta)Sw(s, T_1, T_n)^+ \qquad \text{(A3)}$$

We can now write:

$$P_{1,t} = E_t \left[\int_t^{T_1} h_s \exp\left(-\int_t^s h_u\,du \right) \right.$$

$$\left. \times B(t,s)\left(Sw(s, T_1, T_n) - (1-\delta)Sw(s, T_1, T_n)^+ \right)ds \right]$$

$$+ \sum_{i=1}^{n-1} E_t \left[\int_{T_i}^{T_{i+1}} h_s \exp\left(-\int_t^s h_u \, du \right) \right.$$

$$\left. \times B(t,s)\left(Sw(s,T_1,T_n) - (1-\delta) Sw(s,T_1,T_n)^+ \right) ds \right] \qquad \text{(A4)}$$

The payments when there is no default can be written as:

$$P_{2,t} = \sum_{i=1}^{n} E_t \left[\exp\left(-\int_t^{T_i} (r_u + h_u) \, du \right) \left(L_{T_{i-1}} - \kappa \right) \Delta \right] \qquad \text{(A5)}$$

where $L_{T_{i-1}}$ represents the Libor reference reset in arrears,

$$L_{T_{i-1}} = \left(\frac{1}{B(T_{i-1}, T_i)} \right) \frac{1}{\Delta}$$

and $\Delta = T_i - T_{i-1}$ is the coverage. This expression gives the sum of the discounted future swap cashflows multiplied by the probability of not having defaulted (or equivalently the future swap cashflows discounted at the risky rate).

We can now write an expression for the risky PV, which is simply $P_{1,t} + P_{2,t}$, ie,

$$PV_t^{risky} = E_t \left[\int_t^{T_1} h_s \exp\left(-\int_t^s h_u \, du \right) \right.$$

$$\left. \times B(t,s)\left(Sw(s,T_1,T_n) - (1-\delta) Sw(s,T_1,T_n)^+ \right) ds \right]$$

$$+ \sum_{i=1}^{n-1} E_t \left[\int_{T_i}^{T_{i+1}} h_s \exp\left(-\int_t^s h_u \, du \right) \right.$$

$$\left. \times B(t,s)\left(Sw(s,T_1,T_n) - (1-\delta) Sw(s,T_1,T_n)^+ \right) ds \right]$$

$$\sum_{i=1}^{n} E_t \left[\exp\left(-\int_t^{T_i} (r_u + h_u) \, du \right) \left(L_{T_{i-1}} - \kappa \right) \Delta \right] \qquad \text{(A6)}$$

Next, we cancel the terms that are dependent on the forward value of the swap. The expression simplifies as follows:

$$
\begin{aligned}
PV_t^{risky} = &\sum_{i=1}^{n} E_t \left[\exp\left(-\int_t^{T_i} r_u \, du \right) \left(L_{T_{i-1}} - \kappa \right) \Delta \right] \\
&- (1-\delta) E_t \left[\int_t^{T_1} h_s \exp\left(-\int_t^s h_u \, du \right) B(t,s) Sw(s,T_1,T_n)^+ \, ds \right] \\
&- (1-\delta) \sum_{i=1}^{n-1} E_t \left[\int_{T_i}^{T_{i+1}} h_s \exp\left(-\int_t^s h_u \, du \right) B(t,s) Sw(s,T_1,T_n)^+ \, ds \right]
\end{aligned}
$$

(A7)

The first term in the above expression can be identified as the risk-free PV of the swap. We can therefore interpret the second term as being the expected loss on the contract, ie,

$$
PV_t^{risky} = PV_t^{risk\text{-}free} - EL_t \tag{A8}
$$

$$
\begin{aligned}
EL_t = &(1-\delta) E_t \left[\int_t^{T_1} h_s \exp\left(-\int_t^s h_u \, du \right) B(t,s) Sw(s,T_1,T_n)^+ \, ds \right] \\
&+ (1-\delta) \sum_{i=1}^{n-1} E_t \left[\int_{T_i}^{T_{i+1}} h_s \exp\left(-\int_t^s h_u \, du \right) B(t,s) Sw(s,T_{i+1},T_n)^+ \, ds \right]
\end{aligned}
$$

(A9)

If the current date corresponds to the first fixing date T_0, (this is normally the case to within a few days, unless the swap is forward starting), then we can simply write:

$$
EL_t = (1-\delta) \sum_{i=1}^{n} E_t \left[\int_{T_{i-1}}^{T_i} h_s \exp\left(-\int_t^s h_u \, du \right) B(t,s) Sw(s,T_1,T_n)^+ \, ds \right]
$$

(A10)

To evaluate the above formulae, we assume a piecewise constant hazard rate and an instantaneous risk-free rate, whose dynamics are described by the Hull and White model. These assumptions allow us to compute explicitly the terms in Equation (A6).

The first term is simply equal to a standard swap, ie,

$$\sum_{i=1}^{n} E_t \left[\left(\exp - \int_t^{T_i} r_u \, du \right) \left(L_{i-1} - \kappa \right) \Delta \right]$$

$$= B(t, T_0) - \sum_{i=1}^{n} \kappa \Delta B(t, T_i) - B(t, T_n) \qquad \text{(A11)}$$

The second and third terms correspond to swaption payouts weighted by marginal default probabilities, which may be separated under the independence assumption. The swaption payouts can be written as:

$$E_t \left[\int_t^{T_1} B(t, s) Sw(s, T_1, T_n)^+ \, ds \right]$$

$$= E_t \left[\int_t^{T_1} B(t, s) \left(B(t, T_0) - \sum_{i=1}^{n} \kappa \Delta B(t, T_i) - B(t, T_n) \right)^+ ds \right] \qquad \text{(A12a)}$$

$$E_t \left[\int_t^{T_1} B(t, s) Sw(s, T_{i+1}, T_n)^+ \, ds \right]$$

$$= E_t \left[\int_{T_i}^{T_{i+1}} B(t, s) \left(B(t, T_0) - \sum_{i=1}^{n} \kappa \Delta B(t, T_i) - B(t, T_n) \right)^+ ds \right] \qquad \text{(A12b)}$$

These expressions can be re-written as:

$$E_t \left[\int_t^{T_1} B(t, s) \left(B(t, T_0) - \sum_{i=1}^{n} \kappa \Delta B(t, T_i) - B(t, T_n) \right) 1\{r_s > r_0^*\} \, ds \right]$$

$$\text{(A13a)}$$

$$E_t \left[\int_{T_i}^{T_{i+1}} B(t, s) \left(B(t, T_0) - \sum_{l=i+1}^{n} \kappa \Delta B(t, T_l) - B(t, T_n) \right) 1\{r_s > r_0^*\} \, ds \right]$$

$$\text{(A13b)}$$

where r_i^* represents the exercise boundary (the values such that the swap PV is zero). This can be written using forward neutral expectations to give:

$$B(t,T_0)E_t^{Q^{T_0}}\left[1\{r_s>r_0^*\}\right]$$

$$-\sum_{i=1}^{n}\kappa\Delta B(t,T_i)E_t^{Q^{T_i}}\left[1\{r_s>r_0^*\}\right]-B(t,T_n)E_t^{Q^{T_n}}\left[1\{r_s>r_0^*\}\right]$$

(A14a)

$$B(t,T_0)E_t^{Q^{T_i}}\left[1\{r_s>r_i^*\}\right]$$

$$-\sum_{l=i+1}^{n}\kappa\Delta B(t,T_l)E_t^{Q^{T_l}}\left[1\{r_s>r_i^*\}\right]-B(t,T_n)E_t^{Q^{T_n}}\left[1\{r_s>r_i^*\}\right]$$

(A14b)

where $E_T^{Q^{T_l}}$ denote the expectation under the forward neutral measures associated with the discount bond with maturity T_l and conditional on information available at date T. The computation of the addition terms in the above is given in Appendix C on interest rate swaptions.

APPENDIX B – THE FORMULA FOR THE EXPECTED LOSS ON AN INTEREST RATE CAP OR FLOOR

The expected loss on a cap or floor can be derived following the same lines as for the interest rate swap in Appendix A. Similarly to Equation (A10), we arrive at:

$$EL_t=(1-\delta)\sum_{i=1}^{n}E_t\left[\int_{T_{i-1}}^{T_i}h_s\exp\left(-\int_t^s h_u\,du\right)B(t,s)\mathrm{Opt}(s,T_1,T_n)^+\,ds\right]$$

(B1)

where $\mathrm{Opt}(s,T_1,T_n)$ represents the PV of the cap or floor (with caplet/floorlet maturities ranging from T_1 to T_n) at time s. However, since the PV of a long option position when the premium is paid upfront is always positive, this expression can be simply written as:

$$EL_t=(1-\delta)\sum_{i=1}^{n}E_t\left[\int_{T_{i-1}}^{T_i}h_s\exp\left(-\int_t^s h_u\,du\right)B(t,s)\mathrm{Opt}(s,T_1,T_n)\,ds\right]$$

(B2)

We can therefore use any model for the value of the cap or floor in the above expression.

APPENDIX C – DERIVATION OF THE FORMULA FOR THE EXPECTED LOSS ON AN INTEREST RATE SWAPTION (HULL AND WHITE INTEREST RATE MODEL)

We analyse and derive a pricing formula for a risky European swaption in the Hull and White model. The holder of the swaption has the right to enter into a swap at maturity. This contract can be decomposed into the following payouts:

1. If there is default before the maturity of the swaption, the bank gets the present value of a default-free swaption on a default-free swap multiplied by the recovery rate. This present value is always positive, since it corresponds to the price of an option.
2. If no default happens, the swaption is still alive at maturity. If there is no exercise, no cashflows are exchanged. In case of exercise, we have to distinguish whether there is cash settlement or not.

   ❑ For cash settlement, a value corresponding to the positive part of the present value of the risk-free swap is received.
   ❑ For physical delivery, a defaultable swap is entered and we need to take into account the default risk on all future swapped cashflows.

   Clearly, a risky swaption with physical delivery is worth less than a cash-settled swaption.

We denote the current date by t and the swaption maturity by T. The present value at date s $(t \leq s \leq T)$ of a risk-free swaption on a risk-free swap, which starts at T_1 and ends at T_n, is denoted by $Sn(s, T, T_1, T_n)$. The constant recovery rate is given by δ. The present value at date s $(T \leq s \leq T_n)$ of risk-free and risky swaps with payments starting at T_1 and ending at T_n are denoted by $Sw(s, T_1, T_n)$ and $\tilde{Sw}(s, T_1, T_n)$ respectively.

The price of the first contingent claim (default before swaption maturity) is given by:

$$P_{1,t} = E_t\left[\int_t^T h_s\left(\exp-\int_t^s\left(r_u + h_u\right)du\right)\delta Sn(s, T, T_1, T_n)ds\right] \quad \textbf{(C1)}$$

where E_t is the conditional expectation under the risk neutral probability measure with respect to information available at date t, r_u is the instantaneous risk free rate and h_u is the hazard rate of default.

The price of the second contingent claim (default after swaption maturity) is given by:

$$P_{2,t} = E_t\left[\left(\exp-\int_t^T\left(r_u + h_u\right)du\right)\left(Sw(T, T_1, T_n)\right)^+\right] \quad \textbf{(C2)}$$

in case of cash settlement, and by:

$$P_{2,t} = E_t\left[\left(\exp - \int_t^T (r_u + h_u)\,du\right)\left(\tilde{S}w(T, T_1, T_n)\right)^+\right] \tag{C3}$$

in case of physical delivery.

The price of the swaption at current date t is given by the sum of the two prices $P_{1,t}$ and $P_{2,t}$.

To evaluate the above formulae, we assume a piecewise constant hazard rate and an instantaneous risk-free rate with dynamics that follow the Hull and White model. From the application of Fubini's Theorem we have:

$$P_{1,t} = \int_t^T E_t\left[h_s\left(\exp - \int_t^s (r_u + h_u)\,du\right)\delta Sn(s, T, T_1, T_n)\right]ds \tag{C4}$$

Due to the independence between the hazard rate and the risk-free rate, we may disentangle the default and interest rate parts:

$$P_{1,t} = \int_t^T E_t\left[h_s\left(\exp - \int_t^s h_u\,du\right)\right]E_t\left[\left(\exp - \int_t^s r_u\,du\right)\delta Sn(s, T, T_1, T_n)\right]ds \tag{C5}$$

where the default part, $E_t[h_s(\exp - \int_t^s h_u du)]$, is easily obtained from a default swap stripper (see Chapter 5). The interest rate component is given by:

$$E_t\left[\left(\exp - \int_t^s r_u\,\delta u\right)Sn(s, T, T_1, T_n)\right]$$

$$= E_t\left[\left(\exp - \int_t^s r_u\,\delta u\right)E_s\left[\left(\exp - \int_s^T r_u\,\delta u\right)\left(Sw(T, T_1, T_n)\right)^+\right]\right]$$

$$= E_t\left[\left(\exp - \int_t^T r_u\,\delta u\right)\left(Sw(T, T_1, T_n)\right)^+\right]$$

$$P_{1,t} = \int_t^T E_t\left[h_s\left(\exp - \int_t^s h_u\,\delta u\right)\right]E_t\left[\left(\exp - \int_t^s r_u\,\delta u\right)\left(Sw(T, T_1, T_n)\right)^+\right]\delta s \tag{C6}$$

Hence, the price of the first contingent claim is the price of a default-free swaption multiplied by a weighted average of default probabilities, for which the computations were shown in Appendix A.

For the second contingent claim under cash settlement,

$$P_{2,t} = E_t \left[\left(\exp - \int_t^T (r_u + h_u) \, du \right) \left(Sw(T, T_1, T_n) \right)^+ \right] \tag{C7}$$

which is also the price of a standard swaption. In this case, the computations are no more difficult than for the interest rate swap.

In the case of physical delivery, we need to price a risk-free swaption on a risky swap:

$$P_{2,t} = E_t \left[\left(\exp - \int_t^T (r_u + h_u) \, du \right) \left(\tilde{S}w(T, T_1, T_n) \right)^+ \right] \tag{C8}$$

Here, the computations are more involved. We must once again decompose the risky swap into two contingent claims as before:

$$\tilde{S}w(T, T_1, T_n) =$$

$$E_T \left[\int_T^{T_1} h_s \left(\exp - \int_T^s (r_u + h_u) \, \delta u \right) \right.$$

$$\left. \times \left(\delta \left(Sw(s, T_1, T_n) \right)^+ + \left(Sw(s, T_1, T_n) \right)^- \right) \delta s \right]$$

$$+ \sum_{i=1}^{n-1} E_T \left[\int_{T_i}^{T_{i+1}} h_s \left(\exp - \int_T^s (r_u + h_u) \, \delta u \right) \right.$$

$$\left. \times \left(\delta \left(Sw(s, T_{i+1}, T_n) \right)^+ + \left(Sw(s, T_{i+1}, T_n) \right)^- \right) \delta s \right]$$

$$+ \sum_{i=1}^{n} E_T \left[\left(\exp - \int_T^{T_i} (r_u + h_u) \, \delta u \right) \left(L_{i-1} - \kappa \right) \Delta \right] \tag{C9}$$

In the same way as before (see Appendix A) we obtain:

$$\tilde{S}w(T, T_1, T_n) =$$

$$E_T\left[\int_T^{T_1} h_s\left(\exp -\int_T^s (r_u + h_u)\,du\right)(\delta-1)\big(Sw(s, T_1, T_n)\big)^+ ds\right]$$

$$+\sum_{i=1}^{n-1} E_T\left[\int_{T_i}^{T_{i+1}} h_s\left(\exp -\int_T^s (r_u + h_u)\,du\right)(\delta-1)\big(Sw(s, T_{i+1}, T_n)\big)^+ ds\right]$$

$$+\sum_{i=1}^{n} E_T\left[\left(\exp -\int_T^{T_i} r_u\,du\right)\big(L_{i-1} - \kappa\big)\Delta\right] \qquad \text{(C10)}$$

Due to our assumptions (independence between hazard and interest rates), we may again separate the default and interest rate parts.

We still need to price the interest rate components. The last expression in Equation (C10) is a standard swap:

$$\sum_{i=1}^{n} E_T\left[\left(\exp -\int_T^{T_i} r_u\,du\right)\big(L_{i-1} - \kappa\big)\Delta\right]$$

$$= B(T, T_0) - \sum_{i=1}^{n} \kappa\Delta B(T, T_i) - B(T, T_n) \qquad \text{(C11)}$$

In the case of the Hull–White model, discount bond values will depend on the value of the short term interest rate r_T at date T.

The first and second terms in Equation (C10) are swaption payoffs, which can be written as:

$$E_T\left[\left(\exp -\int_T^s r_u\,du\right)\big(Sw(s, T_1, T_n)\big)^+\right]$$

$$= E_T\left[\left(\exp -\int_T^s r_u\,du\right)\left(B(s, T_0) - \sum_{i=1}^{n} \kappa\Delta B(s, T_i) - B(s, T_n)\right)^+\right] \qquad \text{(C12a)}$$

$$E_T\left[\left(\exp-\int_T^s r_u\,du\right)\left(Sw\left(s,T_{i+1},T_n\right)\right)^+\right]$$

$$=E_T\left[\left(\exp-\int_T^s r_u\,du\right)\left(B(s,T_i)-\sum_{l=i+1}^n \kappa\Delta B(s,T_l)-B(s,T_n)\right)^+\right] \quad \text{(C12b)}$$

Special values of the short-term interest rate will define the exercise regions. Indeed the above expressions can be rewritten:

$$E_T\left[\left(\exp-\int_T^s r_u\,du\right)\left(B(s,T_0)-\sum_{i=1}^n \kappa\Delta B(s,T_i)-B(s,T_n)\right)1\left\{r_s>r_0^*\right\}\right] \quad \text{(C13a)}$$

$$E_T\left[\left(\exp-\int_T^s r_u\,du\right)\left(B(s,T_i)-\sum_{l=i+1}^n \kappa\Delta B(s,T_i)-B(s,T_n)\right)1\left\{r_s>r_0^*\right\}\right] \quad \text{(C13b)}$$

Where the values r_i^* are chosen so that the swap values $B(s,T_i)-\sum_{l=i+1}^n\kappa\Delta B(s,T_l)-B(s,T_n)$ are equal to zero. Recall that all discount bond values are decreasing functions of the instantaneous interest rate r_s in the Hull and White model. Hence, the condition that the swap is positive is equivalent to a condition on the instantaneous interest rate. This condition is that r_s should be greater than the interest rate value r_i^*, making the swap equal to zero. Using forward neutral measures we have:

$$B(T,T_0)E_T^{Q^{T_0}}\left[1\left\{r_s>r_0^*\right\}\right]-\sum_{i=1}^n \kappa\Delta B(T,T_i)E_T^{Q^{T_i}}\left[1\left\{r_s>r_0^*\right\}\right]$$

$$-B(T,T_n)E_T^{Q^{T_n}}\left[1\left\{r_s>r_0^*\right\}\right] \quad \text{(C14a)}$$

$$B(T,T_i)E_T^{Q^{T_i}}\left[1\left\{r_s>r_i^*\right\}\right]-\sum_{l=i+1}^n \kappa\Delta B(T,T_l)E_T^{Q^{T_l}}\left[1\left\{r_s>r_i^*\right\}\right]$$

$$-B(T,T_n)E_T^{Q^{T_n}}\left[1\left\{r_s>r_i^*\right\}\right] \quad \text{(C14b)}$$

where $E_T^{Q^{T_l}}$ denotes the expectation under the forward neutral measures associated with the discount bond with maturity T_l and conditional to information available at date T. Adopting more compact notations we get:

$$\sum_{l=0}^{n} c_l B(T, T_l) E_T^{Q^{T_l}} \left[1\{ r_s > r_0^* \} \right],$$

$$c_0 = 1, c_1 = \ldots = c_{n-1} = -\kappa\Delta, \ c_n = -1 - \kappa\Delta \qquad \text{(C15a)}$$

$$\sum_{l=i}^{n} c_l B(T, T_l) E_T^{Q^{T_l}} \left[1\{ r_s > r_i^* \} \right],$$

$$c_i = 1, c_{i+1} = \ldots = c_{n-1} = -\kappa\Delta, \ c_n = -1 - \kappa\Delta \qquad \text{(C15b)}$$

By gathering all expressions, we have that the defaultable swap value $\tilde{S}w(T, T_1, T_n)$ at date T is equal to:

$$\int_T^{T_1} E_T \left[h_s \exp\left(-\int_T^s h_u \, du \right) \right] (\delta - 1) \sum_{l=0}^{n} c_l B(T, T_l) E_T^{Q^{T_l}} \left[1\{ r_s > r_0^* \} \right] ds$$

$$+ \sum_{i=1}^{n} \int_{T_i}^{T_{i+1}} E_T \left[h_s \exp\left(-\int_T^s h_u \, du \right) \right] (\delta - 1) \sum_{l=i}^{n} c_l B(T, T_l) E_T^{Q^{T_l}} \left[1\{ r_s > r_i^* \} \right] ds$$

$$+ B(T, T_0) - \sum_{i=1}^{n} \kappa \Delta B(T, T_i) - B(T, T_n) \qquad \text{(C16)}$$

All terms in the above formula depend on the value of the instantaneous interest rate r_T at date T.

Let us denote r_T^* the value of this instantaneous interest rate such that the defaultable swap $\tilde{S}w(T, T_1, T_n)$ is zero. We deduce:

$$E_t \left[\left(\exp -\int_t^T r_u \, du \right) \left(\tilde{S}w(T, T_1, T_n) \right)^+ \right]$$

$$= E_t \left[\left(\exp -\int_t^T r_u \, du \right) \left(\tilde{S}w(T, T_1, T_n) \right) 1\{ r_T > r_T^* \} \right] \qquad \text{(C17)}$$

which gives:

$$E_t \left\{ \exp - \int_t^T r_s \, ds \right.$$

$$\times \left[\int_T^{T_1} E_T \left[h_s \exp\left(-\int_T^s h_u \, du \right) \right] \right.$$

$$\times (\delta - 1) \sum_{l=0}^n c_l B(T, T_l) E_T^{Q^{T_l}} \left[1\{ r_s > r_0^* \} \right] ds$$

$$+ \sum_{i=1}^n \int_{T_i}^{T_{i+1}} E_T \left[h_s \exp\left(-\int_T^s h_u \, du \right) \right]$$

$$\times (\delta - 1) \sum_{l=i}^n c_l B(T, T_l) E_T^{Q^{T_l}} \left[1\{ r_s > r_i^* \} \right] ds$$

$$\left. + B(T, T_0) - \sum_{i=1}^n \kappa \Delta B(T, T_i) - B(T, T_n) \right]$$

$$\left. 1\{ r_T > r_T^* \} \right\} \qquad \textbf{(C18)}$$

Again, using the forward neutral measure, we get:

$$\int_T^{T_1} E_T \left[h_s \exp\left(-\int_T^s h_u \, du \right) \right] (\delta - 1) \sum_{l=0}^n c_l B(t, T_l) E_t^{Q^{T_l}}$$

$$\times \left[1\{ r_s > r_0^* \} 1\{ r_T > r_T^* \} \right] ds$$

$$+ \sum_{i=1}^n \int_{T_i}^{T_{i+1}} E_T \left[h_s \exp\left(-\int_T^s h_u \, du \right) \right] (\delta - 1) \sum_{l=i}^n c_l B(t, T_l) E_t^{Q^{T_l}}$$

$$\times \left[1\{ r_s > r_i^* \} 1\{ r_T > r_T^* \} \right] ds$$

$$+ \left\{ B(t, T_0) E_t^{Q^{T_0}} \left[1\{ r_T > r_T^* \} \right] - \sum_{i=1}^n \kappa \Delta B(t, T_i) E_t^{Q^{T_i}} \right.$$

$$\left. \times \left[1\{ r_T > r_T^* \} \right] - B(t, T_n) E_t^{Q^{T_n}} \left[1\{ r_T > r_T^* \} \right] \right\} \qquad \textbf{(C19)}$$

To compute the above expressions, we must compute the joint distribution of the pair (r_s, r_T) under the different forward neutral measures. In the Hull and White model, the instantaneous interest rate follows an Ornstein–Uhlenbeck process with a time-varying drift under the risk neutral measure:

$$dr_t = (\theta(t) - ar_t)dt + \sigma dW_t \qquad (C20)$$

or equivalently in integral form:

$$r_T = e^{-a(T-t)}r_t + \int_t^T \theta(u)e^{-a(T-u)}du + \int_t^T \sigma e^{-a(T-u)}dW_u \qquad (C21)$$

From Girsanov's Theorem, we know that $dW_t^{Q^{T_l}} + dW_t - \sigma(t, T_l)dt$ is a standard Brownian motion. The diffusion term $\sigma(t, T_l)$ is the volatility of the discount bond with maturity T_l – in the extended Vasicek model:

$$\sigma(t, T_l) = -\sigma \frac{1 - \exp(-a(T_l - t))}{a}$$

Hence, we get:

$$dr_t = (\theta(t) + \sigma\sigma(t, T_l) - ar_t)dt + \sigma dW_t \qquad (C22)$$

The integration gives:

$$r_T = e^{-a(T-t)}r_t + \int_t^T \left(\theta(u) + \sigma\sigma(u, T_l)\right)e^{-a(T-u)}du + \int_t^T \sigma e^{-a(T-u)}dW_u \qquad (C23)$$

Hence, we get that the conditional distribution of r_T knowing r_t is a normal distribution:

$$r_T \Big|r_t \sim N\left(e^{-a(T-t)}r_t + \int_t^T \left(\theta(u) + \sigma\sigma(u, T_l)\right)e^{-a(T-u)}du, \right.$$

$$\left. \int_t^T \sigma^2 e^{-2a(T-u)}du \right) \qquad (C24)$$

Of course this expression is also valid for the conditional distribution of r_s knowing r_t. The variance is equal to $\sigma^2\left((1 - e^{-2a(T-t)})/2a\right)$, while

$$\int_t^T \sigma\sigma(u,T_l)e^{-a(T-u)}du$$

$$= -\frac{\sigma^2}{2a^2}\left[2\left(1-e^{-a(T-t)}\right)-\left(e^{-a(T_l-T)}-e^{-a(T+T_l-2t)}\right)\right]$$

In the above expression, $\int_t^T \theta(u)e^{-a(T-u)}du$ is computed as follows. In the Hull and White model, the time varying drift is equal to:

$$\theta(u)=\frac{\partial}{\partial u}f(0,u)+\lambda f(0,u)+\frac{\sigma^2}{2a}\left(1-e^{-2au}\right)$$

where $f(0,u)$ is the instantaneous forward rate at date 0 with maturity u. Using:

$$\int_t^T \frac{\partial}{\partial u}f(0,u)e^{-a(T-u)}du$$

$$=f(0,T)-f(0,t)e^{-a(T-t)}-\int_t^T f(0,u)ae^{-a(T-u)}du \qquad \text{(C25)}$$

from the integration by part formula, we get the simplification:

$$\int_t^T \theta(u)e^{-a(T-u)}du$$

$$=f(0,T)-f(0,t)e^{-a(T-t)}+\int_t^T \frac{\sigma^2}{2a}\left(1-e^{-2au}\right)e^{-a(T-u)}du \qquad \text{(C26)}$$

and finally:

$$\int_t^T \theta(u)e^{-a(T-u)}du$$

$$=f(0,T)-f(0,t)e^{-a(T-t)}+\frac{\sigma^2}{2a^2}\left(1-e^{-a(T-t)}+e^{-2aT}-e^{-a(T+t)}\right)$$

$$\text{(C27)}$$

The distribution of the pair (r_s, r_T) is bivariate Gaussian, and the covariance between r_s and r_T is:

$$\int_t^{\min(T,\,s)} \sigma^2 e^{-a(T-u)} e^{-a(s-u)} \, du = \sigma^2 \, \frac{e^{-a(s-T)} - e^{-a(T+s-2t)}}{2a}$$

The probabilities:

$$E_t^{Q^{T_l}} \left[1\{r_s > r_0^*\} 1\{r_T > r_T^*\} \right] = Q^{T_l}\left(r_s > r_0^*, r_T > r_T^* \right) \qquad \text{(C28a)}$$

$$E_t^{Q^{T_i}} \left[1\{r_T > r_T^*\} \right] = Q^{T_i}\left(r_T > r_T^* \right) \qquad \text{(C28b)}$$

are then immediately given by one minus the cumulative density function of the bivariate and standard normal distribution. Therefore we have an explicit formula for the standalone case in the Hull and White model.

APPENDIX D – DERIVATION OF THE FORMULA FOR THE EXPECTED LOSS ON A CANCELLABLE INTEREST RATE SWAP

We analyse the pricing of a risky interest rate swap with the option to cancel. Since we consider the possibility of default by the counterparty, we need to carefully describe the different cashflows in case of default and no default. We consider only European cancellables, ie, we may only cancel the swap at a single fixed future date.

The cancellable swap is decomposed into two parts:

1. A part corresponding to cashflows that are paid when default occurs before the cancellation date. If the default occurs before the cancellation date, the bank receives the present value of a default free cancellable swap multiplied by the recovery rate when the swap value is positive. If the value of the cancellable swap is negative, the bank has to pay the future cashflows to its counterparty.
2. A part corresponding to cashflows that are paid when the default occurs after the cancellation date. If no default happens before the cancellation date, fixed and floating cashflows are exchanged, and the bank only stays in the risky swap if the value of future cashflows is positive. The exercise of the cancellable feature is equivalent to the exercise of a swaption on a risky swap.

The two aforementioned parts can be valued as follows. We denote the current date by t. The present value at date s of a risk-free and risky swaps, with payments starting at T_1 and ending at T_n are denoted by $Sw(s, T_1, T_n)$ and $\tilde{Sw}(s, T_1, T_n)$ respectively. When a cancellable feature is present, the quantities are represented by $Sw^c(s, T_1, T_n)$ or $\tilde{Sw}^c(s, T_1, T_n)$. The cancellable date is denoted by T_{n^*}, and assumed for simplicity to coincide with a payment date.

1) The first part (default before cancel date) is given by:

$$P_{1,t} = E_t \left[\int_t^{T_1} h_s \left(\exp -\int_t^s (r_u + h_u)\, du \right) \right.$$

$$\left. \times \left(\delta \left(Sw^c(s,T_1,T_n) \right)^+ + \left(Sw^c(s,T_1,T_n) \right)^- \right) ds \right]$$

$$+ \sum_{i=1}^{n^*-1} E_t \left[\int_{T_i}^{T_{i+1}} h_s \left(\exp -\int_t^s (r_u + h_u)\, du \right) \right.$$

$$\left. \times \left(\delta \left(Sw^c(s,T_{i+1},T_n) \right)^+ + \left(Sw^c(s,T_{i+1},T_n) \right)^- \right) ds \right]$$

$$\text{(D1)}$$

where E_t is the conditional expectation under the risk neutral probability measure with respect to information available at date t. As usual, r_u is the instantaneous risk free rate and h_u is the hazard rate of default.

As before, we can represent this as:

$$\delta \left(Sw^c(s,T_1,T_n) \right)^+ + \left(Sw^c(s,T_1,T_n) \right)^-$$

$$= (\delta - 1) \left(Sw^c(s,T_1,T_n) \right)^+ + Sw^c(s,T_1,T_n) \qquad \text{(D2a)}$$

and

$$\delta \left(Sw^c(s,T_{i+1},T_n) \right)^+ + \left(Sw^c(s,T_{i+1},T_n) \right)^-$$

$$= (\delta - 1) \left(Sw^c(s,T_{i+1},T_n) \right)^+ + Sw^c(s,T_{i+1},T_n) \qquad \text{(D2b)}$$

Therefore, in case of default, we have a swaption type payout plus a risk-free cancellable swap.

2) The second part (default after cancel date) is given by:

$$P_{2,t} = \sum_{i=1}^{n^*} E_t \left[\left(\exp -\int_t^{T_i} (r_u + h_u)\, du \right) \left(L_{i-1} - \kappa \right) \Delta \right]$$

$$+ E_t \left[\left(\exp -\int_t^{T_{n^*}} (r_u + h_u)\, du \right) \left(\tilde{S}w(T_{n^*},T_{n^*+1},T_n) \right)^+ \right] \qquad \text{(D3)}$$

Equation (D3), when the default aspect is neglected ($\tilde{S}w(T_{n^*},T_{n^*+1},T_n)$

replaced by $Sw(T_{n*}, T_{n*+1}, T_n))$ is equal to:

$$P_{2,t}^* = \sum_{i=1}^{n} E_t \left[\left(\exp - \int_t^{T_i} (r_u + h_u) \, du \right) \left(L_{i-1} - \kappa \right) \Delta \right]$$

$$+ E_t \left[\left(\exp - \int_t^{T_{n*}} (r_u + h_u) \, du \right) \left(- Sw(T_{n*}, T_{n*+1}, T_n) \right)^+ \right] \quad \text{(D4)}$$

which corresponds to the cashflows of a default-free cancellable swap on the whole period (swap plus swaption payout based on the reverse swap). In that case, by comparing $P_{1,t}$ and $P_{2,t'}$ we see that no matter whether or not default occurs, a default-free cancellable swap is always put in place. It means that the risky cancellable swap can then be decomposed as a sum of swaptions on cancellable swaps and a risk-free cancellable swap, ie, a swap and a swaption on the reverse swap:

$$P_{1,t} + P_{2,t}^* =$$

$$E_t \left[\int_t^{T_1} h_s \left(\exp - \int_t^{s} (r_u + h_u) \, du \right) (\delta - 1) \left(Sw^c(s, T_1, T_n) \right)^+ ds \right]$$

$$+ \sum_{i=1}^{n*-1} E_t \left[\int_{T_i}^{T_{i+1}} h_s \left(\exp - \int_t^{s} (r_u + h_u) \, du \right) (\delta - 1) \left(Sw^c(s, T_{i+1}, T_n) \right)^+ ds \right]$$

$$+ \sum_{i=1}^{n} E_t \left[\left(\exp - \int_t^{T_i} r_u \, du \right) \left(L_{i-1} - \kappa \right) \Delta \right]$$

$$+ Sn^{rev}(t, T_{n*}, T_{n*+1}, T_n) \quad \text{(D5)}$$

Similarly to the standard swap, the above expression can be written as the risk-free PV of the cancellable swap (swap + reverse swaption) minus the expected loss on the cancellable. However, the decomposition in Equation (D5) is not valid if the decision to cancel the swap is made on the basis of the risky present value $\tilde{Sw}(T_{n*}, T_{n*+1}, T_n)$ of the swap in place of the default-free value $Sw(T_{n*}, T_{n*+1}, T_n)$. In this case, the expression for the expected loss will not be so simple, since the following full expression should be used instead:

$$P_{1,t} + P_{2,t} = E_t \left[\int_t^{T_1} h_s \left(\exp - \int_t^s (r_u + h_u)\,du \right) \right.$$

$$\left. \times \left((\delta - 1)\left(Sw^c(s,T_1,T_n) \right)^+ + Sw^c(s,T_1,T_n) \right) ds \right]$$

$$+ \sum_{i=1}^{n^*-1} E_t \left[\int_{T_i}^{T_{i+1}} h_s \left(\exp - \int_t^s (r_u + h_u)\,du \right) \right.$$

$$\left. \times \left((\delta - 1)\left(Sw^c(s,T_{i+1},T_n) \right)^+ + Sw^c(s,T_{i+1},T_n) \right) ds \right]$$

$$+ \sum_{i=1}^{n^*} E_t \left[\left(\exp - \int_t^{T_i} (r_u + h_u)\,du \right) \left(L_{i-1} - \kappa \right) \Delta \right]$$

$$+ E_t \left[\left(\exp - \int_t^{T_{n^*}} (r_u + h_u)\,du \right) \left(\tilde{S}w(T_{n^*},T_{n^*+1},T_n) \right)^+ \right] \qquad \text{(D6)}$$

The previous pricing formula for the cancellable swap can be implemented, assuming a piecewise constant hazard rate and an instantaneous risk-free rate, with dynamics as described by an Ornstein–Uhlenbeck process with time-varying mean (Hull and White or extended Vasicek model). On the basis of these assumptions, we are in fact able to compute an explicit formula.

Let us start with the first two components of Equation (D6). From the application of Fubini's Theorem we have:

$$\int_{T_i}^{T_{i+1}} E_t \left[h_s \left(\exp - \int_t^s (r_u + h_u)\,du \right) \right.$$

$$\left. \times \left((\delta - 1)\left(Sw^c(s,T_{i+1},T_n) \right)^+ + Sw^c(s,T_{i+1},T_n) \right) \right] ds \qquad \text{(D7)}$$

Due to the independence between the hazard rate and the risk-free rate, we may disentangle the default and interest rate parts. This leads to:

$$
\int\limits_{T_i}^{T_{i+1}} E_t \left[h_s \left(\exp - \int\limits_t^s h_u \, du \right) \right]
$$

$$
\times E_t \left[\left(\exp - \int\limits_t^s r_u \, du \right) \right.
$$

$$
\left. \times \left((\delta - 1) \left(Sw^c(s, T_{i+1}, T_n) \right)^+ + Sw^c(s, T_{i+1}, T_n) \right) \right] ds \qquad \text{(D8)}
$$

The default parts $E_t\left[h_s\left(\exp - \int_t^s h_u \, du\right)\right]$ are obtained through the output probabilities given by a default stripper.

The first interest part is given by:

$$
E_t \left[\left(\exp - \int\limits_t^s r_u \, du \right) \left(Sw^c(s, T_{i+1}, T_n) \right)^+ \right]
$$

$$
= E_t \left[\left(\exp - \int\limits_t^s r_u \, du \right) \left(Sw(s, T_{i+1}, T_n) + Sn^{rev}(s, T_{n*}, T_{n*+1}, T_n) \right)^+ \right]
$$

$$
\text{(D9)}
$$

Let us denote r_i^* the value of the instantaneous interest rate at date s, so that the sum of the swap value and the value of the swaption on the reverse swap is zero. We also denote by $\bar{r}_{n*}$ the value of the instantaneous interest rate at date T_{n*}, so that the value of the reverse swap in the swaption is zero. As usual, Q^{T_l} denotes the forward measure associated with the discount bond with maturity T_l. The above expression can be written as:

$$
\sum\limits_{l=i}^{n} c_l B(t, T_l) E_t^{Q^{T_l}} \left[1\{ r_s > r_i^* \} \right]
$$

$$
+ \sum\limits_{l=n*}^{n} d_l B(t, T_l) E_t^{Q^{T_l}} \left[1\{ r_s > r_i^* \} 1\{ r_{T_{n*}} < \bar{r}_{n*} \} \right] \qquad \text{(D10)}
$$

where the cashflows in the swaps are:

$$c_i = 1, c_{i+1} = ... = c_{n-1} = -\kappa\Delta, c_n = -1 - \kappa\Delta \qquad \textbf{(D11a)}$$

$$d_{n*} = -1, d_{n*+1} = ... = d_{n-1} = \kappa\Delta, d_n = 1 + \kappa\Delta \qquad \textbf{(D11b)}$$

The second interest rate part, without the positivity condition, is very similar, except that the condition $1\{r_s > r_i^*\}$ is not present.

The third term in Equation (D6) (due to the independence between the hazard rate and the risk-free rate) is given by:

$$\sum_{i=1}^{n*} E_t\left[\left(\exp - \int_t^{T_i} h_u\, du\right)\right]$$

$$\times E_t\left[\left(\exp - \int_t^{T_i} r_u\, du\right)\left(L_{i-1} - \kappa\right)\Delta\right] \qquad \textbf{(D12)}$$

The default part is again obtained through the output probabilities given by a default stripper, while the interest rate part is a standard swap $\sum_{l=0}^{n*} c_l B(t, T_l)$ with

$$c_0 = 1, c_1 = ... = c_{n*-1} = -\kappa\Delta, c_{n*} = -1 - \kappa\Delta$$

Finally, in the fourth term in Equation (D6), we still need to compute the interest rate part:

$$E_t\left[\left(\exp - \int_t^{T_{n*}} r_u\, du\right)\left(\tilde{S}w(T_{n*}, T_{n*+1}, T_n)\right)^+\right] \qquad \textbf{(D13)}$$

Let us denote $\bar{\bar{r}}_{n*}$ the value of the instantaneous interest rate at date T_{n*}, so that the default swap value $\tilde{S}w(T_{n*}, T_{n*+1}, T_n)$ is zero. This leads to:

$$E_t\left[\left(\exp - \int_t^{T_{n*}} r_u\, du\right)\left(\tilde{S}w(T_{n*}, T_{n*+1}, T_n)\right)1\{r_{T_{n*}} > \bar{\bar{r}}_{n*}\}\right] \qquad \textbf{(D14)}$$

which gives:

$$E_t \left\{ \exp - \int_t^{T_{n^*}} r_s \, ds \right.$$

$$\times \left[\int_{T_{n^*}}^{T_{n^*+1}} E_{T_{n^*}} \left[h_s \exp\left(- \int_{T_{n^*}}^s h_u \, du \right) \right] (\delta - 1) \right.$$

$$\times \sum_{l=n^*}^n c_l B(T_{n^*}, T_l) E_{T_{n^*}}^{Q^{T_l}} \left[1\left\{ r_s > \bar{\bar{r}}_{n^*} \right\} \right] ds$$

$$+ \sum_{i=n^*+1}^n \int_{T_i}^{T_{i+1}} E_{T_{n^*}} \left[h_s \exp\left(- \int_{T_{n^*}}^s h_u \, du \right) \right] (\delta - 1)$$

$$\times \sum_{l=i}^n c_l B(T, T_l) E_{T_{n^*}}^{Q^{T_l}} \left[1\left\{ r_s > \bar{\bar{r}}_i \right\} \right] ds$$

$$+ B(T_{n^*}, T_{n^*}) - \left. \sum_{i=n^*+1}^n \kappa \Delta B(T_{n^*}, T_i) - B(T_{n^*}, T_n) \right]$$

$$\left. \times 1\left\{ r_{T_{n^*}} > \bar{\bar{r}}_{n^*} \right\} \right\} \quad \textbf{(D15)}$$

Again using the forward neutral measure we get:

$$\int_{T_{n^*}}^{T_{n^*+1}} E_{T_{n^*}} \left[h_s \exp\left(- \int_{T_{n^*}}^s h_u \, du \right) \right] (\delta - 1)$$

$$\times \sum_{l=n^*}^n c_l B(t, T_l) E_t^{Q^{T_l}} \left[1\left\{ r_s > \bar{\bar{r}}_{n^*} \right\} 1\left\{ r_{T_{n^*}} > \bar{\bar{r}}_{n^*} \right\} \right] ds$$

$$+ \sum_{i=n^*+1}^n \int_{T_i}^{T_{i+1}} E_{T_{n^*}} \left[h_s \exp\left(- \int_{T_{n^*}}^s h_u \, du \right) \right] (\delta - 1)$$

$$\times \sum_{l=i}^n c_l B(t, T_l) E_t^{Q^{T_l}} \left[1\left\{ r_s > \bar{\bar{r}}_i \right\} 1\left\{ r_{T_{n^*}} > \bar{\bar{r}}_{n^*} \right\} \right] ds$$

$$+\left[B(t,T_{n^*})E_t^{Q^{T_{n^*}}}\left[1\left\{r_{T_{n^*}}>\bar{\bar{r}}_{n^*}\right\}\right]\right.$$

$$-\sum_{i=n^*+1}^{n}\kappa\Delta B(t,T_i)E_t^{Q^{T_i}}\left[1\left\{r_{T_{n^*}}>\bar{\bar{r}}_{n^*}\right\}\right]-B(t,T_n)E_t^{Q^{T_n}}$$

$$\left.\times\left[1\left\{r_{T_{n^*}}>\bar{\bar{r}}_{n^*}\right\}\right]\right]$$

$$(D16)$$

In order to compute the above expressions, we need to exhibit the joint distribution of, for example, the pair $(r_s, r_{T_{n^*}})$ under the different forward neutral measures. In the Hull and White model, the instantaneous interest rate is distributed as an Ornstein–Uhlenbeck process with a time-varying drift under the risk neutral measure:

$$dr_t = (\theta(t) - ar_t)dt + \sigma dW_t \qquad (D17)$$

or equivalently under an integrated form:

$$r_{T_{n^*}} = e^{-a(T_{n^*}-t)}r_t + \int_t^{T_{n^*}}\theta(u)e^{-a(T_{n^*}-u)}du + \int_t^{T_{n^*}}\sigma e^{-a(T_{n^*}-u)}dW_u \quad (D18)$$

From Girsanov's Theorem, we know that $dW_t^{Q^{T_l}} = dW_t - \sigma(t,T_l)dt$ is a standard Brownian motion. The diffusion term $\sigma(t,T_l)$ is the volatility of the discount bond with maturity T_l – in the extended Vasicek model:

$$\sigma(t,T_l) = -\sigma\frac{1-\exp\left(-a(T_l-t)\right)}{a}$$

Hence we get:

$$dr_t = (\theta(t) + \sigma\sigma(t,T_l) - ar_t)dt + \sigma dW_t \qquad (D19)$$

The integration gives:

$$r_{T_{n^*}} = e^{-a(T_{n^*}-t)}r_t$$

$$+\int_t^{T_{n^*}}\left(\theta(u)+\sigma\sigma(u,T_l)\right)e^{-a(T_{n^*}-u)}du + \int_t^{T_{n^*}}\sigma e^{-a(T_{n^*}-u)}dW_u \qquad (D20)$$

Hence, we calculate that the conditional distribution of $r_{T_{n^*}}$ knowing r_t is a normal distribution:

$$r_{T_{n^*}} \bigg|_{r_t} \sim N\left(e^{-a(T_{n^*}-t)} r_t + \int_t^{T_{n^*}} \left(\theta(u) + \sigma\sigma(u,T_l) \right) \right.$$
$$\left. \times e^{-a(T_{n^*}-u)} du, \int_t^{T_{n^*}} \sigma^2 e^{-2a(T_{n^*}-u)} du \right) \qquad \text{(D21)}$$

Of course, this expression is also valid for the conditional distribution of r_s knowing r_t. The variance is equal to $\sigma^2[(1 - e^{-2a(T_{n^*}-t)})/2a]$, while

$$\int_t^{T_{n^*}} \sigma\sigma(u,T_l) e^{-a(T_{n^*}-u)} du$$

$$= -\frac{\sigma^2}{2a^2}\left[2\left(1 - e^{-a(T_{n^*}-t)}\right) - \left(e^{-a(T_l-T_{n^*})} - e^{-a(T_{n^*}+T_l-2t)} \right) \right] \qquad \text{(D22)}$$

In the above expression, $\int_t^{T_{n^*}} \theta(u) e^{-a(T_{n^*}-u)} du$ is computed as follows. In the Hull and White model, the time-varying drift is equal to:

$$\theta(u) = \frac{\partial}{\partial u} f(0,u) + \lambda f(0,u) + \frac{\sigma^2}{2a}\left(1 - e^{-2au}\right)$$

where $f(0,u)$ is the instantaneous forward rate at date 0 with maturity u. Using:

$$\int_t^{T_{n^*}} \frac{\partial}{\partial u} f(0,u) e^{-a(T_{n^*}-u)} du$$

$$= f(0,T_{n^*}) - f(0,t) e^{-a(T_{n^*}-t)} - \int_t^{T_{n^*}} f(0,u) \lambda e^{-a(T_{n^*}-u)} du \qquad \text{(D23)}$$

from the integration by part formula, we get the simplification:

$$\int_t^{T_{n^*}} \theta(u) e^{-a(T_{n^*}-u)} du$$

$$= f(0,T_{n^*}) - f(0,t) e^{-a(T_{n^*}-t)} + \int_t^{T_{n^*}} \frac{\sigma^2}{2a}\left(1 - e^{-2au}\right) e^{-a(T_{n^*}-u)} du \qquad \text{(D24)}$$

and finally:

$$\int_t^{T_{n*}} \theta(u) e^{-a(T_{n*}-u)} du$$

$$= f(0, T_{n*}) - f(0, t) e^{-a(T_{n*}-t)}$$

$$+ \frac{\sigma^2}{2a^2} \left(1 - e^{-a(T_{n*}-t)} + e^{-2aT_{n*}} - e^{-a(T_{n*}+t)} \right)$$

$$(D25)$$

The distribution of the pair $(r_s, r_{T_{n*}})$ is bivariate Gaussian and the covariance between r_s and $r_{T_{n*}}$ is:

$$\int_t^{\min(T_{n*}, s)} \sigma^2 e^{-a(T_{n*}-u)} e^{-a(s-u)} du$$

$$= \sigma^2 \frac{e^{-a(s-T_{n*})} - e^{-a(T_{n*}+s-2t)}}{2a}$$

The probabilities:

$$E_t^{Q^{T_l}} \left[1\left\{ r_s > \bar{\bar{r}}_{n*} \right\} 1\left\{ r_{T_{n*}} > \bar{\bar{r}}_{n*} \right\} \right]$$

$$= Q^{T_l} \left(r_s > \bar{\bar{r}}_{n*}, r_{T_{n*}} > \bar{\bar{r}}_{n*} \right) \qquad (D26a)$$

$$E_t^{Q^{T_l}} \left[1\left\{ r_s > \bar{\bar{r}}_i \right\} 1\left\{ r_{T_{n*}} > \bar{\bar{r}}_{n*} \right\} \right]$$

$$= Q^{T_l} \left(r_s > \bar{\bar{r}}_i, r_{T_{n*}} > \bar{\bar{r}}_{n*} \right) \qquad (D26b)$$

$$E_t^{Q^{T_l}} \left[1\left\{ r_{T_{n*}} > \bar{\bar{r}}_{n*} \right\} \right]$$

$$= Q^{T_i} \left(r_{T_{n*}} > \bar{\bar{r}}_{n*} \right) \qquad (D26c)$$

are then given by one minus the cdf of the bivariate and the standard normal distribution. Similar expressions can be obtained for other probabilities involved in the pricing. Therefore, we have an explicit formula for risky cancellable swap in the Hull and White model.

APPENDIX E – MARKET PARAMETERS USED FOR THE COMPUTATIONS

1. Interest rate parameters.

	Short-rate volatility (σ)	Short-rate mean reversion (α)
US$	1.56%	0.095
euro	1.34%	0.108
UK£	1.58%	0.097
Japan ¥	1.35%	0.053

2. FX parameters

	FX volatility (σ_{FX})
US$/euro	12.2%
US$/UK£	9.1%
US$/Japan ¥	13.4%

7

Credit Risk in Convertible Bonds

In this chapter, we proceed with the next topic: the impact of credit risk on the pricing of convertible bonds. This work has been motivated by the substantial growth of the US high-yield, convertible bond market and the expectation that a similar market will develop in Europe, supported by the advent of a common currency. We restrict the analysis mainly to exploring how credit risk can be incorporated into the relevant pricing models and do not describe the plethora of other products that are traded in this market (eg, Warrants, Dividend Enhanced Common Stock (DECS), Equity Linked Securities (ELKS)). A comprehensive exposition of the latter can be found in recent texts such as Calamos (1998), Connelly (1998) and Nelken (2000).

7.1 INTRODUCTION

This chapter is structured as follows. First, for completeness, we present some standard results on the pricing of convertible bonds that are model independent and assume that the firm will honour its financial obligations. Second, we show how these conditions can be expanded to take credit risk into account. We describe two models with different characteristics, both of which explicitly take credit risk into account. We will refer to them as the "Credit Spread" and the "Firm Value" models. The two models have different specifications, and in a later section of this chapter we show how they can be reconciled and their parameterisations interconnected.

A convertible bond (CB) is an investment vehicle that has features of both debt and equity. Therefore, both the level of the risk-free interest rates and the share price of the issuing firm drive the price of the CB. The pricing of CBs is a two-factor problem that is substantially more complex to solve than the pricing of straight bonds. In addition, for low-graded companies, there might be a significant chance that the issuer will default on the bond payments. To address this element of credit risk, we have to incorporate the credit spread of the issuer in the analysis. This further complicates the pricing theory, since we have to solve a three-factor problem, which can be intractable.

The Credit Spread model

The Credit Spread model, an extension of a two-factor model for the interest rate and stock price, assumes that the credit spread is a function of the latter. Originally, this relationship is assumed deterministic, but later on a stochastic element is introduced. This specification has been motivated by the fact that a decline in the underlying stock price is likely to be accompanied by a deterioration of the credit quality of the issuer. We will concentrate on the modelling of this relationship between the credit spread and the stock price.

The Firm Value model

The Firm Value model is an application of the Black–Scholes–Merton model (Black and Scholes, 1973, and Merton, 1973). It is also based on ideas presented in Brennan and Schwartz (1980). It assumes a certain process for the risk-free interest rates and the value of the issuing firm. A fundamental difference between the two models is the way in which the equity component is described. In the Credit Spread model, the equity is represented by the stock price, whereas in the Firm Value model, it is the value of the firm itself. This leads to different specifications and strengths and weaknesses of the two models, which we will discuss.

7.2 BASIC FEATURES OF CONVERTIBLES

The holder of a CB has the right to convert the bond into a predetermined number of shares of common stock. It is, therefore, a corporate bond with an embedded call option on the underlying stock. The number of shares that the CB holder will receive from conversion of the bond is given by the *conversion ratio*. If the share price rises significantly, there is a considerable probability that the CB will be converted, while if the share does not perform well, there is limited downside since it will be redeemed like an ordinary straight bond. As long as the bond has not been converted, the holder will receive coupons in the usual way.

The conversion privilege is expressed either in terms of the price at which the bonds are convertible into common stock, the *conversion price* (CVP_t) or the number of shares into which each bond is convertible, ie, the *conversion ratio* (q_t). These two measures, which may be specified to change over time, are related by

$$q_t = \frac{Par}{CVP_t} \tag{1}$$

Example: Typical convertible bond
Notional:	US$100
Coupon:	4.5% annual
Conversion price:	US$5

Conversion ratio: 20
Underlying share price: US$4
Maturity: 5 years

Consider the following two possibilities at the maturity of the CB:

1. The share price is US$3. Conversion would yield only US$60 worth of equity. The holder would instead redeem the bond at US$100.
2. The share price is US$8. The holder would convert the bond and receive US$160 worth of equity.

It is the upside potential that can drive the price of the convertible above its par value, even if interest rates are higher than its coupon. Note that conversion can occur at times other than maturity.

CBs are commonly callable by the issuer (and sometimes putable by the holder). This means that the issuer can call the bond for a predetermined price. If a convertible bond is called, then the holder has the option to sell the bond back to the issuer for the *call price* or to convert it into shares of the issuer, indeed a call will normally force conversion. The holder may alternatively decide to put the bond back to the issuer at the *put price*. Finally, convertible bonds are subject to default risk, since the issuer may default at any time during the life of the CB and an amount up to its entire value of the CB at the default time may be lost.

7.3 GENERAL PRICING CONDITIONS

Next, we derive some fundamental boundary conditions satisfied by the CBs that are model independent. The value at time t of the CB, if it has not been called, is given by:

$$C_t = \max\left(HV_t, PP_t, CV_t \right) \tag{2}$$

This states that the holder will choose the highest value between the "hold" value (HV_t) which is the expected value of the bond if not converted or sold, the put price (PP_t) and the conversion value based on the current conversion price ($CV_t = q_t S_t$).

The value at time t of the CB, if it has been called, is given by:

$$C_t = \max\left(CP_t, PP_t, CV_t \right) \tag{3}$$

The holder will choose the highest value among the call price (CP_t), the put price and the conversion value. He can either surrender the CB to the issuer at the call price, he can decide to put it if the put price is higher (it would seem unlikely that a contract would be structured in this way), or he can convert it. Since the CB has been called, he does not have the option to just hold it.

The holder of the CB should put it when its market value falls below the put price. The put condition is therefore $C_t \leq PP_t$. A convertible should be called as soon as its market value is greater than its call price. The call condition is therefore $C_t \geq CP_t$. Both of these conditions assume that the holder and issuer act optimally, ie, to maximise and minimise the price respectively.

We will assume throughout that the issuer will follow a call strategy that will minimise the CB's value and therefore maximise the share price. This is a standard assumption, but we do show how to incorporate the effect of sub-optimal call policies (which is not really a credit issue) in Appendix C. On the other hand, the holder will act optimally as described in Equations (2) and (3) in order to maximise the value of the CB. This jointly optimal behaviour of both parties is described by Equation (5). The "min" operator reflects the behaviour of the issuer, who will call only when the call price is lower than the "hold" value.

$$C_t = \max\left(\min\left(HV_t, CP_t\right), PP_t, CV_t\right) \tag{4}$$

The above equation at maturity T can be simplified as follows:

$$C_T = \max\left(F^C, PP_T, CV_T\right) \tag{5}$$

The holder has the choice among getting the face value F^C, the put price or the conversion value. Equations (4) and (5) implicitly assume that the firm has sufficient funds to meet any payments. In particular, they do not take into account the possibility of default. We will discuss this later.

7.4 INTEREST RATE MODEL

Since there are two sources of uncertainty in the pricing, namely the risk-free interest rate and the firm value or the stock price, we must model these two sources of risk together. For the interest rate, any standard term structure model can be used. We will use the Hull and White model, as we have done in the previous chapter, in which the dynamics of the short rate are:

$$dr_t = \left(\theta(t) - ar_t\right)dt + \sigma_r dz \tag{6}$$

where dz is a Gauss–Wiener process (Brownian motion). The volatility σ_r and the mean-reversion rate a are constants. $\theta(t)$ is chosen to match the initial risk-free term structure (yield curve).

Since a CB is generally callable and convertible at any time, there are embedded American-type options. This means that a finite-difference or tree method must be used, as Monte Carlo is not readily applicable to American features. The interest rate implementation therefore uses a trinomial tree. The extra degree of freedom given by a trinomial tree allows

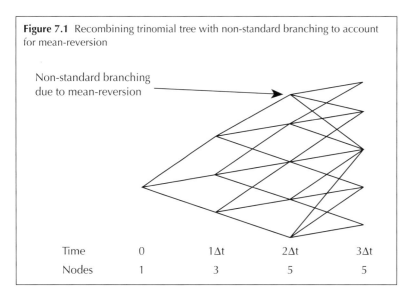

Figure 7.1 Recombining trinomial tree with non-standard branching to account for mean-reversion

Non-standard branching
due to mean-reversion

Time	0	$1\Delta t$	$2\Delta t$	$3\Delta t$
Nodes	1	3	5	5

easier matching of the initial term structure. The procedure described by Hull and White (1993) allows the tree to be built and then displaced so as to match the risk-free term structure. When mean-reversion is used, the tree-building procedure needs to be modified to accommodate non-standard branching when the interest rate is further away from the mean. This ensures that the probabilities are always positive. An illustration of such a trinomial tree is shown in Figure 7.1.

7.5 FIRM VALUE MODEL

In the first instance, we consider directly modelling the evolution of the value of a firm; for ease of exposition, this is assumed to have only common stock, straight debt and convertible debt outstanding. Of course, it is possible to handle more complex capital structures. The advantage of this model is that it provides a comprehensive and self-consistent approach for pricing any security, modelling default and determining the recovery rate and the credit spread volatility. It also incorporates the smile, ie, the dependence of the stock volatility on its price that is endogenous to the Firm Value model. The disadvantage of the model is that we need to estimate the capital structure of the firm (ie, assets/liabilities). Also, the conversion shares must be from the same firm that issued the CB. We assume that the convertible bonds are junior to the straight debt, as is normally the case. For ease of exposition, the straight debt is assumed to have the same maturity as the CBs. Both these assumptions can be lifted. In the next section, we define certain quantities that will be useful in presenting the model. The definitions in this section are independent of the process followed by the firm value.

7.5.1 Model specification

The firm value V_t at time t before conversion of any CBs, equals the sum of the market values of all outstanding securities:

$$V_t = N^B B_t + N^C CV_t + N^S S_t^{BC} \tag{7}$$

B_t – Market value of senior bonds $\qquad N^B$ – Number of senior bonds
CV_t – Market value of convertibles $\qquad N^C$ – Number of convertibles
S_t^{BC} – Share price (before conversion) $\quad N^S$ – Number of shares
Similarly, after conversion, the market value of the firm is given by:

$$V_t = N^B B_t + (N^S + \Delta N^S) S_t^{AC} \tag{8}$$

where ΔN^S is the number of shares issued as a result of conversion and S_t^{AC} is the stock price after conversion has taken place.

Expressed in terms of the conversion ratio, q_t, the total number of new shares issued on conversion (ΔN^S) is given by:

$$\Delta N^S = N^C \times q_t \tag{9}$$

The fraction of the total shares owned by the holder of each convertible after conversion, the so-called dilution ratio (Z_t) is given by the number of shares received by converting a single bond divided by the total number of shares, ie,

$$Z_t = \frac{q_t}{N^S + \Delta N^S} \tag{10}$$

By making the standard assumption that all CBs are converted simultaneously, their individual values after conversion (CV_t) are given by:

$$CV_t = q_t \times S_t^{AC} = \frac{q_t}{N^S + \Delta N^S} \left(V_t - N^B B_t \right) = Z_t \left(V_t - N^B B_t \right) \tag{11}$$

We assume that the firm value (V_t) follows a diffusion process, represented by the following equation:

$$\frac{dV_t}{V_t} = \left(\mu_V - Q(V_t, t) \right) dt + \sigma_V dW_t \tag{12}$$

where μ_V is the total rate of return on the firm's value and σ_V is its volatility. $Q(V, t)$ is the total rate of cash distribution to the firm's security holders in the form of coupon payments (to the senior bondholders and convertible holders) and dividends (to the shareholders).

Based on the Black–Scholes and Merton models, it is possible for

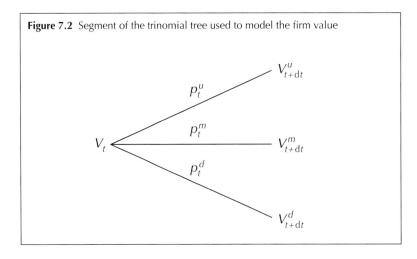

Figure 7.2 Segment of the trinomial tree used to model the firm value

simplified products to derive some closed-form solutions to the PDE for the firm value (we present this in Appendix A). For most products, the solution must be computed numerically and this is our next topic.

7.5.2 Implementation

The evolution of the firm value is modelled using a trinomial tree, as shown in Figure 7.2.

At each node in the tree, the firm value moves for the next period are given by:

$$V_{t+dt}^{u} = V_t\, u \qquad V_{t+dt}^{m} = V_t \qquad V_{t+dt}^{d} = V_t / u \tag{13}$$

where $u = e^{\sigma \sqrt{3 dt}}$.

The three probabilities can be chosen to match the following conditions:

$$p_t^u + p_t^m + p_t^d = 1$$

$$\left(p_t^u\, V_{t+dt}^u + p_t^m\, V_{t+dt}^m + p_t^d\, V_{t+dt}^d\right) = V_t\, e^{\mu_V\, dt}$$

$$p_t^u \left(V_{t+dt}^u\right)^2 + p_t^u \left(V_{t+dt}^u\right)^2 + p_t^u \left(V_{t+dt}^u\right)^2 -$$

$$\left(p_t^u\, V_{t+dt}^u + p_t^m\, V_{t+dt}^u + p_t^d\, V_{t+dt}^u\right)^2 = V_t\, e^{2\mu_V\, dt}\left(e^{\sigma_V^2\, dt} - 1\right) \tag{14.abc}$$

where μ_V and σ_V are as defined above. The solution of the above problem is fairly standard and can be found, for example, in Hull (1996, p. 360). We also show the derivation under more general conditions (including a default leg) in Appendix B. The above choice of the parameter values

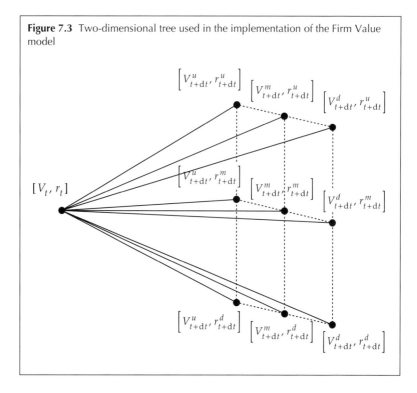

Figure 7.3 Two-dimensional tree used in the implementation of the Firm Value model

allows us to match the mean and the variance of the underlying lognormal process and ensure that the probabilities sum to one.

In order to take into account the stochastic nature of the interest rates and the firm value, we need a two-dimensional tree. This is a discrete time implementation of Equations (6) and (12), using a small time step dt (ie, so that the total number of steps is around 50–200). A representative segment of such a tree is shown in Figure 7.3.

Using backward induction, we can price on the tree any security that depends on the value of the firm and the risk-free interest rates. Therefore, products that can be priced include risky bonds, callable bonds, bond options, warrants and all varieties of convertible securities. This is done by first determining the value of the security at each one of the terminal nodes, using the boundary conditions given by Equation (5). As we move backward through the tree, the price of the security at each node at time t equals its discounted (at r_t) expectation from the nine nodes at time $t + 1$.

$$HV_t = \exp\left(-r_t \, dt\right) \left(\sum_{i,j=1}^{3} p_t^{ij} \, CV_{t+dt}^{ij} \right)$$
(15)

Table 7.1 Illustration of the incorporation of a correlation of ρ via modified transition probabilities in the two-dimensional tree ($\varepsilon = \rho/36$)

		Firm value movement		
		V_{t+dt}^d	V_{t+dt}^m	V_{t+dt}^u
Interest rate	r_{t+dt}^u	$p_t^u \bar{p}_t^d - \varepsilon$	$p_t^u \bar{p}_t^m - 4\varepsilon$	$p_t^u \bar{p}_t^u + 5\varepsilon$
movement	r_{t+dt}^m	$p_t^m \bar{p}_t^d - 4\varepsilon$	$p_t^m \bar{p}_t^m + 8\varepsilon$	$p_t^m \bar{p}_t^u - 4\varepsilon$
	r_{t+dt}^d	$p_t^d \bar{p}_t^d + 5\varepsilon$	$p_t^d \bar{p}_t^m - 4\varepsilon$	$p_t^d \bar{p}_t^u - \varepsilon$

where r_t is the interest rate at the node at time t, CV_{t+1}^{ij} is the value of the convertible at the node (i, j) at time $t + dt$ and p_t^{ij} is the probability of reaching that node. Once HV_t has been computed, we should apply Equation (4) in order to determine whether call, put or conversion is optimal before continuing backwards through the tree.

7.5.3 Correlation
When there is no correlation between the firm value and the interest rates, the two trees can be combined by simply multiplying the corresponding branch probabilities. When there is correlation, the procedure becomes more complex, but can be achieved as described in Hull and White (1994). This involves modifying the transition probabilities, as shown in Table 7.1.

7.5.4 Boundary conditions
Next, we define the boundary conditions in the Firm Value model for valuing CBs at maturity. After the (senior) straight bond principal payments have been made, the amount left to pay the convertible bondholders will be $V_T - N^B(F^B + c^B)$, where F^B and c^B are the face value and coupon of the straight debt. From Equation (5), the value of the convertible at maturity for a given terminal firm value V_T can be expressed as follows:

$$CV_T = \max\left(\left(F^C + c^C\right), PP_T, Z_T\left(V_T - N^B\left(F^B + c^B\right)\right)\right) \tag{16}$$

where F^C and c^C are the face value and the coupon of the convertible debt. However, this expression ignores credit risk. In order to include it, we have to account for the fact that $V_T - N^B(F^B + c^B)$ may not be sufficient to pay the convertible bondholders, ie:

$$CV_T = \min\left(\begin{array}{l} \max\left(\left(F^C + c^C\right), P_T, Z_T\left(V_T - N^B\left(F^B + c^B\right)\right)\right) \\ \max\left(\dfrac{1}{N^C}\left(V_T - N^B\left(F^B + c^B\right)\right), 0\right) \end{array} \right) \tag{17}$$

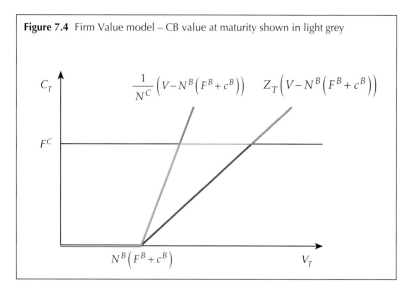

Figure 7.4 Firm Value model – CB value at maturity shown in light grey

The first term in the above equation states the fact that the CB holder will follow the strategy that maximises the CB's payout, ie, redeem it at its face value, put it to the issuer or convert it. The second term simply expresses the fact that the CB holder can only receive what is left after the senior bonds have been redeemed. If the second term is smaller than the first one, then the CB issuer is in default and the recovery amount is

$$\max\left(\frac{1}{N^C}\left(V_T - N^B\left(F^B + c^B\right)\right),\, 0\right)$$

More explicitly the above equation can be rewritten as:

$$CV_T = \begin{cases} Z_T\left(V_T - N^B\left(F^B + c^B\right)\right) & \text{if } Z_T\left(V_T - N^B\left(F^B + c^B\right)\right) \geq \left(F^C + c^C\right) \\[2mm] F^C + c^C & \text{if } Z_T\left(V_T - N^B\left(F^B + c^B\right)\right) \leq F^C \\[2mm] & \leq \frac{1}{N^C}\left(V_T - N^B\left(F^B + c^B\right)\right) \\[2mm] \frac{1}{N^C}\left(V_T - N^B F^B\right) & \text{if } F^C \geq \frac{1}{N^C}\left(V_T - N^B\left(F^B + c^B\right)\right) \geq 0 \\[2mm] 0 & \text{if } V_T \leq N^B\left(F^B + c^B\right) \end{cases} \qquad (18)$$

From top to bottom in Equation (18) the firm value is decreasing. The terms of the equation correspond to conversion, redemption at par, default with recovery (senior bonds fully paid) and default with no recovery (senior bonds defaulted). Figure 7.4 provides a graphical representation of the above equation.

Equation (18) can be modified to give the value of the convertible before maturity. This must account for the call provision and accrued interest. Default can still occur before maturity if coupon payments cannot be made or if the convertible bonds are put by the holders.

7.5.5 Treatment of coupons

The treatment of coupon payments when modelling the firm value directly adds a complexity. Due to the decrease of the value of the firm by a fixed amount at a given point in time, the tree does not recombine. This is analogous to the problem of modelling absolute, rather than proportional dividends as described by Hull (1999, pp. 354–5). The problem can be simplified by assuming that the present value of all future coupons (not necessarily the one at maturity) is non-stochastic and modelling the remaining firm value, denoted by V^*. We therefore assume that the volatility of V^*, rather than V is constant and is denoted by σ^*. We can build a tree for V^* in the usual way, where the starting value is obtained by subtracting the present value of the $N-1$ coupons from the firm value:

$$V_0^* = V_0 - \sum_{i=1}^{N-1} C_i \, Df(t_i) \tag{19}$$

where t_i represents the time at which the ith coupon is paid and $Df(t_i)$ is the discount factor at this time. At a given time point in the tree, t_j, the actual firm value, taking into account the coupons that have not yet been paid is given by:

$$V_t = V_t^* + \sum_{i \geq j}^{N-1} C_i \, Df(t_i) \tag{20}$$

Note that this assumption puts a lower bound on the recovery rate, which is the present value of the coupons (except the one at maturity). As a result, default can occur only at maturity.

Note that if the dividend payment is not chosen to be proportional to the firm value, the tree will not be recombining and we must cope with this in a similar way.

7.5.6 Seniority

We briefly describe how to relax the assumption that the straight debt is strictly senior to the CBs, since in reality there can be some recovery on a note, even if the more senior tranche cannot be repaid fully. Assuming that the firm is in default and denoting the recovery rates for the straight debt and the CBs as δ^B and δ^C respectively, we have to set the recovery rates such that:

$$V_T = N^B \delta^B + N^C \delta^C \qquad (21)$$

We define a parameter α $(0 \le \alpha \le \infty)$ that determines the ratio of the recovery rates of the convertible and straight bonds, ie, $\alpha = \delta^C / \delta^B$. The two recovery rates when default occurs at maturity are determined as follows:

$$\delta^B = \frac{1}{N^B} \max\left(\frac{V_T}{1+\alpha}, \; N^B\left(F^S + c^S\right) \right) \qquad (22)$$

$$\delta^C = \frac{1}{N^C} \max\left(\frac{\alpha V_T}{1+\alpha}, \; \left(V_T - N^B\left(F^S + c^S\right)\right) \right) \qquad (23)$$

For $\alpha = 0$, the straight bond is strictly senior (eg, the recovery rate could be 99% on this bond and 0% on the subordinated convertibles). For $\alpha = \infty$, the convertibles are senior (as is sometimes the case in Asia), while in between these values, there is some sharing of the total recovery amount as is often observed in practice.

7.5.7 Pricing using the stock price
In practice, we observe directly the current stock price and not the firm value, although the latter is the variable that we model. The price of the convertible depends on the value of the firm, but the value of the firm is determined by the actual price of the convertible. The initial value of the firm will be given by $V_0 = N^B B_0 + N^C C_0 + N^S S_0^{BC}$. If $\tilde{C}_0$ represents the convertible value obtained from the model, then in order to match the current stock price, we have to find the initial firm value $\tilde{V}_0$ that satisfies the following equation:

$$\frac{\tilde{V}_0 - N_B B - N_S S^{BC}}{N_C} = \tilde{C}_0(\tilde{V}_0, r, T) \qquad (24)$$

This equation can be solved iteratively to give both the initial firm value and convertible price (several passes through the tree are made changing the initial firm value until convergence is reached).

7.5.8 Examples
We now proceed to give examples of the pricing behaviour of the Firm Value model and perform a sensitivity analysis on the underlying parameters, ie, the volatility of the firm's asset returns and the amount of equity

Table 7.2 Description of the two bonds used for the examples for the Firm Value model

Interest rate	Currency	US$
	Mean-reversion (a)	0.1
	Volatility (σ_r)	1%
Senior bonds	Number (N^B)	5,000
	Face value (F^B)	US$100
	Coupon (c^B)	8.0% (semi-annual)
Convertible bonds	Number (N^C)	2,500
	Par value (F^C)	US$100
	Coupon (c^C)	6.5% (semi-annual)
	Conversion price (CVP_t)	US$25
	Conversion ratio (q_t)	4
	Call price (CP_t)	US$120 (after first year)
Stock	Number (N^S)	200,000
	Dividends	None
	Volatility of firm value (σ_V)	25%

and senior debt outstanding. Also the behaviour of the delta (the hedge ratio) is analysed. We illustrate sub-optimal call strategies and the "smile" implied by the model, but since these are not really credit issues, they are presented in Appendix C. The inputs into the model and the characteristics of the straight debt and the CB are given in Table 7.2. Each calculation was performed using 100 steps on the tree, which took around two seconds on a 600MHz PC.

The dependence of the price and delta of the CB on the underlying stock price is illustrated in Figure 7.5. When the stock price is high, the convertible price approaches the conversion value and its delta is close to 1 (conversion is almost certain). At intermediate stock prices the convertible is insensitive to stock price movements, behaving like a straight bond with a small delta. However, at very low stock prices the CB price falls rapidly and the delta once again increases, as there is a significant chance that the firm will default.

The detailed behaviour of the convertible price as the stock price falls will be determined by the individual characteristics of the issuer. In this model there are three parameters, which determine the behaviour of the convertible price for low stock prices. Namely, the firm value volatility, the amount of equity and the amount of senior debt that the firm has outstanding. We consider these three effects separately.

Figure 7.6 shows the convertible price as a function of the underlying stock price for different firm value volatilities. Increasing the volatility

Figure 7.5 Convertible price and delta as a function of the underlying stock price

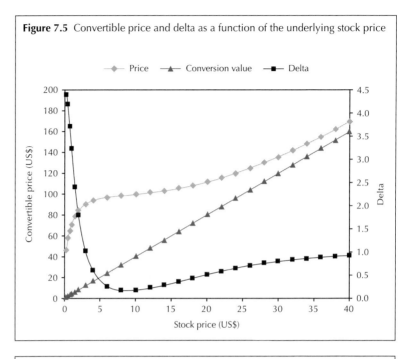

Figure 7.6 Sensitivity of the CB price on the volatility of the firm's asset returns (σ_V in Equation 12)

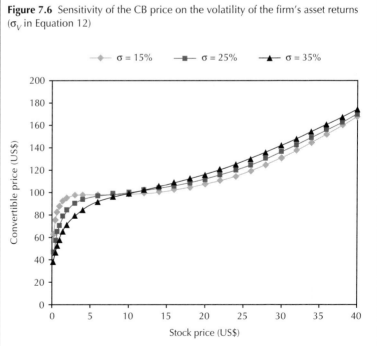

Figure 7.7 Sensitivity of CB's credit quality on the amount of straight debt (N^B) outstanding

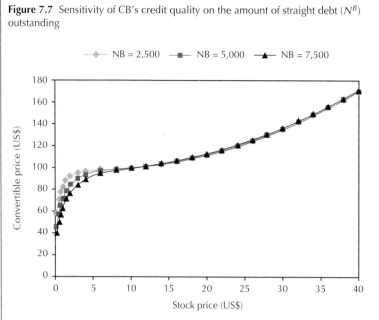

Figure 7.8 Sensitivity of the CB's price on the number of shares (N^S)

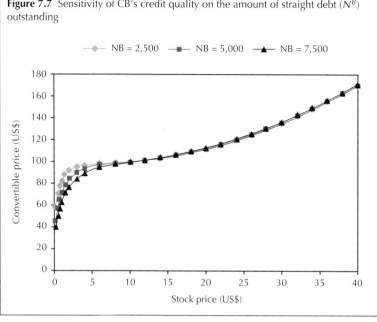

causes the probability of default to increase, but also the probability of conversion to increase. For low stock prices, the former is dominant and the convertible price decreases with increasing volatility. For high stock prices, the latter effect means that the convertible price increases with increasing volatility.

The coupons and principal of the straight bonds are senior to those of the convertibles and are paid first. This means that the more straight bonds there are, the greater the probability of default for the convertibles (which are effectively more subordinated), as illustrated in Figure 7.7. In addition, an increase in the amount of senior debt also increases the debt/equity ratio.

As the amount of equity decreases and the ratio of debt to equity increases, the equity effectively acts as a cushion against default. With less equity to absorb large losses, the probability of default increases and the convertible price therefore falls. This is illustrated in Figure 7.8.

7.6 CREDIT SPREAD MODEL

We now consider a model that follows the more traditional approach of modelling the stock price instead of the value of the firm. The advantages of this model relative to the Firm Value model is that it does not require any firm-specific information and it is more consistent with existing CB models. Its disadvantage is that we either need to impose a direct functional relationship or assume a certain value for the correlation between the stock price and the credit spread. Both approaches are faced with difficult estimation issues.

In a nutshell, the model works as follows: the stock price, conditional on no default, follows a lognormal process. The process is discretised using a trinomial lattice. The lattice is augmented by an additional leg, which corresponds to the default state. In case of default, it is assumed that the stock price is worthless and that the recovery rate of a straight bond is δ. The risk-neutral default probability (q_t) in a small interval is approximately determined by the following equation $q_t = c_t dt/(1 - \delta)$, where c_t is the credit spread. At each node in the tree the rest of the parameters are set, such that the mean and (conditional) variance of the stock price are matched. The credit spread (and therefore the default probability) is modelled as a deterministic function of the random stock price.

An alternative specification of the model would be to model the credit spread as a separate random process that is correlated to the stock price. We do not go into detail, but simply wish to note that such an approach seemingly cannot match prices observed in the market; in particular, it does not generate the rapid decline in the CB price when the stock price is low. Another problem with such an approach is that, numerically, the three-factor problem is much harder to solve.

7.6.1 Model specification

For the interest rate process we use the specification given by Equation (6) and the discretisation presented earlier. Next, we discuss the process followed by the stock price and the process followed by the risk-neutral default probability.

Conditional on no default, the stock price follows a geometric Brownian motion (lognormal distribution). In order to compensate the stockholder for the losses in case of default, the risk-neutral drift of the stock return has to be augmented by the credit spread. Its dynamics are described by the following equation:

$$\frac{dS_t}{S_t} = (r_t + c_t)\,dt + \sigma_S\,dz \tag{25}$$

In the event of default, we assume that the stock price is zero. The reason for doing this is that if an issuer defaults, then all the equity value will be used to repay the debt. Figure 7.9 shows a discretisation of the above process using a trinomial tree.

We assume that the credit spread is related to the stock price according to the following equation[1] (note that we can also use this equation to incorporate correlation between the credit spread and risk-free interest rate, but since this is of secondary importance we do not address it):

$$c_t = \beta_0 + \beta_1 \exp\left(-\beta_2 S_t\right) \tag{26}$$

Figure 7.9 The trinomial tree with default for the stock price process

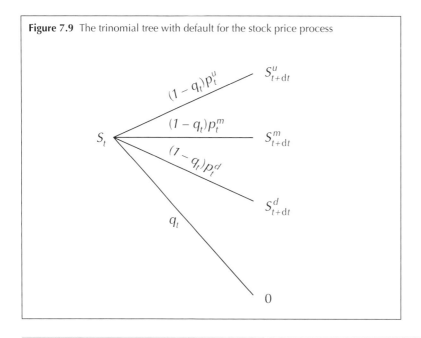

where S_t is the stock price at time t. At any node in the tree, the probability of the default leg is given by $q_t = c_t/(1 - \delta)$. The parameters β_1 and β_2 can be estimated either by using time-series analysis of the credit spreads and stock prices or from observations of convertible prices together with the underlying stock prices (if such data are available). These parameters can be shown to have a nice interpretation in terms of the characteristics of the issuing firm. We discuss interpretation and estimation of the parameters later in the text.

7.6.2 Numerical implementation

For each node in the tree, the possible stock prices in the next period are given by S_{t+dt}^u, S_{t+dt}^m and S_{t+dt}^d. This tree differs from the standard trees in that it has the additional node that corresponds to the default state. The probabilities of the three branches, conditional on no default, must satisfy the following system of equations, which require that the probabilities sum up to unity and that the mean and variance (conditional on no default) of the observed stock price process (Equation 25) are matched:

$$p_t^u + p_t^m + p_t^d = 1$$

$$\left(1 - q_t\right)\left(p_t^u S_{t+dt}^u + p_t^m S_{t+dt}^m + p_t^d S_{t+dt}^d\right) = S_t\, e^{(r_t + c_t)\, dt}$$

$$p_t^u \left(S_{t+dt}^u\right)^2 + p_t^m \left(S_{t+dt}^m\right)^2 + p_t^d \left(S_{t+dt}^d\right)^2 -$$

$$\left(p_t^u S_{t+dt}^u + p_t^m S_{t+dt}^m + p_t^d S_{t+dt}^d\right)^2 = \left(S_t\right)^2 e^{2(r_t + c_t)\, dt}\left(e^{\sigma^2 dt} - 1\right)$$

$$\tag{27abc}$$

It is possible that the solution of the above system of equations produces negative probabilities. In practice this is rare, due to the mean-reversion of the interest rate process. In practice, it can only occur for extreme interest rates or credit spreads.

The reason for using a trinomial tree to model the stock process is to make it possible to choose the values for S_{t+dt}^u, S_{t+dt}^m and S_{t+dt}^d arbitrarily. This ensures that the tree will still recombine, despite there being a probability of default and the interest rates not being constant. The values chosen for the stock branching are $S_{t+dt}^u = S_t u_t$, $S_{t+dt}^m = S_t$ and $S_{t+dt}^d = S_t/u_t$, with $u_t = e^{\sigma_s \sqrt{3dt}}$ chosen as the optimal vertical spacing.

We now need to solve the above equations to determine the probabilities p_t^u, p_t^m and p_t^d. The solution to Equation (27) is given by (see Appendix B):

$$p_d = \frac{(1 - M)(1 + u_t) - (1 - M^2 - V)}{(u_t - 1/u_t) - (1 - 1/u_t^2)}$$

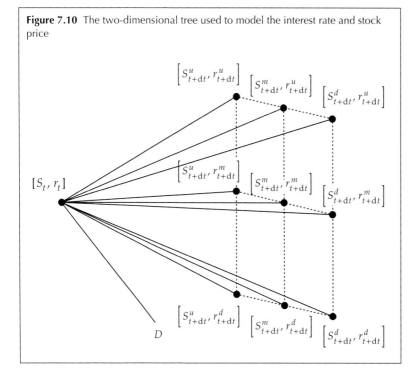

Figure 7.10 The two-dimensional tree used to model the interest rate and stock price

$$p_u = \frac{(1-M)(1+1/u_t) - (1 - M^2 - V)}{(1/u_t - u_t) - (1 - u_t^2)}$$

$$p_m = 1 - p_u - p_d \tag{28abc}$$

where

$$\frac{e^{(r_t + c_t)\, dt}}{1 - q_t} = M \quad \text{and} \quad e^{2(r_t + c_t)\, dt}\left(e^{\sigma_S^2\, dt} - 1\right) = V$$

The next step is to combine the interest rate (Figure 7.1) and the stock price trees (Figure 7.9) to create a two-dimensional tree. Since the constituent trees are both trinomial and recombining, the new tree has nine paths emanating from each node and is also recombining. There is also the additional path that corresponds to default. The probability of each path is the product of the probabilities of the corresponding paths of the two trinomial trees if the stock price and the interest rates are independent. If there is correlation, the procedure is more complex, as discussed previously for the Firm Value model. However, the fact that a default state has been added to the tree does not complicate matters further.

Recall that the value of the convertible at maturity is given by the following expression:

$$C_T = \max\left(F^C, PP_T, CV_T\right) \tag{29}$$

where PP_T is the put price, S_T is the stock price and CV_T is the conversion value. The above equation arises from the assumption that the issuer will pay the minimum of the par value and call value, while the holder will choose the maximum of the conversion value, the put price and the payment from the issuer.

As we move backwards through the tree, the CB value at each node at time t is given by the discounted expectation from the 10 nodes at time $t + 1$ that follow that node. Therefore, the CB "hold" value at time t is given by:

$$HV_t = \exp\left(-r_t \, dt\right)\left(\sum_{i,j} p_t^{i,j}\, CV_{t+1}^{i,j}\right) + \exp\left(-r_t dt\right) p_d\, \delta F^C \tag{30}$$

Here, $p_t^{i,j}$ is the probability of moving up to node with stock price S_{t+1}^i and interest rate r_{t+1}^j and $CV_{t+1}^{i,j}$ is the value of the convertible at that node (see below). Equation (30) incorporates the assumption that in the event of default, the convertible holder receives δF^C (a fraction of the par value) immediately. At any node on the tree, the value of the convertible bond is given by Equation (4), which is reproduced below, with accrued interest included:

$$CV_t = \max\left(\min\left(HV_t, (CP_t + AI_t)\right), (PP_t + AI_t), CV_t\right) \tag{31}$$

where AI_t denotes the accrued interest received if the bond is sold back to the issuer (as a result of a call or put).

7.6.3 Example
We describe the results of an example using the two-dimensional tree for pricing a convertible bond and a straight bond with the same par value and coupon rate. The characteristics of these bonds are given in Table 7.3.

In Figure 7.11, we show the variation of the value of a riskless convertible with the stock price. As the stock price falls, the convertible value approaches the present value of the coupons and principal, since there is an insignificant probability that conversion will be optimal at any point in the lifetime of the convertible. At high stock prices, the price of the convertible approaches the conversion value as there is almost 100% chance that it will be exchanged into equity. The delta therefore increases from almost zero to 1, as the convertible price approaches the conversion value.

Figure 7.12 shows the variation of the value of a risky convertible with the stock price and parameters of $\beta_0 = 0.0$, $\beta_1 = 0.2$ and $\beta_0 = 0.6$. For high

Table 7.3 Parameters for the examples

Interest rate process	Currency	US$
	Mean-reversion (a)	0.1
	Volatility (σ_r)	1%
Bond characteristics	Par value (F^C)	US$100
	Coupon (c^C)	6.5% (semi-annual)
	Conversion price (CVP_t)	US$25
	Conversion ratio (q_t)	4
	Call price (CP_t)	US$120 (after first year)
Stock parameters	Dividends	None
	Volatility (σ_S)	25%

stock prices, there is no difference between the risky and riskless convertibles. However, for low stock prices, the risky convertible falls in price much faster and its delta increases rapidly.

Figure 7.13 and Figure 7.14 show the impact of the parameters of Equation (26) on the price of the CB. We see that the absolute level and the slope of the convertible price for low stock prices can be controlled with these parameters. It should, therefore, be possible to estimate them using

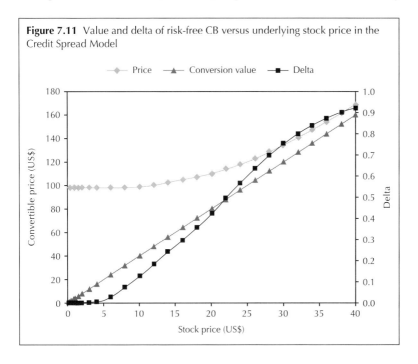

Figure 7.11 Value and delta of risk-free CB versus underlying stock price in the Credit Spread Model

265

joint observations of the price of convertible bonds together with the underlying stock price.

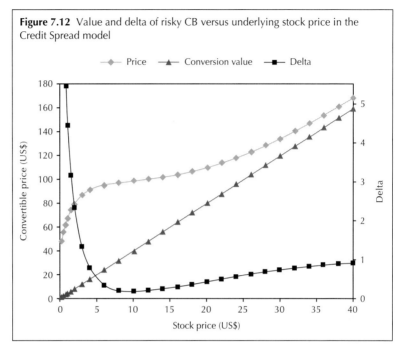

Figure 7.12 Value and delta of risky CB versus underlying stock price in the Credit Spread model

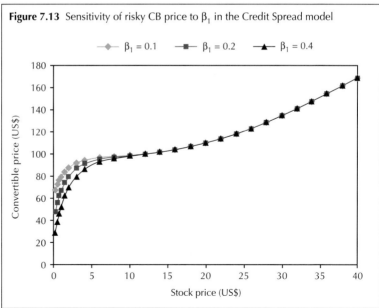

Figure 7.13 Sensitivity of risky CB price to β_1 in the Credit Spread model

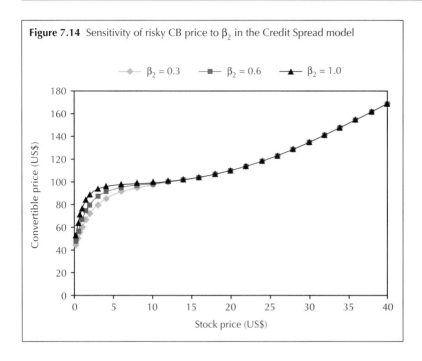

Figure 7.14 Sensitivity of risky CB price to β_2 in the Credit Spread model

7.6.4 Stochastic credit spread

In Equation (26), we assume that the credit spread is a deterministic function of the stock price. This is clearly not realistic, but accounting for the volatility of the credit spread in the three-factor model is not easy. One simple way to add credit spread volatility is to introduce a random term so that the credit spread becomes stochastic, ie,

$$c_t = \beta_0 + \beta_1 \exp(-\beta_2 S_t) + \sigma_c c_t dW_t \tag{32}$$

where σ_c is the credit spread volatility, which will be greater when the stock price is low (high credit spread). An example of the impact on the price of the CB is illustrated in Figure 7.15. The introduction of stochastic spread has important implications for hedging, as we will discuss later.

7.6.5 Intuitive discussion of parameters

What follows is an intuitive discussion of the parameters in the Credit Spread model.

Clearly, as the stock price increases, the exponential term in Equation (26) approaches zero. Therefore β_0 represents the minimum credit spread attainable. By making this parameter time dependent, we can match the credit spread term structure. β_1 determines the maximum value of the credit spread, which is $(\beta_0 + \beta_1)$ as S_t tends to zero. We should, therefore, note that β_1 is related to the recovery rate δ. This is so because in case of default, we think of the bond as being worth a fraction δ of the par value, but we could equivalently represent it as if trading at a very large credit spread. Hence, if we know δ we can estimate β_1.

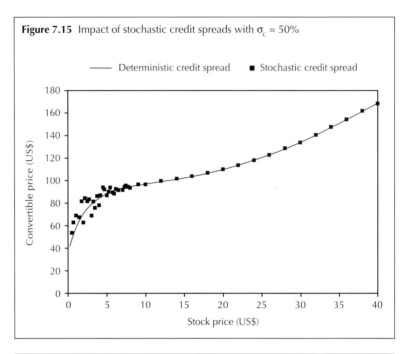

Figure 7.15 Impact of stochastic credit spreads with $\sigma_c = 50\%$

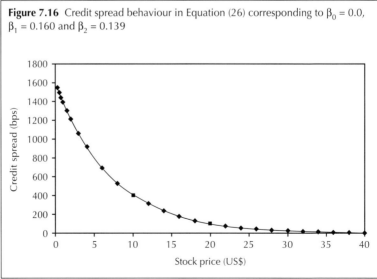

Figure 7.16 Credit spread behaviour in Equation (26) corresponding to $\beta_0 = 0.0$, $\beta_1 = 0.160$ and $\beta_2 = 0.139$

The interpretation of β_2 is not so clear and it does not have the units of a credit spread. This parameter will determine the behaviour of the credit spread between the upper and lower limits, defined by β_1 and β_2. We will give a clear interpretation of the role of this parameter in the next section. For now, we note that an easy way to estimate β_2 is by imposing a view on how the credit spread will behave between the upper and lower limits (β_1 and β_0).

For example, suppose that the stock price is US$20, the initial credit spread 100bps, the minimum credit spread 20bps – this means that we immediately have $\beta_0 = 0.002$. Suppose also that we believe that if the stock price falls to US$15, the credit spread will widen to 400bps. This gives two simultaneous equations from Equation (26), which can be solved to give $\beta_1 = 0.160$ and $\beta_2 = 0.139$. We will see in the next section that these are not unreasonable parameters. The credit spread behaviour for these parameters is shown in Figure 7.16.

7.7 COMPARISON OF THE TWO MODELS

7.7.1 Overview of models

In Table 7.4, we briefly compare the characteristics, advantages and disadvantages of the two models.

7.7.2 Intuitive "link" between models

Next, we briefly discuss how the parameters in Equation (26) can be interpreted using properties of the firm – ie, debt to equity ratio, senior debt outstanding, etc. We first show that the price behaviour of the CB in the

Table 7.4 Comparison of the two convertible pricing models

Credit Spread model	Firm Value model
Models interest rate and stock price	Models interest rate and firm value
Default process defined exogenously with credit spread determined from current stock price and interest rate	Default process specified endogenously within the model
Recovery rate fixed parameter	Recovery rate endogenous
Need to estimate parameters for credit spread	Need to know details of issuing firm (amount of equity and senior debt)
Underlying equity can be of any kind	Underlying equity must be from same issuing firm as convertibles
No smile	Direct incorporation of smile
Price computed directly	Price obtained iteratively when stock price is input – slower computation

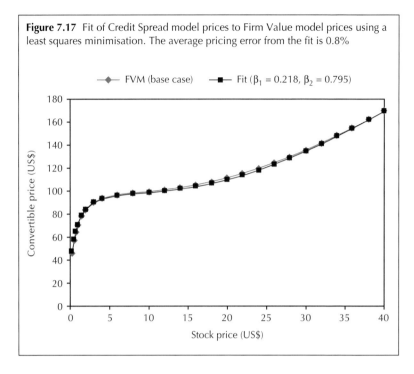

Figure 7.17 Fit of Credit Spread model prices to Firm Value model prices using a least squares minimisation. The average pricing error from the fit is 0.8%

Firm Value model in the example illustrated in Figure 7.5 can be matched. A least-squares fit with $\beta_0 = 0.0$ gives parameters $\beta_1 = 0.218$, $\beta_2 = 0.795$ and an average error of only 0.8%. The fit is shown in Figure 7.17.

The parameter β_1 is a proxy for the amount of senior straight debt outstanding. As the amount of senior debt increases, the more risky the convertible becomes and its credit quality deteriorates[2]. Therefore, its price would decrease faster as the stock price decreases. We can illustrate this by changing the amount of senior debt shown in Figure 7.7 and refitting the prices shown in Figure 7.17, only by changing the value of β_1 (all other parameters held fixed). Again, we get a good fit, as shown in Figure 7.18.

As discussed previously, β_2 determines the convexity or rate at which the slope (delta) of the convertible price increases with decreasing stock price. By performing a similar analysis to that for β_1 (see Figure 7.19), we can show that this parameter is naturally related to the amount of equity within the firm. If there is less equity, then a decrease in the stock price will cause a larger decline in the convertible price, since there is a smaller buffer against potential losses due to default. In the Credit Spread model this is captured via a significant widening of the credit spread for low stock prices.

Figure 7.18 Fit of Credit Spread model prices to Firm Value model prices (while changing only the parameter β_1), using a least squares minimisation for different amounts of senior debt – 2,500 straight bonds (top) and 10,000 straight bonds (bottom). The average pricing errors from the fits are 1.8% and 1.3% respectively

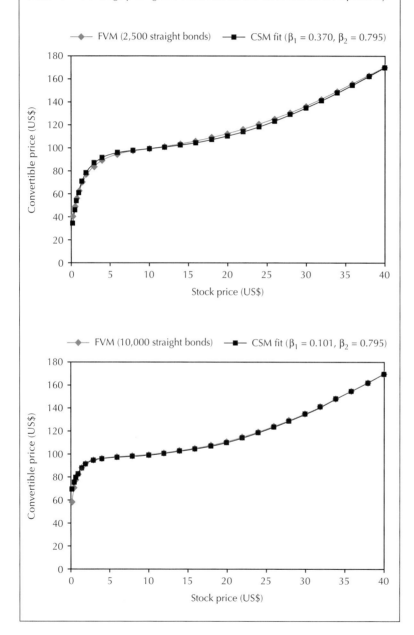

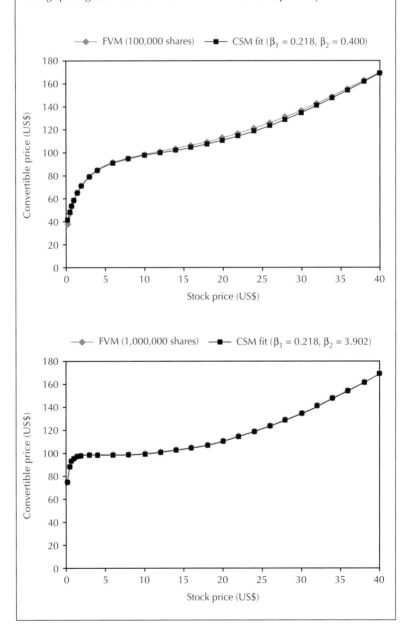

Figure 7.19 Fit of Credit Spread model prices to Firm Value model prices (while changing only the parameter β_2), using a least squares minimisation for different amounts of equity – 100,000 shares (top) and 1,000,000 shares (bottom). The average pricing errors from the fits are 2.0% and 0.2% respectively

7.8 HEDGING OF CREDIT RISK

Before concluding, we make some brief remarks regarding the hedging of credit risk in convertible bonds. We recall from discussions in the previous two chapters that there are two elements of risk that need to be hedged: credit spread volatility and default events. The hedging strategies we outline below are general and do not make particular reference to either model.

7.8.1 Hedging with underlying stock

From observing the magnitude of the delta in some of the examples given in the last two sections, it can be suggested that the credit exposure can be hedged with the underlying stock. We can hedge against an increase in the credit spread by holding a short position in the issuing firm's equity. If the credit spread widens and the CB price decreases, the stock price will have decreased and we will gain on the short position. One particularly attractive feature of this is that (for once) it is theoretically possible to hedge the credit risk with an instrument that is liquid. However, there are two obvious disadvantages of this hedging strategy, which we describe below.

1. The above strategy is very model dependent. At low stock prices, the delta can vary considerably with the parameters of the model (this is true for either model). Even if we believe that we can estimate the parameters quite accurately, there is generally additional volatility in the credit spread of CBs, similar to the behaviour shown in Figure 7.15. Any additional credit spread movements not driven by the underlying stock price are not hedged using this approach.
2. We emphasise that this strategy does not protect against a sudden default. If default is represented by a gradual (continuous) decline of the stock price to zero, then we will short a larger amount of the stock and hedge the decrease in the CB price. However, if default is sudden, as is the case in practice, we will most probably not have a sufficiently large short position to cover the loss.

7.8.2 Hedging with default swaps

By using default swaps it is possible to hedge against default events. As above, this would be a dynamic strategy, very similar to that presented in the hedging section of the last chapter. We do not discuss this issue again, but simply recall that the amount of default swaps held is determined in order to protect against default, while the maturity of the default swaps is set to hedge changes in the credit spread. However, there is one issue that should be mentioned: the recovery rate on the convertible may be less than the recovery rate on the underlying bond in the default swap contract. Indeed, it may even be possible that the convertible defaults, while a more senior bond does not and therefore no payment is due under the terms of the default swap contract.

7.9 CONCLUSION

We presented two models for pricing convertible bonds in the presence of credit risk: the Firm Value and the Credit Spread model. The Credit Spread model, an extension of a two-factor model for the interest rate and stock price, assumes that the credit spread is a function of the latter. This specification has been motivated by the fact that a decline in the underlying stock price is likely to be accompanied by a deterioration of the credit quality of the issuer. The Firm Value model is an application of the Black–Scholes–Merton model. It assumes a certain process for the risk-free interest rate and the value of the issuing firm. The fundamental difference between the two models is the way in which the equity component is described. We have discussed their advantages and disadvantages, the estimation of their parameters as well as the relationship between the two parameterisations. They should not be viewed as two competing models, but rather as complementary. In particular, the insight we get by comparing the model parameterisations can be particularly useful in model calibration. This could partly compensate for the lack of available data.

APPENDIX A. FIRM VALUE MODEL – ANALYTIC PRICING FORMULAE

The following results can be found in Ingersoll (1977a).
1. For a zero-coupon bond in the Firm Value model, when the firm consists of a single stock and a single zero-coupon bond, the solution to the PDE is simply a transformation of the Black–Scholes equation:

$$B(F, V, r, \tau, \sigma) = F \exp(-r\tau) \left[\Phi(h_2) + d^{-1}\Phi(h_1) \right] \tag{A1}$$

with

$$d = \frac{F \exp(-r\tau)}{V} \tag{A2}$$

$$h_1 = \left(\log d - \frac{1}{2}\sigma^2\tau \right) \Big/ \sigma\sqrt{\tau} \tag{A3}$$

$$h_2 = -\left(\log d + \frac{1}{2}\sigma^2\tau \right) \Big/ \sigma\sqrt{\tau} \tag{A4}$$

Here, r represents the interest rate, τ the maturity, σ the volatility, F the par value and V the firm value and $\Phi(\cdot)$ is the cumulative normal distribution function.
2. For a non-callable, convertible zero-coupon bond, the price can be treated as that of the ordinary discount bond. On top of that, the CB holder is entitled to purchase the same fraction of the equity of the company with an exercise price equal to the notional of the bond. It can be

shown that early exercise is sub-optimal, which leads to the following formula (zero-coupon bond plus call option):

$$CB(F, V, r, \tau, \sigma) = B(F, r, \tau, \sigma, V) + c(\gamma V, r, \tau, \sigma, B) \tag{A5}$$

where $c(\gamma V, r, \tau, \sigma, B)$ is the basic Black–Scholes option pricing formula:

$$c(S, r, \tau, \sigma, X) = S\Phi(x_1) - E\exp(-r\tau)\Phi(x_2) \tag{A6}$$

with

$$x_1 = \left[\log(S/E) + \left(r + \frac{1}{2}\sigma^2\right)\tau\right]/\sigma\sqrt{\tau} \quad \text{and} \quad x_2 = x_1 - \sigma\sqrt{\tau} \tag{A7}$$

APPENDIX B. DERIVATION OF FORMULAE FOR TRINOMIAL TREE WITH DEFAULT BRANCH

In Figure 7.9, we showed the structure of a trinomial tree incorporating default. It is the same as a standard trinomial tree, except that each node leads also to an additional "default state", in which the stock price is zero. For a description of the procedure for a trinomial tree without default, the reader is referred to a standard text such as Hull (1996, p. 360).

The default probability q_t is determined from the credit spread as discussed in the main text. We can use the following conditions to determine the other probabilities in the tree.

1. The probabilities must sum to one (note that we multiply the probabilities below by $(1 - q_t)$):

$$q_t + (1 - q_t)\left(p_t^u + p_t^m + p_t^d\right) = p_t^u + p_t^m + p_t^d = 1 \tag{B1}$$

2. The expected value of the stock price at the end of a short time interval dt is matched:

$$(1 - q_t)\left(p_t^u S_{t+dt}^u + p_t^m S_{t+dt}^m + p_t^d S_{t+dt}^d\right) = S_t e^{(r_t + c_t)\,dt} \tag{B2}$$

3. The unconditional variance of the stock price at the end of a short time interval dt is matched (recall that the variance of a random variable X is given by $E[X^2] - E[X]^2$):

$$p_t^u\left(S_{t+dt}^u\right)^2 + p_t^m\left(S_{t+dt}^m\right)^2 + p_t^d\left(S_{t+dt}^d\right)^2 -$$

$$\left[p_t^u S_{t+dt}^u + p_t^m S_{t+dt}^m + p_t^d S_{t+dt}^d\right]^2$$

$$= S_t e^{(r_t + c_t)\,dt}\left(e^{\sigma_S^2 dt} - 1\right) \tag{B3}$$

Using the imposed conditions $S_{t+dt}^u = S_t u_t$, $S_{t+dt}^m = S_t$ and $S_{t+dt}^d = S_t/u_t$, we can simplify Equations (B2) and (B3) as follows:

$$\left(p_t^u u + p_t^m + p_t^d / u \right) = \frac{e^{(r_t + c_t)\, dt}}{1 - q_t} = M \tag{B4}$$

$$\left(p_t^u u^2 + p_t^m + p_t^d / u^2 \right) = e^{2(r_t + c_t)\, dt} \left(e^{\sigma_S^2\, dt} - 1 \right) + M^2 = V + M^2 \tag{B5}$$

so that M and V represent the mean and variance of the lognormal process. We can solve the above equations for the probabilities quite easily. Firstly, taking (B4) and (B5) away from (B1) gives:

$$p_t^u (1 - u_t) + p_t^d (1 - 1/u_t) = 1 - M \tag{B6}$$

and

$$p_t^u \left(1 - u_t^2 \right) + p_t^d \left(1 - 1/u_t^2 \right) = 1 - V - M^2 \tag{B7}$$

Multiplying Equation (B6) by a factor of $(1 + u)$ can be shown to give:

$$p_t^u \left(1 - u_t^2 \right) + p_t^d \left(u_t - 1/u_t \right) = (1 - M)(1 + u_t) \tag{B8}$$

We can now subtract Equation (B7) from Equation (B8) and rearrange to obtain:

$$p_d = \frac{(1 - M)(1 + u_t) - (1 - M^2 - V)}{\left(u_t - 1/u_t \right) - \left(1 - 1/u_t^2 \right)} \tag{B9}$$

Multiplying Equation (A5) by a factor of $(1 + 1/u_t)$ and subtracting (B7) as before and rearranging gives:

$$p_u = \frac{(1 - M)\left(1 + 1/u_t \right) - (1 - M^2 - V)}{\left(1/u_t - u_t \right) - \left(1 - u_t^2 \right)} \tag{B10}$$

Finally, of course:

$$p_m = 1 - p_u - p_d \tag{B11}$$

APPENDIX C. EFFECT OF SUB-OPTIMAL CALL POLICY

There has been a significant amount of work that has highlighted the possibility of firms following sub-optimal call policies for various reasons (eg, call notice, cost of issuing debt, tax). Here we present the fundamental ideas. A more thorough discussion can be found in Ingersoll (1977b). We describe a simple way to investigate the effect of sub-optimal call policies. We assume that the probability of the bond being called increases progressively to one as the value of the convertible increases above the call value according to the following relationship:

$$
P_t^{call} = \begin{cases} 1 - \exp\left[\lambda \dfrac{(C_t - CP_t)}{CP_t}\right] & C_t > CP_t \\ \\ 0 & C_t \leq CP_t \end{cases} \tag{C1}
$$

This means that as λ increases, the call condition approaches a step function. The value chosen for λ therefore determines the premium that will be incorporated into the convertible price as a result of the assumed sub-optimal call strategy. For a discussion of the effects of sub-optimal call policies on convertible prices, see Ingersoll (1997b).

We show the impact of a sub-optimal call policy in Figure C1. For low stock prices, the bond is very unlikely to be called and so the price of the CB is not sensitive to the call policy. For high stock prices, the bond is almost certain to be called since the value of the CB is well above the call price. Therefore, again, the sensitivity to the call policy is minimal. At intermediate stock prices, the convertible assuming a sub-optimal call policy should trade at a slight premium, since there is a chance that even if its value is above the call threshold, it may not be called.

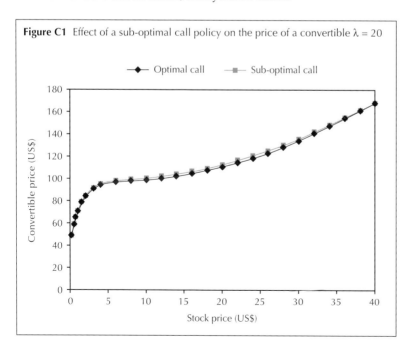

Figure C1 Effect of a sub-optimal call policy on the price of a convertible $\lambda = 20$

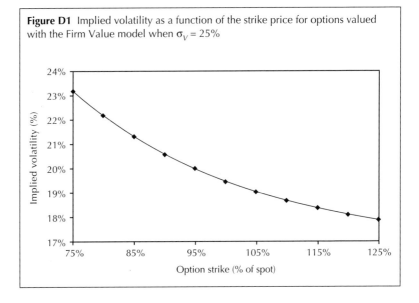

Figure D1 Implied volatility as a function of the strike price for options valued with the Firm Value model when $\sigma_V = 25\%$

APPENDIX D. INCORPORATION OF "SMILE" IN THE FIRM VALUE MODEL

As shown in Figure D1, the Firm Value model directly incorporates volatility smile. This occurs because the volatility of the underlying stock is negatively correlated with the firm value. When the firm value decreases, leverage (the ratio of debt to equity) increases and the volatility of the stock also increases. We can illustrate this effect by calculating the value of the conversion options within the Firm Value model and then comparing their implied volatilities (calculated using the Black–Scholes equation). The volatility is higher for options with low strikes, because the firm value volatility is high for low firm values.

---

1   For an example of empirical firm-specific study on the relationship between stocks and bonds, see Kwan (1996). This functional relationship was chosen after analysing the historical data for a number of different CBs. It proved most flexible in describing the decline of the convertible prices when stock prices fall. Further justification is provided above.

2   If the convertible debt is senior, this effect will be reversed but the analogy remains valid.

BIBLIOGRAPHY

Black, F., and M. Scholes, 1973, "The Pricing of Options and Corporate Liabilities", *Journal of Political Economy* 81, pp. 637–59.

Brennan, M. J., and E. S. Schwartz, 1977, "Convertible Bonds: Valuation and Optimal Strategies for Call and Conversion", *Journal of Finance* 32(5), (December), pp. 1699–715.

Brennan, M. J., and E. S. Schwartz, 1980, "Analyzing Convertible Bonds", *Journal of Financial and Quantitative Analysis* 15(4), (November), pp. 907–29.

Calamos, J. P., 1998, *Convertible Securities: The Latest Instruments, Portfolio Strategies, and Valuation Analysis*, Second Edition (New York, NY: McGraw-Hill).

Connolly, K. B., 1998, *Pricing Convertible Bonds* (New York, NY: John Wiley and Sons).

Hull, J. C., 1996, *Options, Futures, and Other Derivatives*, Third Edition (Englewood Cliffs, NJ: Prentice-Hall International).

Hull, J., and A. White, 1993, "One Factor Interest Rate Models and the Valuation of Interest Rate Derivative Securities", *Journal of Financial and Quantitative Analysis* 28, pp. 235–54.

Hull, J., and A. White, 1994, "Numerical Procedures for Implementing Term Structure Models II: Two-Factor Models", *Journal of Derivatives* (Winter), pp. 235–54.

Ingersoll, J., 1977a, "A Contingent Claims Valuation of Convertible Securities", *Journal of Financial Economics* 4, pp. 289–322.

Ingersoll, J., 1977b, "An Examination of Corporate Call Policies on Convertible Securities", *Journal of Finance* 32(2), pp. 463–78.

Kwan, S. H., 1996, "Firm-Specific Information and the Correlation Between Individual Stocks and Bonds", *Journal of Financial Economics* 40, pp. 63–80.

Merton, R. C., 1973, "Theory of Rational Option Pricing", *Bell Journal of Economics and Management Science* 4, pp. 141–83.

Nelken, I. (ed), 2000, *Handbook of Hybrid Instruments: Convertible Bonds, Preferred Shares, Lyons, Elks, Decs and Other Mandatory Convertible Notes* (New York, NY: John Wiley and Sons).

8

Market Imperfections

In the last chapter, we digressed slightly from our main theme to discuss three topics related to credit: impact of market illiquidity, non-continuous rebalancing of hedging portfolios and asymmetric information among market participants. In economic terms, the above would be referred to as market imperfections. In order to keep the mathematics simple, we have decided to present the first two applications in an equity context. These market imperfections are prevalent to a smaller or higher extent in most markets, but tend to be important in most credit markets. Though we have not yet applied these ideas to credit, we believe that they can provide more realistic models that emulate more closely the functioning of the real markets. Of course, we realise that their complexity and difficult calibration issues could limit their applicability.

We can simply define liquidity risk as: the inability to transact at substantial volumes at the prevailing market price. The market price reflects the cash amount we can expect to pay or receive for small transactions. In a market that does not have a lot of depth, the "market price" for large transactions can be substantially different from the above, which penalises the investor. To take this potential inability to trade into account, we need to adjust the price of the securities by a liquidity spread. This liquidity spread does not reflect the default probability, but rather the potential lack of a sufficient number of market participants with which to transact. We demonstrate these ideas in the pricing of collateralised loans, where equity is held as collateral. If the borrower fails to post margin, we may need to liquidate the collateral in a short period of time, adversely impacting the market price.

A side effect of market illiquidity is the inability to adjust the hedges continuously when implementing a dynamic hedging strategy. The Black–Scholes price is strictly valid only when the hedge is continuously rebalanced, as dictated by the model. This could be true also for small transactions, eg, as in the presence of substantial transaction costs. It is even possible that the underlying does not trade continuously, as is the case for indices on funds. We will demonstrate the effect of discrete hedging by analysing a call option on a stock, where the hedge is rebalanced only at discrete time points. It is interesting to note that the "residual variance" is substantial, even if the rebalancing frequency is high.

Asymmetric information, the third issue we are addressing, is again closely related to market liquidity. In a market where information is freely available, we expect risk-averse investors to transfer risk to institutions with high risk-tolerance. In the capital markets, information on frequently traded liquid instruments is publicly available and is reflected in the price. Access to information has been a catalyst for the phenomenal increase in trading volumes in recent years. In illiquid markets, certain investors have superior information and a premium is charged for transacting with them. This additional cost, due to asymmetric information, can make trading costs prohibitive and prevent otherwise mutually beneficial exchange of risk. In this chapter, we propose a contingent fee structure that partly resolves the asymmetric information problem and then demonstrate the hedge in the following context. An importer of hardware equipment pays for imported goods in US dollars and receives revenues in local currency. Business at this stage is minimal, but it is expected to grow substantially if the economy improves. In the latter case, the country's credit rating can be used as a proxy. At the current volume, the importer would not want to hedge their foreign exchange exposure, but if business grows, they may want to enter into a series of forward contracts. This is similar to the contingent contracts discussed in Chapter 5. In this section, we propose an entirely different risk management technique. We will be referring to this as a conditional financial hedge.

8.1 LIQUIDITY RISK

Liquidity risk can be defined as the inability to transact at substantial volumes at the prevailing market price. For example, when we want to buy or sell on-the-run (the current issue) US Treasury securities, it is always possible to execute at practically any volume. In other words, US Treasury securities are very liquid. This is not the case for most corporate bonds. In past credit crises, the market had dried out and it had become almost impossible for financial institutions to sell out without incurring very large losses. Because of that possibility, the price of illiquid securities should be adjusted to take into account the fact that when we want to receive cash for our securities, we may not be able to–at least not if we insist to receive the current "market price". The reason for this is not the possibility of default, but the lack of sufficient potential buyers to transact with. This effect, even though related to credit risk, is definitely different. Liquidity risk has attracted a lot of attention both from academics and practitioners alike, but only a few models have been developed that could possibly be of practical use.

Furthermore, we digress from fixed income instruments and model the pricing of an equity-backed security structure, a collateralised loan. This structure is commonly used and we think that it will be of interest to the reader. If the collateral deteriorates in value and the counterparty fails to make the subsequent margin call, the lender will have to liquidate it. If the amount of collateral held is large, the market will not be able to readily absorb the sale without an adverse price change. We present a liquidation model that estimates the loss incurred when liquidating. The model is calibrated on parameters that are related to the liquidity of the market. To estimate the impact on the market price, we model the behaviour of the economic agents and their interaction. The model is tested against a real liquidation event. The ideas presented, appropriately modified, can be applied to a different context.

8.1.1 Illiquid markets

The issue we address is as follows: if we have collateral that we want to liq-uidate in large volume because the borrower has failed a margin call, what is a realistic price that we can expect to achieve if we know the current mar-ket price? The market price reflects the cash amount we can expect to receive for small transactions. If the market has a lot of depth, ie, it is very liquid, we could liquidate very large volumes at that price. Here, we assume that this is not the case and that the size of the trade could be of similar magnitude to the issue size. This is of practical interest, since even a whole issue can be given as collateral. We present these ideas using equi-ties, but they are readily applicable to other types of instruments. It would be necessary to amend some of the stochastic processes describing the evo-lution of the collateral's market price. Explicitly, we model how trading volume and new transactions are generated. The basic idea is that a change of price generates an additional trade. This assumption is a good description of the behaviour of the market, in particular for transactions of substantial size. We assume a linear relationship between price changes and trading volume. The ratio (or sensitivity) of additional trading volume to price change is assumed to be a constant of the market. It is a parameter of the model, which can be estimated from the observed distribution of the daily volume, as explained below.[1]

It is difficult to incorporate into the model the factors that entice investors to buy or sell, or, in other words, to model explicitly the investor behaviour that triggers changes in the market price. For this reason, it is customary to specify a stochastic process for the market price that is exogenous to the model. In other words, we do not justify the stochastic process followed by the market prices based on the behaviour of the eco-nomic agents. In economic terms, this is a partial – as opposed to a general – equilibrium model. When there are not any buy or sell orders of very large size, price changes can be fairly well described to occur randomly, and to follow a lognormal distribution, reflecting the arrival of random shocks in the market. This is the process we have assumed before a large liquidation order comes into the market. In the framework of this model, these price changes generate proportional random volumes, the daily aggregation of which is an observable distribution. Using the moments of this distribution, we can estimate the sensitivity of additional traded volume to a change in the price of the collateral. If this sensitivity is low, a large reduction in the price will be necessary to sell the target volume.

8.1.2 Collateralised loan

Consider making a loan to a counterparty of average credit quality and taking collateral against this position. Despite having a cushion to cover the possibility of default on the loan, there is still risk, since the value of the collateral may deteriorate and the counterparty may then fail to post margin. If this happens, it will be necessary to liquidate the collateral. Large-scale liquidation could result in a potential loss if the market is not liquid and deep. The price of the collateral will have to decline for the market to absorb the sale and for a new equilibrium to be reached. This chapter introduces a model that estimates the adverse price change that we are likely to experience as a result of the insufficient liquidity and depth of the market.

Using the model, we can then calculate the liquidity spread that should be charged to cover this additional risk. We assume a worst-case scenario such that the counterparty will default on the first margin call,[2] and we estimate the expected loss when liquidating. To compute the liquidity spread, we simply multiply the expected loss by the probability that the margin call will occur, and divide it by the maturity and size of the loan. We conservatively ignore time value, ie, we do not discount the expected loss.

Probability of margin call
Assume that we issue a loan of constant amount L and take collateral of value C_0 against this position. The amount $(C_0 - L)$ is the "haircut". The value of the collateral is assumed to follow a lognormal random walk, the same as the assumption underlying the Black–Scholes model:

$$dC_t = \mu_C C_t \, dt + \sigma_C C_t \, dW_t \tag{1}$$

where μ_c and σ_c represent the expected return and the volatility of the collateral and dW_t is a Brownian motion. μ_c for a stock can be set equal to the risk-free interest rate reduced by the stock's dividend yield. This specification of the drift is consistent with risk-neutral pricing.

The lognormality assumption is an adequate approximation for our purposes, since the most significant factor for determining the liquidity spread is the adverse stock price movement during collateral liquidation. Another good reason to select a lognormal process is that it allows us to compute analytically the probability of a margin call.

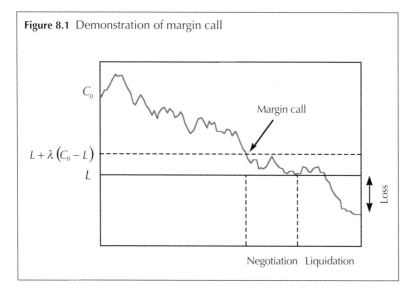

Figure 8.1 Demonstration of margin call

We assume that a margin call will be made when the value of the collateral equals the margin call level:

$$C_\tau = L + \lambda(C_0 - L) \tag{2}$$

where λ is a threshold between 0 and 1. This is shown in Figure 8.1. Given the maturity of the loan (T) and under the lognormality assumption, we can calculate analytically the probability p_{mc} that a margin call will be made at any time before T. Indeed, this probability is also the price of an American digital with zero interest rates (ie, no discounting).

The probability of a margin call p_{mc} is given by (eg, see Wilmott, 1998):

$$p_{mc} = N(-d_2) + \left(\frac{C_\tau}{C_0}\right)^{\frac{2\mu_C}{\sigma^2} - 1} N(-d_3)$$

$$d_2 = \frac{\ln\left(\frac{C_0}{C_\tau}\right) + (\mu_C - \sigma^2/2)T}{\sigma\sqrt{T}}$$

$$d_3 = \frac{\ln\left(\frac{C_0}{C_\tau}\right) - (\mu_C - \sigma^2/2)T}{\sigma\sqrt{T}} \tag{3}$$

Liquidation process
We next compute the expected loss during liquidation, conditional on a

margin call having been made. We assume that following the margin call, there will be a period of negotiation, after which the counterparty will fail to provide more collateral, while the one held will have to be sold. The liquidation period is normally one week.

It is likely that liquidating a large position compared to the size of the market will drive the market price down and result in a loss. To estimate the impact on the market price, we have to take into account the characteristics of the market and derive liquidity measures. A simple lognormal model cannot describe the behaviour of the market price during the liquidation. Indeed, such a model is based on the assumption that market participants can buy or sell infinitely large amounts without affecting the market price.

To estimate the impact of the liquidation on the market price, we need a model that explains why and how trading volume (or new transactions) is generated. One obvious factor that triggers a new transaction is a price change. What matters is the absolute size of the price change and not its direction (increase or decrease). We assume that all transactions are only the effect of changes in price. This assumption is a good description of the behaviour of the market, especially for large transactions. For instance, a large buy order is executed when the investor that places it accepts offers at substantially higher levels than the prevailing market price indicated by the last trade. The same holds, of course, for a large sell order, with lower bids having to be accepted. Therefore, large transactions occur simultaneously with large changes in price and they also drive the price.

The model then assumes that price changes generate proportional trading volumes. The ratio (or sensitivity) of additional trading volume to price change is assumed to be a constant of the market. It is a parameter of the model, which can be estimated from the observed distribution of the daily volume, as explained later.

In the absence of bid–ask spreads, the change in price ΔS when liquidating an amount L is simply equal to L divided by the "ratio" or sensitivity $\sigma[Vd]/S_0\sigma_C$. Equation (4) is derived later in the text.

$$\Delta S = -\frac{L}{\sigma[V_d]} \times S_0 \sigma_C \times \sqrt{1-\frac{2}{\pi}} \qquad (4)$$

S_0 is the stock price prevailing at the beginning of liquidation, σ_C the daily volatility of the collateral and $\sigma[V_d]$ the standard deviation of the daily volume. We see that the price change does not depend directly on the average daily volume, but on the standard deviation of the daily volume. It is a direct function of $\sigma[Vd]/S_0\sigma_C$, which is the ratio of the standard deviation of the daily volume to the standard deviation of the collateral price. If this ratio is low, large changes in price will not lead to additional large volumes, while the loss suffered in the liquidation is high. The inverse of this ratio is a measure of the liquidity of the market, which is more accurate than the average daily volume itself.

When the bid–ask spread is significant, we must expect to pay at least a portion of the prevailing spread. Let β be the bid–ask spread expressed in percentage terms. In order to be conservative, we add the full spread to the right-hand side of Equation (4), resulting in the following expression:

$$\Delta S = -\frac{L}{\sigma\left[V_d\right]} \times S_0 \sigma_C \times \sqrt{1 - \frac{2}{\pi}} - \beta \times S_0 \qquad (5)$$

Expected loss and liquidity spread

In Equations (4) and (5) we have not incorporated the impact of the additional uncertainty due to the finite liquidation period. This effect constitutes a real source of additional risk, since the daily price volatility can easily be around 10%. The simplest way to take this effect into account is to assume that there is a liquidation loss distribution, with mean ΔS, and standard deviation

$$S_{\text{at margin call}} \times \sigma_C \times \sqrt{\text{liquidation period}}$$

which is the standard deviation of the collateral value over the liquidation period. ΔS is computed in Equations (4) and (5) by substituting S_0 with $S_0 = S_{\text{at margin call}}$ ($= L + \lambda(C_0 - L)$). This means that we assume that liquidation causes a negative drift on the stock price, but that its standard deviation is unaltered.

We use this distribution to calculate the expected loss after liquidation EL_{liq}, conditional on a margin call being made. This is given by Equation (6), where C_l denotes the value of the collateral after liquidation:

$$EL_{\text{liq}} = E\left[\left(L - C_l\right)^+\right] \qquad (6)$$

The liquidity spread that should be charged to account for the possibility of making a loss on the collateralised position is then approximately given by

$$s = \frac{p_{\text{mc}} \cdot EL_{\text{liq}}}{L.T} \qquad (7)$$

where p_{mc} is the probability of a margin call given by Equation (3). Once again, we do not discount the expected loss in order to be conservative. Note that since $EL_{\text{liq}} \leq L$, the maximum possible credit spread is given by $s = p_{\text{mc}}/T$. The liquidity spread is always a decreasing function of the haircut and generally a decreasing function of λ (the "cushion"). When λ increases, the expected loss at liquidation decreases, but the probability of a margin call increases, usually by a smaller proportion.

Hedging a collateralised loan

The next step is to develop a strategy for hedging the potential loss during liquidation. Note that this quantity has been computed by pricing a barrier option: on the condition we hit the margin call level, we get long the shares, which we liquidate at a loss. A natural hedging strategy would then be to short the shares close to the barrier, thereby substantially reducing the risk during the liquidation period.

It is important to remember, however, that we have assumed the counterparty will fail to post margin. If the margin is posted when it is called, this hedging strategy will result in an unwanted risky short position in the shares. The optimal amount of shares to be shorted could be computed by minimising the variance of the hedged portfolio, as a function of the probability of failing to post margin, and possibly, of the correlation between a margin call being made and the failure to post margin. Certainly, this is not a perfect hedging strategy, and there will be residual risk, which will, on certain occasions, be substantial.

Another issue of practical interest is finding the most efficient way to liquidate the collateral. In the framework of our model, the optimum strategy is to sell the collateral as soon as practically possible. This is because the adverse price movement is assumed to be linear with respect to the size of the collateral to be sold. Because of this assumption, if we liquidate over time, the mean of the liquidation price will be the same, but with higher variance. In other words, the loss distribution will have the same mean but bigger variance.

Model derivation

Figure 8.2 depicts the collateral demand, D_t, and offer, O_t, curves. The two curves are determined by the aggregated buy and sell orders respectively. S_t is the current market price, being the price at which the last trade was executed. As can be seen from this figure, no more trades will be executed at this price. The two curves are represented as straight lines, since we have made the assumption that the response to a price change is linear and that, therefore, only the slope of these curves is significant. If the bid–ask spread were not zero, the demand curve would have its origin to the left and the offer curve to the right of S_t.

Suppose that the buyers are not willing to increase their bid, so that sellers decide to lower their ask: the offer curve shifts to the left (as shown on the graph). We suppose that the slopes of the curves remain stable, if the "offer shock" is fairly weak. Then, in order to sell a fixed targeted volume $\delta V = L$, the new price has to be such that:

$$\delta V = D_t' \times \delta S \text{ with } \delta S = (S_{t+dt} - S_t) < 0 \tag{8}$$

In Equation (8), the price change is assumed to be stochastic, meaning,

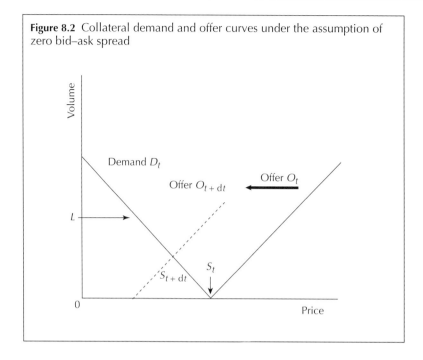

Figure 8.2 Collateral demand and offer curves under the assumption of zero bid–ask spread

therefore, that the trading volume is also stochastic. The stochastic change in price can be the result of a stochastic "shift in the demand or offer curve", or, in other words, a stochastic "demand or offer shock".

In particular, if the slope of the demand curve is small (elasticity of demand with respect to price is low), the sellers have to accept a significant reduction in price in order to sell the target amount. Similar results hold for a buy order, where the demand curve is shifted to the right. In case of liquidation, only the slope of the demand curve matters.

The daily traded volume in this model consists of all the trades resulting from shifts of one of the two curves. We suppose that the curves have constant and equal slopes. This assumption should hold at least on average in real markets, and therefore the elasticity of demand and offer would tend to be equal over time in order to guarantee equilibrium. The daily trading volume would be proportional to the sum of the intra-day price changes:

$$V_d = \left[\sum_i \left| S_{i+1} - S_i \right| \times \left| D_i' \right| \right]_{\text{sell orders}}$$

$$+ \left[\sum_i \left| S_{i+1} - S_i \right| \times \left| O_i' \right| \right]_{\text{buy orders}} \tag{9a}$$

$$V_d \approx \left(\sum_i \left| S_{i+1} - S_i \right| \right) \times \varepsilon \qquad (9b)$$

Empirical evidence, presented later on, is consistent with the above equations. The evidence consists of a histogram of the simulated weighted sum of intra-day price changes (absolute values) of a lognormal asset, which is compared with a typical histogram of the daily trading volume actually observed in the market.

For liquidating a small volume L:

$$\Delta S \approx -\frac{L}{\varepsilon} \qquad (10)$$

In this equation, both the change in price ΔS and the trading volume L are deterministic. This is a consequence of the demand-offer model described above, which only states the relationship between the trading volume and the price change, but without specifying what causes the shift in demand or offer – ie, what causes the trade to occur.

Suppose also that a trade occurs every dt, a fixed time step. Then, assuming lognormal returns for the asset, and making the additional assumption that the price during one day remains close to a price S_0 (the last assumption only simplifies computations), we get for the price change:

$$\left| S_{i+1} - S_i \right| \approx S_0 \sigma_C \sqrt{dt} \times \left| N_i \right| \qquad (11)$$

where N_i is a normal deviate. $S_0 \sigma_C$ is approximately the daily volatility expressed in absolute amount, rather than in percentage terms.

Since the daily volume is proportional to the sum of the absolute price changes, we have:

$$V_d \sim \sum_i \left| N_i \right| S_0 \sigma_c \sqrt{dt} \qquad (12)$$

Next, we compute the first two moments of the above distribution:

$$E\left[\sum_{i=1 \text{ to } N} \left| S_{i+1} - S_i \right| \right] = S_0 \sigma_C \sqrt{N} \times \sqrt{\frac{2}{\pi}} \qquad (13a)$$

$$\sigma\left[\sum_{i=1 \text{ to } N} \left| S_{i+1} - S_i \right| \right] = S_0 \sigma_C \times \sqrt{1 - \frac{2}{\pi}} \qquad (13b)$$

We can also estimate the first two moments of the distribution of the daily volume $E[V_d]$ and $\sigma[V_d]$. Matching the standard deviation, we get the following expression for the price change:

$$\Delta S = -\frac{L}{\varepsilon} = -\frac{L}{\sigma [V_d]} \times S_0 \sigma_C \times \sqrt{1 - \frac{2}{\pi}} \qquad (14)$$

The elasticity ε is defined as:

$$\varepsilon = \frac{\sigma [V_d]}{S_0 \sigma_C \times \sqrt{1 - \frac{2}{\pi}}} \qquad (15)$$

Therefore, the elasticity is proportional to the volatility of the daily traded volume. As a result, the absolute value of the price change is lower when the volatility of the daily traded volume is higher. A market where the same volume is always trading is not likely to absorb easily an additional large size. The inverse of ε is then a measure of liquidity or depth of the market.

As already mentioned, the bid–ask spread is the distance between the offer and the demand curves. To execute a sell order, a fraction of the bid–ask spread has at least to be paid to sell the first unit of collateral. If β is the spread expressed in percentage terms, adding the full spread to be conservative we get:

$$\Delta S = -\frac{L}{\varepsilon} - \beta \times S_0 = -\frac{L}{\sigma [V_d]} \times S_0 \sigma_C \times \sqrt{1 - \frac{2}{\pi}} - \beta \times S_0 \qquad (16)$$

The liquidation is not supposed to affect the sensitivity or slope of the offer curve. This allows us to estimate this sensitivity from historical data preceding liquidation. In order to incorporate the potential convexity of this curve – ie, the effect of the liquidation on the offer curve – we can assume a wider spread, which would emulate a shift of the offer curve to a lower price region.

8.1.3. Example

We have tested this liquidation model against a reduction in the share price of an an Internet company ("company"), triggered by the liquidation of 2% of its outstanding shares by a Japanese bank ("bank"), a major holder of Internet stocks. The price reduction predicted by Equation (16) was remarkably close to the one that was actually observed in the market, which was 9.5%.

The bank, in a single day, cut its holdings from 30% to 28% of the outstanding shares of the company, resulting in a continuous price reduction during the day. The percentage price reduction of the company was approximately 10%. On that date, the Nasdaq closed with marginal losses. Based on the Capital Asset Pricing Model (CAPM) the expected price reduction would have been much lower than the one actually observed.

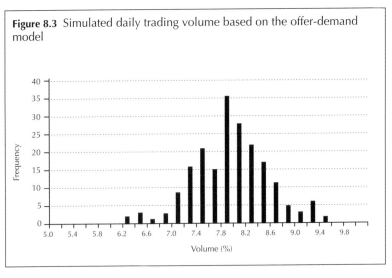

Figure 8.3 Simulated daily trading volume based on the offer-demand model

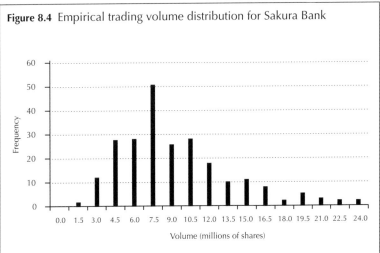

Figure 8.4 Empirical trading volume distribution for Sakura Bank

The percentage price reduction predicted by Equation (16) is 7.2%, remarkably close to the one observed in the market. Since the bank is the main shareholder of the company, the price might also have suffered from fears of information asymmetry and possible further liquidations. It is not possible to distinguish between the liquidity and the information effects without putting additional structure into the model.

In Figure 8.3, a histogram shows the daily trading volume resulting from simulating Equation (12), where the price S follows a lognormal process as described by Equation (1). In Figure 8.4, we provide, for comparison purposes, an empirical histogram for the observed daily volume for Sakura bank (this is not the bank holding the internet stock). The histogram we obtain from the actual distribution of the daily trading volume has a similar shape to the one predicted by the model by simulating the intra-day price changes. In particular, they both exhibit a positive skew.

8.2 DISCRETE HEDGING

In Chapters 5 and 6, we discussed the hedging of credit derivatives and fixed income derivatives subject to credit risk, respectively. Throughout, we made the assumption that the default swaps used for hedging could be traded continuously. It is well known that this is not the case and that this discreteness in hedge rebalancing would reduce the effectiveness of the hedge. The corresponding situation in equity derivatives is the adjustment of the Black–Scholes price to take into account non-continuous trading.

A fundamental assumption in standard financial theory (martingale pricing and in the Black–Scholes formula) is that prices of derivative instruments can be completely replicated by continuously trading a set of fundamental underlying securities. The prices of these reference securities are determined by the preferences of the investors, while derivative securities can be priced using arbitrage arguments. Investor preferences in this framework are not relevant when pricing derivative instruments. This result breaks down when continuous trading and complete replication are not possible. In this section, we make the assumption that we can only rebalance the hedge at discrete time points. In order to price derivatives in this incomplete market framework and to derive a hedging strategy, we employ techniques from dynamic programming. We consider a European option on a stock S with payoff $g(S)$ occurring at maturity T. The underlying can only be traded on pre-specified discrete time points $0 = t_0, t_1, \ldots, t_n = T$. We derive the optimal delta hedging variance-minimisation strategy, which minimises the uncertainty of the aggregate cashflows of the hedged position during the life of the option.

8.2.1. Recursive delta hedging conditions

Consider buying Δ_m units of stock at time t_m and selling them at time t_{m+1}, where $0 \leq m \leq n$. Denote by Y_m the sum of the option payoff and the net expenditure on the last $(n - m)$ hedging transactions, discounted to time t_m. The risk-free discount factor for the interval $[t_l, t_k]$ is written $\beta_{l,k}$. Then we define:

$$Y_n = g(S_n)$$

$$Y_m = \beta_{m,n} g(S_n) - \sum_{k=m}^{n-1} \Delta_k \beta_{m,k} (\beta_{k,k+1} S_{k+1} - S_k) \tag{17}$$

Y_0 is the sum of the cashflows from rebalancing the hedge and the call payoff. This is a random variable, since its constituent parts are random. The information that has been revealed at time t_m is denoted by F_m. The mean and the variance conditional on the information set F_m will be denoted by $\mathbf{E}_m$ and $\mathbf{V}_m$ respectively. Using this notation, the problem we want to solve can be reformulated as follows:

$$\text{Find } C_0, \ (\Delta_m)_{m=0}^{n-1} \ \text{ that minimise } \ \mathbf{E}_0 \left[(C_0 - Y_0)^2 \right]$$

$$\text{with each } \Delta_m \in F_m \tag{18}$$

C_0 is the fair value of the option. Note that $Y_m \notin F_m$.

In order to solve the problem depicted by Equation (18), we employ dynamic programming, where we work backward in time. First we solve for Δ_{n-1}, given F_{n-1}. This is easy to do, since the previous Δ_ms are in F_{n-1} and therefore fixed. Next, we solve for Δ_{n-2} given F_{n-2}. We use the optimal Δ_{n-1}, computed in the previous step. By iteratively applying this optimisation technique, we solve for the optimal hedging strategy across time. This is computationally efficient because we have simplified a complex minimisation problem with respect to n variables into a series on n minimisation problems with respect to one variable. The latter is much simpler to solve. Next, we make these computations explicit. Note that these are true for any hedging strategy, even if it is not the optimal variance minimisation strategy. For example, the Δ_ms could be equal to the Black–Scholes delta (note that this choice would not be optimal and that the solution to the following problem would not be the Black–Scholes price).

It is clear that:

$$Y_{m-1} = \beta_{m-1, m} Y_m - \Delta_{m-1} (\beta_{m-1, m} S_m - S_{m-1})$$

Now, at time t_{m-1} we have to solve the following minimisation problem:

$$\text{Determine } C_{m-1}, \ \Delta_{m-1}$$

$$\text{in order to minimise } \mathbf{E}_{m-1} \left[(C_{m-1} - Y_{m-1})^2 \right]$$

$$\text{where } \Delta_{m-1}, C_{m-1} \in F_{m-1} \tag{19}$$

Minimise with respect to C_{m-1} first. The optimal C_{m-1} is given by:

$$C_{m-1} = \mathbf{E}_{m-1} \left[Y_{m-1} \right]$$

The optimisation of Δ_{m-1} is dealt with in the next section. Using the recursion for Y we get:

$$C_{m-1} = \beta_{m-1,m} \, \mathbf{E}_{m-1} \left[C_m \right]$$

$$- \Delta_{m-1} \left(\beta_{m-1,m} \, \mathbf{E}_{m-1} \left[S_m \right] - S_{m-1} \right) \tag{20}$$

The residual error variance in solving the problem in Equation (19) is:

$$R_{m-1} = \mathbf{V}_{m-1} \left[Y_{m-1} \right]$$

To find its recursion, we use the iteration formula for the variance operator to deduce:

$$R_{m-1} = \left(\mathbf{E}_{m-1} \, \mathbf{V}_m + \mathbf{V}_{m-1} \, \mathbf{E}_m \right)$$

$$\times \left[\beta_{m-1,m} \, Y_m - \Delta_{m-1} (\beta_{m-1,m} \, S_m - S_{m-1}) \right]$$

$$= \beta_{m-1,m}^2 \left\{ \mathbf{E}_{m-1} \left[R_m \right] + \mathbf{V}_{m-1} \left[C_m - \Delta_{m-1} S_m \right] \right\} \tag{21}$$

The initial conditions are:

$$C_n = \varphi(S_n) \quad \text{and} \quad R_n = 0$$

8.2.2. Optimal hedge ratios

The variance minimisation hedge ratio can be obtained by optimising Equation (21)

$$\Delta_{m-1} = \frac{\mathbf{cov}_{m-1} \left[C_m, S_m \right]}{\mathbf{V}_{m-1} \left[S_m \right]} \tag{22}$$

where Δ_{m-1} is the optimal hedge ratio. By substituting the optimal hedge ratio into Equation (21) we get:

$$R_{m-1} =$$

$$\beta_{m-1,m}^2 \left\{ \mathbf{E}_{m-1} \left[R_m \right] + \mathbf{V}_{m-1} \left[C_m \right] - \Delta_{m-1}^2 \, \mathbf{V}_{m-1} \left[S_m \right] \right\} \tag{23}$$

We assume that the stock price follows a lognormal random walk with drift μ and variance σ^2. We can use a tree to discretise this process. Construction of stock trees is discussed in some detail in Chapter 7.

8.2.3 Examples

Consider an at-the-money call option, ie, where the strike price is equal to the stock forward value $S_0 e^{rT}$. In the examples that follow, we set the

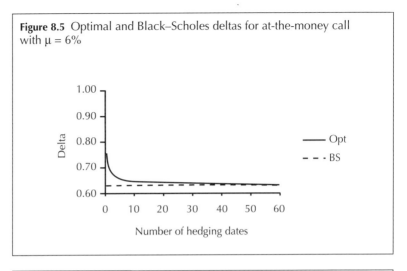

Figure 8.5 Optimal and Black–Scholes deltas for at-the-money call with $\mu = 6\%$

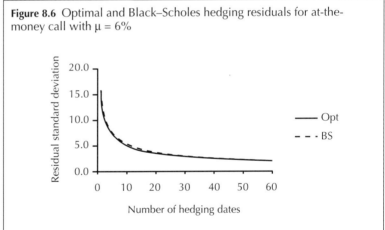

Figure 8.6 Optimal and Black–Scholes hedging residuals for at-the-money call with $\mu = 6\%$

maturity of the option equal to five years and the strike price to 100. The annual stock return volatility is assumed to be $\sigma = 30\%$ and the risk-free interest rate 6%.

In Figures 8.5 –8.8, we see the hedging strategy and the hedging residuals for growth rates μ of 6% and 14%. The results are shown for optimal and Black–Scholes hedging strategies. The number of hedging dates on the x-axis is the number of dates on which the underlying can be traded over the life of the option.

As expected, the Black–Scholes delta is the same in both Figures 8.5 and 8.7, since it does not depend on the growth rate μ. But since the hedge is rebalanced at discrete time points, changing μ affects the optimal hedge. As can be seen from Figures 8.6 and 8.8, it also affects the hedging residuals in

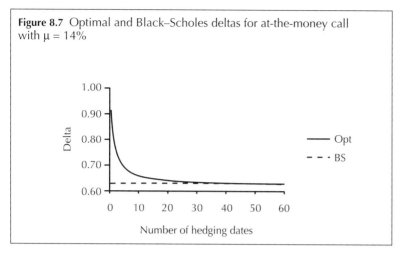

Figure 8.7 Optimal and Black–Scholes deltas for at-the-money call with μ = 14%

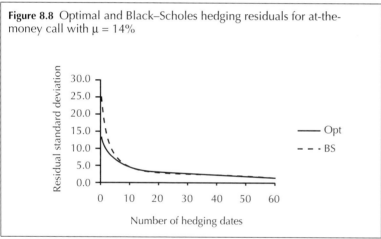

Figure 8.8 Optimal and Black–Scholes hedging residuals for at-the-money call with μ = 14%

both strategies. The optimal delta is higher because the writer has unlimited liability if the stock price increases and must guard himself against this. Notice how slowly the residual standard deviation decays with the number of hedging dates. Even for monthly hedging there is significant uncertainty. The option price is about 20, so the uncertainty is a significant proportion of this, and the 95% confidence interval of "plus or minus two standard deviations" represents about ±20% of the option price for monthly hedging.

The above effects are even more pronounced for out-of-the-money calls, when the assumed growth rate is high and the hedging is infrequent. In Figures 8.9–8.12, we show similar results for out-of-the-money call options, where the forward is 80 and the strike 100.

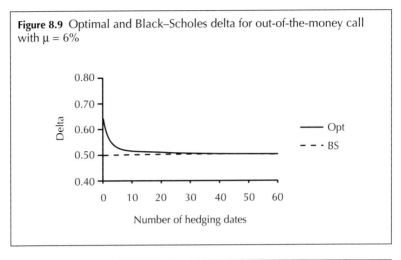

Figure 8.9 Optimal and Black–Scholes delta for out-of-the-money call with μ = 6%

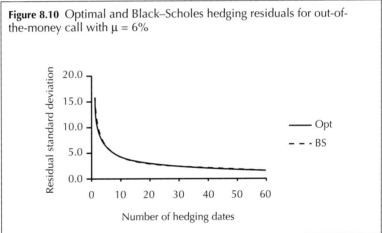

Figure 8.10 Optimal and Black–Scholes hedging residuals for out-of-the-money call with μ = 6%

Notice, as before, the significant hedging residual whichever strategy is used. Now that the option price is about 11, the 95% confidence interval of "plus or minus two standard deviations" represents about ±35% of the option price for monthly hedging.

8.3 ASYMMETRIC INFORMATION

In a market where information is freely available, we expect risk-averse investors to transfer risk to institutions with high-risk tolerance. In the capital markets, information regarding frequently traded liquid instruments is publicly available. Access to information has been a catalyst for the phenomenal increase in trading volumes in recent years. In illiquid markets, certain investors have superior information and a premium is charged for

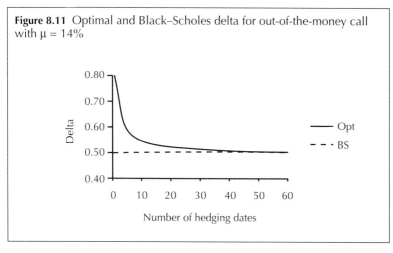

Figure 8.11 Optimal and Black–Scholes delta for out-of-the-money call with μ = 14%

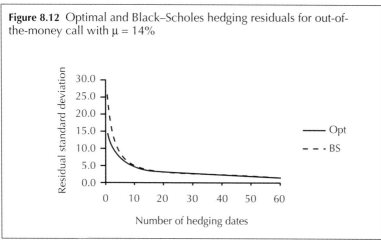

Figure 8.12 Optimal and Black–Scholes hedging residuals for out-of-the-money call with μ = 14%

transacting with them. This is, for example, true in the credit markets. Insiders in companies that are not followed closely by analysts tend to have significant information regarding the risks they face that is not available to the public. An institution that provides a financial hedge to these clients is exposed to asymmetric information, which is reflected in the pricing. This additional cost can make trading costs prohibitive and prevent otherwise mutually beneficial exchange of risk. The impact of asymmetric information is even more pronounced when dealing with non-financial risks. An institution that hedges a client against certain business or insurance risks is subject to moral hazard and adverse selection. Non-linear pricing, the use of deductibles, screening and scoring techniques are standard in the insurance industry. Sellers of insurance hold large portfolios of relatively small contracts and charge premiums according to average losses. Not knowing the exact probability of a specific policyholder suffering a loss is not crucial. However, if contracts are relatively large or their risk is non-diversifiable, asymmetric information presents a serious pricing dilemma. In this chapter, we present a more general solution to the pricing of risk with asymmetric information. We propose charging two fees: a fee paid upfront and a fee conditional on a specific event occurring.

Many contracts with asymmetric information contain more than one source of risk, one of which is often an event. Some examples of "conditional" or "dual-trigger" contracts follow:

❑ A corporate that invests its profits in the stock market would like to be hedged against "double jeopardy" – a decrease in sales volume and a simultaneous stock market crash that may be detrimental to the financial viability of the company. The corporate would enter into a conditional contract at time 0 to sell forward a stock market index at time t, only if the sales volume during a certain period falls below a trigger level. This can be viewed as a hedge against bankruptcy.

❑ An airline would like to hedge against the simultaneous decrease in the number of passengers and an increase in the oil price, which would result in increased operational costs. The airline could enter into a conditional forward contract or buy conditional options to hedge against increasing oil prices.

❑ A pharmaceutical company in the US wishes to build or expand a plant in Europe, depending on a drug's success in clinical trials, which requires financing in euros. A very good hedge for this company would be a conditional cross-currency swap.

❑ An importer of computer hardware equipment pays for imported goods in US dollars and receives revenues in the local currency. Business at this stage is minimal, but is expected to grow substantially if the economy improves. In the latter case, they are willing to use the country's credit rating as a proxy. At the current volume, they do not want to hedge their foreign exchange exposure, but if business is to grow, they should enter into a series of forward contracts.

We will demonstrate the conditional hedge and its performance in the context of the last example. The theoretical framework we use is expected utility maximisation, although the main results are not specific to this choice. The magnitude of the fees are chosen so that the financial institution is indifferent to the outcome of the event and is therefore immunised against asymmetric information. The probability of the event occurring is not needed for pricing, since the financial institution will be appropriately compensated for the variance whatever the outcome of the event. This is similar to risk-neutral valuation in standard option pricing.

The section is structured as follows. First, we discuss pricing in incomplete markets and introduce the notion of indifference price for pricing residual variance. We then present a simple hedging strategy that the client could execute without complex financial engineering. We analyse the conditional hedge and the fee structure that the financial institution could offer. Then we discuss the conditions under which the client would be willing to pay the fees for the structured hedge, instead of entering into the simple one.

8.3.1 Pricing partially hedgeable risks

In incomplete markets, arbitrage pricing is no longer valid. Either there is no exhaustive set of fundamental securities that span all the states of the world or continuous rebalancing is not possible. Under these assumptions, the individual preferences and therefore attitude towards risk cannot be ignored when pricing derivative instruments. In the problem at hand, we are facing both of the above problems. Also, we are faced with asymmetric information because the client has better information, about the probability of the occurrence of the trigger event.

We develop a pricing structure based on the hypothesis of utility maximisation (see Von Neumann and Morgenstern, 1947), which is a standard framework for making investment decisions. We emphasise that utility-based pricing provides a sound framework for our purposes, but it is not the only one. Several other alternatives are commonly accepted (see Chapter 4, Bühlmann, 1970). A utility function describes an investor's preferences and can be used to rank the desirability of different payoffs. It is an increasing function – more is always preferred to less. It is concave, ie, the marginal utility from one more unit of wealth decreases as wealth increases. The shape of the utility function describes the investor's risk tolerance. A risk-averse investor has a concave utility function, indicating that more significance is attached to losses over gains. The risk-neutral investor has a linear utility function and is indifferent to risk.

Utility theory can be used to calculate the fair premium α, for an instrument with an uncertain payout x under the agent's subjective probability, in the absence of complete replication:

$$E\left[u\left(W+a+x\right)\right]=u\left(W\right) \tag{24}$$

where W represents the initial wealth of the agent. In economics, such a price is referred to as the *indifference price*, since an agent with utility $u(W)$ is indifferent to holding an asset with random payoff x and receiving a premium a.

It can be shown (Lukacs, 1952), that the indifference price can be written in the form:

$$a(x) = \sum_{n=1}^{\infty} c_n \kappa_n \qquad (25)$$

where the cs are constants that depend on the utility function and the κs are the cumulants of the distribution $F(x)$, under the agent's subjective probability. This equation shows that there is a price assigned by the risk-averse investor to each moment of the distribution. We should not only charge for the mean but also for the variance, skew, kurtosis, etc. As a continuity condition, we shall require that $c_1 = -1$, since this ensures that a certain payoff will be priced appropriately. If the distribution of x is normal, all the cumulants higher than the second are zero and Equation (25) simplifies to:

$$a(x) = -m + c\sigma^2, \quad \text{where } c > 0 \qquad (26)$$

The price will depend on only the mean and variance of the distribution. This is true for any utility function. It is reasonable to assume that c will be positive and will increase with risk aversion (as should be the case for any reasonable concave utility function), so that the investor will be compensated for bearing risk (variance).

In the analysis that follows, we assume that pricing is based on variance, ignoring the terms from any higher-order cumulants. This means that maximising the agent's utility corresponds to minimising the variance of the distribution of x. Although this is strictly valid only for a normal distribution (or a quadratic utility function), it will simplify the discussion and allow us to derive some important intuitive results.

8.3.2 Simple hedge as a standard forward

As already discussed, we present the contingent fee structure in the following context of an importer. For simplicity, we assume that they will enter only into one contract to sell the local currency with one-year maturity. We denote by p the real probability and by q the importer's subjective probability that the country will be upgraded (a "trigger event"). It is reasonable to assume that the importer is better informed than the financial institution and therefore that the latter is subject to asymmetric information. The asymmetric information issue would be even more severe if the trigger event were the actual performance of the importer's business. Let the binary variable Λ represent the outcome of the trigger event (Λ is 1 if the country upgrades and 0 otherwise), with $E[\Lambda] = p$.

In the absence of any bespoke financial product, the importer could sell forward an amount q of the foreign currency. We denote the forward exchange rate by F and the actual future spot exchange rate at the maturity of the forward contract by f. Depending on whether or not the country is upgraded, the importer's realised possible gains or losses are shown in Table 8.1.

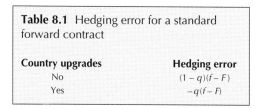

Table 8.1 Hedging error for a standard forward contract

Country upgrades	Hedging error
No	$(1 - q)(f - F)$
Yes	$-q(f - F)$

The importer's indifference price is given by the unconditional variance of the partially hedged position multiplied by his risk-aversion coefficient c, ie,

$$cV\left(p(1-q)^2 + (1-p)q^2 \right) \tag{27}$$

where $V = \sigma^2$ and σ is the volatility of the foreign exchange rate. In order to derive Equation (27), we have assumed that $E(f) = F$. With no hedge, we see from Equation (27) that the variance of his position is pV. Figure 8.13 shows the variance of the hedged position relative to that of the unhedged position. It is clear that if the importer does not have reliable information

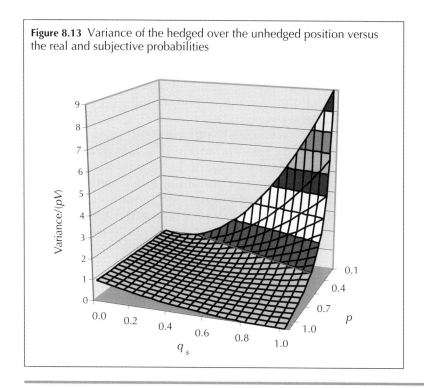

Figure 8.13 Variance of the hedged over the unhedged position versus the real and subjective probabilities

on the probability p, it may be inadvisable to hedge. This is especially important when p is small, where a slight hedging error can increase the variance substantially. It can be shown that it is only beneficial to hedge if $q < 2p$ (see the straight line in Figure 8.13). It can be easily shown that the optimum hedge is obtained by choosing $q_{opt} = p$.

8.3.3 Contingent hedge as a conditional forward

Next, we discuss the pricing of a product that completely immunises the importer against foreign exchange volatility. The product is a forward contract that is conditional on the trigger event occurring. If the country does not upgrade, then the forward will be cancelled. The product is structured and priced so that the financial institution does not need to know the probability p. This is fundamental for the viability of the product, since, otherwise, the provider of the financial hedge would suffer from asymmetric information and would probably need to offer a prohibitively expensive price. The foreign exchange exposure will be transferred from the client to the financial institution if the country's credit rating improves. The financial institution should charge for the variance that is transferred, since it cannot hedge it perfectly with existing market instruments.

Assume that the financial institution hedges by selling forward an amount q_f of the local currency, where q_f is the financial institution's subjective probability that the trigger event will occur. The resulting hedging error is the same as shown in Table 8.1 after substituting q for q_f. If the financial institution knew that the country would be upgraded, it would charge $c_f V (1 - q_f)^2$, where c_f represents its risk-aversion coefficient. On the other hand, if the financial institution knew that the country would not be upgraded, it would charge $c_f V q_f^2$. The financial institution's indifference price, which in this case is stochastic, is given by Equation (28):

$$ c_f V \left((1 - \Lambda) q_f^2 + \Lambda \left(1 - q_f \right)^2 \right) \tag{28} $$

If the financial institution could charge the price given above, regardless of the outcome Λ, it would be indifferent as to the value of the probability p.

Consider now that two fees are charged: one up-front, which is unconditional f_u, and a second one, f_c, which is conditional on the occurrence of the trigger event, ie,

$$ f_u + \Lambda f_c = (1 - \Lambda) f_u + \Lambda \left(f_u + f_c \right) \tag{29} $$

By equating the terms in Equations (28) and (29) we obtain:

$$ f_u = c_f V q_f^2 \quad \text{and} \quad f_c = c_f V \left(1 - 2 q_f \right), \quad 0 \le q_f \le 1 \tag{30} $$

The real probability p is now unimportant in the analysis as far as the financial institution is concerned. Four extreme examples will help to illustrate this. The crucial point is the ability to charge an additional fee if the country upgrades.

❑ *Example 1*. Assume $q_f = 1$ and $p = 1$. The fees will then be $f_u = c_f V$ and $f_c = -c_f V$. The event is certain to occur and the financial institution hedges the full amount and it is exposed to no variance. The net fee is zero.

❑ *Example 2*. Assume $q_f = 0$ and $p = 1$. The fees will then be $f_u = 0$ and $f_c = c_f V$. The event is certain to occur and the financial institution does not hedge as it is exposed to a variance V and will be appropriately compensated by the conditional fee.

❑ *Example 3*. Assume $q_f = 0$ and $p = 0$. The fees will then be $f_u = 0$ and $f_c = c_f V$. The event is certain not to occur. The financial institution does not hedge and is exposed to no variance. The net fee is zero.

❑ *Example 4*. Assume $q_f = 1$ and $p = 0$. The fees will then be $f_u = c_f V$ and $f_c = -c_f V$. The event is certain not to occur, but the financial institution hedges and is exposed to a variance V, and will be appropriately compensated for this by the unconditional fee.

Note that although the client is fully hedged against foreign exchange volatility when the country's credit rating improves, he is subject to a new risk because of the uncertain fee. However, the total variance has been substantially reduced. A sensible way to structure the product is to offer a range of fees, corresponding to different values of q_f in Equation (30). We emphasise that this is done only to allow the client to choose the most desirable fee structure. The financial institution is indifferent about the contract that will be chosen. If the importer chooses fees that give the financial institution a higher variance for the hedged position, he will expect to pay higher fees as compensation.

8.3.4 Simple hedge versus contingent fee

Next, we compare the conditional hedge with the simple hedge from the importer's point of view and investigate the circumstances under which they will be willing to enter into the conditional hedge, rather than simply trading a forward for a fraction of the notional.

The client's indifference price, if he follows the simple hedging strategy, is given by Equation (27), which is reproduced below:

$$cV\left(p(1-q)^2 + (1-p)q^2 \right)$$

where q represents the notional of the forward contract. As noted before, the client can maximise his utility by minimising Equation (27) with respect to q, ie, $q_{\text{opt}} = p$.

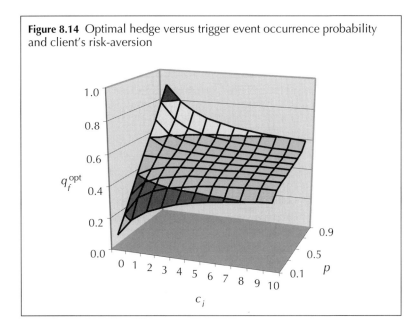

Figure 8.14 Optimal hedge versus trigger event occurrence probability and client's risk-aversion

If the importer agrees to enter into a conditional hedge with the financial institution and pay fees f_u and f_c as given by Equation (30), his indifference price will be:

$$c_f V \left(q_f^2 + p\left(1 - 2q_f\right)\right) + c(c_f V)^2 p(1-p)(1-2q_f)^2 \qquad (31)$$

where c and c_f are determined by the client's and the financial institution's utility function respectively.

The client can again maximise his utility by choosing the fees to minimise his indifference price given by Equation (31). The optimal value of the notional of the hedge is given below by Equation (32):

$$q_f^{opt} = \frac{p + 2cc_f Vp(1-p)}{1 + 4cc_f Vp(1-p)} \qquad (32)$$

If either the importer or the financial institution is risk-averse, then from Equation (32) we get that $q_f^{opt} = p$. The same result is true if $p = 50\%$. The importer evaluates Equation (32) by substituting p with q, his subjective probability that the trigger event will occur. A very risk-averse importer will choose q_f^{opt} close to 50% for any p in order to minimise the variance of the fees. If p is less than 50%, the optimal q_f^{opt} is greater than p as shown in Figure 8.14.

Note that the product $c_f V$ affects the choice of q_f^{opt} through its effect on the fee structure. The product pc corresponds to the risk-neutral probability in standard option pricing theory. The financial institution cannot deduct p from the choice of fees, since it does not know c and vice versa. This corresponds to the fact that we cannot deduce the real probabilities from asset prices, unless we make an assumption about the risk premiums. In this example, q_f corresponds to asset prices, since it determines the fees. It is worth emphasising that from knowing q_f the financial institution cannot even determine the "risk-neutral probability" pc. The financial intuition is that we are in an incomplete market framework and there is a charge for variance.

8.3.5 Minimum risk-aversion to induce trading

The contingent forward hedge transfers volatility from the importer to the financial institution. Because of the positive expected fee, for this exchange of risk to be viable, the importer should be more risk-averse than the financial institution. Assuming that the importer cannot split the trade, he can maximise his utility by choosing the minimum indifference price from entering into the standard or the conditional forward. The client should then only trade with the financial institution if the price in Equation (27) is greater than that given by Equation (31), after substituting for $q = q^{\text{opt}}$ and $q_f = q_f^{\text{opt}}$. This defines the minimum value of $c = c^m$ for the client to trade:

$$c^m = \frac{2\sqrt{1+\gamma\left[12\tilde{p}-1\right]+\gamma^2}\,\cos\left(\dfrac{\beta-\pi}{3}\right)-(2-\gamma)}{12\,c_f\,V\tilde{p}}$$

$$\beta = a\cos\left(\frac{-(2-\gamma)\left(1-\gamma(1+36\tilde{p})-2\gamma^2\right)-108\,\gamma\tilde{p}}{2\left(1+\gamma(12\tilde{p}-1)+\gamma^2\right)^{3/2}}\right)$$

$$\tilde{p} = p(1-p) \quad \gamma = c_f^2 V \tag{33}$$

This relationship is shown in Figure 8.15. For illustration purposes, assume that $p = 50\%$. If the importer enters into a standard forward, then from Equation (27), it can be seen that his indifference price is $0.25cV$. If he enters into the contingent forward, we deduce from Equation (31) that his indifference price is $0.25c_fV$. Therefore, he will only trade with the financial institution as long as $c_f \le c$.

If p is not 50%, the fees are random and the financial institution has to be less risk-averse than the importer, since his indifference price will increase due to the variance of the fees.

If we relax the assumption that the importer has to choose either the standard or the conditional forward for 100% of his hedge, then we also

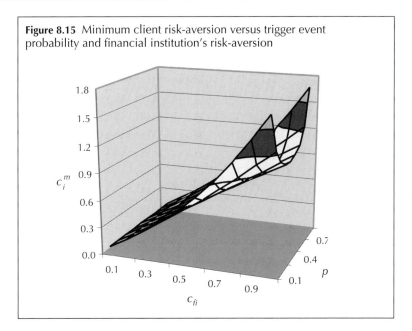

Figure 8.15 Minimum client risk-aversion versus trigger event probability and financial institution's risk-aversion

assume that they have the option to split the hedge between the two contracts as they consider optimal. They enter into a conditional hedge for a fraction α of the notional and he follows a simple hedging strategy for the remaining $(1 - \alpha)$, ie,

$$c(1-\alpha)^2 \, Vp(1-p) + c_f \alpha^2 V \left(q^2 + p(1-2q) \right)$$

$$+ c(c_f \alpha^2 V)^2 \, p(1-p)(1-2q)^2 \tag{34}$$

By choosing α in order to minimise the above expression, the importer will maximise their utility. The solution to the above can be written as:

$$\alpha_m = \left(a - \sqrt{a^2 + b^3} \right)^{\frac{1}{3}} - b \left(a - \sqrt{a^2 + b^3} \right)^{-\frac{1}{3}}$$

$$a = \frac{\left(1 + 4c_f c V\tilde{p} \right)^2}{4c\gamma(1-2p)^2}$$

$$b = \frac{\left(c_f + 8c\gamma\tilde{p} + 4c^2 c_f V\gamma\tilde{p} + c\left(1 + 4c_f c V\tilde{p} \right)^2 \right)}{6\gamma(1-2p)^2} \tag{35}$$

Figure 8.16 shows the optimal fraction of the notional for which the

Figure 8.16 α_m versus the client's and the financial institution's risk aversion (note the scale is logarithmic)

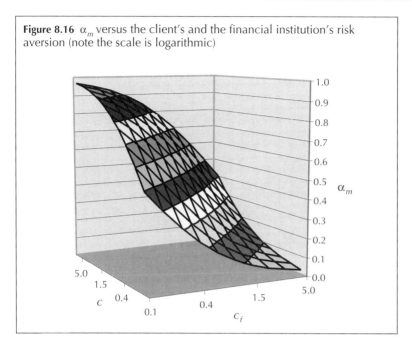

importer should enter into a conditional forward. It shows that, unless the difference in risk aversion coefficients is large, the optimal value is close to 50%. The reason for this is that, by splitting the notional in this way, the variance (and consequently the price) is almost halved. The result of charging based on variance is that the importer will try and split the notional over as many contracts as possible.

For a closer look at the risk management of a portfolio of "dual" trigger contracts, see Arvanitis and Lasry (1999) or Arvanitis (*et al*, 2000).

8.4 CONCLUSION

Market imperfections affect, to a greater or lesser extent, the functioning of most markets, especially in their early stage of development, as in the case for credit derivatives and other credit related products. The term "market imperfections" encompasses attributes of the market that make trading expensive, reduce trading volume and make pricing less transparent. Among those most commonly addressed in the financial literature are market illiquidity, transaction costs, infrequent trading and asymmetric information. High transaction costs and limited flow of information adversely impact the liquidity of the market. A certain issue can also become illiquid when it has small outstanding notional, is held in investment portfolios, or is traded by only a few market participants. Securities that differ only in liquidity, having similar cashflows and credit risk profiles, will trade at a different price; the illiquid one is going to be cheaper.

A simple example can be taken from the US Treasury market, where off-the-run (old issue) treasuries are cheap compared to on-the-run (current issue) ones, since the latter are more actively traded. In illiquid markets, the market maker charges a higher bid–ask spread to compensate for the uncertainty in the price at which he will be able to unwind his position.

Arbitrage-free pricing of derivative instruments is based on the assumption that continuous trading of the underlying securities and perfect replication of the derivative payoff are possible. The impact of these assumptions is that as far as pricing and hedging are concerned, neither investor preferences nor the actual distributions of the market variables are important. In this new expanded framework this is no longer the case. The payoffs of derivative securities cannot be perfectly replicated by trading the underlying security and therefore it is not possible to unload all the risks in the market. The investor is left with some residual volatility for which they should be compensated. Investor preferences and future evolution of market variables now become essential in pricing derivative instruments. The notion of a "universally" accepted price of a derivative breaks down, since every investor will value it using their own utility function, even if they agree on the "real" distribution of the underlying market variables. To complicate the issue further, financial institutions may use as a pricing criterion the condition that they be compensated for the marginal increase in capital consumption required to enter the new deal. Under any reasonable pricing system, derivatives should be priced such that financial institutions, being risk-neutral compared to their clients, will accept taking on risk while being compensated with additional expected gains. The mathematical framework applied to solving these problems is stochastic optimal control.

When applying this expanded class of models, we are faced with difficult estimation issues. We need to estimate the distributions of market variables. In illiquid markets it is very likely that transaction data will be scarce and that there will therefore not be much confidence on the values of the estimated parameters. It is also well known that financial time series are unstable, since they are greatly affected by the business cycle. For example, the real default probabilities will depend on where we are in the business cycle, which is generally not known at present. Note that arbitrage-free pricing does not suffer from this drawback. In this example, the risk-neutral default probabilities would be derived from default swap quotes. Estimating utility functions is even more difficult, unstable and very much model dependent. Furthermore, we may hope to estimate the utility function of the representative agent, but this is not what we are after. We want the utility function of the specific agent with whom we transact.

In incomplete markets, we lose universal pricing of derivatives, which can make risk management very complex. That is why in most markets, even if we know that they are not perfect, we prefer to use standard pricing and make rule of thumb adjustments that satisfy us. We believe that arbitrage-pricing theory will remain at the core of applied financial engineering, because of its simplicity, universality and its broad acceptance, even if its assumptions do not always reflect the functioning of the real markets. Alternatively, models of incomplete markets have a role to play too and we expect to see more development in the future. Their broader framework can provide a good environment for testing the assumptions of the arbitrage pricing theory and to perform theoretically justifiable sensitivity analysis and stress testing. These models can help intuition and provide guidance for adjusting the arbitrage-free prices to take into account market imperfections.

1   This parameter is simply the slope of the demand curve for the asset, assumed to be constant and equal to the slope of the offer curve.

2   In other words, we assume 100% correlation between default of the counterparty and value of the collateral.

BIBLIOGRAPHY

Arvanitis, A., J. Gregory and R. Martin, 2000, "Hedging Financial Risks with Asymmetric Information", *The Journal of Risk Finance*, Winter, pp. 9–18.

Arvanitis, A., and J-M. Lasry, 1999, "Hedging under Asymmetry", *Risk* 12(6), pp. 62–7.

Boyle, P., and D. Emanuel, 1980, "Discretely Adjusted Option Hedges", *Journal of Financial Economics* 8, pp. 259–82.

Bühlmann, H., 1970, *Mathematical Methods of Risk Theory* (New York: Springer-Verlag).

Fleming, W. H., and R. W. Rishel, 1975, *Dynamic & Stochastic Optimal Control* (New York: Springer-Verlag).

Gilster, J. E., 1997, "Option Pricing Theory: Is 'Risk-Free' Hedging Feasible?", *Financial Management* 26(1), pp. 91–105.

Kamal, M., and E. Derman, 1999, "Correcting Black–Scholes", *Risk* 12(1), pp. 82–5.

Lukacs, E., 1952, "An Essential Property of the Fourier Transforms of Distribution Functions", *Proceedings of the American Mathematical Society*, pp. 481–92.

Von Neumann, J., and O. Morgenstern, 1947, *Theory of Games and Economic Behaviour*, Second Edition (Princeton University Press).

Wilmott, P., S. Howison and J. Dewynne, 1995, *The Mathematics of Financial Derivatives* (Cambridge University Press), p. 186.

Wilmott, P., 1998, *Derivatives: The Theory and Practice of Financial Engineering* (John Wiley & Sons).

Press, W. H., et al., 1993, *Numerical Recipes in C*, Second Edition (Cambridge University Press).

Appendix

Credit Swap Valuation

Darrell Duffie

This review of the pricing of credit swaps, a form of derivative security that can be viewed as default insurance on loans or bonds, begins with a description of the credit swap contract, turns to pricing by reference to spreads over the risk-free rate of par floating-rate bonds of the same quality, and then considers model-based pricing. The role of asset swap spreads as a reference for pricing credit swaps is also considered.

Credit swaps pay the buyer of protection a given contingent amount at the time of a given credit event, such as a default. The contingent amount is often the difference between the face value of a bond and its market value and is paid at the time the underlying bond defaults. The buyer of protection pays an annuity premium until the time of the credit event or the maturity date of the credit swap, whichever is first. The credit event must be documented with a notice, supported with evidence of public announcement of the event in, for example, the international press. The amount to be paid at the time of the credit event is determined by one or more third parties and based on physical or cash settlement, as indicated in the confirmation form of the OTC credit swap transaction, a standard contract form with indicated alternatives.

The term "swap" applies to credit swaps because they can be viewed, under certain ideal conditions to be explained in this article, as a swap of a default-free floating-rate note for a defaultable floating-rate note.

Credit swaps are currently perhaps the most popular of credit derivatives.[1] Unlike many other derivative forms, in a credit swap, payment to the buyer of protection is triggered by a contractually defined event that must be documented.

This paper was first published in the *Financial Analysts Journal* 55(1), 1999, pp. 73–87, and is reprinted with the permission of the Association for Investment Management and Research. Since it was written, some notable developments have accompanied the rapid growth in the size of the credit-swap market. One such development is the appearance of "clean asset swaps", structured as a traditional asset swap, with the exception that the embedded interest-rate swap terminates with default. A clean asset swap is therefore more like a true par floating-rate note than is a traditional asset swap, and offers better guidance on default swap rates. A second development is some tension over whether restructuring is included as a default event in the ISDA default swap contract. This tension arises from the distinction between the expected recoveries at restructuring between loans and bonds, with loans viewed by some as superior. This difference may encourage the delivery of bonds by buyers of protection, and thus introduce some basis risk. ISDA has recently attempted to maintain some degree of standardization over this issue in order to foster further improvement in the size and liquidity of default swaps, which might be hampered by fragmentation over the contractual definition of which default events are covered.

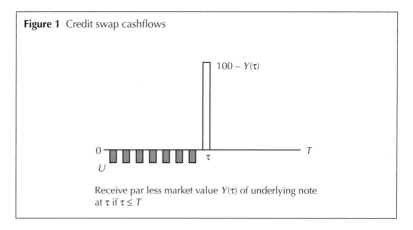

Figure 1 Credit swap cashflows

Receive par less market value $Y(\tau)$ of underlying note at τ if $\tau \leq T$

THE BASICS

The basic credit swap contract is as follows. Parties A and B enter into a contract terminating at the time of a given credit event or at a stated maturity, whichever is first. A commonly stipulated credit event is default by a named issuer – say, Entity C, which could be a corporation or a sovereign issuer. Credit events may be defined in terms of downgrades, events that could instigate the default of one or more counterparties, or other credit-related occurrences.[2] Swaps involve some risk of disagreement about whether the event has, in fact, occurred, but in this discussion of valuing the credit swap, such risk of documentation or enforceability will be ignored.

In the event of termination at the designated credit event, Party A pays Party B a stipulated termination amount. For example, in the most common form of credit swap, called a "default swap", if the termination is triggered by the default of Entity C, A pays B an amount that is, in effect, the difference between the face value and the market value of the designated note issued by C.

In compensation for what it may receive in the event of termination by a credit event, until the maturity of the credit swap or termination by the designated credit event, Party B pays Party A an annuity at a rate called the "credit swap spread" or, sometimes, the "credit swap premium".

The cashflows of a credit swap are illustrated in Figure 1, where U is the swap's annuity coupon rate, τ is the default event time, $Y(\tau)$ is the market value of the designated underlying note at time τ, and T is the maturity date. The payment at credit event time τ, if before maturity T, is the difference, D, between the underlying note's face value – 100 units, for example – and $Y(\tau)$, or in this case, $D = 100 - Y(\tau)$.

For instance, in some cases, the compensating annuity may be paid as a spread over the usual plain-vanilla (non-credit) swap rate.[3] For example, if the five-year fixed-for-floating interest rate swap rate is 6% versus Libor and B is the fixed-rate payer in the default swap, then B pays a fixed rate higher than the usual 6%. If, for example, B pays 7.5% fixed versus Libor and if the C-issued note underlying the default swap is of the same notional amount as the interest rate swap, then in this case, the default swap spread is 150 basis points. If B is the floating-rate payer on the interest rate swap, then B pays floating plus a spread in return for the usual market fixed rate on swaps or, in effect, receives fixed less a spread. The theoretical default swap spread is not necessarily the same in the case of B paying fixed as in B paying floating.

In general, combining the credit swap with an interest rate swap affects the quoted credit swap spread because an interest rate swap whose fixed rate is the at-market swap rate for maturity T but has a random early termination does not have a market value of zero. For example, if the term structure of forward rates is steeply upward sloping, then an at-market interest rate swap to maturity T or the credit event time, whichever is first, has a lower fixed rate than a plain-vanilla at-market interest rate swap to maturity T. A credit spread of 150 bp over the at-market plain-vanilla swap rate to maturity T, therefore, represents a larger credit spread than does a credit swap without an interest rate swap that pays a premium of 150 bp.

Apparently, when corporate bonds are the underlying securities, default swaps in which the payment at default is reduced by the accrued portion of the credit swap premium are not unusual. This variation is briefly considered later.

In short, the classic credit swap can be thought of as an insurance contract in which the insured party pays an insurance premium in return for coverage against a loss that may occur because of a credit event.

The credit swap involves two pricing problems:

❏ At origination, the standard credit swap involves no exchange of cash-flows and, therefore (ignoring dealer margins and transaction costs), has a market value of zero. One must, however, determine the at-market annuity premium rate, U, for which the market value of the credit swap is indeed zero. This at-market rate is the credit swap premium, sometimes called the "market credit swap spread".

❏ After origination, changes in market interest rates and in the credit quality of the issuing entity, as well as the passage of time, typically change the market value of the credit swap. For a given credit swap with stated annuity rate U, one must then determine the current market value, which is not generally zero.

When making markets, the first pricing problem is the more critical. When hedging or marking to market, the second problem is relevant. Methods for solving the two problems are similar. The second problem is generally the more challenging because off-market default swaps have less liquidity and because pricing references, such as bond spreads, are of relatively less use.

This chapter considers simple credit swaps and their extensions.[4] In all the following discussions, the credit swap counterparties A and B are assumed to be default-free in order to avoid dealing here with the pricing impact of default by counterparties A and B, which can be treated by the first-to-default results in Duffie (1998b).

SIMPLE CREDIT SWAP SPREADS

For this section, the contingent payment amount specified in the credit swap (the amount to be paid if the credit event occurs) is the difference between the face value of a note issued by Entity C and the note's market value $Y(\tau)$ at the credit event time, τ – that is, the contingent-payment amount is $D = 100 - Y(\tau)$.

Starter case

The assumptions for this starter case are as follows:

❑ The swap involves no embedded interest rate swap. That is, the default swap is an exchange of a constant coupon rate, U, paid by Party B until termination at maturity or at the stated credit event (which may or may not be default of the underlying C-issued note.) This constraint eliminates the need to consider the value of an interest rate swap with early termination at a credit event.

❑ There is no payment of the accrued credit swap premium at default.

❑ The underlying note issued by C is a par floating-rate note (FRN) with the maturity of the credit swap. This important restriction will be relaxed later.

❑ For this starter case, the assumption is that an investor can create a short position by selling today the underlying C-issued note for its current market value and can buy back the note on the date of the credit event, or on the credit swap maturity date, at its then-current market value, with no other cashflows.

❑ A default-free FRN exists with floating rate R_t at date t. The coupon payments on the FRN issued by C (the C-FRN) are contractually specified to be $R_t + S$, the floating rate plus a fixed spread, S. In practice, FRN spreads are usually relative to Libor or some other benchmark floating rate that need not be a pure default-free rate. Having the pure default-free floating rate and reference rate (which might be Libor) differ by a constant poses no difficulties for this analysis. (Bear in mind that the short-term US Treasury rate is not a pure default-free interest rate because of repo (repurchase agreement) "specials" (discussed later) and the "moneyness" or tax advantages of Treasuries.[5] A better benchmark for risk-free borrowing is the term general collateral rate, which is close to a default-free rate and has typically been close to

Libor, with a slowly varying spread to Libor in US markets.) For example, suppose the C-FRN is at a spread of 100 bps to Libor, which is at a spread to the general collateral rate that, although varying over time, is approximately 5 bp. Then, for purposes of this analysis, an approximation of the spread of the C-FRN to the default-free floating rate would be 105 bp.

❑ In cash markets for the default-free note and C-FRN, there are no transaction costs, such as bid–ask spreads. In particular, at the initiation of the credit swap, an investor can sell the underlying C-FRN at its market value. At termination, the assumption is that an investor can buy the C-FRN at market value.

❑ The termination payment if a credit event occurs is made at the immediately following coupon date on the underlying C-issued note. (If not, the question of accrued interest arises and can be accommodated by standard time value of money calculations, shown later.)

❑ If the credit swap is terminated by the stated credit event, the swap is settled by the physical delivery of the C-FRN in exchange for cash in the amount of its face value. (Many credit swaps are settled in cash and, so far, neither physical nor cash settlement seems to have gained predominance as the standard method.)

❑ Tax effects can be ignored. (If not, the calculations to be made are applied after tax and using the tax rate of investors that are indifferent to purchasing the default swap at its market price.)

With these assumptions, one can "price" the credit swap; that is, one can compute the at-market credit swap spread on the basis of a synthesis of Party B's cashflows on the credit swap, by the following arbitrage argument.

An investor can short the part C-FRN for an initial cash receivable of, say, 100 units of account and invest the 100 units in a par default-free FRN. The investor holds this portfolio through maturity or the stated credit event. In the meantime, the investor pays the floating rate plus spread on the C-FRN and receives the floating rate on the default-free FRN. The net paid is the spread.

If the credit event does not occur before maturity, both notes mature at par value and no net cashflow occurs at termination.

If the credit event does occur before maturity, the investor liquidates the portfolio at the coupon date immediately following the event and collects the difference between the market value of the default-free FRN (which is par on a coupon date) and the market value of the C-FRN – in this example, the difference is $D = 100 - Y(\tau)$. (Liquidation calls for termination of the short position in the C-FRN, which involves buying the C-FRN in the market for delivery against the short sale through, for example, the completion of a repo contract.)

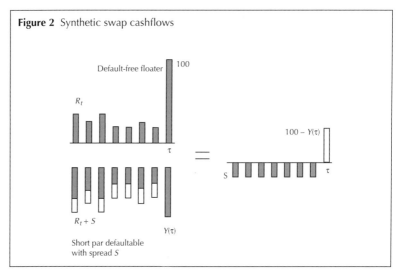

Figure 2 Synthetic swap cashflows

Because this contingent amount, the difference D, is the same as the amount specified in the credit swap contract, the absence of arbitrage implies that the unique arbitrage-free at-market credit swap spread, denoted U, is S, the spread over the risk-free rate on the underlying floating-rate notes issued by C. (That is, combining this strategy with Party A's cashflows as the seller of the credit swap results in a net constant annuity cashflow of $U-S$ until maturity or termination. Therefore, in the absence of other costs, for no arbitrage to exist, U must equal S.)

This arbitrage under its ideal assumptions, is illustrated in Figure 2.

Extension: the reference par spread for default swaps

Provided the credit swap is, in fact, a default swap, the restrictive assumption that the underlying note has the same maturity as the credit swap can be relaxed. In this case, the relevant par spread for fixing the credit swap spread is that of a (possibly different) C-issued FRN that is of the same maturity as the credit swap and of the same priority as the underlying note. This note is the "reference C-FRN". As long as absolute priority applies at default (so that the underlying note and the reference note have the same recovery value at default), the previous arbitrage pricing argument applies. This argument works, under the stated assumptions, even if the underlying note is a fixed-rate note of the same seniority as the reference C-FRN.

Some cautions are in order here. First, often no reference C-FRN exists. Second, absolute priority need not apply in practice. For example, a senior short-maturity FRN and a senior long-maturity fixed-rate note may represent significantly different bargaining power, especially in a re-organisation scenario precipitated by default.

Extension: adding repo specials and transaction costs

Another important and common relaxation of the assumptions in the starter case involves the ability to freely short the reference C-FRN. A typical method of shorting securities is via a reverse repo combined with a cash sale. That is, through a reverse repo, an investor can arrange to receive the reference note as collateral on a loan to a given term. Rather than holding the note as collateral, the investor can immediately sell the note. In effect, the investor has then created a short position in the reference note through the term of the repo. As shown in the top part of Figure 3 (with Dickson as the investor), each repo involves a collateralised interest rate, or repo rate, R. A loan of L dollars at repo rate R for a term of T years results in a loan repayment of $L(1 + RT)$ at term. As shown in the bottom part of Figure 3, the repo counterparty – in this case, Jones – who is offering the loan and receiving the collateral may, at the initiation of the repo, sell the collateral at its market value, $Y(0)$. Then, at the maturity date of the repo contract, Jones may buy the note back at its market value, $Y(T)$, so as to return it to the original repo counterparty, in this case, Dickson. If the general prevailing interest rate, r, for such loans, called the

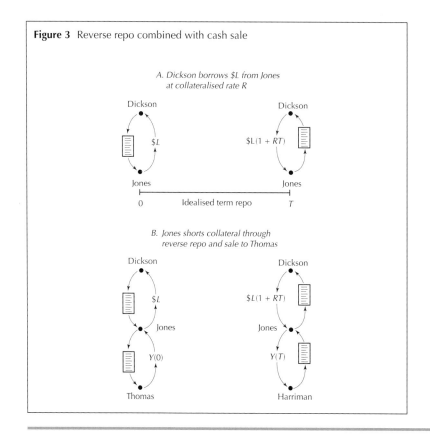

Figure 3 Reverse repo combined with cash sale

"general collateral rate", is larger than the specific collateral rate R for the loan collateralised by the C-issued note in question, Jones will have suffered costs in creating the short position in the underlying C-issued note.[6]

In many cases, one cannot arrange a reverse repo at the general collateral rate (GCR). If the reference note is "scarce", an investor may be forced to offer a repo rate that is below the GCR in order to reverse in the C-FRN as collateral. This situation is termed a repo special (see, eg, Duffie, 1996). In addition, particularly with risky FRNs, a substantial bid–ask spread may be present in the market for the reference FRN at initiation of the repo (when one sells) and at termination (when one buys).

Suppose that a term reverse repo collateralised by the C-FRN can be arranged, with maturity equal to the maturity date of the credit swap. Also suppose that default of the collateral triggers early termination of the repo at the originally agreed repo rate (which is the case in many jurisdictions). The term repo special, Z, is the difference between the term GCR and the term specific collateral rate for the C-FRN. Shorting the C-FRN, therefore, requires an extra annuity payment of Z. The arbitrage-based default swap spread would then be approximately $S + Z$. If the term repo does not necessarily terminate at the credit event, this spread is not an exact arbitrage-based spread. Because the probability of a credit event occurring well before maturity is typically small, however, and because term repo specials are often small, the difference may not be large in practice.[7]

Now consider the other side of the swap. For the synthesis of a short position in the credit swap, an investor purchases the C-FRN and places it into a term repo to capture the term repo special.

If transaction costs in the cash market are a factor, the credit swap broker/dealer may incur risk from uncovered credit swap positions, transaction costs, or some of each, and may, in principle, charge an additional premium. With two-sided market making and diversification, how quickly these costs and risks build up over a portfolio of positions is not clear.[8]

The difference between a transaction cost and a repo special is important. A transaction cost simply widens the bid–ask spread on a default swap, increasing the default swap spread quoted by the broker/dealer who sells the default swap and reducing the quoted default swap spread when the broker/dealer is asked by a customer to buy a default swap from the customer. A repo special, however, is not itself a transaction cost; it can be thought of as an extra source of interest income on the underlying C-FRN, a source that effectively changes the spread relative to the default-free rate. Substantial specials, which raise the cost of providing the credit swap, do not necessarily increase the bid–ask spread. For example, in synthesising a short position in a default swap, an investor can place the associated long position in the C-FRN into a repo position and profit from the repo special.

In summary, under the assumptions stated up to this point, a dealer can broker a default swap (that is, take the position of Party A) at a spread of approximately $S + Z$ with a bid–ask spread of K, where

❑ S is the par spread on a reference floating-rate note issued by a named entity, called here Entity C, of the same maturity as the default swap and of the same seniority as the underlying note;
❑ Z is the term repo special on par floating-rate notes issued by C or else an estimate of the annuity rate paid, throughout the term of the default swap, for maintaining a short position in the reference note to the termination of the credit swap; and
❑ K contains any annuitised transaction costs (such as cash market bid–ask spreads) for hedging, any risk premium for unhedged portions of the risk (which would apply in imperfect capital markets), overhead and a profit margin.

In practice, estimating the effective term repo special is usually difficult, because default swaps are normally of much longer term than repo positions. In some cases, liquidity in the credit swap market has apparently been sufficient to allow some traders to quote term repo rates for the underlying collateral by reference to the credit swap spread.

Extension: payment of accrued credit swap premium
Some credit swaps, more frequently on underlying corporate rather than sovereign bonds, specify that, at default, the buyer of protection must pay the credit swap premium that has accrued since the last coupon date. For example, with a credit swap spread of 300 bp and default one-third of the way through a current semi-annual coupon period, the buyer of protection would receive face value less recovery value of the underlying asset less one-third of the semi-annual annuity payment, which would be 0.5% of the underlying face value.

For reasonably small default probabilities and intercoupon periods, the expected difference in time between the credit event and the previous coupon date is approximately half the length of an intercoupon period. Thus, for pricing purposes in all but extreme cases, one can think of the credit swap as equivalent to payment at default of face value less recovery value less one-half of the regular default swap premium payment.

For example, suppose there is some risk-neutral probability $h > 0$ per year for the credit event.[9] Then one estimates a reduction in the at-market credit swap spread for the accrued premium that is below the spread that is appropriate without the accrued-premium feature – approximately $hS/2n$, where n is the number of coupons per year of the underlying bond. For a pure default swap, spread S is smaller than h because of partial recovery, so this correction is smaller than $h^2/2n$, which is negligible for small h. For example, at semi-annual credit swap coupon intervals and for a risk-neutral mean arrival rate of the credit event of 2% per year, the correction for the accrued-premium effect is less than 1 bp.

Extension: accrued interest on the underlying notes

For calculating the synthetic arbitrage described previously, the question of accrued interest payment on the default-free floating rate note arises. The typical credit swap specifies payment of the difference between face value without accrued interest and market value of the underlying note. However, the arbitrage portfolio described here (long a default-free floater, short a defaultable floater) is worth face value plus accrued interest on the default-free note less recovery on the underlying defaultable note. If the credit event involves default of the underlying note, the previous arbitrage argument is not quite right.

Consider, for example, a one-year default swap with semi-annual coupons. Suppose the Libor rate is 8%. Then, the expected value of the accrued interest on the default-free note at default is approximately 2% of face value for small default probabilities. Suppose the risk-neutral probability of occurrence of the credit event is 4% per year. Then, the market value of the credit swap to the buyer of protection is reduced roughly 8 bp of face value and, therefore, the at-market credit swap spread is reduced roughly 8 bp.

Generally, for credit swaps of any maturity with relatively small and constant risk-neutral default probabilities and relatively flat term structures of default-free rates, the reduction in the at-market credit swap spread for the accrued-interest effect, below the par floating rate-spread plus effective repo special, is approximately $hr/2n$, where h is the annual risk-neutral probability of occurrence of the credit, r is the average of the default-free forward rates through credit swap maturity, and n is the number of coupons per year of the underlying bond. Of course, one could work out the effect more precisely with a term-structure model, as described later.

Extension: approximating the reference floating-rate spread

If no par floating-rate note of the same credit quality is available whose maturity is that of the default swap, then one can attempt to "back out" the reference par spread, S, from other spreads. For example, suppose C issues an FRN of the swap maturity and of the same seniority as the underlying note and it is trading at a price, p, that is not necessarily par and paying a spread of $\hat{S}$ over the default-free floating rate.

Let AP denote the associated annuity price – that is, the present value of an annuity paid at a rate of 1 unit until the credit swap termination (default of the underlying note or maturity).

For reasonably small credit risks and interest rates, AP is close to the default-free annuity price because most of the market value of the credit risk of an FRN is associated in this case with potential loss of principal. A more precise computation of AP is considered later.

The difference between a par and a non-par FRN with the same maturity is the coupon spread (assuming the same recovery at default); therefore,

$$p - 1 = AP(\hat{S} - S)$$

where S is the implied reference par spread. Solving for the implied reference par spread produces

$$S = \hat{S} + \frac{1-p}{AP}$$

With this formula, one can estimate the reference par spread, S.

If the relevant price information is for a fixed-rate note issued by C of the reference maturity and seniority, one can again resort to the assumption that its recovery of face value at default is the same as that of a par floater of the same seniority (which is again reasonable on legal grounds in a liquidation scenario). And one can again attempt to "back out" the reference par floating-rate spread.

Spreads over default-free rates on par fixed-rate notes and par floating-rate notes are approximately equal.[10] Thus, if the only reference spread is a par fixed-rate spread, F, using F in place of S in estimating the default swap spread is reasonably safe.

An example in Figure 4 shows the close relationship between the term structures of default swap spreads and par fixed-coupon yield spreads for

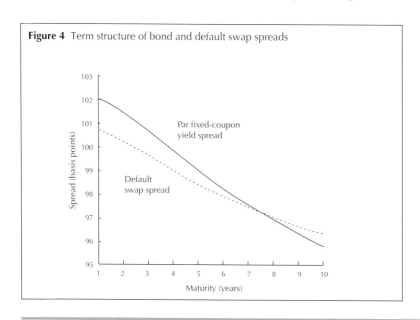

Figure 4 Term structure of bond and default swap spreads

the same credit quality.[11] Some of the difference between the spreads shown in Figure 4 is, in fact, the accrued-interest effect discussed in the previous subsection.

If the reference pricing information is for a non-par fixed-rate note, then one can proceed as before. Let p denote the price of the available fixed-rate note, with spread $\hat{F}$ over the default-free rate. Then,

$$p - 1 = AP(\hat{F} - F)$$

where AP is again the annuity price to maturity or default. So, with an estimate of AP, one can obtain an estimate of the par fixed spread, F, which is a close approximation of the par floating-rate spread, S, the quantity needed to compute the default swap spread.[12]

ESTIMATING HAZARD RATES AND DEFAULTABLE ANNUITY PRICES
The hazard rate for the credit event is the arrival rate of the credit event (in the sense of Poisson processes). For example, a constant hazard rate of 400 bps represents a mean arrival rate of 4 times per 100 years. The mean time arrival, conditional on no event arrival data by T, remains 25 years after T for any T. Begin by assuming a constant risk-neutral hazard rate, h, for the event. In this simple model (to be generalised shortly), at any time, given that the credit event has not yet occurred, the amount of time until it does occur is risk-neutrally exponentially distributed with parameter h. For small h, the probability of defaulting during a time period of small length, Δ, conditional on survival to the beginning of the period, is then approximately $h\Delta$. This section contains some intermediate calculations that can be used to estimate implied hazard rates and the annuity price.

The case of constant default hazard rate
Suppose default by Entity C occurs at a risk-neutral constant hazard rate of h. In that case, default occurs at a time that, under "risk-neutral probabilities", is the first jump time of a Poisson process with intensity h. Let

❑ $a_i(h)$ be the value at time zero of receiving 1 unit of account at the ith coupon date in the event that default is after that date and
❑ $b_i(h)$ be the value at time zero of receiving 1 unit of account at the ith coupon date in the event that default is between the $(i-1)$th and the ith coupon date.

Then,

$$a_i(h) = \exp\{-[h + y(i)]T(i)\}$$

where $T(i)$ is time to maturity of the ith coupon date and $y(i)$ is the continuously compounding default-free zero-coupon yield to the ith coupon date. Similarly, under these assumptions,

$$b_i(h) = \exp\left[-y(i)T(i)\right]\left\{\exp\left[-hT(i-1)\right] - \exp\left[-hT(i)\right]\right\}$$

The price of an annuity of 1 unit of account paid at each coupon date until default by C or maturity $T(n)$ is

$$A(h, T) = a_1(h) + \cdots + a_n(h)$$

The market value of a payment of 1 unit of account at the first coupon date after default by C, provided the default date is before maturity date $T(n)$, is

$$B(h, T) = b_1(h) + \cdots + b_n(h)$$

Now, consider a classic default swap:

❑ Party B pays Party A a constant annuity U until maturity T or the default time τ of the underlying note issued by C.
❑ If $\tau \leq T$, then at τ, Party A pays Party B 1 unit of account minus the value at τ of the underlying note issued by C.

Suppose now that the loss of face value at default carries no risk premium and has an expected value of f.[13] Then, given the parameters (T, U) of the default swap contract and given the default-risk-free term structure, one can compute the market value of the classic default swap as a function of any assumed default parameters h and f:

$$V(h, f, T, U) = B(h, T)f - A(h, T)U$$

The at-market default swap spread, $U(h, T, f)$, is obtained by solving $V(h, f, T, U) = 0$ for U, leaving

$$U(h, T, f) = \frac{B(h, T)}{A(h, T)}$$

For more accuracy, one can easily account for the difference in time between the credit event and the subsequent coupon date. At small hazard rates, this difference is slightly more than half the intercoupon period of the credit swap and can be treated analytically in a direct manner. Alternatively, one can make a simple approximating adjustment by noting that the effect is equivalent to the accrued-interest effect in adjusting the par floating-rate spread to the credit swap spread. As mentioned previously, this adjustment causes an increase in the implied default swap spread that is on the order of $hr/2n$, where r is the average of the intercoupon default-free forward rates through maturity. (One can obtain a better approximation for a steeply sloped forward-rate curve.)

Estimates of the expected loss, f, at default and the risk-neutral hazard rate, h, can be obtained from the prices of bonds or notes issued by Entity C, from risk-free rates, and from data on recovery values for bonds or notes of the same seniority.[14] For example, suppose a C-issued FRN, which is possibly different from the note underlying the default swap, sells at a price p, has maturity $\hat{T}$, and has spread $\hat{S}$. And suppose the expected default loss of this note, relative to face value, is $\hat{f}$. Under the assumptions stated here, a portfolio containing a risk-free floater and a short position in this C-issued FRN (with no repo specials) has a market value of

$$1 - p = A(h, \hat{T})\hat{S} + B(h, \hat{T})\hat{f}$$

This equation can be solved for the implied risk-neutral hazard rate, h.

Provided the reference prices of notes used for this purpose are near par, a certain robustness is associated with uncertainty about recovery. For example, an upward bias in f results in a downward bias in h and these errors (for small h) approximately cancel each other out when the mark-to-market value of the default swap, $V(h, f, T, U)$, is being estimated. To obtain this robustness, it is best to use a reference note of approximately the same maturity as that of the default swap.

If the C-issued note that is chosen for price reference is a fixed-rate note with price p, coupon rate c, expected loss $\hat{f}$ at default relative to face value, and maturity $\hat{T}$, then h can be estimated from the pricing formula

$$p = A(h, T)c + B(h, \hat{T})(1 - \hat{f})$$

To check the sensitivity of the model to choice of risk-neutral default arrival rate and expected recovery, one can use the intuition that the coupon yield spread of a fixed-rate bond is roughly the product of the mean default intensity and the fractional loss of value at default. This intuition can be given a formal justification in certain settings, as explained in Duffie and Singleton (1997). For example, Figure 5 contains plots of the risk-neutral mean (set equal to initial default) intensity $\bar{h}$ implied by the term-structure model and that mean intensity implied by the approximation $S = f\bar{h}$, for various par 10-year coupon spreads S at each assumed level of expected recovery of face value at default, $w = (1 - f)$.

Figure 5 shows that, up to a high level of fractional recovery, the effects of varying h and f are more or less offsetting in the fashion previously suggested. (That is, if one overestimates f by a factor of 2, even a crude term-structure model will underestimate h by a factor of roughly 2 and the implied par-coupon spread will be relatively unaffected, which means

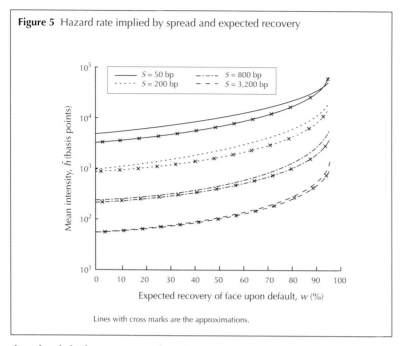

Figure 5 Hazard rate implied by spread and expected recovery

Lines with cross marks are the approximations.

that the default swap spread is also relatively unaffected.) This approximation is more accurate for shorter maturities. The fact that the approximation works poorly at high spreads is mainly because par spreads are measured on the basis of bond-equivalent yield (compounded semi-annually), whereas the mean intensity is measured on a continuously compounded basis.

If multiple reference notes with maturities similar to that of the underlying default swap are available, an investor might average their implied hazard rates, after discarding outliers, and then average the rates. An alternative is to use non-linear least-squares fitting or some similar pragmatic estimation procedure. The reference notes may, however, have important institutional differences that will affect relative recovery. For example, in negotiated workouts, one investor group may be favoured over another for bargaining reasons.

Default swaps seem to serve, at least currently, as a benchmark for credit pricing. For example, if the at-market default swap quote, U^*, is available and an investor wishes to estimate the implied risk-neutral hazard rate, the process is to solve $U(h, T, f) = U^*$ for h. As suggested previously, the model result depends more or less linearly on the modelling assumption for the expected fractional loss at default. Sensitivity analysis is warranted if the objective is to apply the hazard-rate estimate to price an issue that has substantially different cashflow features from those of the reference default swap.

The term structure of hazard rates

If the reference credit's pricing information is for maturities different from the maturity of the credit swap, an investor is advised to estimate the term structure of hazard rates. For example, one could assume that the hazard rate between coupon dates $T(i-1)$ and $T(i)$ is $h(i)$. In this case, given the vector $h = [h(1),\ldots,h(n)]$, and assuming equal intercoupon time intervals, we have the more general calculations:

$$a_i(h) = \exp\left\{-[H(i) + y(i)]T(i)\right\}$$

where

$$H(i) = \frac{h_1 + \cdots + h_i}{i}$$

and

$$b_i(h) = \exp[-y(i)T(i)]\left\{\exp[-H(i-1)T(i-1)] - \exp[-H(i)T(i)]\right\}$$

Following these changes, the previous results apply.

Because of the well-established dependence of credit spreads on maturity, the wise analyst will consider the term structure when valuing credit swaps or inferring default probabilities from credit swap spreads.

When information regarding the shape of the term structure of hazard rates for the reference entity C is critical but not available, a pragmatic approach is to assume that the shape is that of comparable issues. For example, one might use the shape implied by Bloomberg par yield spreads for issues of the same credit rating and sector and then scale the implied hazard rates to match the pricing available for the reference entity. This ad hoc approach is subject to the modeller's judgement.

A more sophisticated approach to estimating hazard rates is to build a term-structure model for a stochastically varying risk-neutral intensity process, as in Duffie (1998a), Duffie and Singleton (1997), Jarrow and Turnbull (1995), or Lando (1998). Default swap pricing is reasonably robust, however, to the model of intensities, calibrated to given spread correlations and volatilities. For example, Figure 6 shows that default swap spreads do not depend significantly on how much the default arrival intensity is assumed to change with each 100 bp change in the short-term rates. The effect of default-risk volatility on default swap spreads becomes pronounced only at relatively high levels of volatility of h, as indicated in Figure 7. For this figure, volatility was measured as percentage standard deviation, at initial conditions, for an intensity model in the style of Cox–Ingersoll–Ross. The effect of volatility arises essentially from Jensen's inequality.[15]

Even the general structure of the defaultable term-structure model may not be critical for determining default swap spreads. For example,

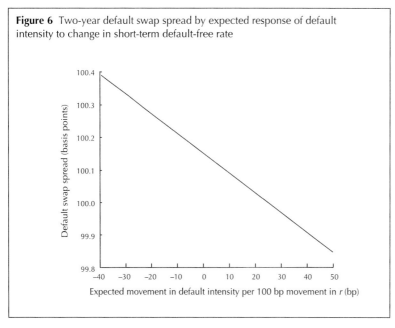

Figure 6 Two-year default swap spread by expected response of default intensity to change in short-term default-free rate

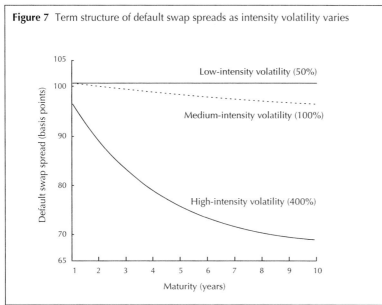

Figure 7 Term structure of default swap spreads as intensity volatility varies

Figure 8 shows par coupon yield spreads for two term-structure models. One, the RMV model, is based on Duffie and Singleton (1997) and assumes recovery of 50% of *market value* at default. The other, the RFV model, assumes recovery of 50% of *face value* at default. Despite the differ-

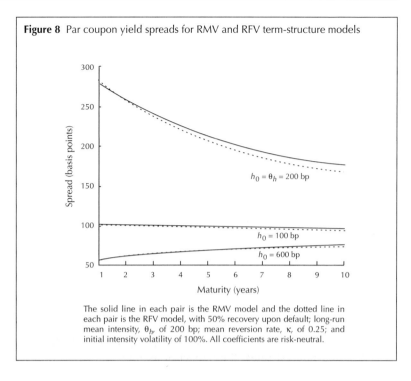

Figure 8 Par coupon yield spreads for RMV and RFV term-structure models

The solid line in each pair is the RMV model and the dotted line in each pair is the RFV model, with 50% recovery upon default; long-run mean intensity, θ_h, of 200 bp; mean reversion rate, κ, of 0.25; and initial intensity volatility of 100%. All coefficients are risk-neutral.

ence in recovery assumptions, with no attempt to calibrate the two models to given prices, the implied term structures are similar. With calibration to a reference bond of maturity similar to that of the underlying bond, the match of credit swap spreads implied by the two models would be even closer. (This discussion does not, however, address the relative pricing of callable or convertible bonds with these two classes of models.) Some cautions or extensions are as follows:

❑ The risk-neutral hazard-rate need not be the same as the hazard rate under an objective probability measure. The "objective" (actual) hazard rate is never used here.

❑ Even if hazard rates are stochastic, the previous calculations apply as long as they are independent (risk-neutrally) of interest rates. In such a case, one simply interprets $h(i)$ to be the rate of arrival of default during the ith interval, conditional only on survival to the beginning of that interval. This "forward default rate" is by definition deterministic.[16]

❑ If the notes used for pricing reference are on special in the repo market, an estimate of the "hidden" specialness, Y, should be included in the preceding calculations as an add-on to the floating-rate spreads, S, or the fixed-rate coupon, c, when estimating the implied risk-neutral hazard rate, h.

❑ If necessary, one can use actuarial data on default incidence for comparable companies and adjust the estimated actual default arrival rate by a multiplicative corrective risk-premium factor, estimated cross-sectionally perhaps, to incorporate a risk premium.[17]

❑ If one assumes "instant" payment at default, rather than payment at the subsequent coupon date, the factor $b_i(h)$ is replaced by

$$b_i^*(h) = \exp\left\{-\left[y(i-1) + H(i-1)\right]T(i-1)k_i[h(i)]\right\}$$

where

$$k_i[h(i)] = \frac{h(i)}{h(i)+\varphi(i)}\left\langle 1 - \exp\left\{-[h(i)+\varphi(i)][T(i)-T(i-1)]\right\}\right\rangle$$

is the price at time $T(i-1)$, conditional on survival to that date, of a claim that pays one unit of account at the default time provided the default time is before $T(i)$ and where φ_i is the instantaneous default-free forward interest rate, assumed constant between $T(i-1)$ and $T(i)$. This equation can be checked by noting that the conditional density of the time to default, given survival to $T(i-1)$, is over the interval $[T(i-1), T(i)]$. For reasonably small intercoupon periods, default probabilities and interest rates, the impact of assuming instant recovery rather than recovery at the subsequent coupon date is relatively small.

THE ROLE OF ASSET SWAPS

An asset swap is a derivative security that can be viewed in its simplest version as a portfolio consisting of a fixed-rate note and an interest rate swap that pays the fixed rate and receives the floating rate to the stated maturity of the underlying fixed-rate note. The fixed rate on the interest rate swap is conventionally chosen so that the asset swap is valued at par when traded. An important aspect is that the net coupons of the interest-rate swap are exchanged through maturity even if the underlying note defaults and its coupon payments are thereby discontinued.

Recently the markets for many fixed-rate notes have sometimes been less liquid than the markets for associated asset swaps, whose spreads are thus often used as benchmarks for pricing default swaps. In fact, because of the mismatch in termination with default between the interest rate swap embedded in the asset swap and the underlying fixed-rate note, the asset swap spread does not on its own provide precise information for default swap pricing. For example, as illustrated in Figure 9, a synthetic credit swap cannot be created from a portfolio consisting of a default-free floater and a short asset swap.

The asset swap spread and the term structure of default-free rates together, however, can be used to obtain an implied par floating-rate

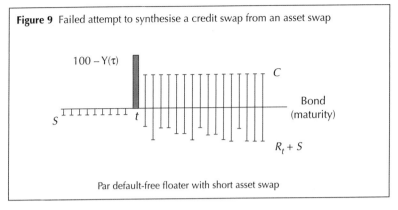

Figure 9 Failed attempt to synthesise a credit swap from an asset swap

spread from which the default swap spread can be estimated. For example, suppose an asset swap is at quoted spread $\hat{S}$ to the default-free floating rate. (In the following, repo specials and transaction costs are ignored, but they can easily be added.) Suppose the stated underlying fixed rate on the note is c and the at-market default-free interest-rate swap rate is c^*. Then, the interest rate swap underlying the asset swap is an exchange of the floating rate for $c - \hat{S}$. An analyst can compute the desired par fixed-rate spread, F, over the default-free coupon rate of the same credit quality from the relationship implied by the price of a portfolio consisting of the asset swap and a short position in a portfolio consisting of a par fixed-rate note of the same credit quality as the underlying C-issued fixed-rate note combined with an at-market interest rate swap. This portfolio is worth

$$1 - 1 = 0$$

$$= AP(c - F) + AP^*(c^* - c + \hat{S})$$

where AP is the defaultable annuity price described previously and AP^* is the default-free annuity price to the same maturity. All the variables c, c^*, $\hat{S}$, and AP^* are available from market quotes. Given the defaultable annuity price AP, which can be estimated as discussed previously, an analyst can thus solve this equation for the implied par fixed-rate spread:

$$F = c - \frac{AP^*}{AP}(c - \hat{S} - c^*)$$

The implied par rate F is approximately the same as the par floating-rate spread, S, which is then the basis for setting the default swap spread. For small default probabilities, under the other assumptions given here, the default swap spread S and the par asset swap spread are approximately the same.

To assume that the asset swap spread is a reasonable proxy for the

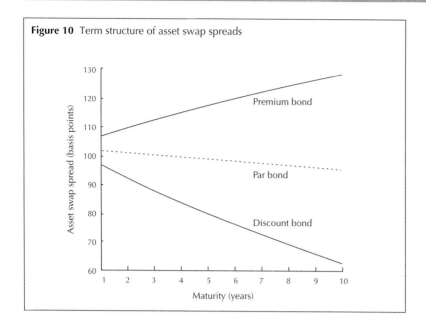

Figure 10 Term structure of asset swap spreads

default swap spread is dangerous, however, for premium or discount bonds. Figure 10 shows the divergence between the term structures of asset swap spreads for premium bonds (coupon rate 400 bp above the par rate), par bonds and discount bonds (coupon rate 400 bp under the par rate).

CONCLUDING REMARKS

This article has explained how the superficially simple arbitrage pricing (and synthesis) of a credit swap through a portfolio of default-free and defaultable floating-rate notes may, in fact, be difficult. Key concerns are, first, the ability to short the underlying note without incurring the cost of repo specials, and second, the valuation and recovery of reference notes used for pricing purposes in relation to the actual note underlying the swap. Model-based pricing may be useful because it adds discipline to the measurement and use of default probabilities and recoveries. For additional modelling of default swaps, see Davis and Mavroidis (1997).

1 Key credit derivatives in addition to credit swaps include total-return swaps, which pay the net return of one asset class over another (if the two asset classes differ mainly in terms of credit risk, such as a US Treasury bond versus a corporate bond of similar duration, then the total-return swap is a credit derivative); collateralised debt obligations, which are typically tranches of a structure collateralised by a pool of debt whose cashflows are allocated according to a specified priority schedule to the individual tranches of the structure; and spread options, which typically convey the right to trade bonds at given spreads over a reference yield, such as a Treasury yield.

2   At a presentation at the March 1998 International Swap Dealers Association conference in Rome, Daniel Cunningham of Cravath, Swaine, and Moore reviewed the documentation of credit swaps, including the specification of such credit event types as "bankruptcy, credit event upon merger, cross-acceleration, cross-default, downgrade, failure to pay, repudiation, or restructuring".

3   My discussions with a global bank indicate that of more than 200 default swaps, approximately 10% of the total were combined with an interest rate swap.

4   I do not consider here "exotic" forms of credit swaps, such as "first-to-default" swaps, for which credit event time t is the first of the default times of a given list of underlying notes or bonds, with a payment at the credit event time that depends on the identity of the first of the underlying bonds to default. For example, the payment could be the loss relative to face value of the first bond to default.

5   The moneyness of Treasuries refers to their usefulness as a medium of exchange in, for example, securities transactions that are conducted by federal funds wire or for margin services. This usefulness conveys extra value to Treasury securities.

6   As to the costs, a haircut would normally apply. For example, at a haircut of 20%, a note trading at a market value of $100 would serve as collateral on a loan of $80. At a general collateral rate of 5%, a specific collateral rate of 1%, and a term of 0.5 year, Jones incurs an extra shorting cost of which the present value is $80 \times (5\% - 1\%) \times [0.5/1 + 5\% \times 0.5)] = \$1.56$.

7   If the term repo rate applies to the credit swap maturity, then $S + Y$ is a lower bound on the theoretical credit swap premium.

8   This article does not consider these effects directly, but traders have noted that, in practice, the credit swap spread for illiquid entities can vary substantially from the reference par FRN spread.

9   This rate may be interpreted as a Poisson arrival rate, in the sense of hazard rates explained later in the chapter.

10 The floating-rate spread is known theoretically to be slightly higher than the fixed-rate spread in the case of the typical upward-sloping term structure, but the difference is typically on the order of 1 bp or less on a five-year note per 100 bp of yield spread to the default-free rate. See Duffie and Liu (1997) for details.

11 Figures 4–10 are based on an illustrative correlated multi-factor Cox–Ingersoll–Ross model of default-free short rates and default arrival intensities. The short-rate model is a three-factor Cox–Ingersoll–Ross model calibrated to recent behaviour in the term structure of Libor swap rates. The model of risk-neutral default-arrival intensity is set for an initial arrival intensity of 200 bp, with 100% initial volatility at 25% per year to 200 bp until default. Recovery at default is assumed to be 50% of face value. For details, see Duffie (1998b). The results depend on the degree of correlation, mean reversion and volatility among short-term rates and default-arrival intensities.

12 Sometimes the statement is made that if the underlying asset is a fixed-rate bond, the reference par floating-rate spread may be taken to be the asset swap spread. The usefulness of this assumption is considered in the last section of this article.

13 Recovery risk is sometimes viewed as reasonably diversifiable and relatively unrelated to the business cycle. No rigorous test of these hypotheses is available.

14 Sources of recovery data include annual reports by Moody's Investors Service and Standard & Poor's Corporation, Altman (1993) for bonds, and Carey (1998) and sources cited in it for loans. The averages reported are typically by seniority.

15 The risk-neutral survival probability to term T for a risk-neutral intensity process h under standard regularity assumptions is given by

$$E^* \left\{ \exp \left[-\int_0^T h(t)\, dt \right] \right\}$$

where E^* denotes risk-neutral expectation. See Lando for a survey. Because $\exp(\cdot)$ is convex, more volatility of risk-neutral intensity causes, other things being equal, a higher risk-neutral survival probability and thus narrower credit spreads.

16 This idea is based on the "forward default probability" introduced by Litterman and Iben (1991).

17 Multiplicative factors are preferred to additive factors in light of general economic considerations and the form of Girsanov's Theorem for point processes, as in Protter (1990). Fons (1994) provides information on the pricing of notes at actuarially implied default rates, but Fons does not provide an estimate of default arrival intensity.

BIBLIOGRAPHY

Altman, E., 1993, "Defaulted Bonds: Demand, Supply and Performance 1987–1992", *Financial Analysts Journal* 49(3), pp. 55–60.

Carey, M., 1998, "Credit Risk in Private Debt Portfolios", *Journal of Finance* 53(4), pp. 1363–88.

Davis, M., and T. Mavroidis, 1997, "Valuation and Potential Exposure of Default Swaps", Technical Note RPD-18 (Tokyo: Mitsubishi International).

Duffie, D., 1998a, "Defaultable Term Structure Models with Fractional Recovery of Par", Working paper, Graduate School of Business, Stanford University.

Duffie, D., 1998b, "First-to-Default Valuation", Working paper, Graduate School of Business, Stanford University.

Duffie, D., 1996, "Special Repo Rates", *Journal of Finance* 51(2) June, pp. 493–526.

Duffie, D., and J. Liu, 1997, "Floating-Fixed Credit Specials", Working paper, Graduate School of Business, Stanford University.

Duffie, D., and K. Singleton, 1997, "Modeling Term Structures of Defaultable Bonds", Working paper, Graduate School of Business, Stanford University (forthcoming in *Review of Financial Studies*).

Fons, J., 1994, "Using Default Rates to model the Term Structure of Credit Risk", *Financial Analysts Journal* 50(5), pp. 25–32.

Jarrow, R., and S. Turnbull, 1995, "Pricing Derivatives on Financial Securities Subject to Default Risk," *Journal of Finance* 50(1), pp. 53–86.

Lando, D., 1998, "On Cox Processes and Credit Risky Securities", Working paper, Department of Operations Research, University of Copenhagen (forthcoming in Review of Derivatives Research).

Litterman, R., and T. Iben, 1991, "Corporate Bond Valuation and the Term Structure of Credit Spreads", *Journal of Portfolio Management* 17(3), pp. 52–64.

Protter, P., 1990, *Stochastic Integration and Differential Equations* (New York: Springer-Verlag).

Practical Use of Credit Risk Models in Loan Portfolio and Counterparty Exposure Management

Robert A. Jarrow and Donald R. van Deventer

The state of the art in credit risk modelling is advancing rapidly, with a wide variety of improvements, generalisations and extensions made to the original Merton model since its publication in 1974.[1] The Merton model is called a "structural" model of credit risk. "Structural" because the assumptions underlying the model are imposed on the firm's balance sheet – the firm's structure. An alternative approach to credit risk modelling, called the "reduced-form approach", was introduced by Jarrow and Turnbull (1995) just over two decades later. "Reduced form" because the assumptions underlying the model are imposed on the prices of the firm's traded liabilities that can be deduced from the structural models – the reduced form. A recent survey summarises the characteristics of 13 different credit models that have been introduced since 1993.[2]

Given the plethora of credit risk models now available, how should a banker who seeks to use them in credit risk management assess their relative performance and, then, implement them in practice? The answer to this difficult question is the subject of this chapter.

The form of the chapter is as follows. The first section briefly reviews the various credit risk models available. In the second section we discuss how these models should be evaluated, arguing that they need to be verified on the basis of their ability to hedge market prices and not through comparison of implied default probabilities with historic default probabilities. The third section illustrates this assertion with a short empirical study involving the Merton model, and a fourth section concludes the paper.

THE CREDIT RISK MODELS

Selection of the appropriate credit risk model is an important aspect of credit risk management. An inappropriate model contains model error, and model error introduces risk into the credit risk management process. This model risk is as "real" in terms of profit/loss volatility as is market, credit, liquidity or operational risk.

For example, a recent $80 million loss at the New York branch of a major international bank stemmed from a derivatives dealer's activities who believed that his pricing model was better than "the market". Generating biased quotes outside the rest of the market, the model caused his trades to dominate new transactions. This imbalanced position continued until outside auditors called a halt to his trading activity.

Historically, the first class of credit risk models to be formulated was based on the structural approach. Such models include the original Merton model (1974) and the extension of this model to random interest rates by Shimko, Tejima and van Deventer (1993). This class of models imposes assumptions on the evolution of the value of the firm's underlying assets. The liability structure of the firm, in conjunction with the firm's asset value fluctuations, determines the occurrence of bankruptcy and the payoffs (recovery rates) in the event of default. See Jones, Mason and Rosenfeld (1984), *Risk* Magazine (September, 1998) and Jarrow and van Deventer (1998) for a summary of the empirical results relating to this class of models.

Extensions of the structural approach, assuming exogenous recovery rates, include the work by Nielsen, Saá-Requejo and Santa Clara (1993) and Longstaff and Schwartz (1995). The Longstaff and Schwartz paper contains some empirical results.

The original Merton model, like the Black–Scholes model, assumed constant interest rates. Constant interest rates are inconsistent with market realities, and this assumption is one of the reasons why implementations of the original Merton model have not performed well in empirical tests.

Random interest rates, from both an intuitive and a theoretical perspective, should be an essential feature of any credit risk model. Indeed, the US taxpayers' trillion dollar experience with the interest rate-induced failures of many banks in the savings and loan industry provides anecdotal evidence for the validity of this claim. More anecdotal evidence also comes from the current troubles experienced by firms in Asia, where high interest rates (used to defend national currencies) have triggered record bankruptcies. Random interest rates, in fact, have been a standard assumption underlying all recent models of the credit risk process.[3]

It was the desire to include random interest rates and the discovery of the Heath–Jarrow–Morton (1992) term structure modelling technology that led to the reduced-form approach to modelling credit risk (Jarrow and Turnbull, 1995, and Jarrow, Lando and Turnbull, 1997). Empirical verification of these models is just becoming available, for which see Duffee (1999) and references therein.

Reduced-form models impose their assumptions directly on the prices of the firm's traded liabilities – primarily its debt – and on the default-free term structure of interest rates. Intuitively, the assumptions on the firm's debt prices relate to the credit spread, which is decomposable into the probability of bankruptcy (per unit time) multiplied by the loss (per promised dollar) in the event of bankruptcy. Exogenous assumptions are imposed on these quantities (the bankruptcy and recovery rate process) directly. This procedure gives the reduced-form models added flexibility in fitting market realities.

This is especially true of the implicit assumptions embedded in the structural approach regarding corporate capital structure policy. The structural approach assumes that the corporate capital structure policy is static, with the liability structure fixed and unchanging. For example, the Merton model (and its extension by Shimko, Tejima and van Deventer, 1993) assumes that management puts a debt structure in place and leaves it unchanged even if the value of corporate assets (and therefore equity) has doubled. This is too simplistic to realistically capture management behaviour and the dynamics of bankruptcy. It is our belief that management attempts to maintain a more constant debt/equity ratio across time. For example, a real estate entrepreneur would confirm that, when a building purchased for $100 million and financed with an $80 million loan doubles in value, he would refinance for $160 million. The Merton model cannot capture this behaviour, whereas the reduced-form model can.

The common implementation of the Merton model uses accounting data and equity prices to estimate the relevant parameters. The common implementation of the reduced-form models uses Treasury and corporate debt prices. Reduced-form models have been criticised for this reason because corporate debt markets are known to be less liquid than equity markets (with a scarcity of available quotes and wider bid/ask spreads), the implication being that corporate debt prices are useless and that they contain little if any useful information. This is a narrow point of view, not reflecting market efficiency. All corporate securities contain some information concerning the potential default of the issuer. Although perhaps noisier than equity prices, debt prices do provide valuable information.

To accommodate the wider bid-offered spreads in thinly traded debt, reduced-form models need to model liquidity risk explicitly. Then, however, they can reliably use debt prices to extract relevant information. In fact, such models, if properly constructed, can be used to extract implied parameters from all or any subset of the available market prices: equity prices, debt prices, subordinated debt prices or credit derivative prices.

EVALUATION OF CREDIT RISK MODELS

All credit risk models are based on the option pricing technology underlying the famous Black–Scholes formula. This technology is sometimes called the "risk-neutral" valuation technology. But, regardless of its name, the basic framework underlying these models is the same. Derivatives are priced by synthetic replication in complete markets that are arbitrage-free. Pricing by "synthetic replication" means that a derivative is priced by determining the cost of synthetically constructing the derivative using other traded securities. For example, a call option on a stock is priced in a Black–Scholes model by determining the cost of constructing the option using a dynamic portfolio of the underlying stock and riskless borrowing.

This means that a model is valid if and only if its implied "hedge" works.[4] The implied "hedge" is the synthetic replication portfolio used in reverse. This insight implies that the only valid way to test the outputs[5] of a credit risk model is to test its hedging performance. Hence, a model that fails a hedging test is misspecified. A misspecified model, if used to infer default probabilities, will only generate misspecified estimates.

It could be argued that the implicit default probabilities obtained from a credit risk model could be empirically verified by comparing them to historical default frequencies. In theory this is correct, but in practice it does not work. In Japan, for instance, Nippon Credit Bank and Long-Term Credit Bank of Japan were both nationalised and neither defaulted. A hedging test of the pricing of both firms' equity and bonds would have provided an informative test of model performance. No test based on default experience could have been performed. As with this example, empirical comparisons of estimated and historical default probabilities do not work for one of two reasons.

One, it can be argued that standard statistical procedures do not apply. Indeed, default is a firm-specific event that has not yet occurred. Since it has not, there are no historical data of relevance. For example, how many IBMs are there, or have there been?

Two, it can be argued that even if standard statistical procedures apply, default is a rare event and not enough observations are available to obtain reliable estimates. Indeed, if one believes that existing firms are samples from a population of similar firms, some of which have defaulted in the past, then statistical methods do apply. But here defaults are so rare that the standard errors of the default likelihoods are too large and the power of standard statistical procedures is too small. The bottom line is that any reasonable estimate of default probability is consistent with the data. Therefore, comparisons of estimates with historical default probabilities are not very informative.

To illustrate this last point, we perform an empirical investigation of the Merton model to demonstrate the wide range of default probabilities that are consistent with a reasonable specification of the model's parameters, thereby casting doubt on the reliability of the estimates obtained.

AN EMPIRICAL INVESTIGATION OF THE MERTON MODEL

This section presents an empirical investigation of the Merton model using a unique data set to determine the implied default probabilities. The unique data set employed is the First Interstate Bancorp data set previously used by Jarrow and van Deventer (1998). The set contains weekly quotes on potential new issues of various maturity bonds of First Interstate Bancorp from January 3, 1986, to August 20, 1993. For this illustration the two-year debt issue is employed. For these data, we show that the range of the implied default probabilities obtained for reasonable specifications of the input parameters is too wide and too time-varying to be verifiable using historical default data. This evidence casts doubt on the reliability of using historical default data to test a credit risk model.

DEFAULT PROBABILITIES FROM MERTON'S MODEL

Merton's model of risky debt views debt as a put option on the firm's value. In this simple model debt is a discount bond (no coupons) with a fixed maturity. Firm value is represented by a single quantity that is interpreted as the value of the underlying assets of the firm. The firm defaults at the maturity of the debt if the asset value is less than the promised payment. Using the Black–Scholes technology, an analytic formula for the debt's value can easily be obtained. In this solution it is well known that the expected return on the value of the firm's assets does not appear. In fact, it is this aspect of the Black–Scholes formula that has made it so useable in practice.

From Merton's risky debt model, one can infer the implied *pseudo* default probabilities. These probabilities are not those revealed by actual default experience but those needed to do a valuation. They are sometimes called *martingale* or *risk-adjusted* probabilities because they are the empirical probabilities, after an adjustment for risk, used for valuation purposes. If we are to compare implied default probabilities from Merton's model with historical default experience, we need to remove this adjustment.

Removal of the adjustment is akin to inserting expected returns back into the valuation procedure. To do this, we need a continuous-time equilibrium model of asset returns consistent with the Merton risky debt structure. Merton's (1973) intertemporal capital asset pricing model provides such a structure. We now show how to make this adjustment.

Let the value of the ith firm's assets at time t be denoted by $V_i(t)$, with its expected return per unit time denoted by a_i and its volatility per unit time denoted by σ_i. Under the Merton (1974) structure, we have that

$$V_i(t) = V_i(0)e^{\mu_i t + \sigma_i Z_i(t)}$$

where $\mu_i = a_i - \sigma_i^2/2$ and $Z_i(t)$ is a normally distributed random variable with mean 0 and variance t.

The evolution of $V_i(t)$ above is under the empirical probabilities.[6] In Merton's (1973) equilibrium asset pricing model, when interest rates and the investment opportunity set[7] are constant, the expected return on the ith asset is equal to

$$a_i = r + \frac{\sigma_i \rho_{iM}}{\sigma_M}\left(a_M - r\right)$$

where r is the risk-free rate,[8] the subscript M refers to the "market" portfolio or, equivalently, the portfolio consisting of all assets of all companies in the economy, and ρ_{iM} denotes the correlation between the return on the asset value of firm i and the market portfolio.

Using this equilibrium relationship, the drift term on the ith company's assets can be written as

$$\mu_i = -\frac{1}{2}\sigma_i^2 + \left(1 - b_i\right)r + b_i a_M$$

where $b_i = \sigma_i \rho_{iM}/\sigma_M$ is the ith firm's beta.

For expositional purposes, we parameterise the expected return on the market, a_M, as equal to a constant, k, times the risk-free interest rate, r:

$$a_M = kr$$

This is without loss of generality. Using this relation, we have that

$$\mu_i = -\frac{1}{2}\sigma_i^2 + \left(1 - b_i + b_i k\right)r$$

In Merton's risky debt model, the firm defaults at the maturity of the debt if the firm's asset value is below the face value of the debt. We now compute the probability that this event occurs.

Let t be the maturity of the discount bond and let B be its face value. Bankruptcy occurs when $V_i(t) < B$; formally,

$$\text{Probability}\left(\text{Default}\right) = \text{Probability}\left(V_i(t) < B\right)$$

$$= N\left(\frac{\ln\left(B/V_i(0)\right) - \mu_i t}{\sigma_i \sqrt{t}}\right)$$

where $N(\cdot)$ represents the cumulative normal distribution function.

We see from this expression that default probabilities are determined given the values of the parameters $(B, V_i(0), \sigma_i, r, \sigma_M, \rho_{iM}, k)$. The estimation of these parameters is discussed in the next section.

EMPIRICAL ESTIMATION OF THE DEFAULT PROBABILITIES

As mentioned previously, this estimation is based on First Interstate Bancorp bond data. The time period covered is from January 3, 1986, to August 20, 1993. Over this period the bank solicited weekly quotes from various investment banks regarding new issue rates on debt issues of various maturities. The two-year issue is employed in the analysis that follows; see Jarrow and van Deventer (1998) for additional details.

To estimate the default probabilities, we need to estimate the seven parameters $(B, V_i(0), \sigma_i, r, \sigma_M, \rho_{iM}, k)$.

The face value of the firm's debt, B, can be estimated using balance sheet data. To do this, we choose B to be equal to the total value of all of the bank's liabilities, compounded for two years at the average liability cost for First Interstate.

Table 1 Merton model default probabilities (%)

Correlation of asset returns with market returns	Ratio of expected return on market to risk-free rate				
	5.00	4.00	3.00	2.00	1.00
1.00	0.06	0.49	2.57	9.09	22.83
0.75	0.49	1.76	5.06	11.79	22.83
0.50	2.57	5.06	9.09	14.99	22.83
0.25	9.09	11.79	14.99	18.67	22.83
0.00	22.83	22.83	22.83	22.83	22.83
−0.25	43.08	37.64	32.38	27.42	22.83
−0.50	64.78	54.16	43.08	32.38	22.83
−0.75	82.14	69.70	54.16	37.64	22.83
−1.00	92.68	82.14	64.78	43.08	22.83

Date: November 17, 1898; actual credit spread, 1.220%.

The firm value at time 0, $V_i(0)$, and the firm's volatility parameter, σ_i, are both unobservable. This is one of the primary difficulties with using Merton's model and with the structural approach in general. For this reason, both the market value of First Interstate's assets and the firm's asset volatility were implied from the observable values of First Interstate common stock and First Interstate's credit spread for a two-year straight bond issue. We choose those values that minimise the sum of squared errors of the market price from the theoretical price (see Jarrow and van Deventer, 1998, for details).

The spot rate, r, is observable and the volatility of the market portfolio, σ_M, can easily be estimated from market data. As a proxy for the market portfolio we used the S&P500 index. The volatility of the index over the sample period was 15.56%.

This leaves two parameters: the expected return on the market and the correlation between the firm's assets and the market portfolio. As both quantities are unobservable and arguably difficult to estimate, we allow them to be "free" parameters. That is, we leave them unspecified and estimate default probabilities for a range of their values. The range of values we use for the correlation, ρ_{iM}, is from −1 to 1, and the range of ratios, k, of the market return to the risk-free rate is from 1 to 5.

Finally, in order to compare the derived two-year default probabilities with the observable credit spread, which is quoted on an annual basis, we convert the actual two-year default probability to a discrete annual basis using the following conversion formula:

$$\text{Probability}\left[\text{Annual}\right] = 1 - \sqrt{1 - \text{Probability}\left[\text{Two year}\right]}$$

Table 2 Standard deviation of Merton default probabilities, 1986–93 (%)

Correlation of asset returns with market returns	Ratio of expected return on market to risk-free rate				
	5.00	4.00	3.00	2.00	1.00
1.00	0.48	1.13	2.34	4.10	6.41
0.75	1.13	1.98	3.16	4.61	6.41
0.50	2.34	3.16	4.10	5.17	6.41
0.25	4.10	4.61	5.17	5.76	6.41
0.00	6.41	6.41	6.41	6.41	6.41
−0.25	9.52	8.68	7.87	7.11	6.41
−0.50	12.56	11.16	9.52	7.87	6.41
−0.75	13.84	13.10	11.16	8.68	6.41
−1.00	12.88	13.84	12.56	9.52	6.41

Table 3 Ratio of standard deviation of Merton default probabilities to standard deviation of credit spread, 1986–93 (%)

Correlation of asset returns with market returns	Ratio of expected return on market to risk-free rate				
	5.00	4.00	3.00	2.00	1.00
1.00	84	200	413	723	1131
0.75	200	350	557	815	1131
0.50	413	557	723	912	1131
0.25	723	815	912	1017	1131
0.00	1131	1131	1131	1131	1131
−0.25	1680	1533	1390	1256	1131
−0.50	2218	1971	1680	1390	1131
−0.75	2443	2312	1971	1533	1131
−1.00	2274	2443	2218	1680	1131

Table 1 gives these annualised default probabilities for November 17, 1989.[9] One can see the surprisingly wide range of default probabilities that are possible as we vary the free parameters. Across the entire table the annualised default probability varies from 0.06% to 92.68%. For a correlation of 1 (the typical asset),[10] the range of default probabilities for a market return to risk-free rate ratio, k, of between 2 and 3 is 9.09% to 2.57%. These ranges are quite large and they cast doubt on our abilities to validate the model credibly using historical default frequencies.

More insight into the imprecision of the Merton default probability estimates can be obtained by looking at the variability of these estimates across time. For illustrative purposes, we set the correlation between First Interstate assets and the market portfolio to be 1. We look at the two extreme market return to risk-free rate ratios $k = 5$ and $k = 1$.

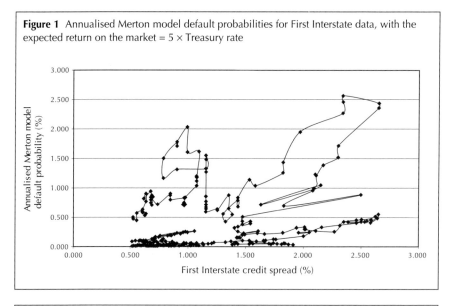

Figure 1 Annualised Merton model default probabilities for First Interstate data, with the expected return on the market = 5 × Treasury rate

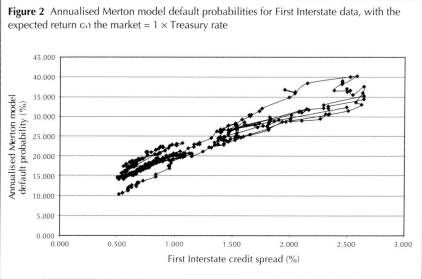

Figure 2 Annualised Merton model default probabilities for First Interstate data, with the expected return on the market = 1 × Treasury rate

Time-series graphs of the annualised default probabilities are displayed in Figures 1 and 2.[11] The line connecting the data is drawn chronologically from point to point. The highest end of the line represents the newest data points. The primary observation from these graphs is the high degree of instability that the estimates exhibit across time. This is especially true for the larger market return to risk-free rate ratio, $k = 5$. The more stable estimates for $k = 1$, however, appear to be implausibly high.

To obtain a better sense of the magnitude of the variability in these default probability estimates, we computed the standard deviations of the estimates across time. The results are given in Table 2, from which they can be seen to be quite large. To put them in perspective, the standard deviation of First Interstate Bancorp's two-year credit spread over the sample period was only 0.566%.

In Table 3 we consider the ratio of the annualised default probability standard deviations to the standard deviation of First Interstate's two-year credit spread. The results emphasise further the instability of the estimated default probabilities. Except for the case where the correlation coefficient is 1 and the market return to risk-free rate ratio, k, is 5, the variation in default probabilities far exceeds the volatility of the underlying credit spread.

In summary, given the wide variation in default probabilities for small changes in the input parameters, this illustration supports the statement that comparing estimated default probabilities with historical default frequencies does not provide a very powerful test of a credit risk model.

CONCLUDING COMMENTS

The successful implementation and practical use of a credit model involves critical choices. In these choices, bank management and bank regulators have a fiduciary responsibility to shareholders and depositors to completely "vet" or audit all the models that are used. A black box approach to modelling fails this test. All credit models used should be subjected to critical analysis and review, either publicly or privately.

All models should be tested "out of sample" by the user (or an auditor employed by the user). The richest tests involve historical periods with substantially different market conditions (say the high-interest period 1979–85 in the United States) or tests based on other countries with quite different market conditions. Japan and the rest of Asia over the last decade, for example, provide a much better testing ground than just using the almost 15 years of prosperity in the United States.

All models have weaknesses, and it is better to seek them out aggressively than to identify them after a problem has occurred. An ideal credit risk management system should perhaps utilise many credit models to help to "diversify" this model risk. Such a system would allow the user full control of the model audit and performance testing process. This kind of system would end the debate about relative model performance because it is "agnostic". Through its use the user would obtain definitive proof of "best model performance".

Despite their inherent difficulties, models are the key ingredient of a successful credit risk management system. This is because they can be used to estimate true credit-adjusted valuations that correctly reflect the risk-adjusted value of a borrower's promise to repay. Such credit-adjusted valuations can and should be used for:

❏ all major derivative exposures;
❏ callable bonds;
❏ standby letters of credit;
❏ other contingent credit lines;
❏ all value-at-risk calculations;
❏ all risk-adjusted capital calculations;
❏ middle office exposure management;
❏ mark-to-market real-time trade authorisations;
❏ net income simulation with default adjustment.

Finally, a good credit risk model should be rich enough to allow extension to retail credit scoring as well as small-business credit scoring.

Credit model risk management has much in common with loan portfolio management. Diversification of model risk is essential, and so is the transparency and comprehensiveness of the analytics used. The pursuit of perfection in credit risk modelling will continue for decades, and practical bankers should plan for and implement smooth transitions from one model to the next as the state of the art improves.

1   See Chen *et al.* (1998).
2   *Ibid.*, p. 100.
3   *Ibid.*
4   It is sometimes believed that if a derivatives model matches market prices correctly, the model is "proven". This is not a sufficient test. Any reasonable model (with enough time-varying parameters) can be calibrated to match the relevant market prices. Given that this is true for many models, matching market prices cannot be used to differentiate them.
5   It can be argued that another way to test a model is to test its inputs – ie, its assumptions. For example, if the model assumes constant interest rates, one can test to see if this assumption is empirically valid.
6   Under the pseudo-probabilities $a_i = r$.
7   The investment opportunity set is the means and covariances of all the assets' returns. This implies that the mean and covariances with the market return are also deterministic.
8   In this structure this is the spot rate of interest on default-free debt.
9   This date was chosen because it is the mid-point of the First Interstate data set.
10 The typical asset has a beta of 1. If the volatility of the market and the firm's asset are equal, the correlation is one as well.
11 As in Jarrow and van Deventer (1998), we omit two outlying data points August 14 and 21, 1992.

BIBLIOGRAPHY

Chen, D. H., H. H. Huang, R. Kan, A. Varikooty and H. N. Wang, 1998, "Modelling and Managing Credit Risk", in *Asset & Liability Management: A Synthesis of New Methodologies* (London: Risk Publications), pp. 97–115.

Duffee, G., 1999, "Estimating the Price of Default Risk", *Review of Financial Studies* 12(1), pp. 197–226.

Russian Federation's massive US$9.7 billion default, this represents increases of 97% in issuer terms and 115% in terms of the dollar amount of defaulted debt from 1997, when 70 issuers defaulted on US$9.3 billion. While total default activity was fairly steady throughout the year, US-issuer defaults were clustered toward the end of the year with 25, or 47%, occurring in the fourth quarter. Of particular note in 1998 were its three sovereign defaults: Venezuela, the Russian Federation, and Pakistan.[1]

In 1998 we saw approximate doubling in both the number and magnitude of bond defaults which, tempered by robust growth in issuance, produced percentage increases of 63% and 87% for the all-corporate and speculative-grade default rates, respectively. Moody's trailing 12-month default rate for all corporate issuers jumped from 0.68% at the start of 1998 to 1.27% at the start of 1999 after holding steady at around 1.0% for most of the year. Moody's speculative-grade trailing 12-month default rate ended the year at 3.31% versus 2.02% for 1997 (see Figure 1). These rates remain below the averages since January 1970 of 1.04% for all corporates and 3.37% for speculative-grade. For US-only speculative-grade issuers, the trailing 12-month default rate climbed to 3.84% as of January 1, 1999, versus 2.14% a year ago.

DEFAULTS AND DEFAULT RATES SINCE 1920

Moody's bases the results of its default research on a proprietary database of ratings and defaults for industrial and transportation companies, utilities, financial institutions, and sovereigns that have issued long-term debt to the public. In total, the data cover the credit experiences of over 15,200 issuers that sold long-term debt publicly at some time between 1919 and the start of 1999. As of January 1, 1999, over 4,600 of those issuers held Moody's ratings. These issuers account for the bulk of the outstanding dol-

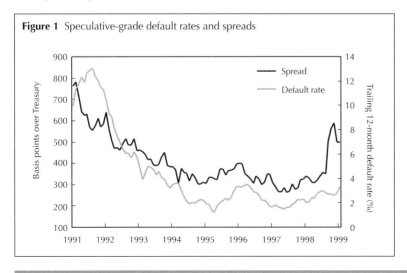

Figure 1 Speculative-grade default rates and spreads

lar amount of US public long-term corporate debt and a substantial part of public issuance abroad.

Moody's considers an obligation, including the 3,200 long-term bond defaults in our database, to be in default if there has been any missed or delayed disbursement of interest and/or principal, bankruptcy, receivership, or distressed exchange where (i) the issuer offered bondholders a new security or package of securities that amount to a diminished financial obligation (such as preferred or common stock, or debt with a lower coupon or par amount) or (ii) the exchange had the apparent purpose of helping the borrower avoid default. To calculate default rates, we use the issuer as the unit of study rather than individual debt instruments or outstanding dollar amounts of debt.

The incidence of default by both rated and unrated issuers is spread unevenly over this century, with large numbers of defaults in the 1920s, the depression of the 1930s, and again in the late 1980s and early 1990s, as portrayed in Figure 2. January 1920 through mid-1929 was a period of cyclical and declining default risk that resembled the 1980s in terms of the average default rate. However, the next period, from mid-1929 through December 1939, produced the heaviest default activity of this century. The Great Depression generated a 79-year high, one-year corporate default rate of 9.2% in July 1932, indicating that nearly one in 10 of Moody's-rated corporate issuers defaulted over the following year.

The severity of the depression and its characteristic asset depreciation ensured that such high rates of default did not quickly subside. For the eight-year period beginning in January 1930, the default rate averaged 3.7% – nearly as high as the recent 4.1% peak set in July 1991. The default rate jumped again at the beginning of World War II, reflecting the war-related defaults of Italian, German, French, Japanese, Czechoslovakian, and Austrian companies. Following the war, however, default risk subsided to very low levels. These low levels persisted until 1970, when the defaults of Penn Central Railroad and 25 of its affiliates shook fixed-income markets. After 1970, default risk again ebbed and was moderate to low by historical standards until 1982, when the modern period of relatively high default risk began.

Figure 2 also plots the US Industrial Production Index (IP) in terms of its deviation from trend,[2] whose correlation with the all-corporate default rate is a fairly weak –0.14. From 1920 through 1965 significant increases in the default rate were typically preceded by weakness in the overall economy as reflected in total IP. Since 1965, it has more often been the case that increases in the default rate occur in advance of a weakening in the general economy. For example, in the worst episode of the postwar era, the default rate began to rise in June 1988 rising from 0.85% to its peak of 4.08% in July 1990. IP, on the other hand, peaked in January 1989 but did not fall below trend until July 1989. While the default rate returned to its pre-junk bond

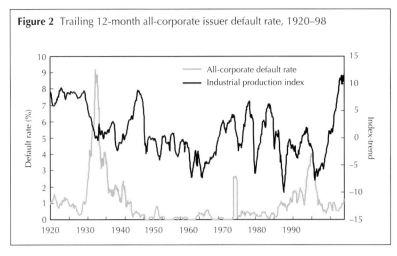

Figure 2 Trailing 12-month all-corporate issuer default rate, 1920–98

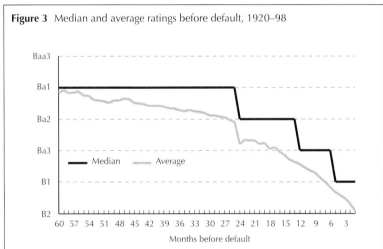

Figure 3 Median and average ratings before default, 1920–98

collapse levels by July 1991, IP remained weak through the end of 1993. More recently, robust economic growth and low default rates have gone hand in hand. Nevertheless, the shifting of this lead–lag relationship is a typical example of the instability of the relationship between corporate bond default rates and macroeconomic variables generally.

To summarise the advance warning of default risk provided by ratings, we calculated the median and average[3] senior or implied senior unsecured rating of issuers up to five years before default, shown in Figure 3.

Five years prior to default, the median rating of defaulting companies is speculative-grade. The downward slope indicates that, as a group, these future defaulters have systematically experienced downward rating pressure five years in advance of default.

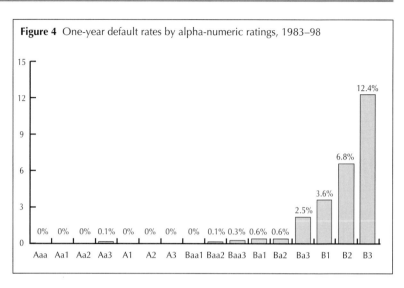

Figure 4 One-year default rates by alpha-numeric ratings, 1983–98

The weighted average default rates shown in Figure 4 clearly show an increased risk of default associated with lower rating categories. Since 1970, an average of 3.27% of speculative-grade issuers have defaulted per year, compared with just 0.17% of investment-grade issuers. For all but 28 of the past 79 years, the one-year default rate for the investment-grade sector was zero. From the relatively high default risk period extending from 1983 through the present, average one-year default rates climb from 0.0% for Aaa to 12.4% for B3.

In June 1997, Moody's announced the assignment of numerical modifiers to long-term issues rated Caa. These rating categories were expanded to include three numerical modifiers each in order to provide finer gradations of credit risk evaluation. Caa rated issues are characterised by high levels of risk with respect to principal and interest payments. Issuers include both young companies whose credit histories are sparse, as well as established players with declining fundamentals. The Caa category also encompasses defaulted obligations with high expected recoveries.

Figure 5 shows default rates for the numerically modified Caa ratings for 1998, the first and only cohort year for these sub-categories, as well as the B3 category for the same period. The default rates increase smoothly over the entire range, from B3 through Caa3.

Although the one-year default rates presented up to this point are of greatest interest to many market participants, some find default rates for longer time horizons more relevant. A 10-year default rate, for example, estimates the share of a portfolio of bonds that can be expected to default over a 10-year period.

Figure 6 presents average cumulative default rates for five-, 10-, 15-, and 20-year time horizons based on all data available since 1920. It shows that

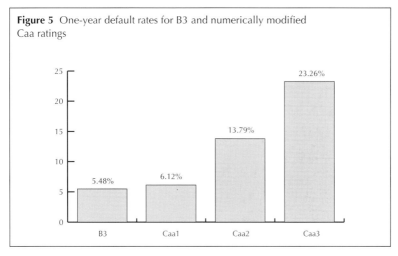

Figure 5 One-year default rates for B3 and numerically modified Caa ratings

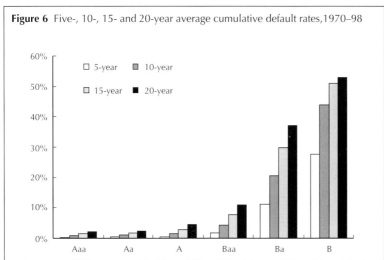

Figure 6 Five-, 10-, 15- and 20-year average cumulative default rates,1970–98

higher default risk for lower rating categories remains evident over investment periods as long as 20 years. For example, average default rates for five-year holding periods climb from 0.1% for the Aaa rating category to 27.7% for the B rating category. Figure 6 also shows that the pattern recurs for average default rates for 10-year and 15-year holding periods.

Moody's default rates characterise the relationship between the credit rating of issuers at a point in time and the probability of default over different time horizons, with lower ratings generally linked to higher defaults rates. However, default rate statistics calculated using our cohort methodology do not identify the relationship between default frequency and the life-cycle of corporate bond issuers. We attempt to identify regularities in

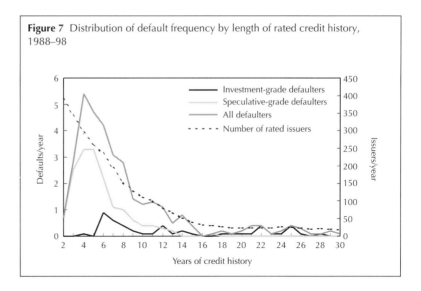

Figure 7 Distribution of default frequency by length of rated credit history, 1988–98

default dynamics by describing the time spent by an issuer in the healthy group before default occurs. Thus we are considering the hazard rate of issuer default.

Figure 7 shows the hazard rate of default for issuers at different stages of their credit history, plotted against the length of credit history, for the period 1988–1998. If the curve were perfectly flat, then the risk of default would be constant over the issuer's life. The default rate is quite low for issuers in their first two years as rated borrowers, reflecting the fact that their initial rating is usually accompanied by a successful debt issue, bolstering their financial position in the short run. Default risk increases sharply in the third year, reaching a peak in the fourth year and tapering off thereafter. For guidance purposes, the dashed line represents the average annual number of issuers for a given length of credit history.

RATING MIGRATION

In order to measure general trends in the credit quality of the Moody's-rated corporate universe through time, we consider annual rating drift and rating activity. Rating drift summarises the overall increase or decrease in the credit quality of the rated universe as a percentage of one rating grade per issuer. We calculate annual rating drift as the number of upgrades less downgrades (weighted by the number of ratings changed per upgrade) per year divided by the number of non-defaulted issuers at risk of a rating change during the course of the year. Rating activity is the sum of all rating changes (weighted by the number of ratings changed) divided by the number of non-defaulted issuers. It shows the pace at which ratings change, based on units of ratings changed per issuer.

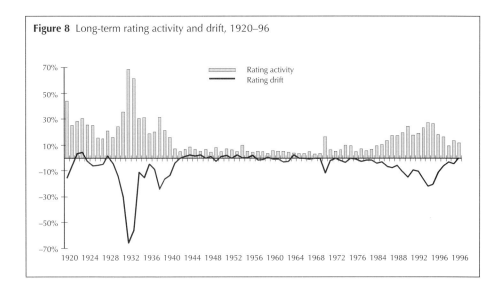

Figure 8 Long-term rating activity and drift, 1920–96

Figure 8 shows annual rating drift and activity from 1920 through 1996 and is based upon letter rating changes as opposed to changes in alpha-numeric ratings.[4]

The negative average annual drift for the 1930s reflects the most severe economic contraction of this century, coupled with severe asset deflation. This combination put even highly creditworthy borrowers at considerable risk of default, and was reflected by an increase in the incidence and size of downgrades relative to upgrades. The significant credit deterioration beginning in 1980 was the result of a myriad of special events and an over-all trend towards increased corporate leverage. The recession of 1982 proved to be the most severe of the post-World War II era. Sharply lower oil prices in the mid-1980s prompted large numbers of industrial and finan-cial company downgrades. Concerns about problem loans in the banking system led to numerous downgrades in 1989, just one year before the onset of another recession.

Table 1 displays the frequency of rating revisions by the magnitude of change for the entire period spanned by our database. We define the mag-nitude of a rating change as the number of rating categories that a rating change spans. For example, an upgrade from Ba to Baa covers one letter rating category while a downgrade from Ba to Caa covers two categories. This same concept applies analogously to our alpha-numeric ratings.

Changes of smaller magnitude are relatively more frequent than are large rating revisions. Rating changes of three ratings or more have occurred historically only about 2% of the time. For the alpha-numeric ratings, changes of more than four rating notches have occurred histori-cally only about 3% of the time.

Table 1 Frequency of rating change magnitudes

	Letter ratings (rating grades) (%)*	Alpha-numeric ratings (notches) (%)**
1	89	62
2	9	26
3	2	7
>3	0	4

*January 1920 to March 1997.
**April 1982 to March 1997.

Unlike Table 1, an average transition matrix is a concise representation not only of the size, but also of the direction of typical rating changes. Table 2 depicts an average rating transition matrix defined for a one-year time horizon. Each row indicates the rating group at the beginning of a one-year time period. Each column corresponds to a rating group, default, or withdrawn rating ("WR") as of the end of the one-year period. Each cell entry, excluding the "Default" and "WR" columns, is the average fraction of issuers who held the row rating at the beginning of the time period and the column rating or status at the end of the time period.

The upper left-hand corner, for example, indicates that on average over the period from 1920 to the present, 88.32% of Aaa's have remained at that level over the course of one year. The next percentage to the right indicates that 6.15% of Aaa's have, on average, suffered a downgrade to Aa. Also, by way of example, the table indicates that 2.30% of all A rated companies enjoyed a net improvement of one letter rating (to Aa) by the end of any one-year period.[5]

The largest values in the transition matrix are along the diagonal, indicating that the most likely rating for an issuer at the end of a one-year time horizon is the rating with which the issuer started the period. Moving off of the diagonal, the values fall off very quickly as very large changes in credit quality over a one-year period are infrequent.

The withdrawn rating category (column heading "WR") in the preceding (average) rating transition matrices corresponds to cases where Moody's has withdrawn all of an issuer's ratings. The likelihood of a rating withdrawal generally increases as credit quality decreases. Table 2 indicates that over a one-year time period, Aaa rated issuers have an average 4.29% risk of rating withdrawal while B rated issuers have more than double the risk, 10.53%. At least part of the reason for this pattern is that private debt markets are relatively more attractive for many of the smaller borrowers that generally carry lower ratings. Consequently, such issuers have been more likely to replace rated public bonds with unrated private debt.

Of the over 35,000 withdrawn long-term individual debt ratings considered, 92% were withdrawn because either an issue had matured or had

Table 2 Average one-year rating transition matrix, 1920–96

		Rating to:							Default	WR
		Aaa	Aa	A	Baa	Ba	B	Caa-C	Default	WR
Rating from:	Aaa	88.32%	6.15%	0.99%	0.23%	0.02%	0.00%	0.00%	0.00%	4.29%
	Aa	1.21%	86.76%	5.76%	0.66%	0.16%	0.02%	0.00%	0.06%	5.36%
	A	0.07%	2.30%	86.09%	4.67%	0.63%	0.10%	0.02%	0.12%	5.99%
	Baa	0.03%	0.24%	3.87%	82.52%	4.68%	0.61%	0.06%	0.28%	7.71%
	Ba	0.01%	0.08%	0.39%	4.61%	79.03%	4.96%	0.41%	1.11%	9.39%
	B	0.00%	0.04%	0.13%	0.60%	5.79%	76.33%	3.08%	3.49%	10.53%
	Caa-C	0.00%	0.02%	0.04%	0.34%	1.26%	5.29%	71.87%	12.41%	8.78%

Figure 9 Frequency of rating changes following Watchlist assignment

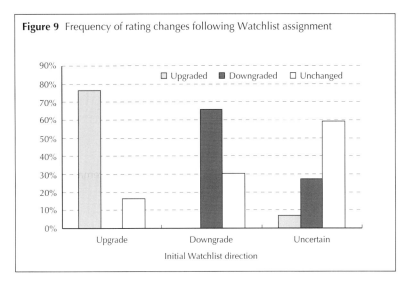

been called. In the remaining 8% of cases, the reason for the withdrawn rating was not specified or the rating withdrawal was associated with any of a variety of situations, including conversions, mergers, defeasances, bankruptcies, or the lack of sufficient information to accurately rate the debt. Just 1% of the total number of withdrawals occurred for reasons that could be connected with negative credit developments (eg insufficient information to maintain the rating or an indenture amendment).

Moody's rating process includes both the initial assignment of ratings and the monitoring of those ratings over the life of the security. Ratings are monitored continuously and, when circumstances warrant, are raised or lowered. As part of the rating monitoring process, an issue may be placed on a formal "rating review",[6] typically for upgrade or downgrade, although the direction may also be uncertain. A rating's Watchlist status has important implications for rating migrations. Issues placed on review for rating change experience rating changes in the expected direction at a

Table 3 One-year rating transition matrices for Watchlisted issuers, January 1, 1992 to December 31, 1997

Issuers placed on review for upgrade (%)

	Aaa	Aa	A	Baa	Ba	B	Caa-C	Default
Aaa	NA	NA	NA	NA	NA	NA	NA	NA
Aa	17.54	82.46	0.00	0.00	0.00	0.00	0.00	0.00
A	0.78	22.66	75.78	0.78	0.00	0.00	0.00	0.00
Baa	0.46	2.29	48.17	48.62	0.46	0.00	0.00	0.00
Ba	0.00	0.51	9.18	40.31	50.00	0.00	0.00	0.00
B	0.72	0.72	2.88	8.63	41.73	45.32	0.00	0.00
Caa-C	0.00	0.00	0.00	4.17	4.17	45.83	41.67	4.17

Issuers placed on review for downgrade (%)

	Aaa	Aa	A	Baa	Ba	B	Caa-C	Default
Aaa	27.14	70.00	2.86	0.00	0.00	0.00	0.00	0.00
Aa	0.00	52.99	45.38	1.63	0.00	0.00	0.00	0.00
A	0.00	0.48	67.57	26.36	5.27	0.32	0.00	0.00
Baa	0.00	0.00	2.02	60.52	31.12	4.90	0.86	0.58
Ba	0.00	0.00	0.36	1.08	60.65	26.35	8.66	2.89
B	0.00	0.00	1.48	0.00	2.22	54.81	23.70	17.78
Caa-C	0.00	0.00	0.00	0.00	0.00	0.00	42.86	57.14

Issuers placed on review with direction uncertain (%)

	Aaa	Aa	A	Baa	Ba	B	Caa-C	Default
Aaa	0.00	0.00	0.00	0.00	0.00	0.00	0.00	0.00
Aa	0.00	100.00	0.00	0.00	0.00	0.00	0.00	0.00
A	0.00	8.11	86.49	5.41	0.00	0.00	0.00	0.00
Baa	0.00	0.00	18.75	65.63	12.50	3.13	0.00	0.00
Ba	0.00	0.00	0.00	11.76	67.65	20.59	0.00	0.00
B	0.00	0.00	6.90	3.45	6.90	68.97	6.90	6.90
Caa-C	0.00	0.00	0.00	0.00	0.00	20.00	60.00	20.00

greater rate than the population of bonds as a whole (see Figure 9). Given the significant percentage of issues that are on the Watchlist at any time – approximately 10% since 1995 – a detailed measurement and description of these rating dynamics is an important input to the understanding and management of credit risk for a portfolio of rated securities.

Table 3 presents one-year average rating transition matrices for bonds which have been placed on rating review. These are constructed with the initial rating on the left vertical axis and the final rating on the horizontal axis.

Table 3 also demonstrates that for each rating category the direction in which the review is assigned gives a good indication that the rating will be changed in that direction. In all but one case (Aa2 bonds on review for upgrade), there has been better than 50% frequency of the rating being changed as indicated. There have been very few instances of the rating being changed in the opposite direction, although the chances of this are slightly better if the initial direction is down. As shown in Table 3, bonds placed on review with direction uncertain have a higher probability than other Watchlist bonds of not experiencing a rating change. Where they do, bonds rated Baa2 and higher tend to have a greater likelihood of being downgraded, while bonds rated Ba3 and lower are more likely to be upgraded.

Table 3 also shows that rating dynamics for issuers on Moody's Watchlist are different from those not on the Watchlist. Rating dynamics have important consequences for the measurement of bond and bond portfolio credit risk. An example is afforded by JP Morgan's approach to portfolio credit risk measurement, ie the reliance of CreditMetrics on rating migration matrices.

CREDIT QUALITY CORRELATION
The rating transition matrices above (Table 3) summarise the average risk of changes in credit quality over a specified time period. However, the risk of a change of credit quality varies from year to year as unexpected changes in macroeconomic variables and the business environment in general alter firms' credit outlooks. Consequently, there is volatility in rating transition rates from year to year. The average rating transition matrices reported above are calculated over as many as 77 years, smoothing over variations in the year-to-year rating transition rates caused by fluctuating macroeconomic and business conditions.

To investigate rating transition rate volatility, we have, by way of example, expanded the average, one-year, A-to-Baa transition rate into its 77 constituent observations – one for each year since 1920, as shown in Figure 10. The grey bars indicate years for which the annual growth rate of real US GDP was negative, hinting at downgrade risk counter-cyclicality – that is, economic contractions seem to be associated with greater downgrade risk. Since growth is a common risk factor to firms within a particular economy, this is evidence of credit quality correlation.

To examine the question of whether credit quality is correlated across firms, we first examine the patterns in the co-movements of ratings that we would expect to see if credit quality were not correlated. We then examine actual rating co-movements in our database of rating histories. Finally, we compare the two results to answer the question of whether the credit qualities of different firms is likely to be correlated or not.

Consider, for example, two issuers with Baa rated senior unsecured debt. Historically, over the course of one year, Baa rated issuers have maintained the same rating, moved to another rating category, or defaulted with the probabilities reported in the Baa row of the one-year transition matrix in Table 2. Because there are eight possible transitions (seven different rating groupings plus default) for each of the two issuers, there are a total of 64

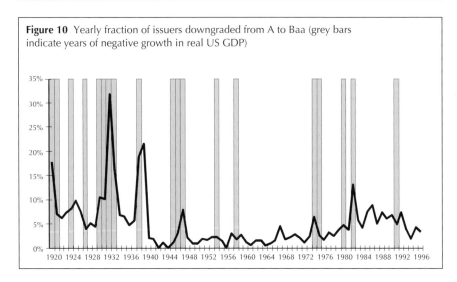

Figure 10 Yearly fraction of issuers downgraded from A to Baa (grey bars indicate years of negative growth in real US GDP)

(8 × 8) possible credit quality combinations for the two issuers at the end of one year. If we impose the assumption that the credit qualities of these issuers are uncorrelated, then the likelihoods of each possible credit quality combination for the two issuers at the end of one year are easily calculated. They are simply the products of the likelihoods of each issuer making the specified transition. If we perform this calculation for each of the 64 possible rating combinations, then we obtain a matrix describing the joint probability distribution of rating migrations for the portfolio of two issuers at the end of one year. These are detailed in Table 4.

Each cell entry of Table 4 is an estimate of the likelihood that the first Baa rated issuer will move to the corresponding row rating and the second issuer will move to the corresponding column rating. The first row of numbers represents the sum of each column of probabilities and identically sums to our likelihood estimate that a Baa rated issuer will move to the corresponding column rating over the course of one year (the Baa row of the one-year rating transition matrix of Table 2).[7] Similarly, the first column of numbers represents the sum of each row of probabilities and also sums to our likelihood estimate that a Baa rated issuer will move to the corresponding row rating over the course of one year. The 64 interior cells of the joint rating transition matrix in Table 4 sum to 100%. They describe completely the probabilities associated with the range of possible joint rating outcomes at the end of one year for the two Baa rated issuers under the assumption that their credit qualities are not correlated.

We derived Table 4 under the assumption of zero credit quality correlation. We obtain evidence about the true nature of credit quality correlation by comparing these results with those we obtained directly from our database of rating histories. In Table 5 we estimate directly an empirical joint

Table 4 Joint rating transition matrix assuming no credit quality correlation (two, initially Baa rated issuers; based on data available since 1920)

			Aaa	Aa	A	Baa	Ba	B	Caa-C	Default
			0.04	0.27	4.22	89.16	5.25	0.68	0.07	0.31
	Aaa	0.04	0.00	0.00	0.00	0.03	0.00	0.00	0.00	0.00
	Aa	0.27	0.00	0.00	0.01	0.24	0.01	0.00	0.00	0.00
	A	4.22	0.00	0.01	0.18	3.76	0.22	0.03	0.00	0.01
	Baa	89.16	0.03	0.24	3.76	79.49	4.68	0.61	0.06	0.28
	Ba	5.25	0.00	0.01	0.22	4.68	0.28	0.04	0.00	0.02
	B	0.68	0.00	0.00	0.03	0.61	0.04	0.00	0.00	0.00
	Caa-C	0.07	0.00	0.00	0.00	0.06	0.00	0.00	0.00	0.00
	Default	0.31	0.00	0.00	0.01	0.28	0.02	0.00	0.00	0.00

Left axis: First issuer's end-of-period rating (%)
Top heading: Second issuer's end-of-period rating (%)

Table 5 Empirical joint rating transition matrix (two, initially Baa rated, issuers; based on data available since 1920)

			Aaa	Aa	A	Baa	Ba	B	Caa-C	Default
			0.04	0.27	4.22	89.16	5.25	0.68	0.07	0.31
	Aaa	0.04	0.00	0.00	0.00	0.03	0.00	0.00	0.00	0.00
	Aa	0.27	0.00	0.00	0.03	0.21	0.03	0.00	0.00	0.00
	A	4.22	0.00	0.03	0.36	3.46	0.31	0.04	0.00	0.02
	Baa	89.16	0.03	0.21	3.46	80.50	4.14	0.52	0.05	0.25
	Ba	5.25	0.00	0.03	0.31	4.14	0.63	0.10	0.01	0.04
	B	0.68	0.00	0.00	0.04	0.52	0.10	0.02	0.00	0.01
	Caa-C	0.07	0.00	0.00	0.00	0.05	0.01	0.00	0.00	0.00
	Default	0.31	0.00	0.00	0.02	0.25	0.04	0.01	0.00	0.00

Left axis: First issuer's end-of-period rating (%)
Top heading: Second issuer's end-of-period rating (%)

rating transition matrix without imposing the assumption of zero correlation. To do that, we formed a dataset of all possible pairs of Baa rated issuers as of the start of each year since 1920 and then examined the ratings combinations of those pairs at the end of each one-year period. The relative frequency of the actual historically observed ratings co-movements for each pair of issuers are estimates of the joint migration probabilities.

The first row and the first column of numbers are the same as those of Table 4 and give the "stand-alone" likelihood of each issuer moving to each rating category. Each cell entry gives an estimate of the probability that, of a pair of Baa rated issuers, the first will move to the row rating while the second will move to the column rating.

A comparison of Table 4 with Table 5 provides evidence that the credit qualities of these two Baa rated issuers are positively correlated. The shaded cells in the upper left-hand quadrants of Tables 4 and 5 correspond to the probabilities that both issuers will experience an improvement in their credit ratings. The shaded cells in the lower right-hand quadrants correspond to the probabilities that both issuers will experience a deterioration in their credit ratings. If the credit quality of Baa rated obligors is positively correlated, then the total likelihood that both obligors' ratings improve (the sum of the shaded cells in the upper left-hand corner) or deteriorate (the sum of the shaded cells in the lower right-hand corner) should be larger than those calculated under the assumption of no correlation. The total likelihood of an upgrade for both issuers under the assumption of no correlation is 0.21%, versus the 0.42% actually observed. The total likelihood of downgrades or default for both issuers under the assumption of no correlation is 0.40% versus the 0.97% actually observed.

The joint rating transition matrix derived under the assumption of zero credit quality correlation and the empirical joint rating transition matrix, together with the issuer counts used to generate them, can be combined into a more rigorous statistical test of the assumption of no credit quality correlation.[8] Under this test, we can reject the hypothesis of zero credit quality correlation at the 1% level of confidence.

DEFAULT SEVERITY AND RECOVERY RATES

A critical aspect of a corporate bond default is the severity of the loss incurred. Eventually, most bond default resolutions provide bondholders with some amount of recovery, which may take the form of cash, other securities, or even a physical asset. The recovery rate, defined here as the percentage of par value returned to the bondholder, is a function of several variables. These variables include the seniority of the issue within the issuer's capital structure, the quality of collateral (if any), the overall state of the economy, and the market for corporate assets.

We use the trading price of the defaulted instrument as a proxy for the present value of the ultimate recovery. To do so, we collected from several sources prices for many of the bonds that defaulted between January 1, 1920 and December 31, 1998. For each defaulted issue we considered the seniority, date of default, and the price approximately one month after default. Although this information provides only an estimate of the actual recovery, it has the advantage of being the definite measure of the recovery realised by those debt-holders who liquidated a position soon after default.

Figure 11 breaks out the average recovery estimates since 1970 by seniority of claim and includes Moody's estimate of the recovery investors can expect to receive on senior secured bank loans and preferred stock.[9] Recoveries, on average, decline as priority of claim declines, lending support to Moody's practice of assigning lower ratings to an issuer's

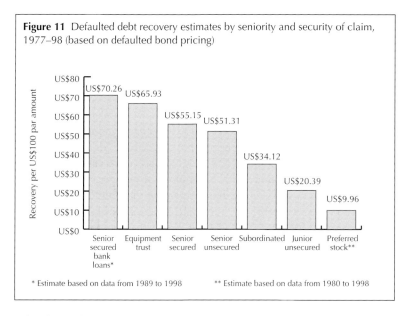

Figure 11 Defaulted debt recovery estimates by seniority and security of claim, 1977–98 (based on defaulted bond pricing)

* Estimate based on data from 1989 to 1998   ** Estimate based on data from 1980 to 1998

subordinated debt. The average senior secured bank loan recovery estimate is US$70 per US$100 defaulted par amount. Considering prices for 118 senior secured bonds, our recovery estimate is US$55; prices for 338 senior unsecured bonds generate a recovery estimate of US$51. The 252 subordinated bonds sold for US$39 on average, while 19 junior subordinated bonds sold for US$20 on average. Preferred stock holders can only expect to retrieve about US$10 per US$100 par on liquidation value of defaulted preferred stock.

The recoveries shown in Figure 11 clearly show that bonds with higher claims to a firm's assets enjoy greater recoveries, on average. However, these rates are only indirect estimates of the relative value of a bond's seniority. The decision between investing at the senior versus the subordinated level for a particular issuer is largely dependent on a comparison of the incremental yield promised on the subordinated debt with the decreased recovery that can be expected in the event of a default. In order to more directly estimate the effect of a bond's seniority provisions on recovery, we compared the prices of bonds of different seniorities, but for the same issuing firm. Table 6 presents the average difference between the prices for a defaulted issuer's relatively senior (row) debt and relatively junior (column) debt.

The entry in the second row under the "Subordinated" column heading indicates that, for the 39 issuers in our database for which we have defaulted bond prices for both senior unsecured and subordinated issues, the average difference between the senior unsecured bond prices and the subordinated bond prices is US$20. That is to say, the senior unsecured

Table 6 Average difference between senior and subordinated defaulted bond prices

	Senior unsecured (US$)	Subordinated (US$)
Senior secured	17	30
Senior unsecured	–	20

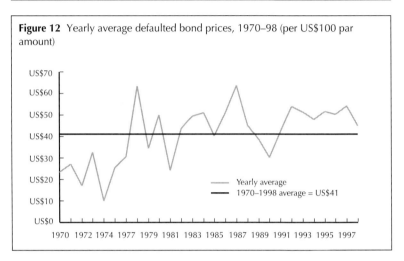

Figure 12 Yearly average defaulted bond prices, 1970–98 (per US$100 par amount)

debt of an issuer can be expected to recover 20% more of principal than the subordinated issue.

An additional important consideration in assessing recovery rates is the variability of defaulted bond prices. As shown in Figure 12, the average defaulted bond price for the 79-year period from 1970 to 1998 is US$41, although recovery values over various shorter time horizons vary significantly. The problem then with choosing averages as an indicator is that they approximate the most likely bond price to arise from a particular default, but they do not convey the range of possible outcomes. For example, while the estimated recovery for all subordinated bonds is US$34 per US$100 par amount, one of the underlying issues had a price of just US$1, while several had prices above par.

Table A1 in the appendix provides additional statistics describing the distribution of defaulted debt prices. Equipment trust obligations have median post-default prices significantly higher than other debt classes. This reflects, in part, bankruptcy statutes that accelerate the transfer of assets pledged as security when those assets consist of transportation equipment, the main type of asset used to support equipment trust issues. Across debt types, median prices of defaulted bonds tend to fall as seniority declines, while variances first widen and then tighten. This pattern of greater variance on senior unsecured bonds reflects, in part, the greater number of defaults involving this type of bond relative to equipment trusts and junior subordinated bonds. It also suggests that although the more subordinated investor can expect to receive less in the event of default, there is less uncertainty as to how much the defaulted bond price will vary from its mean. Subordinated debt prices also exhibit a number of high value outliers, indicating that subordination by itself does not always lead to economic loss in the event of default.

The recovery rates calculated above are ratios of the post-default instrument market values to their par amounts. Using market valuations in this way has several benefits. First, this use captures recoveries for investors unwilling or unable to maintain their claim through the workout process. Second, it permits market participants to estimate recovery rates particular to their own circumstances. As an example of this second point, consider the following. Moody's has published recovery rates as the ratio of an instrument's post-default market value to its par value. This calculation would likely underestimate recoveries likely to be realised for investors purchasing distressed debt at a discount. The recovery rate these investors need might then be calculated – based on the price-based recovery data – as the ratio of the defaulted instrument's expected market price and its purchase price. Finally, the use of market pricing to estimate recoveries has the advantage of being implementable in practice.

However, relying on market valuations as recovery indicators does not allow us to describe the timing, value, and nature of debt-holders' realised recoveries. This section is concerned with the recoveries actually experienced by a sample of corporate obligations.[10] It analyses the value (as of the date of emergence from bankruptcy) of actual payouts associated with the bankruptcy's resolution.

The recovery rate in this section is defined as the value of the payout to each obligation in accordance with the resolution of the firm's bankruptcy presented as a fraction of the obligation's pre-petition claim amount. Our results are based on a dataset of 829 financial obligations associated with the 159 bankruptcy cases of 155 borrowers.

Almost by definition, bankruptcy resolution requires the relaxation of the current financial commitments of the firm.[11] Financial reorganisation typically requires extending debt maturity, eliminating, diminishing, deferring, or otherwise modifying interest payable (eg making pay-in-kind); and diminishing the principal or replacing the claim with contracts that place less strain on the firm's short-term contractual cash flow (eg preferred stock, equity, warrants, right, options, or other derivative instruments).

Table 7 summarises how often the bankruptcy claims of debt of differing security and type were resolved using various types of financial instruments. Claims may be paid through a variety of new securities, in cash, by "other" payments, or the claim could be cancelled outright. The "other" category is composed of various types of assets, including securing col-

Table 7 Instrument use in bankruptcy resolution

WEIGHTED BY RECOVERY INSTRUMENT TYPE

Claim type:	Claim satisfied with:									
	Bank loans (%)	Public bonds (%)	Private debt (%)	Trade claims (%)	Preferred stock (%)	Equity (%)	Options (%)	Other (%)	Cash (%)	Claim cancelled (%)*
Secured bank loans	35.9	4.5	3.7	0.0	0.4	16.3	1.6	4.1	33.5	0.0
Secured public bonds	3.4	28.6	4.1	0.0	3.4	25.9	2.0	1.4	31.3	0.0
Secured private placements	1.7	14.3	31.1	0.0	0.0	26.9	2.5	5.9	17.6	0.0
Unsecured bank loans	7.9	7.9	2.6	0.0	10.5	23.7	0.0	2.6	39.5	5.3
Unsecured public bonds	0.0	14.9	0.2	0.0	7.9	42.3	12.8	2.5	18.0	1.4
Unsecured private placements	0.9	11.2	1.7	0.0	6.0	40.5	12.9	0.9	20.7	5.2
Trade claims	0.0	0.0	4.2	8.3	0.0	29.2	0.0	0.0	58.3	0.0
Preferred stock	0.0	2.2	1.1	0.0	2.2	46.1	20.2	2.2	2.2	23.6

WEIGHTED BY RECOVERY VALUE

Claim type:	Claim satisfied with:									
	Bank loans (%)	Public bonds (%)	Private debt (%)	Trade claims (%)	Preferred stock (%)	Equity (%)	Options (%)	Other (%)	Cash (%)	Claim cancelled (%)*
Secured bank loans	42.8	11.4	8.1	0.0	0.0	15.1	0.2	1.9	20.4	0.0
Secured public bonds	2.4	55.8	4.8	0.0	2.0	13.0	0.0	0.4	21.5	0.0
Secured private placements	0.1	7.1	24.1	0.0	0.0	10.4	0.5	0.2	57.6	0.0
Unsecured bank loans	7.4	44.3	1.1	0.0	6.3	8.9	0.0	0.3	31.7	5.3
Unsecured public bonds	0.0	41.3	0.1	0.0	2.8	36.4	1.8	0.6	17.1	1.4
Unsecured private placements	0.1	16.2	0.0	0.0	0.8	56.5	2.1	7.5	16.8	5.2
Trade claims	0.0	0.0	0.3	6.9	0.0	41.0	0.0	0.0	51.9	0.0
Preferred stock	0.0	0.8	0.9	0.0	0.4	25.9	3.4	64.1	4.6	23.6

*Percentage of issues cancelled.

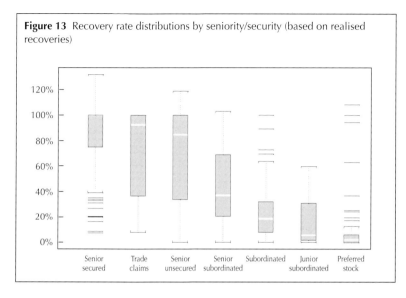

Figure 13 Recovery rate distributions by seniority/security (based on realised recoveries)

lateral or claims to income generated by future legal settlements. The first part of Table 7 shows how often the claim type in the left-most column was satisfied by the payment type in the top row. The second part shows how often asset claims were satisfied as a percentage of recovery value. For example, 35.9% of the claims secured by the bank were satisfied with new bank loans (see the upper left corner of the first part); as a percentage of the recovery value, though, senior secured bank loans were satisfied with new bank loans 42.8% of the time (see the upper left corner of the second part).

Equity and equity-like assets, such as warrants and options, were more frequently used to satisfy claims as one moves down the capital structure. Equity was used only 25.9% of the time to satisfy the claims of secured public bonds, compared with 46.1% for preferred stock claims. The use of equity is also strongly correlated with a claim's security. Of the unsecured public bond claims, 42.3% were paid in new equity securities. The same pattern holds for private debt. Secured private debt was paid in new equity only 26.9% of the time; this figure rises to 40.5% for senior unsecured private debt.

Security also plays an important role in the percentage of claims cancelled outright. Preferred stocks showed the highest cancellation rate, 23.6%. Secured claims and trade claims were not cancelled in our sample. The cancellation rate for unsecured claims, on the other hand, was not trivial. Of unsecured bank loans, 5.3% were cancelled outright, which is very close to the 5.2% cancellation rate for unsecured private debt. Unsecured public bonds showed a cancellation rate of only 1.4%, however.

The shape of the distribution implies that firm-level recovery rates can fall into one of three regimes: the extremely low (less than 10%) with low likelihood; the "normal" (between 10% and 89%) occurring most often; and the extremely high (90% or greater), also with low likelihood.

The patterns of the distributions of recovery rates according to seniority and security in Figure 13 corroborate our findings using recovery rates based on market prices above. As expected, an obligation's position in the capital structure of a bankrupt firm has a direct effect on its recovery rate: the more senior/secure an issue, the higher its recovery rate.

There is a smooth monotonic relationship between median and average recovery rates and seniority/security. Senior and secured obligations' median recovery rate is 100%, or 84.3% on average. The median recovery rate falls to 85.6% (70.1% average) for senior unsecured obligations, 37% (43.1% average) for senior subordinated assets, 18.7% (25.3% average) for subordinated, and 5.8% (18% average) for junior subordinated obligations. Trade claims generated a relatively high median recovery rate of 92.4% (74% average), falling between the median recovery rates for senior secured and senior unsecured obligations. Preferred stock's median recovery, on the lowest rung of the capital structure ladder in our sample, was only 2.2%, or 11.6% on average.

CONCLUSION

This chapter encapsulated a broad cross-section of recent Moody's default and credit research that spans the period from 1920 to the present. As the management of credit risk in financial institutions moves closer to adopting quantitative modelling techniques, the statistics presented in this chapter represent not only interesting historical information about credit risk, but useful quantitative inputs for the accurate pricing of credit instruments with default risk, swaps, and other credit derivatives.

APPENDIX: STATISTICAL TABLES OF DEFAULT RATES AND RECOVERY ESTIMATES

Table A1 Descriptive statistics for defaulted bond prices, 1977–98

Seniority and security	Number	Average (US$)	Standard deviation (US$)
Senior secured bank loans*	98	70.26	21.33
Equipment trust	27	65.93	28.55
Senior secured public debt	118	55.15	24.31
Senior unsecured public debt	338	51.31	26.30
Senior subordinated public debt	252	39.05	24.39
Subordinated public debt	405	31.66	20.58
Junior subordinated public debt	19	20.39	15.36
All subordinated public debt	675	34.12	22.35
All public debt	1113	45.02	26.77

*Data cover the years 1989–96.

Table A2 One-year default rates by year and letter rating, 1970–98 (%)

Rating	1970	1971	1972	1973	1974	1975	1976	1977	1978	1979	1980	1981	1982	1983	1984
Aaa	0.00	0.00	0.00	0.00	0.00	0.00	0.00	0.00	0.00	0.00	0.00	0.00	0.00	0.00	0.00
Aa	0.00	0.00	0.00	0.00	0.00	0.00	0.00	0.00	0.00	0.00	0.00	0.00	0.00	0.00	0.00
A	0.00	0.00	0.00	0.00	0.00	0.00	0.00	0.00	0.00	0.00	0.00	0.00	0.26	0.00	0.00
Baa	0.27	0.00	0.00	0.45	0.00	0.00	0.00	0.27	0.00	0.00	0.00	0.00	0.30	0.00	0.36
Ba	4.12	0.42	0.00	0.00	0.00	1.02	1.01	0.52	1.08	0.49	0.00	0.00	2.73	0.91	0.83
B	23.38	4.00	7.41	3.92	10.34	6.15	0.00	3.39	5.56	0.00	5.06	4.60	2.41	6.36	6.78
Investment grade	0.14	0.00	0.00	0.23	0.00	0.00	0.00	0.11	0.00	0.00	0.00	0.00	0.21	0.00	0.09
Speculative grade	9.12	1.11	1.88	1.24	1.31	1.74	0.88	1.35	1.79	0.42	1.61	0.70	3.54	3.82	3.32
US only speculative grade	9.72	1.52	1.94	1.28	1.36	1.79	0.89	1.36	1.80	0.42	1.62	0.71	3.58	3.90	3.40
All corporates	2.72	0.28	0.45	0.45	0.27	0.36	0.17	0.35	0.35	0.09	0.34	0.16	1.02	0.95	0.91

Rating	1985	1986	1987	1988	1989	1990	1991	1992	1993	1994	1995	1996	1997	1998
Aaa	0.00	0.00	0.00	0.00	0.00	0.00	0.00	0.00	0.00	0.00	0.00	0.00	0.00	0.00
Aa	0.00	0.00	0.00	0.00	0.61	0.00	0.00	0.00	0.00	0.00	0.00	0.00	0.00	0.00
A	0.00	0.00	0.00	0.00	0.00	0.00	0.00	0.00	0.00	0.00	0.00	0.00	0.00	0.00
Baa	0.00	1.33	0.00	0.00	0.60	0.00	0.28	0.00	0.00	0.00	0.00	0.00	0.00	0.12
Ba	1.75	2.05	2.72	1.24	2.98	3.32	5.25	0.30	0.55	0.23	0.67	0.00	0.19	0.61
B	8.28	11.80	5.86	6.02	9.17	16.11	14.66	9.00	5.76	3.81	4.84	1.45	2.10	4.08
Investment grade	0.00	0.32	0.00	0.00	0.28	0.00	0.07	0.00	0.00	0.00	0.00	0.00	0.00	0.04
Speculative grade	3.90	5.67	4.10	3.47	6.02	9.80	10.45	4.83	3.50	1.93	3.30	1.66	2.02	3.31
US only speculative grade	4.24	5.82	4.04	3.77	5.75	9.85	10.53	5.13	3.84	2.07	3.65	1.92	2.14	3.84
All corporates	1.06	1.89	1.44	1.31	2.42	3.51	3.29	1.33	0.96	0.57	1.07	0.54	0.68	1.27

Table A3 One-year default rates by year and alpha-numeric rating, 1983–98 (%)

	1983	1984	1985	1986	1987	1988	1989	1990	1991	1992	1993	1994	1995	1996	1997	1998
Aaa	0.00	0.00	0.00	0.00	0.00	0.00	0.00	0.00	0.00	0.00	0.00	0.00	0.00	0.00	0.00	0.00
Aa1	0.00	0.00	0.00	0.00	0.00	0.00	0.00	0.00	0.00	0.00	0.00	0.00	0.00	0.00	0.00	0.00
Aa2	0.00	0.00	0.00	0.00	0.00	0.00	0.00	0.00	0.00	0.00	0.00	0.00	0.00	0.00	0.00	0.00
Aa3	0.00	0.00	0.00	0.00	0.00	0.00	1.40	0.00	0.00	0.00	0.00	0.00	0.00	0.00	0.00	0.00
A1	0.00	0.00	0.00	0.00	0.00	0.00	0.00	0.00	0.00	0.00	0.00	0.00	0.00	0.00	0.00	0.00
A2	0.00	0.00	0.00	0.00	0.00	0.00	0.00	0.00	0.00	0.00	0.00	0.00	0.00	0.00	0.00	0.00
A3	0.00	0.00	0.00	0.00	0.00	0.00	0.00	0.00	0.00	0.00	0.00	0.00	0.00	0.00	0.00	0.00
Baa1	0.00	0.00	0.00	0.00	0.00	0.00	0.00	0.00	0.00	0.00	0.00	0.00	0.00	0.00	0.00	0.00
Baa2	0.00	0.00	0.00	0.00	0.00	0.00	0.00	0.00	0.76	0.00	0.00	0.00	0.00	0.00	0.00	0.33
Baa3	0.00	0.00	0.00	0.00	0.00	0.00	1.07	0.00	0.00	0.00	0.00	0.00	0.00	0.00	0.00	0.00
Ba1	0.00	1.06	0.00	4.82	0.00	0.00	0.80	2.69	0.00	0.00	0.00	0.00	0.00	0.00	0.00	0.00
Ba2	0.00	1.16	1.63	0.88	3.73	0.00	0.80	2.74	1.07	0.00	0.81	0.00	0.00	0.00	0.00	0.58
Ba3	2.61	1.61	3.77	1.21	0.96	2.58	1.82	3.90	9.73	0.73	0.75	0.59	1.71	0.00	0.47	1.09
B1	0.00	5.84	4.38	7.61	4.93	4.34	6.24	8.59	6.04	1.03	3.32	1.93	4.43	1.19	0.00	2.09
B2	11.11	20.00	7.69	16.67	4.30	6.90	8.16	21.82	12.58	1.54	4.96	3.61	6.31	0.00	1.48	7.16
B3	17.91	2.90	13.86	16.07	8.89	9.59	19.40	28.93	28.42	24.24	11.29	7.84	4.10	3.38	7.49	5.48
Investment grade	0.00	0.09	0.00	0.32	0.00	0.00	0.28	0.00	0.07	0.00	0.00	0.00	0.00	0.00	0.00	0.04
Speculative grade	3.82	3.32	3.90	5.67	4.10	3.47	6.02	9.80	10.45	4.83	3.50	1.93	3.30	1.66	2.02	3.31
All corporates	0.95	0.91	1.06	1.89	1.44	1.31	2.42	3.51	3.29	1.33	0.96	0.57	1.07	0.54	0.68	1.27

Table A4 Average cumulative default rates by letter rating from 1 to 20 years, 1970–98 (%)

Rating	1	2	3	4	5	6	7	8	9	10
Aaa	0.00	0.00	0.00	0.04	0.14	0.24	0.35	0.47	0.61	0.77
Aa	0.03	0.04	0.09	0.23	0.36	0.50	0.64	0.80	0.91	0.99
A	0.01	0.06	0.20	0.35	0.50	0.68	0.85	1.05	1.29	1.55
Baa	0.12	0.38	0.74	1.24	1.67	2.14	2.67	3.20	3.80	4.39
Ba	1.29	3.60	6.03	8.51	11.10	13.37	15.20	17.14	18.91	20.63
B	6.47	12.77	18.54	23.32	27.74	31.59	35.04	37.97	40.70	43.91
Investment grade	0.05	0.15	0.33	0.58	0.81	1.06	1.34	1.63	1.94	2.27
Speculative grade	3.82	7.69	11.27	14.44	17.49	20.14	22.33	24.46	26.38	28.32
All corporates	1.15	2.30	3.37	4.33	5.21	5.99	6.66	7.31	7.93	8.55

Rating	11	12	13	14	15	16	17	18	19	20
Aaa	0.94	1.13	1.35	1.47	1.59	1.73	1.88	2.05	2.05	2.05
Aa	1.08	1.18	1.30	1.56	1.63	1.72	1.92	2.04	2.17	2.32
A	1.81	2.09	2.35	2.56	2.86	3.19	3.52	3.86	4.24	4.45
Baa	5.04	5.71	6.35	7.02	7.72	8.46	9.19	9.88	10.44	10.89
Ba	22.50	24.54	26.55	28.21	29.86	31.70	33.28	34.66	35.88	36.99
B	45.98	47.25	48.53	49.69	51.07	52.20	52.90	52.90	52.90	52.90
Investment grade	2.62	2.99	3.35	3.72	4.10	4.52	4.95	5.36	5.73	5.99
Speculative grade	30.16	31.96	33.74	35.23	36.74	38.36	39.73	40.87	41.87	42.80
All corporates	9.17	9.77	10.37	10.91	11.47	12.07	12.65	13.16	13.62	13.98

Table A5 Average cumulative default rates from 1 to 8 years, 1983–98 (%)

	1	2	3	4	5	6	7	8
Aaa	0.00	0.00	0.00	0.07	0.22	0.30	0.40	0.53
Aa1	0.00	0.00	0.00	0.25	0.25	0.42	0.42	0.42
Aa2	0.00	0.00	0.07	0.23	0.50	0.61	0.74	0.89
Aa3	0.07	0.11	0.21	0.32	0.45	0.61	0.61	0.61
A1	0.00	0.03	0.37	0.59	0.75	0.93	1.01	1.10
A2	0.00	0.03	0.16	0.43	0.66	0.88	1.01	1.38
A3	0.00	0.15	0.28	0.38	0.45	0.60	0.88	0.99
Baa1	0.04	0.29	0.59	1.02	1.45	1.66	2.05	2.36
Baa2	0.08	0.28	0.41	0.85	1.29	1.84	2.24	2.40
Baa3	0.31	0.75	1.28	2.21	2.79	3.65	4.53	5.39
Ba1	0.64	2.14	3.77	6.11	8.45	10.93	12.63	14.30
Ba2	0.59	2.84	5.46	7.75	9.66	11.22	12.76	13.77
Ba3	2.55	6.95	11.76	16.38	20.76	24.66	28.40	32.39
B1	3.56	9.17	15.03	20.36	25.56	30.85	35.90	39.70
B2	6.85	13.83	19.85	24.78	28.52	31.34	32.93	34.34
B3	12.41	20.97	27.79	32.56	37.49	40.55	43.75	48.34
Caa1-C	18.31	25.94	31.38	35.76	38.30	42.79	42.79	47.37
Investment grade	0.04	0.15	0.32	0.59	0.82	1.06	1.27	1.47
Speculative grade	3.67	8.19	12.60	16.58	20.26	23.54	26.44	29.17
All corporates	1.18	2.59	3.95	5.19	6.25	7.17	7.94	8.64

1 For an overview of the long-term history of sovereign defaults on bonds and loans see Truglia (1995).

2 The trend here is estimated as a smooth function of time. The correlation between the index and this trend is 0.993.

3 The average rating is constructed by translating Moody's rating symbols onto a scale from 1 to 21 where Aaa = 1 and C = 21 and simply taking the average of the numbers to produce a smooth series. Thus, while the value of this "average rating" has no simple interpretation, it can be translated back onto the original symbolic scale and its changes do reflect improvement and deterioration in the underlying pool of future defaulters, capturing finer gradations than does the median rating.

4 Moody's modified its long-term rating scale in April 1982. The traditional nine-tiered letter rating scale (Aaa, Aa, A, Baa, Ba, B, Caa, Ca, C) was expanded by attaching three numerical modifiers (a "1," "2," or "3," in order of increasing credit risk) to each of the ratings from Aa through B. The new alpha-numeric rating system is comprised of 19 grades (Aaa, Aa1, Aa2, Aa3, A1, ...etc.). Because the alpha-numeric ratings did not exist before April 1982, none of the statistics reported for these rating categories are based upon pre-April, 1982 ratings data. Statistics reported for the original letter rating scale are extended through the post-April 1982 period by collapsing the alpha-numeric ratings into the original letter rating categories. For example, the Baa1, Baa2, and Baa3 ratings would all be simply considered Baa.

5 The increase in credit quality is net since a rating transition matrix is a snapshot of the evolution of the rating profile at a specific point in time. Therefore, they do not address the dynamics of how the hypothetical A-rated issuer arrived at the Aa rating one year later. It may well have been upgraded to Aaa and then downgraded to Aa between the beginning and end of the one-year period.

6   The terms "on the Watchlist", and "on rating review" are equivalent and are used interchangeably in this report.

7   The columns of this matrix, as reported here, do not all sum exactly to the corresponding entry of the first row because of the roundoff error associated with reporting only 4 decimal points of accuracy.

8   We used Pearson's Chi-square statistic to test the hypothesis of no credit quality correlation.

9   See December 1994 Moody's Special Comment, "Preferred Stock Dividend and Credit Risk" and the November 1996 Moody's Special Comment, "Defaulted Bank Loan Recoveries."

10 This section is drawn from Carty et al (1998) and Hamilton and Carty (1999).

11 Exceptions could occur in cases where firms strategically file for court protection though financially solvent (eg Johns Manville).

BIBLIOGRAPHY

Altman, E. I., 1988, "Measuring Corporate Bond Mortality and Performance", *Journal of Finance*, February.

Carty, L. V., 1997a, "An Empirical Investigation of Default Risk Dynamics", Columbia University, doctoral thesis.

Carty, L. V., 1997b, "Moody's Rating Migration and Credit Quality Correlation, 1920–1996", *Moody's Special Comment*, July.

Carty, L. V., *et al*, 1998, "Bankrupt Bank Loan Recoveries", *Moody's Special Comment*, June.

Hamilton, D. T. and L. V. Carty, 1999, "Debt Recoveries for Corporate Bankruptcies", *Moody's Special Comment*, June.

Keenan, S. C., *et al*, 1998a, "Moody's Preferred Stock Ratings and Credit Risk", *Moody's Special Comment*, March.

Keenan, S. C., J. S. Fons and L. V. Carty, 1998b, "An Historical Analysis of Moody's Watchlist", *Moody's Special Comment*, October.

Truglia, V., D. Levey and C. Mahoney, 1995, "Sovereign Risk: Bank Deposits vs Loans", *Moody's Special Comment*, October.

Modelling Credit Migration

Bill Demchak

Credit models are increasingly concerned not only with the probability of default, but also with what happens to a credit on its way to default. Attention is being focused on the probability of moving from one credit level, or rating, to another. One convenient way of expressing this information is through a transition matrix. The primary source for these probabilities has been the rating agencies. As an example, Table 1 contains the historical frequency of annual transitions based on Standard & Poor's (S&P) observations from 1981 to 1998.

There are, however, difficulties involved in applying historical matrices in practice:

❏ In spite of the large number of observations, some measurements have low statistical significance, particularly the investment-grade default frequencies. For example, the BBB default statistic is 0.24% a year, while its value at the 95% confidence interval is more than 200% greater.[1]
❏ The observations are based on seven major rating categories. Many applications require a finer granularity in credit levels.
❏ Historical observations do not reflect the current credit environment.
❏ Historical observations are primarily US-based and are inappropriate for emerging markets.
❏ History only provides an assessment of real probabilities. Pricing models need probabilities that are adjusted for risk (risk-neutral) and are consistent with observed prices in the market.

This article discusses a method for modelling credit migration and default probability. The goal in developing this model was to address the

Table 1 S&P average one-year transition rates (adjusted for the not-rated category)

Initial rating	Rating at year end (%)							
	AAA	AA	A	BBB	BB	B	CCC	Default
AAA	91.93	7.46	0.48	0.08	0.04	0.00	0.00	0.00
AA	0.64	91.81	6.76	0.60	0.06	0.12	0.03	0.00
A	0.07	2.27	91.68	5.12	0.56	0.25	0.01	0.04
BBB	0.04	0.27	5.56	87.87	4.83	1.02	0.17	0.24
BB	0.04	0.10	0.61	7.75	81.48	7.90	1.11	1.01
B	0.00	0.10	0.28	0.46	6.95	82.80	3.96	5.45
CCC	0.19	0.00	0.37	0.75	2.43	12.13	60.44	23.69

issues discussed above using a simple framework with broad pricing and risk management application. The following are highlights of our work:

❏ Rather than being confined to historical rating transitions, the data set is expanded to include historical cumulative default statistics as well as current credit spreads. As will be shown, any one of these three sources is inadequate to paint a reliable picture of credit transitions. In aggregate, however, they provide a more robust result.

❏ Integrating spreads into the analysis requires a means of translating between real and risk-neutral probabilities. The approach used here is based on the capital asset pricing model (CAPM) and derivatives pricing. The end result will be two sets of transition probabilities, one "real" and one risk-neutral.

❏ The number of credit levels is expanded to a much larger set, limited only by computational power.

❏ The process for credit migration is specified in six parameters. An additional seven are used to map the process to the standard rating categories. This represents a large reduction in the number of free variables used in previous work.[2]

❏ The model can be used for a wide range of risk management and pricing applications. In particular, it lends itself to portfolio applications by providing a means for determining loss and return distributions.

This work extends the reduced-form framework of Jarrow, Lando and Turnbull (1997) in several ways. In particular, the number of free parameters is reduced by the introduction of a jump–diffusion process, additional data sources are used to bolster confidence in the results and the model uses a new approach for risk-neutral pricing.

The next section describes the credit process and steps through the procedure for calibrating this process to historical observations. Subsequent sections extend the technique to risk-neutral space and add spreads to the calibration procedure. Fit results are described throughout.

THE PROCESS

The basic underlying or state variable in this model is the one-period default probability.[3] This default rate undergoes changes in accordance with a probability distribution. For credit markets, distributions are highly skewed. For example, the upside of a loan or bond is limited whereas the downside has a significant tail due to defaults. Jump–diffusion processes are well suited to the asymmetric, fat-tailed distributions of credit. Therefore, the default rate is modelled here as a logarithmic jump–diffusion process.

The rows of an historical transition matrix are not dramatically different from one another, suggesting that the same process might successfully characterise each row. There is one exception to this statement – higher-

Figure 1 Probability distribution for changes in the default rate

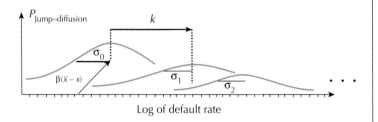

Log of default rate

The jump–diffusion process, conditional on no default, is

$$dx = \beta(\bar{x} - x)dt + \sigma_0 dz + Y dq$$

where x is the log of the instantaneous default rate, dz is standard Brownian motion and dq is the jump event

$$dq = \begin{cases} 1 & \text{with } p = \lambda dt \\ 0 & \text{with } p = 1 - \lambda dt \end{cases}$$

In the event of a jump, Y is normally distributed with mean k and standard deviation Δ_k.

In converting to discrete time, the probability of n jumps occurring over the period is determined from a Poisson likelihood:

$$P_n(\lambda) = \frac{\lambda^n e^{-\lambda}}{n!}$$

Let x_0 be the log of the one-period default rate at the start of the period and x its value at the end of the period. If n jumps have occurred, the conditional distribution for x is normal with mean

$$\beta(\bar{x} - x_0) + nk$$

and standard deviation

$$\sigma_n = \sqrt{\sigma_0^2 + n\Delta_k^2}$$

rated credits have a greater downgrade likelihood than lower-rated credits. Evidence of this "mean-reversion" effect can be observed in the S&P matrix, where a single-A is twice as likely to downgrade as to upgrade, in contrast to the reverse behaviour for a single-B.[4] For this reason, the model includes a mean-reversion parameter.

The continuous credit process is described in Figure 1. The following parameters characterise this process:

❏ The diffusion volatility, σ_0.
❏ The jump probability density, λ.
❏ The expected jump size, k.
❏ The standard deviation of jump size, Δ_k.

Two parameters determine the drift as a function of the state:

❏ The state in which the diffusion drift is zero, $\bar{x}$.
❏ The mean-reversion parameter, β.

Although the process for state changes is a continuous one, it is convenient to work with a version that is discrete in both time and space. In its discrete form, all transition probabilities are contained within a matrix. This greatly eases the computational burden. For example, the 10-year default probabilities are obtained by raising the one-year matrix to the tenth power. The continuous version, by contrast, requires either multiple integrals for each rating state or time-consuming Monte Carlo simulations. The conversion to discrete time is also described in Figure 1.

Each discrete state corresponds to an interval on the continuous axis, as illustrated in Figure 1 by the tick marks on the x-axis. The probability of transition to a discrete state is given by the probability of landing in the corresponding interval. For the results in this article, the space was divided into 40 discrete states, although in practice a larger number could be used.

Except for its drift, the distribution of credit migration is the same for all initial credit levels. Due to mean-reversion, highly rated firms expect an increase in default rate while lower-rated firms expect a decrease.

FITTING THE DATA

Three sources of data will be used to fit the model: annual historical rating transitions, cumulative defaults and credit spreads. As a first step, it is useful to fit the model to the historical data without the credit spreads. Later, after the risk-neutral adjustment is introduced, credit spreads will be added to the optimisation.

For calibrating to S&P data, the seven standard rating categories are mapped to default probabilities. Although this mapping could be done by judgement, here additional fit parameters are introduced for this purpose. These mapping parameters represent the bounds for the default probabilities of each rating category. For example, the BBB rating category might correspond to default probabilities falling between 0.15% and 0.70%.

In total, six fit parameters characterise the process and seven parameters map the S&P rating categories into default probability intervals. The optimum selection of these 13 free variables occurs by minimising the deviation of the model predictions from the input data. The deviation is quantified by the objective function

$$\text{Objective function} = \sum_k \omega_k \times \left(\text{Data}_k - \text{Model}_k\right)^2$$

where Data_k represents the kth data value (whether it is a transition probability, a default probability or a spread) and Model_k represents the corresponding theoretical value predicted by the model. The weights, ω_k, are directly related to the confidence level of the kth data value.

In practice, the selection of ω_k requires judgement. For example, many of the one-year transitions are small numbers with low statistical significance. Therefore, among the transition weights a strong emphasis will be placed on the tri-diagonal elements (ie, no rating change or a single upgrade or downgrade). In addition, the weights can be used to place relative emphasis on the data sources: one-year transitions, multi-year defaults and credit spreads.

RESULTS: HISTORICAL DATA ONLY
This section contains the results of an optimisation to historical data from S&P (1999). The one-year transition results are given in Table 2 and cumulative defaults are listed in Table 3.

If the process were to be fitted to the one-year data alone, a set of fit parameters could be found that faithfully reproduced the transition matrix. However, the one-year transitions and the multi-year defaults cannot be perfectly fit simultaneously because these two data sets are inconsistent with each other.

Table 2 History only: theoretical one-year "real" transition matrix

Rating	AAA	AA	A	BBB	BB	B	CCC	Default
AAA	92.97	3.34	2.67	0.91	0.09	0.01	0.00	0.00
AA	2.60	89.20	4.71	2.97	0.46	0.04	0.01	0.01
A	0.70	2.25	89.77	5.33	1.69	0.19	0.03	0.04
BBB	0.07	0.28	2.47	90.75	4.74	1.24	0.23	0.20
BB	0.00	0.01	0.16	4.56	87.89	4.21	1.95	1.33
BB	0.00	0.00	0.01	0.21	9.05	78.51	6.00	6.23
CCC	0.00	0.00	0.00	0.02	0.38	15.28	64.19	20.14

Table 3 Cumulative default probabilities (%)

		Data	Model prediction		
			History	History and spreads	
		S&P	only	Jul 1999	Oct 1998
Four-year	AA	0.15	0.15	0.18	0.18
	A	0.36	0.42	0.66	0.77
	BBB	1.5	1.6	2.1	2.3
	BB	9.4	7.4	6.7	7.8
	B	24	23	19	24
Eight-year	AA	0.77	0.72	0.57	0.52
	A	1.3	1.7	1.7	1.9
	BBB	4.1	5	4.6	5.2
	BB	20	17	13	15
	B	38	38	31	38

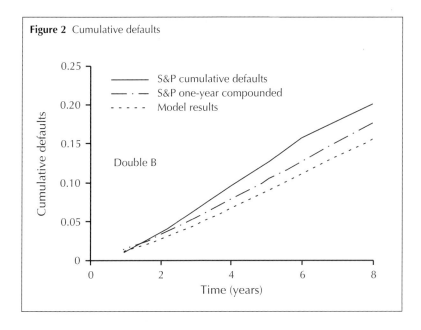

Figure 2 Cumulative defaults

If the historical process is Markovian, a one-year transition matrix already implies future multi-year default levels (as the T-year default probabilities are obtained by raising the one-year matrix to the Tth power).[5] Figure 2 is a comparison for a double-B credit. The cumulative defaults implied from the S&P one-year matrix are shown by the dotted line. S&P's actual cumulative default experience is shown by the solid line. The one-year matrix understates their cumulative observations. The model results fall between these two, representing a compromise between the fit to the default probabilities on the one hand and the transition probabilities on the other.

One explanation for such a data discrepancy is simple statistical error. This would not warrant any adjustment to the weightings. However, the weights can be adjusted if the user has greater confidence in one source over the other. By placing equal aggregate weight on transitions and cumulative defaults, the fit here can be considered a well-behaved Markovian version of all of the S&P historical observations.

THE RISK-NEUTRAL ADJUSTMENT

In this section, market spreads are added to the optimisation. That is, the process is fitted to market prices as well as historical defaults and transitions. Thus far, the model specifies real probabilities. Two additional parameters are needed to get from real probabilities to market prices: a recovery rate, RR, and a market risk premium, θ. The recovery rate is the fraction of notional assumed to be paid upon default.[6] The market risk premium is the

---

PANEL A: RISK-NEUTRAL TRANSLATION

The capital asset pricing model is used for the risk-neutral translation. Asset returns are assumed to be normally distributed and are measured in units of standard deviations from the mean.[1] The risk premium is proportional to the correlation to the market, ρ, and is given by $\rho\theta$. The risk-neutral probability distribution for these assets is the true distribution translated by the risk premium. Thus, the risk-neutral probability, p^{RN}, of one period return, R, falling below some barrier, b, is given by the cumulative normal, N, of the shifted barrier, $b + \rho\theta$:

$$p^{RN}(R < b) = N(b + \rho\theta)$$

For example, suppose a firm has a 2% probability of default and a risk premium, $\rho\theta$, of 0.35. Default will occur if return is below $N^{-1}(0.02) = -2.05$, where N^{-1} is the inverse of the standard cumulative normal distribution. The risk-neutral probability of default is then $p^{RN}(R < -2.05) = N(-1.7) = 4.4\%$.

For the transition probabilities, let q_{ij} represent the probability that a credit at level i at the beginning of the period is at level j or below at the end of the period ($j = 0$ represents default). The risk-neutral transitions are given by

$$p_{ij}^{RN} = q_{ij}^{RN} - q_{ij-1}^{RN}$$

where, from above,

$$q_{ij}^{RN} = N\left[N^{-1}\left(q_{ij}^{real}\right) + \rho\theta\right]$$

and q_{ij}^{real} is the real transition probability from state i to state j or below.

1   Although the asset distribution assumption is different from the jump–diffusion used for credit migration, it results in only limited pricing distortion

---

excess expected return on the market as a fraction of the standard deviation of its return, commonly referred to as the Sharpe ratio. It will be crucial in converting real probabilities into risk-neutral probabilities.

The pricing of credit (a bond or loan) requires risk-neutral default probabilities and a recovery rate (see Panel A for details). Risk-neutral default probabilities are obtained through a two-step process. First, the real one-year transition matrix is transformed to a risk-neutral equivalent. Then this one-period matrix is raised to successive powers to determine the cumulative probabilities.

The risk-neutral transformation is accomplished in a structural framework where all transitions from one credit level to another are driven by the assets of a firm.[7] In this framework a default occurs when the firm's assets drop below some level. The risk-neutral probability distribution is the real distribution translated by the risk premium. This approach is based on the CAPM and has its origins in the seminal Black and Scholes (1973) paper (see Panel B for details).[8]

PANEL B: PRICING OF A CREDIT

$$\text{Price}(C,T) = \sum_{i=1}^{T} Z_i \times \left[C \times \left(1 - p_i^{RN}\right) + RR \times \left(p_i^{RN} - p_{i-1}^{RN}\right) \right] + Z_T\left(1 - p_T^{RN}\right)$$

where C is the coupon, T the time to maturity, Z_i the present value of the risk-free zero-coupon price for maturity i and p_i the risk-neutral cumulative default probability for maturity i. Defaults are implicitly assumed to be uncorrelated with interest rates. The par coupon is derived by setting the price to par and solving for the coupon. The theoretical spread is then the excess of the risky par coupon over the risk-free par coupon. For spread measurements made in this article, agencies are used for the risk-free yield instead of government bonds, whose liquidity and tax advantage have distorting effects.

This approach to risk contrasts with previous work. For example, Jarrow, Lando and Turnbull (1997) make the adjustment to risk-neutral probabilities by increasing the variance of the real probability distribution. As a result, all risk-neutral off-diagonal elements are greater than their real counterparts, including the upgrade probabilities. This is equivalent to the risk-neutral probability of a positive return being greater than its true probability, which goes against intuition. By using a shift in distribution as opposed to an increase in the variance, the CAPM approach avoids this anomaly.

This approach also has the advantage of leading directly to multi-name applications. For example, joint default can be viewed as the event of asset returns for each name being below their respective default levels. Its probability is given by a bivariate normal distribution.

THE ROLE OF RISK PREMIUM

The market risk premium can take on two different roles. It could be used as another fit parameter, allowing more flexibility in fitting both history and current spread levels. Alternatively, it can be fixed at some level (eg, historical average), and the other parameters can be optimised on that basis. As will be shown, spreads will have more leverage on the implied credit process in the latter approach. The right approach depends on the application:

❏ For pricing, where the fit to spreads is primary, the model should solve for the risk premium.
❏ For risk management, the goal is not fitting to spreads but in making the best characterisation of the true credit environment. Fixing the risk premium in this case allows spreads to influence this characterisation.

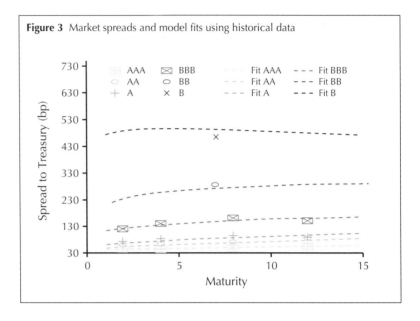

Figure 3 Market spreads and model fits using historical data

THE ROLE OF SPREADS

Although spreads are important for risk management applications and critical for pricing, they are by themselves insufficient. Were the model to fit purely to spreads, we would find that extremely wide ranges of parameters provide equally good fits to the data. These, in turn, would imply very different loss distributions, with different implications for pricing and risk management. The historical data are needed here to lend stability to the solution and the shape of the distribution.

In this article, corporate spreads are measured relative to US agencies rather than to government bonds. Because of their liquidity and tax advantage, a portion of spread over governments is actually non-default related. This is particularly significant for investment-grade spreads. Using spreads over agencies avoids this problem.

Table 4 Spread fit assumptions

Recovery rate 50%

Market risk premium (q) 0.7

Spreads Excess of Merrill Lynch corporate bond yields over US agencies

Equal aggregate weights on spreads, one-year transitions and cumulative defaults

Asset correlations with market range from AAA = 65% to B = 40% (based on KMV data)

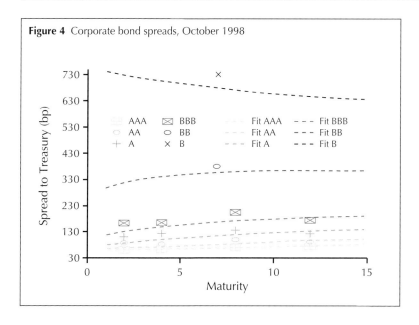

Figure 4 Corporate bond spreads, October 1998

SPREAD RESULTS

The previous historical fit has already provided a process. This process, combined with a given risk premium, implies a set of theoretical spreads. To the extent that the market spreads differ from these predictions, the market is providing new information. The optimiser will seek a compromise between current spreads and history.

In the following two examples, the model is fitted to spread data as well as historical data. Spreads are taken from October 1998 and July 1999, and are represented by the symbols in Figures 3 and 4. Table 4 details the optimisation assumptions.

Table 5 History and July 1999 spreads: theoretical one-year "real" transition matrix

Rating	AAA	AA	A	BBB	BB	B	CCC	Default
AAA	90.04	9.24	0.54	0.14	0.02	0.00	0.00	0.00
AA	1.89	92.39	4.83	0.62	0.17	0.05	0.01	0.03
A	0.27	3.65	91.19	3.85	0.58	0.29	0.05	0.12
BBB	0.05	0.37	5.77	89.80	2.45	0.82	0.27	0.46
BB	0.01	0.09	0.39	9.89	84.81	2.36	0.86	1.58
B	0.00	0.02	0.11	0.42	9.17	82.56	2.09	5.64
CCC	0.00	0.00	0.01	0.08	0.22	10.99	66.76	21.94

July 1999 represents a period when the market was reasonably calm. On average, the model is able to characterise all three data sources well. The model spreads (curves in Figure 3) are close to the data values and the one-year transitions (Table 5) and multi-year defaults (Table C) are not far off their historical values. Some deviations do exist. For example, the model results suggest that the market is not pricing in the single-B default risk suggested by history – the single-B spread curve overshoots the data point, while the single-B cumulative defaults undershoot the historical observations. The opposite is true for the short-term single-A results.

October 1998 represents a large deviation between spreads and history across all ratings. During this period, spreads blew out by almost 40% because of fears of a pending global credit crisis. The model reacts by increasing default probabilities, as can be seen in Table C. The resulting theoretical spreads (Figure 4) are below the market.

Had the model been allowed to fit for the October risk premium, the changes in spread levels would have been reflected in a large increase in the premium, but they would have much less of an effect on the default probabilities that gauge the true riskiness of the credit environment. A fixed risk premium together with an equal weighting scheme (on spreads versus history) will produce results that are sensitive to current conditions but are dampened to market overreaction.

It is worth noting the choice of market risk premium, or Sharpe ratio, used in these fits. We measured premiums on credit risk over various time periods, with different sources of spreads, and consistently found values between 0.7 and 0.8 existing in normal market environments. A premium of 0.7 is high compared with the equity or interest rate market, where values around 0.4 are more typical. Perhaps credit premiums are high due to the huge skew of credit risk compared with that of market risk.

CONCLUSION

This model is used at JP Morgan primarily to determine loss distributions for risk management and pricing and to provide default rates that are sensitive to current credit conditions. Market spreads are assumed to be the best indicators of concurrent loss probability. Conditioning probabilities is important because default likelihoods change significantly through the credit cycle.

The model has been applied to the following situations:

❏ Allowance for credit losses – to determine the cumulative default probabilities used to project expected future losses.
❏ Economic capital requirement – to determine the transition matrix used to generate the credit portfolio loss distribution.

❏ Stress-testing – to set credit spreads for use in firm-wide stress testing.
❏ Pricing structured deals – to determine a risk-neutral transition matrix for generating portfolio loss distribution and timing.

Several lessons have been learned through applications of the model:

❏ The model's output is stable and reasonable over various spread environments (ie, stressed and unstressed) and sources of historical default information (ie, US versus emerging markets).
❏ Combining historical data with current market spreads results in more reasonable and credible estimates of transition and default likelihood than either source alone.
❏ Where credit risks are being hedged, this model improves the consistency and accuracy of hedges.
❏ It is beneficial from a management viewpoint to have a set of consistent default probabilities that can be used across various applications, such as credit derivatives pricing, the allowance for credit losses and the economic capital for the credit portfolio. This increases management confidence in the credibility of complex credit models.
❏ Management judgement is still important, particularly the relative weighting given to historical default information versus market credit spreads.

Based on these observations, we expect the model to be used even more broadly in the future.

1 The methodology for this assessment closely resembles that described in Kealhofer, Kwok and Weng (1998). This assumes a 35% asset cross-correlation, which is close to average for BBB.
2 Examples include Jarrow, Lando and Turnbull (1997) and Arvanitis, Gregory and Laurent (1999).
3 A one-year period is used in the examples here. In theory, any time interval can be used. With a few modifications, the process can be adapted to a continuous-time framework, as in Jarrow, Lando and Turnbull (1997).
4 Downgrade here does not include default.
5 Because of the discreteness of the rating categories, the transitions cannot be truly Markovian. This effect, however, is fairly small and is not sufficient to explain the discrepancy described in this paragraph.
6 In theory, rating-specific (or even name-specific) recovery rates could be used. For this article, a uniform recovery rate of 50% is used across all credits.
7 More generally, this can be viewed as assets relative to liabilities.
8 Black and Scholes (1973) present an alternative derivation of their formula based on CAPM. The implications for risk-neutral probabilities are equivalent to the shift adjustment described here.

BIBLIOGRAPHY

Arvanitis, A., J. Gregory and J. Laurent, 1999, "Building Models for Credit Spreads", *Journal of Derivatives*, Spring, pp. 27–43.

Black, F., and M. Scholes, 1973, "The Pricing of Options and Corporate Liabilities", *Journal of Political Economy* 81, pp. 637–59.

Jarrow, R., D. Lando and S. Turnbull, 1997, "A Markov Model for the Term Structure of Credit Risk Spreads", *Review of Financial Studies* 10(2), pp. 481–523.

Kealhofer, S., S. Kwok and W. Weng, 1998, "Uses and Abuses of Bond Default Rates", *Credit Metrics Monitor*, First Quarter, pp. 37–55.

Standard & Poor's, 1999, "Ratings Performance 1998, Stability & Transition", Report, March, p. 12.

Haircuts for Hedge Funds

Ray Meadows

Those hedge funds that invest in bonds often borrow money against their positions to increase their potential returns on capital. Usually the fund borrows using a repurchase agreement whereby the fund sells the bond to a broker and simultaneously agrees to repurchase it for a fixed price. The broker mitigates repayment risk by "haircutting" the price paid to the fund by a certain percentage. In addition, the broker can call for additional collateral to maintain the haircut percentage. Brokers typically set haircuts at some confidence level (eg, the ninety-ninth percentile) of historical returns or choose a level subjectively. This article describes a method for determining haircuts that explicitly takes into account the risk return trade-off. Specifically, haircuts are set such that the minimum pricing level will just cover the cost of credit risk implied by the haircut and counterparty characteristics.

Although this paper shows how detailed information about the counterparty and the portfolio can be used to set haircuts, in practice it will be difficult to estimate all the parameters. The advantage of the model in this paper over existing methods is that it makes estimates explicit and shows how they affect haircuts.

The basic premise is the higher the spread earned on a loan, the more credit risk a firm should be willing to take, and therefore the lower the haircut taken when financing a bond. Spreads can be seen as compensation for two cost components associated with the credit risk in a portfolio:

❏ expected losses from default; and
❏ the cost of capital required to support the risk of the portfolio.

In turn, there are four factors that affect credit risk and determine the cost of risk:

❏ the level of over-collateralisation (otherwise known as the haircut);
❏ the distribution of possible returns on the asset being financed;
❏ the probability of the counterparty defaulting when the loan exceeds the collateral value; and
❏ the correlation of default across counterparties in the portfolio.

All factors other than the first are outside the control of the credit risk manager. By controlling haircuts, however, the risk manager has a very powerful control on risk because the over-collateralisation of the loan determines both the probability of default and the loss given default.

THE COLLATERAL SETTING PROCESS

The following sections provide details of a pricing model that describes the relationship between the four credit risk factors mentioned above, and the resulting expected losses and capital costs. The process for setting haircuts using the model is straightforward: we choose a minimum haircut such that the resulting required spread (to cover expected losses and cost of capital) is less than or equal to that which will be charged for the loan. The haircut set in this way does not take into account thresholds or minimum call amounts; an additional cushion should be added to account for the minimum call amount.

Using empirical distributions

To quantify the effects of the second and third risk factors above we must model the distributions of the financed bond's returns and the rest of the counterparty's portfolio. For each of these, we can either use the observed historical returns as an empirical proxy of the future distribution or we can specify a mathematical model of the distribution. Unfortunately, historical data can overstate the future volatility of returns as they do not account for the shortening maturity or the changes in the relative value of partial guarantees. Ideally, a mathematical model incorporating the effects of ageing should be used to maximise the usefulness of the data available. In this paper's simple implementation, we have chosen to use five years of historical returns for a group of the most frequently traded Latin bonds. Returns on this group proxy for the rest of the counterparty's portfolio.

Setting levels by analogy

For newly issued bonds or seasoned bonds where there is insufficient data, we must find a similar bond or bonds for which we have sufficient historical returns data. We can then set haircuts for an entire class of bonds with similar characteristics. In defining a class of bonds, the characteristics that determine the distribution of returns include: the rating; the country of issuer; the maturity band (ie, less than one year, one to five years, six to 10 years, etc); the currency; and the liquidity.

CALCULATING EXPECTED LOSSES

Given information about the counterparty's balance sheet, we determine the probability of default as a function of the return on the asset being financed. The relevant period for determining this relationship is the assumed delay between collateral call and liquidation: five business days.[1] Note that the risk period affects the results; we cannot generalise across risk periods. The return distributions mentioned above give us the probability of each return occurring over a given five-day period assuming that the counterparty has not previously defaulted. Conversion of this into an annual probability requires that we take into account the probability of a prior default for each of the 52 five-day periods. The probability of a potential loss being realised is thus the expected annual frequency of the collateral deficiency occurring, multiplied by the probability that the counterparty defaults at that particular level of deficiency. Notice that losses can only occur when the loan amount exceeds the collateral. Given that X is the return on the counterparty's position and HC is the haircut, our potential loss, as a negative number, is $\min(0, HC + X)$. In this model, hedge funds meet collateral calls so long as their total assets exceed total liabilities. Consequently, when they default, our only recovery will be the value of collateral pledged. Multiplying every potential loss by its probability of realisation and summing over all potential losses gives us the expected loss.

Determining the probability of default given the return on the asset financed

Given our assumptions, the probability of default given a deficiency is equal to the probability that the client's assets are less than his liabilities given the market move that led to the deficiency. This quantity, in turn, depends on the distribution of returns on the counterparty's total asset portfolio and the degree of leverage employed by the counterparty. We use the following definitions in our calculations:

- X is the (random) return on the asset being financed (which we are setting the haircut for).
- Y is the (random) return on the client's portfolio other than the asset being financed.
- σ_x and σ_y are the volatilities of X and Y respectively.
- Wx is the percentage of the client portfolio invested in the asset being finance (whose return is X).
- $Wy = (1 - Wx)$ is the percentage invested in assets with return Y.
- Pxy is the correlation between the returns X and Y.
- V is the (random) return component of Y uncorrelated with X.
- $Fv(x^*)$ is the cumulative probability that $V \leq x^*$, where x^* is a given return.
- CE is the counterparty's equity as a percentage of assets.

We assume that, over the term of the trade, we know the values for Wx, Wy, Pxy and CE, and that the distribution of Y is known.[2] The residuals from regressing Y on X give us $Fv(x^*)$. Except for the distribution of Y and related parameters, all other quantities could be known precisely, given full disclosure by the client.

Given the above assumptions, Panel 1 ("Calculating the conditional default probability") shows that the probability of default, conditional on $X = x^*$, is given by:[3]

$$\pi(x^*) = Fv\left[-\left(\frac{CE}{Wy}\right) + \frac{Wx}{Wy}x^* + Pxy\frac{\sigma_y}{\sigma_x}x^*\right] \tag{1}$$

Determining the probability of a particular five-day return on the asset financed

Our calculations require individual instances of asset returns. In practice, this means return bins, where a bin is any return that falls between the upper and lower boundary of the bin.[4] Let x_j^* be the jth return bin for the asset being financed (expressed as a percentage of market value) and let y_j represent the five-day probability of a return in bin j. The first step in calculating the probability of a particular five-day return (occurring sometime in 52 periods) is to calculate π, the unconditional probability of default over five days. We find this value by multiplying each conditional default probability (as defined by Equation (1)) by the probability of the return x_j^* (the conditioning variable), and summing across all possible values of the return. This is given by:

$$\pi\sum_j\pi\left(x_j^*\right)y_j \tag{2}$$

For any of the 52 periods indexed by t, the probability of no previous default is given by $(1-\pi)^{t-1}$ and the annual probability of default, Π_A, is given by:

$$\Pi_A = 1-(1-\pi)^{52} \tag{3}$$

Pulling it all together

Equations (1) and (2) allow us to calculate the expected loss for each return bin for each of the 52 weeks. Summing across all bins and all 52 weeks gives us the annual expected losses (defined as a positive number):

$$E(L) = -\sum_{t=1}^{52}\sum_j\left[\pi\left(x_j^*\right)y_j\left(\frac{\min\left(0, HC+x_j^*\right)}{100\% - HC}\right)(1-\pi)^{t-1}\right] \tag{4}$$

The denominator of the third term is a scaling factor to convert the unit of measure from a percentage of market value to a percentage of the loan amount. This is necessary because both x_j^* and HC are expressed as percentages of the market value of the security financed. The inner summation adds losses for every bin for a particular week. The expected losses for each week, one through 52, are then added together in the outer summation. The term $(1-\pi)^{t-1}$ summed over the 52 weeks is the expected number of weeks out of 52 in which we will not have previously observed a default. If

$\pi = 0$, this will equal 52, otherwise this sum is equal to Π_A/π. Thus Equation (4) simplifies to:

$$E(L) = -\sum_j \left[\frac{\pi\left(x_j^*\right) y_j}{\pi} \left(\frac{\min\left(0, HC + x_j^*\right)}{100\% - HC} \right) \Pi_A \right] \qquad (5)$$

CALCULATING CAPITAL REQUIREMENTS

When determining pricing we must be concerned with both regulatory capital and the economic capital. Economic capital is required to cover "unexpected losses", meaning any losses in excess of the average amount expected. Although economic capital is the minimum necessary capital for the risk of a given transaction, a higher regulatory capital requirement will (effectively) impose regulatory costs over and above the true economic cost of risk. Therefore we use the larger of regulatory or economic capital to evaluate the risk reward trade-off of a proposed transaction.

Regulatory capital

The Bank for International Settlements (BIS) requires that banks hold capital equal to 8% of risk-weighted assets. The amount of the loan at risk when financing readily tradeable assets is calculated as: $\max(0, 10\% - HC)$ × *Asset value*. Banks are risk weighted at 20%; hedge funds are weighted at 50%. For example, if there was a 5% haircut on Brady bonds financed by a hedge fund, the regulatory capital requirement as a percentage of the financed asset value would be $(95\% - 90\%) \times 50\% \times 8\% = 0.2\%$. Dividing by $(1 - haircut)$ we find capital is 0.21%.

Economic capital

The consulting firm Oliver, Wyman & Company (OWC) has developed a methodology for calculating the economic capital requirements for a lending portfolio. The methodology relates the potential "unexpected loss"[5] (UL) from the distribution of potential credit losses on a portfolio to the capital required to maintain a given credit rating. Using this methodology, OWC conducted a study of the capitalisation of more than 60 large US and European banks in the period 1990–1994. They imputed UL for each bank and compared it with book equity. Based on this study, OWC concluded that a bank needed to hold capital equal to 6.5 times the portfolio UL to maintain a credit rating of "A". Consequently, the economic capital required for an individual loan of an A-rated bank would be equal to 6.5 times the unexpected loss contribution (ULC) of that particular loan. This paper applies the same concept to lending under repurchase agreements. The ULC from the potential exposure of a particular transaction i is given by the following equation:

$$ULC_i = N_i \frac{UL_i \, p_i}{\sqrt{P_A}} \tag{6}$$

where:

❑ ULC_i is the unexpected loss contribution (in dollars) of transaction i to the portfolio unexpected loss;

❑ N_i is the ith loan amount in dollars;

❑ p_i is the weighted average correlation of the loss on transaction i with losses on the other transactions in the portfolio;

❑ P_A is the weighted correlation of default across all transactions in the portfolio; and

❑ UL_i is the unexpected loss (as a percentage of the loan) for transaction i on a stand-alone basis.

The unexpected loss (standard deviation) for transaction i is:

$$UL_i = \sqrt{\operatorname{var}\left(L_i\right)} = \sqrt{E\left(L_i^2\right) - \left(E\left(L_i\right)\right)^2} \tag{7}$$

where:

❑ $\operatorname{var}(L_i)$ is the variance of the loss on transaction i as a percentage of the loan amount;

❑ $E(L_i)$ is the expected loss as calculated in Equation (5);

❑ $E(L_i^2)$ is the expectation of the squared loss on transaction i expressed as a percentage of the loan amount.

Thus we calculate economic capital as a percentage of the loan as:

$$Capital = 6.5 \times \sqrt{E\left(L_i^2\right) - \left(E\left(L_i\right)\right)^2} \; \frac{p_i}{\sqrt{P_A}} \tag{8}$$

The expectation of the squared loss, $E(L_i^2)$, is the squared deficiency for bin j, multiplied by the probability of default (conditional on $X = x^*$) and by the expected annual frequency of bin j occurring. Recalling our notation from the above section, we can simply square the loss term in Equation (5) to obtain our result:

$$E\left(L^2\right) = \sum_j \left[\frac{\pi\left(x_j^*\right) y_j}{\pi} \left(\frac{\min\left(0, HC + x_j^*\right)}{100\% - HC} \right)^2 \right] \Pi_A \tag{9}$$

The only remaining unknowns are p_i and P_A. These parameters are given by:

$$p_i = \frac{\displaystyle\sum_{j=1}^{n} UL_j\, p_{ij}}{\displaystyle\sum_{j=1}^{n} UL_j} \quad \text{and} \quad P_A = \frac{\displaystyle\sum_{i=1}^{n}\sum_{j=1}^{n} UL_i\, UL_j\, p_{ij}}{\displaystyle\sum_{i=1}^{n}\sum_{j=1}^{n} UL_i\, UL_j} \qquad \text{(9a)}$$

where p_{ij} is the correlation between losses on transactions i and j. If possible, we estimate p_i using current positions and historical data. If this proves impractical we can simplify things by assuming that $p_i = P_A$. Ideally, we would derive P_A from an analysis of our portfolio. Information on the correlation across clients' portfolios could be used to derive a model of default correlation that would serve to refine the choice of this parameter. The OWC methodology provides the mathematics necessary to turn asset correlations into default correlations. All that is needed is data on the counterparty's holdings.

Given our assumptions for p_i and P_A, we can plug the results of Equations (5) and (9) into Equation (8) and calculate the required economic capital. Sensitivity analysis on a sample of Brady bonds showed that required spreads would change about 1 basis point for each 2% change in the correlation parameters.[6]

CALCULATING SPREAD REQUIREMENTS

The required spread combines the expected losses and cost of the capital for a given transaction. Notation is as follows:

❑ *Funding* = the cost of borrowing money to fund the loan.[7]
❑ *SP* = the required spread over funding cost.
❑ *E(L)* = expected losses as calculated in "Calculating expected losses".
❑ *Capital* = max(regulatory capital, economic capital) is the required equity as a percentage of the loan.
❑ *ROE* = the firm's required return on equity.
❑ *Tax* = the firm's marginal tax rate.
❑ *NI* = net income for the loan as a percentage.

Since the portion of the loan funded by borrowing is (1 − *Capital*), income on the loan is:

$$NI = \left[\left(Funding + SP - E(L)\right) - Funding\left(1 - Capital\right)\right]\left(1 - Tax\right) \qquad \text{(10)}$$

Our *ROE* goal requires that *NI* = *ROE* × *Capital*. Substituting into (10) and solving for *SP* gives:

$$SP = E(L) + \frac{\left(ROE \times Capital\right)}{\left(1 - Tax\right)} - Capital \times Funding \qquad \text{(11)}$$

PANEL A:

ASSUMPTIONS

❑ The return on the counterparty's portfolio of assets can be closely approximated by the return on a portfolio of two assets: security x, the security being financed, and security y, representing all of the counterparty's other positions.

❑ Returns on security y are a linear combination of the returns on x and an uncorrelated component v: $Y = BX + V$.

NOTATION

❑ X, V and Y are the (random) returns on securities x, v and y respectively.

❑ p is the correlation of X and Y.

❑ σ_x and σ_y are the volatilities of X and Y respectively.

❑ B is the regression coefficient for Y regressed on X:

$$B = \frac{\text{cov}(X,Y)}{\text{var}(X)} = p\frac{\sigma_y}{\sigma_x}$$

❑ Wx and Wy are the percentages of counterparty assets invested in securities x and y respectively.

❑ CE is the counterparty's equity as a percentage of assets (= 1 − leverage %).

❑ x^*, y^* and v^* are given returns (defined as return bins or ranges).

❑ $\pi(x^*)$ is the probability of default, conditional on the return x^*. This is what we will derive.

❑ Pr( ) is the probability operator.

❑ $fx(x^*)$, $fy(y^*)$ and $fv(v^*)$ are the probability density functions for X, Y and V respectively, evaluated for specific return bins.

❑
$$Fx(x^*) = \int_{-\infty}^{x^*} fx(z)\,dz = \Pr(X \le x^*)$$

is the cumulative probability function for X evaluated at x^*.

❑ $Fv(v^*)$ is the cumulative probability function for V evaluated at v^*.

DERIVING THE DISTRIBUTION

First we derive the distribution of Y conditional on $X = x^*$. Using Bayes' rule, we see that:

$$\Pr\left(Y = y^* \middle| X = x^*\right) = \frac{\Pr\left(Y = y^*, X = x^*\right)}{\Pr\left(X = x^*\right)}$$

Substituting $BX + V$ in for Y yields:

$$\frac{\Pr\left(BX + V = y^*, X = x^*\right)}{\Pr\left(X = x^*\right)}$$

Substituting x^*, the value of X, on the left and noting that V and X are independent, results in:

CALCULATING THE CONDITIONAL DEFAULT PROBABILITY

$$\frac{\Pr\left(Bx^*+V=y^*\right)\Pr\left(X=x^*\right)}{\Pr\left(X=x^*\right)}$$

Rearranging and cancelling terms gives us:

$$\Pr\left(V=y^*-Bx^*\right)$$

Given our notational conventions, the above probability is equivalent to:

$$fv\left(y^*-Bx^*\right)=\Pr\left(Y=y^*\middle|X=x^*\right)=fy\left(y^*\middle|X=x^*\right) \tag{1A}$$

Now we will use the above probability function to determine the probability of default. Since the counterparty defaults when losses exceed equity, the probability of default is:

$$\Pr\left(WxX+WyY+CE<0\right)=\Pr\left(WxX+WyY<-CE\right)$$

We are interested in the probability of defaulting when we know that $X = x^*$. Substituting in and rearranging to isolate the random variable Y on the left side in the brackets gives the conditional probability of default:

$$\pi(x^*)=\Pr\left[Y<\frac{-\left(CE+Wxx^*\right)}{Wy}\right]$$

In terms of the probability density function this is:

$$\pi(x^*)=\int_{-\infty}^{A}fy\left(y^*\middle|X=x^*\right)dy^* \tag{2A}$$

where:

$$A=\frac{-\left(CE+Wxx^*\right)}{Wy}$$

Substituting (1A) into (2A) give us:

$$\pi(x^*)=\int_{-\infty}^{A}fv\left(y^*-Bx^*\right)dy^*=Fv\left(A-Bx^*\right) \tag{3A}$$

Expanding this out (and substituting for B) yields:

$$\pi(x^*)=Fv\left[-\left(\frac{EC}{Wy}+\frac{Wx}{Wy}(x^*)+p\frac{\sigma_y}{\sigma_x}x^*\right)\right] \tag{4A}$$

as the probability of default conditional on $X = x^*$.

Table 1 Example parameters

Return on equity (*ROE*) goal	15.00%
Effective tax rate	36.00%
Assumed funding cost	5.25%
Assumed leverage	85.00%
Assumed percentage of "other" assets (Wy)	90.00%
Weighted average correlation of transaction (p_i)	10.00%
Weighted average correlation of portfolio (P_A)	10.00%

Table 2 Example bond portfolio

Bond	Beta	15bp haircut	30bp haircut
Argentina discount	0.78	18%	16%
Argentina FRB	0.88	10%	7%
Brazil C bond	0.63	17%	14%
Brazil DCB	0.65	25%	24%
Brazil discount	0.87	14%	11%
Brazil el	0.75	26%	25%
Brazil exit	0.75	19%	17%
Brazil IDU	1.23	12%	11%
Brazil new new money	0.65	29%	28%
Mexico discount	0.95	18%	17%
Mexico par	0.88	17%	16%

RESULTS FOR LATIN BRADY BONDS

The model was implemented using the parameters in Table 1. In addition, the distribution of Y was assumed to correspond to the distribution of returns on an equally weighted portfolio of the example bonds. Table 2 shows the beta of the index returns relative to each particular bond and haircuts implied by spreads of 15 and 30 basis points.

CONCLUSION

The model presented in this paper provides a basic framework for tying haircuts to pricing. Some parameters will not be easy to calibrate. Initially, these can be set using judgement or intuition. Later, as more information is available, estimates can be refined using statistical analysis.

Note in particular that the methodology described here does not use counterparty ratings because ratings do not tell us what we need to know: the probability of default given that the collateral has declined in value below the loan balance. The default model used here builds on the work of Merton (1974),[8] who first modelled default as a put on the firm's assets. This model implies that default is related to the volatility of the client's assets and the amount of leverage (as a percent of assets).[9] Thus the riskiness of a counterparty is calibrated using parameters such as leverage, correlation of asset returns, and the assumed distribution of other assets' returns.

According to the model, different institutions should set different haircuts if they have different levels of diversification. The "market" haircut for a trade should thus be set by the institution with the least concentration of risk. An uncompetitive haircut implies concentration risk higher than the market. In this case economic efficiency requires that the risk reside elsewhere.

Although the data analysis challenges are formidable, the benefits are significant: the ability to quantify how much risk is justified by the spreads being earned by the securities financing desk.

1 The five-day delay assumption comes from the following timeline: on the first day, the market declines and a collateral call is made. On the second day, the counterparty disputes the mark-to-market to delay payment. On the third day, the counterparty claims that he has sent funds and we have lost them. Management begins discussing whether to liquidate the client's portfolio. On the fourth day, the client says that the operational problem was at their end and they will send money immediately. On the fifth day, it is clear the client is stalling, liquidation is authorised and positions are sold by the end of the day. For bonds with low liquidity or for large positions relative to volume, this assumption should be modified.

2 In particular, we could assume Y has the same distribution as an index of securities in the area of the hedge fund's specialisation.

3 Note that the term multiplying x^*:

$$Pxy\frac{\sigma_y}{\sigma_x}$$

is the regression coefficient for Y regressed on X.

4 For example, suppose that a particular bin is for returns between −10.1% and −9.9%. We seek to calculate the probability that a loss within this range will occur over the next year.

5 Unexpected loss is defined as the standard deviation of the distribution of losses.

6 This analysis was carried out assuming correlations in the 7–13% range with haircuts corresponding to a minimum spread of 15bp. The results would vary for different minimum spreads (haircut levels).

7 In our implementation, we found it convenient to assume a constant funding cost over the term of the transaction. Relaxing this assumption would add considerable complexity.

8 Merton R., 1974, "On the Pricing of Corporate Debt: The Risk Structure of Interest Rates", *Journal of Finance* 29, pp. 449–70.

9 KMV's default risk analysis tools are also based on this framework.

Generalising with HJM

Dmitry Pugachevsky

In this paper, we apply the Heath, Jarrow and Morton (1992) term-structure framework to a credit risk model. Maksymiuk and Gatarek (1999) dealt with the forward probability of default when there is no correlation between default and risk-free rates. With the approach we take in this paper, we are able to tackle the case of non-zero correlation. When default and risk-free rates are independent, both results coincide. Numerical results show that the effect of correlation on the drift of the spread can be significant.

First, we introduce notations for the risk-free market and show how the Heath–Jarrow–Morton result for risk-free bonds follows from the theorem proved by Maksymiuk and Gatarek. In the second section, we introduce a risky bond and express its price through risky forward rates. Then we derive a relationship between its drift and volatility terms. A similar result was also obtained by Duffie and Singleton (1999) by modelling hazard rates. The risky model can now be built by direct application of this result. But more common in the literature is the so-called spread approach, where the modelling quantity is the spread between risky and non-risky rates (eg, Longstaff and Schwartz, 1995; Pugachevsky, 1996; Jarrow, Lando and Turnbull, 1997; and Schönbucher, 1998). Using the obtained result for the risky forward rate and the Heath–Jarrow–Morton condition, we derive the general relationship between drift and volatility terms for the spread between forward rates. In the last section, we discuss the case of non-zero recovery and show that in the special case of recovery of treasury (Duffie and Singleton, 1999), the price of a risky bond is the linear combination of prices of a risk-free bond and a risky bond with zero recovery.

NOTATIONS AND PRELIMINARY RESULTS

Let us first consider a risk-free market. Denote the instantaneous forward rate measured at time t and characterising investment at time T ($T > t$) as $f(t, T)$, and the price at time t of a zero-coupon bond maturing at time T as $P(t, T)$. Then the well-known relationship between them is:

$$P(t,T) = \exp\left[-\int_t^T f(t,u)\,du \right] \tag{1}$$

The risk-free short rate $r(t)$ can be expressed through the forward rate as:

$$r(t) = f(t,t) \qquad (2)$$

and it defines the value of the money market account $B(t)$ as:

$$B(t) = \exp\left[-\int_0^t r(t)\,dt \right] \qquad (3)$$

An arbitrage-free argument defines $P(t,T)$ as the expectation of discounting on time interval $[t,T]$:

$$P(t,T) = E\left(\frac{B(t)}{B(T)} \middle| F_t \right) \qquad (4)$$

where expectation is taken under the risk-neutral measure conditional on information at time t.

Assume now that the instantaneous forward rate is the solution of the following stochastic differential equation:

$$df(t,T) = \alpha(t,T)\,dt + \sigma^*(t,T)\,dW_t \qquad (5)$$

where $\alpha(t,T)$ and $\sigma(t,T)$ are one-dimensional and d-dimensional stochastic processes, respectively, W_t is a d-dimensional Brownian motion under the risk-neutral measure and * means "transpose".

The Heath–Jarrow–Morton relationship between drift and volatility terms of $f(t,T)$:

$$\alpha(t,T) = \sigma^*(t,T) \int_t^T \sigma(t,u)\,du \qquad (6)$$

can be also obtained from the following statement.

Maksymiuk and Gatarek's theorem says that if there exists a process $Y(t)$ of bounded variation, such that processes:

$$X(t,T) = Y(t) \exp\left[-\int_t^T f(t,u)\,du \right] \qquad (7)$$

and:

$$M(t) = Y(t) + \int_0^t Y(u) f(u,u)\,du \qquad (8)$$

are both martingales, then the following relationship holds:

$$\int_t^T \alpha(t,u)\,du = \frac{1}{2}\left|\int_t^T \sigma(t,u)\,du\right|^2 \tag{9}$$

To apply this theorem, let us take:

$$Y(t) = \frac{1}{B(t)} \tag{10}$$

which has bounded variation. Equation (4) implies that

$$X(t,T) = \frac{P(t,T)}{B(t)} = E\left(\frac{1}{B(t)}\Big|F_t\right) \tag{11}$$

therefore it is a martingale. It also follows from equations (2) and (3) that:

$$M(t) = \frac{1}{B(t)} + \int_0^t \frac{f(u,u)}{B(u)}\,du = 1 \tag{12}$$

is a martingale.

Thus, the theorem immediately implies formula (9), which, by differentiation in T, can be rewritten in the Heath–Jarrow–Morton form (6).

RISKY FORWARD RATE FRAMEWORK

Let us now consider the risky market where there always exists the possibility of default. Let us denote the time of default as t and the event of no default before time t as $N(t)$, ie:

$$N(t) = 1_{\{\tau > t\}} \tag{13}$$

Let us denote the price at time t of the risky (defaultable) zero-coupon bond maturing at time T as $\tilde{P}(t,T)$. Assume for now that the recovery value is zero, and therefore the value of the bond at maturity T is one if there is no default before T and zero if default happens. Then arbitrage-free argument defines the bond price as:

$$\tilde{P}(t,T) = E\left(\frac{B(t)}{B(T)}N(T)\Big|F_t\right) \tag{14}$$

Since the price at time t is zero if default happens before t, it can be rewritten as:

$$\tilde{P}(t,T) = N(t)Q(t,T) \tag{15}$$

where $Q(t,T)$ is the discounted probability of no default before time T measured at time t and conditional on there being no default before time

t. Thus it is decreasing in T and increasing in t. Assume it can be represented as:

$$Q(t,T)=\exp\left[-\int_t^T \tilde{f}(t,u)\,du\right] \tag{16}$$

where we define the stochastic process $\tilde{f}(t,u)$ as the "risky" instantaneous forward rate. Assume that it satisfies the following stochastic differential equation:

$$d\tilde{f}(t,T)=\tilde{\alpha}(t,T)\,dt+\tilde{\sigma}^*(t,T)\,d\tilde{W}_t \tag{17}$$

where $\tilde{\alpha}(t,T)$ and $\tilde{\sigma}(t,T)$ are stochastic processes and $\tilde{W}_t$ is a $\tilde{d}$-dimensional Brownian motion under the risk-neutral measure.

Let us introduce the process:

$$\tilde{Y}(t)=\frac{N(t)}{B(t)} \tag{18}$$

which obviously has bounded variation. Also, let us define:

$$\tilde{X}(t,T)=\tilde{Y}(t)\exp\left[-\int_t^T \tilde{f}(t,u)\,du\right] \tag{19}$$

Then it follows from equations (14) and (15) that:

$$\tilde{X}(t,T)=\frac{N(t)}{B(t)}Q(t,T)=\frac{\tilde{P}(t,T)}{B(t)}=E\left(\frac{N(T)}{B(T)}\Big|F_t\right) \tag{20}$$

therefore it is a martingale under the risk-neutral measure.

Let us now consider the process defined by the following equation:

$$\tilde{M}(t)=\tilde{Y}(t)+\int_0^t \tilde{Y}(u)\tilde{f}(u,u)\,du \tag{21}$$

Intuitively, because $\tilde{f}(t,t)$ is the intensity of the process $N(t)/B(t)$, this process is a martingale. This result can be proved rigorously, but the proof is rather technical and we do not give it here.

Therefore, we can apply the theorem to show that:

$$\int_t^T \tilde{\alpha}(t,u)\,du=\frac{1}{2}\left|\int_t^T \tilde{\sigma}(t,u)\,du\right|^2 \tag{22}$$

or in the form similar to (6):

$$\tilde{\alpha}(t,T) = \tilde{\sigma}^*(t,T)\int_t^T \tilde{\sigma}(t,u)\,du \tag{23}$$

This result allows one to build the risky term structure by defining the volatility structure of risky forward rates, and can be especially useful for the problems where we do not have to consider risk-free rates. The problem here may arise because there is no guarantee that bond prices in risky markets will be always below bond prices in risk-free markets. The solution to this problem is to model the risky term structure as a risk-free rate plus a stochastic positive spread. This approach is considered below.

SPREAD MODEL

Let us rewrite the expression for the risky zero-coupon bond (15) in the form:

$$\tilde{P}(t,T) = N(t)P(t,T)A(t,T) \tag{24}$$

where the process $A(t,T)$ is the probability of no default before T measured at time t and conditional on no default before time t. Note that this probability is now under the forward measure. The process $A(t,T)$ is decreasing in T, increasing in t and we assume it can be represented as:

$$A(t,T) = \exp\left[-\int_t^T \lambda(t,u)\,du\right] \tag{25}$$

where we define the stochastic process as "spread between forward rates". Assume that spread satisfies the following stochastic differential equation:

$$d\lambda(t,T) = b(t,T)\,dt + \gamma^*(t,T)\,d\hat{W}_t \tag{26}$$

where $b(t,T)$ and $\gamma(t,T)$ are one-dimensional and m-dimensional stochastic processes, respectively, and $\hat{W}_t$ is an m-dimensional Brownian motion under the risk-neutral measure. Assume also that R is the $d \times m$ matrix of time-independent correlations between processes in (5) and (26), ie:

$$R_{i,j} = \text{corr}\left(dW_t^{(i)}, dW_t^{(j)}\right) \tag{27}$$

Comparing (15) and (24), it follows that:

$$Q(t,T) = P(t,T)A(t,T) \tag{28}$$

then representations (1), (16), and (25) imply that the risky forward rate is the sum of the non-risky forward rate and the spread:

$$\tilde{f}(t,T) = f(t,T) + \lambda(t,T) \tag{29}$$

This defines the following equation for the risky forward rate:

$$d\tilde{f}(t,T) = \Big(\alpha(t,T) + b(t,T)\Big)dt + \sigma^*(t,T)dW_t + \gamma^*(t,T)d\hat{W}_t \tag{30}$$

Comparing with (17) and taking into account that Brownian motions W_t and $\hat{W}_t$ are cross-correlated, we can use equation (22) to obtain the following formula:

$$\int_t^T \big[\alpha(t,u) + b(t,u)du\big] = \frac{1}{2}\left|\int_t^T \sigma(t,u)du\right|^2$$

$$+ \int_t^T \sigma^*(t,u)du R \int_t^T \gamma(t,u)du + \frac{1}{2}\left|\int_t^T \gamma(t,u)du\right|^2 \tag{31}$$

This and the Heath–Jarrow–Morton condition (9) together produce the final expression for the drift of the spread:

$$\int_t^T b(t,u)du = \int_t^T \sigma^*(t,u)du R \int_t^T \gamma(t,u)du + \frac{1}{2}\left|\int_t^T \gamma(t,u)du\right|^2 \tag{32}$$

Differentiating with respect to T, it can be rewritten in the form:

$$b(t,T) = \sigma^*(t,T) R \int_t^T \gamma(t,u)du +$$

$$\int_t^T \sigma^*(t,u)du R\gamma(t,T) + \gamma^*(t,T)\int_t^T \gamma(t,u)du \tag{33}$$

Assume for simplicity that the expressions for the spread (26) and non-risky forward rate (5) are both one-factor stochastic differential equations, and the correlation between Brownian motions is:

$$\rho = \text{corr}\Big(dW_t, d\hat{W}_t\Big) \tag{34}$$

Then Equation (33) becomes:

B

Back-testing the validation of a model by feeding it historical data and comparing the model's results with the historical reality.

Banking book *see* trading book

Bankruptcy the liquidation of a firm's assets when it is unable to meet its financial obligations; distinct from default.

Basis risk in a futures market, the basis risk is the risk that the value of a futures contract does not move in line with the underlying exposure.

Basis swap an interest rate basis swap or a cross-currency basis swap is one in which two streams of floating-rate payments are exchanged.

Basket default swap *see* credit default swap

Basket swap a swap in which the floating leg is based on the returns on a basket of underlying assets, such as equities, commodities, bonds or swaps.

Bermudan option the holder of a Bermudan option, also known as a limited-exercise, mid-Atlantic or semi-American option, has the right to exercise it on one or more possible dates prior to its expiry.

Beta the beta of an instrument is its standardised covariance with its class of instruments as a whole. Thus the beta of a stock is the extent to which that stock follows movements in the overall market.

Beta distribution a family of parametric probability distributions with two degrees of freedom defined on the interval [0,1]. One of the Weibull class of distributions.

Beta trading used by currency traders if they take the volatility risk of one currency in another. Eg, rather than hedge one US dollar/ECU option with another, a trader, either because of liquidity constraints or because of lower volatility, might hedge with US dollar/Deutschmark options.

Bilateral netting agreement between two counterparties whereby the value of all in-the-money contracts is offset by the value of all out-of-the-money contracts, resulting in a single net exposure amount owed by one counterparty to the other.

Binary option unlike simple options, which have continuous payout profiles, that of a binary option is discontinuous and pays out a fixed amount if the underlying satisfies a predetermined trigger condition but nothing otherwise. Binary options are also known as digital or all-or-nothing options.

Binomial tree/binomial lattice discrete-time model for describing the evolution of a random variable that is permitted to rise or fall with given probabilities. After the initial rise, two branches will each have two possible outcomes and so the process will continue.

Black–Scholes model original closed-form solution to option pricing developed by Fischer Black and Myron Scholes in 1973. In its simplest form it offers a solution to pricing European-style options on assets with interim cash payouts over the life of the option.

Building-block approach an approach to calculating capital adequacy that is the basis for the quantitative requirements of the European Union's Capital Adequacy Directive (CAD). This approach recognises to some extent the risk reduction that arises from offsetting positions but treats individual market risks as additive, and further distinguishes between general market risk and specific risk, the latter reflecting risks specific to individual securities.

Brownian motion type of Markov process that is used to specify the stochastic process of asset prices – also known as the Wiener process.

C

Calibration (of a model) *see* parameterisation

Call option contract giving purchaser the right to buy an underlying at a certain price on or before a certain date. *See also* put option

Cancellable swap interest rate swap in which the fixed-rate payer has the right to terminate the swap after a certain time if rates fall.

Cap contract whereby the seller agrees to pay to the purchaser, in return for an upfront premium or a series of annuity payments, the difference between a reference rate and an agreed strike rate when the reference exceeds the strike.

Capital Adequacy Directive (CAD) European Union directive that became law across the European Union on January 1, 1996. It requires banks to separate trading book risk from more generalised banking book risk and to apply the building-block approach to interest rate and equity risk in the trading book, as well as foreign exchange risk across both books.

Capped swap interest rate swap with an embedded cap in which the floating payments of the swap are capped at a certain level. A floating-rate payer can thereby limit its exposure to rising interest rates.

Cashflow-at-risk application of value-at-risk (VAR) methodology to a non-financial firm's business operations. In this context, it is defined in terms of earnings or cashflow and expressed as the probability that a firm will fail to meet its business targets.

Cash market an underlying, as opposed to a futures market.

Closed-form models these can usually be evaluated much more quickly than numerical models, which are sometimes far more computationally intensive.

Closed-form solution also called an analytical solution. An explicit solution of, for example, an option pricing problem by the use of formulas involving only simple mathematical functions, for example, Black–Scholes, Vasicek models.

Collar the simultaneous purchase of an out-of-the-money call and sale of an out-of-the-money put (or cap and floor in the case of interest rate options). The premium from selling the put reduces the cost of purchasing the call. The amount saved depends on the strike rate of the two options.

Complete markets if markets are complete, any contingent claim can be hedged exactly using tradable assets.

Confidence interval degree of certainty one has that estimated value-at-risk will not be exceeded by actual losses. For example, if a 95% confidence interval is used for a VAR estimate, actual losses should exceed estimates only on one day out of 20 on average. The greater the confidence interval, the higher the VAR.

Contingent capital note special case of a credit-linked note. In this case, a dealer or corporate founds a highly collateralised special-purpose trust and issues units of the trust in the form of high-yielding notes.

Contingent claim the term used to mean a derivative instrument in mathematical models.

Contingent swap the generic term for a swap activated when rates reach a certain level or a specific event occurs. Swaptions are often considered to be contingent swaps.

Convertible bond a bond issued by a company that must be exchanged for a set number of that company's shares at a predetermined price. Because the bond embeds a call option on the company's equity, convertibles carry much lower rates of interest than traditional debt and is therefore a cheap way for companies to raise debt.

Convexity a bond's convexity is the amount that its price sensitivity differs from that implied by the bond's duration. Fixed-rate bonds and swaps have positive convexity: when rates rise the rate of change in their price is slower than suggested by their duration; when rates fall it is faster.

Correlation measure of the degree to which changes in two variables are related, normally expressed as a coefficient between plus one, which means variables are perfectly correlated (in that they move in the same direction to the same degree), and minus one, which means they are perfectly negatively correlated (in that they move in opposite directions to the same degree).

Cost of carry if the cost of financing an asset is lower than the interest received, the asset is said to have a positive cost of carry; if higher, the cost of carry is negative. The cost of carry is determined by the opportunities for lending the asset and the shape of the yield curve.

Cox–Ingersoll–Ross model in its simplest form this is a lognormal one-factor model of the term structure of interest rates, which has the short rate of interest as its single source of uncertainty. The model allows for interest rate mean-reversion and is also known as the square root model because of the assumptions made about the volatility of the short-term rate.

Correlation of credit quality the correlation of the credit ratings or rating changes of entities in a portfolio.

Correlation of default *see* default correlation

Coupon interest rate payment on a bond.

Credit concentration *see* credit risk concentration; *see also* credit paradox

Credit default note *see* credit-linked note

Credit default swap also known as credit default puts, as they share characteristics of both swaps and options. Irrespective of their exact pedigree, they pay out if a credit event occurs.

Credit derivative specific class of financial instruments whose value is derived from an underlying market instrument driven primarily by the credit risk of private or government entities.

Credit event any event that affects the credit rating or creditworthiness of an entity. Credit events that constitute trigger conditions for credit derivatives include bankruptcy or insolvency, a ratings agency downgrade, default on debt obligations or a specified decline in the price of a reference security.

Credit-linked note /credit default note) created by the securitisation of a credit default swap. Generally the purchaser will buy a coupon-paying note from a special-purpose trust which is collateralised with highly rated securities.

CreditMetrics framework used by JP Morgan for quantifying credit risk in portfolios of credit products, fixed-income instruments and financial instruments subject to counterparty default.

Credit migration short of a default, the extent to which the credit quality of an obligor or counterparty improves or deteriorates.

Credit paradox the dramatic rise in the loan spreads required as exposure to the same obligor increases. The phenomenon forces many banks to take on larger amounts of credit exposure in search of larger spreads, thereby exposing themselves to an even larger probability of suffering from default. *See also* credit risk concentration.

Credit quality credit quality of a firm at a specific point in time is measured by the probability that it will be able to pay off its contractual obligations. The first instance of failure to do so is defined as default.

Credit repo credit repurchase agreement.

Credit (or default) risk risk that a loss will be incurred if a counterparty to a transaction does not fulfil its financial obligations in a timely manner.

Credit risk assessment extent of a firm's credit risk is usually measured in terms of exposure. The current exposure associated with a derivative instrument – its replacement cost – is the present value of the expected future net cashflows of that instrument.

Credit risk concentration/concentration risk if a loan portfolio is highly concentrated in terms of exposure to a specific industry or country, it is highly susceptible to correlated default and credit migration events.

Credit risk models models that attempt to quantify credit risk – eg, value of the firm models; recovery of promised payoff models; instantaneous risk of default models.

Credit spread interest rate spread between two debt issues of similar maturity and duration. This spread reflects the relative creditworthiness of the issuers; the reference issue is generally a government security. The credit spread is often used as a measure of creditworthiness; a reduction in the credit spread reflects an improvement in the borrower's creditworthiness.

Credit spread forward forward on the credit spread between two debt issues. *See also* credit spread option

Credit spread option option on the credit spread between two debt issues. The option will pay out the difference between the credit spread at maturity and a strike spread determined at the outset. *See also* credit spread forward, credit derivatives

Cross-currency swap involves the exchange of cashflows in one currency for those in another. Unlike single-currency swaps, cross-currency swaps often require an exchange of principal.

Current exposure another name for replacement cost. *See also* exposure

D

Default failure of a firm to make a payment on a coupon or reimburse its debt.

Default correlation degree to which the default of one obligor is related to the default of another. The quantity that ties the risk contribution of a risky asset to the portfolio.

Default probability *see* expected default frequency

Default put *see* credit default swap

Default swap *see* credit default swap

Delta delta of an option describes its premium's sensitivity to changes in the price of the underlying. An option's delta will be the amount of the underlying necessary to hedge changes in the option price for small movements in the underlying.

Delta-hedging an option is said to be delta-hedged if a position has been taken in the underlying in proportion to its delta.

Density function (of a distribution) the area under the density curve across an interval represents the probability over that interval.

Derivative a derivative instrument or product is one whose value changes with changes in one or more underlying market variables, such as equity or commodity prices, interest rates or foreign exchange rates. Basic derivatives include forwards, futures, swaps, options, warrants and convertible bonds.

Distribution the probability distribution of a variable describes the probability of the variable attaining a certain value. Assumptions about the distribution of the underlying are crucial to option models because the distribution determines how likely it is that the option will be exercised.

Dynamic hedging *see* delta-hedging

Dynamic replication to replicate the payout

of an option by buying or selling the underlying (or, for some markets, because of cheaper transaction costs, futures) in proportion to an option's delta.

E

Economic capital capital necessary for the bank to remain solvent in the event of extreme loss. Economic capital is the number of standard deviations away from the expected loss that is necessary to protect the bank from insolvency in the event of extreme losses in the bank's portfolio due to default risk. Also known as "risk capital". *See also* value-at-risk

Equilibrium model model that specifies processes for the underlying economic variables and the extra risk premium investors require for risky assets. The evolution of asset prices and their risk premiums can then be derived from the model thus specified.

European-style options options where purchasers may take delivery of the underlying only at the end of the option's life. *See* option

Expected default frequency (EDF) the probability that an obligor will default before the maturity of the contracted obligation to pay. Such probabilities can be estimated from historical data or analytically using options theory.

Expected exposure amount the bank can expect to lose, on average, over the period of time in which it extends credits.

Expected loss (EL) average loss the bank can expect to incur on an asset over the period up to a specified horizon. *See also* unexpected loss

Exposure vulnerability to loss from unanticipated events.

Extreme loss loss arising from defaults of catastrophic magnitude, which tend to occur more frequently when market conditions deteriorate beyond a certain point.

Extreme value theory actuarial science that focuses on extreme events and their associated tail probabilities; it looks explicitly at extreme outcomes and provides a series of natural models for them.

F

Floating–floating swap *see* basis swap

Forward (transaction) agreement to exchange a predetermined amount of currency, commodity or other financial instrument at a specified future date and at a predetermined rate.

Forward rate agreement (FRA) allows purchasers/sellers to fix the interest rate for a specified period in advance. One party pays fixed, the other an agreed variable rate. Maturities are generally out to two years and are priced off the underlying yield curve. The transaction is done on a nominal amount and only the difference between contracted and actual rates is paid. If rates have risen by the time of the agreement's maturity, the purchaser receives the difference in rates from the seller, and vice versa.

Forward start option option that gives the purchaser the right to receive, after a specified time, a standard put or call option. The option's strike price is set at the time the option is activated, rather than when it is purchased. The strike level is usually set at a certain fixed percentage in- or out-of-the-money relative to the prevailing spot rate at the time the strike is activated.

Forward swap swap in which rates are fixed before the start date. If a company expects rates to rise soon but only needs funds later, it may enter into a forward swap.

Fréchet distribution an extreme value distribution with unbounded support to the right. *See also* generalised Pareto distribution

G

Gamma rate of change in the delta of an option for a small change in the underlying. The rate of change is greatest when an option is at-the-money and decreases as the price of the underlying moves further away from the strike price in either direction; gamma is therefore ∩-shaped.

Gaussian *see* distribution

Generalised Pareto distribution class of theoretical distributions of extreme values with three degrees of freedom parameterised as scale, location and shape. Includes the Gumbel (double exponential), Fréchet and Weibull distributions. *See* extreme value theory

Geometric Brownian motion model frequently used for the diffusion process followed by asset prices. Standard Brownian motion is a random walk process with Gaussian increments; that is, changes in the asset price are normally distributed. The term geometric means that it is the proportional change in the asset price (as opposed to the absolute level) which is normally distributed. *See also* random walk, stochastic process

Gumbel (double exponential) distribution an extreme value distribution. Includes the normal, exponential, gamma and lognormal distributions. *See also* generalised Pareto distribution

H

Hedge strategy to reduce exposure by effecting a transaction that offsets an existing position.

Historical simulation method of calculating value-at-risk that uses historical data to assess the effect of market moves on a portfolio. The first step is to record the changes in the relevant market factors over a given historical period, where each change occurs over a constant holding period. The next step is to revalue the portfolio for each change in market factors, as if such change were to occur in the future. The result is a distribution of possible profits and losses on the portfolio over the holding period, from which it is possible to calculate the maximum loss at a given confidence level.

Historical volatility measure of the volatility of an underlying instrument over a past period. It can be used as a guide to pricing options but is not necessarily a good indicator of future volatility. Volatility is normally expressed as the annualised standard deviation of the log relative return.

Hull–White model extension of the Vasicek model for interest rates, the main difference being that mean-reversion is time-dependent. Both are one-factor models. The Hull–White model was developed using a trinomial lattice, although closed-form solutions for European-style options and bond prices are possible.

I

Implied repo rate the return earned by buying a cheapest-to-deliver bond for a bond futures contract and selling it forward via the futures contract.

Interest rate risk the risk to borrowing or investment posed by interest rate changes.

Interest rate swap agreement to exchange net future cashflows. Interest rate swaps most commonly change the basis on which liabilities are paid on a specified principal. They are also used to transform the interest basis of assets. In its commonest form, the fixed–floating swap, one counterparty pays a fixed rate and the other pays a floating rate based on a reference rate, such as Libor. There is no exchange of principal – the interest rate payments are made on a notional amount.

In-the-money an option whose strike price is advantageous compared with the current market price of the underlying. The more an option is in-the-money, the higher its intrinsic value and the more expensive it becomes.

Intrinsic value amount by which an option is in-the-money, that is, its value relative to the current forward market price. Option premiums comprise intrinsic value and time value.

J

Joint distribution a multivariate distribution that depends on two or more variables.

Joint probability of default the probability that one obligor will default if another defaults.

K

Kurtosis measure of how fast the tails or wings of a probability distribution approach zero, evaluated relative to a normal distribution. The tails are either fat-tailed (leptokurtic) or thin-tailed (platykurtic). Markets are generally leptokurtic.

L

Leverage either the opportunity for large gains or losses from a small initial investment as widely associated with derivatives or the relationship between a firm's equity and its debt.

Liquidity risk risk that the market might dry up and make it impossible to sell out of a position without incurring large losses.

Loan agreement whereby one party provides monies to another party for a set period in return for regular payment of interest and principal.

Loan portfolio collection of illiquid assets, eg loans, held by an institution in its banking book.

Lognormal distribution *see* distribution

Longstaff–Schwartz model a two-factor model of the term structure of interest rates. It produces a closed-form solution for the price of zero-coupon bonds and a quasi-closed-form solution for options on zero-coupon bonds. The model is developed in a Cox–Ingersoll–Ross framework with short interest rates and their volatility as the two sources of uncertainty in the equation.

M

Market risk exposure to a change in the value of some market variable, such as interest rates or foreign exchange rates equity or commodity prices.

Mark-to-market valuation valuing securities on the basis of the current market values of a counterparty's obligations.

Martingale property posits that the conditional expectation of a future value of that random variable is the current one.

Mean excess function graphical method of determining the threshold in an extreme value distribution; an empirical estimate of the expected overshoot of a threshold when exceedance occurs. *See also* extreme value theory

Mean-reversion phenomenon whereby interest rates and volatility appear to move back to a long-run average level. Interest rates' mean-reverting tendency is one explanation for the behaviour of the volatility term structure. Some interest rate models incorporate mean-reversion, such as Vasicek and Cox–Ingersoll–Ross, in which high interest rates tend to go down and low ones up.

Model risk risk arising from the misuse of financial models, including mis-calibration and incorrect specification.

Monte Carlo simulation technique used to determine the likely value of a derivative or other contract by simulating the evolution of the underlying variables many times over. The discounted average outcome of the simulation gives an approximation of the derivative's value. Monte Carlo simulation can be used to estimate the value-at-risk (VAR) of a portfolio. Here, it generates a simulation of many correlated market movements for the markets to which the portfolio is exposed, and the positions in the portfolio are revalued repeatedly in accordance with the simulated scenarios. This results in a probability distribution of portfolio gains and losses from which the VAR can be determined.

Multi-factor model any model in which there are two or more uncertain parameters in the option price (one-factor models incorporate only one cause of uncertainty: the future price).

N

Netting the offsetting of transactions between two parties with settlement of the net difference.

Notional amount quantity of an underlier (the primary instrument or variable) to which a derivative contract applies.

O

One-factor model model or description of a system where the model incorporates only one variable or uncertainty: the future price. These are simple models, usually leading to closed-form solutions, such as the Black–Scholes model or the Vasicek model.

Operational risk risk run by a firm that its internal practices, policies and systems are not sufficiently rigorous or sophisticated to cope with adverse market conditions or human or technological errors.

Option contract that gives the purchaser the right, but not the obligation, to buy or sell an underlying at a certain price (the exercise or strike price) on or before an agreed date (the exercise period). For this right, the purchaser pays a premium to the seller. The seller (writer) of an option has a duty to buy or sell at the strike price should the purchaser exercise his right.

OTC *see* over the counter

Out-of-the-money an option whose underlying is below the strike price in the case of a call, or above it in the case of a put. The more the option is out-of-the-money, the cheaper it is (since the chances of it being exercised get slimmer).

Over the counter (OTC) security or instrument which is traded by private negotiation rather than in a supervised environment such as a derivatives exchange. The range of instruments available OTC is typically wider and more tailored than in organised markets.

P

Parameterisation the subjective choice of parameters used as inputs to a risk model; also known as "calibration".

Par bond a bond selling at par.

Pareto distribution *see* generalised Pareto distribution

Path-dependent option option that has a payout that is directly related to movements in the price of the underlying during the option's life. By contrast, the payout of a standard European-style option is determined solely by the price at expiry.

Portfolio expected loss simple sum of individual expected losses from all the risky assets in a portfolio.

Portfolio unexpected loss loss that is unexpected at portfolio level. Unlike portfolio expected loss, this loss is not equal to the linear sum of the individual unexpected losses of the risky assets making up the aggregate portfolio. Because of diversification effects, the portfolio unexpected loss is very much smaller than the sum of the individual unexpected losses.

Put option option contract that gives the holder the right to sell the underlying security at a specified price for a fixed period of time.

Q

Quanto product an asset or liability denominated in a currency other than that in which it is usually traded – typically equity index futures, equity index options, equity index swaps, bond options and interest rate swaps (differential swaps).

R

Random walk series of values taken by a random variable with the progress of some parameter such as time. Each new value (each new step in the walk) is selected randomly and describes the path taken by the underlying variable. *See also* geometric Brownian motion, stochastic process.

RAPM *see* risk-adjusted performance measurement

RAROC *see* risk-adjusted return on capital

Rating evaluation of an issuer's investment quality by a rating agency.

Recovery rate extent to which the face value of an obligation can be recovered once the obligor has defaulted.

Regulatory capital sufficient capital imposed by regulators on banks that must be maintained to provide a cushion to absorb losses that would otherwise cause a bank to fail.

Replacement cost often used in terms of credit exposure; the replacement cost of a financial instrument is its current value in the market – in other words, what it would cost to replace a given contract if the counterparty to the contract defaulted.

Replication replicating the payout of an option by buying or selling other instruments. Creating a synthetic option in this way is always possible in a complete market. In the case of dynamic replication this involves dynamically buying or selling the underlying (or normally, because of cheaper transaction costs, futures) in proportion to an option's delta. In the case of static replication the option is hedged with a basket of standard options whose composition does not change with time.

Required spread spread the bank needs to charge given a particular level of return.

Risk-adjusted performance measurement (RAPM) calculation of performance using a risk adjustment (ie, risk-weighted) process.

See also risk-adjusted return on capital

Risk-adjusted return on capital (RAROC) expected spread over economic capital, calculated for individual assets or portfolios.

Risk capital *see* economic capital

Risk contribution incremental risk that the exposure of a single asset contributes to the portfolio's total risk.

Risk-free rate a theoretical interest rate at which an investment may earn interest without incurring any risk.

Risk measurement assessment of a firm's exposure to risk. *See also* credit risk assessment, value-at-risk

Risk-neutral a theoretical condition whereby investors require no compensation for taking risk

S

Securitisation *see* asset securitisation

Skew a skewed distribution is one that is asymmetric. Skew is a measure of this asymmetry. A perfectly symmetrical distribution has zero skew, whereas a distribution with positive (negative) skew is one where outliers above (below) the mean are more probable.

Specific risk risk of changes in the value of an individual security due to factors related to the individual issuer of the security (eg, credit quality and liquidity) that are outside of broad market movements.

Stochastic process process that can be described by the evolution of some random variable over some parameter, which may be either discrete or continuous. Geometric Brownian motion is an example of a stochastic process parameterised by time. Stochastic processes are used to develop models of the future price of an instrument in terms of the spot price and some random variable; or, analogously, the future value of an interest rate or foreign exchange rate.

Swaption an option to enter an interest rate swap. A payer swaption gives the purchaser the right to pay fixed; a receiver swaption gives the purchaser the right to receive fixed (pay floating).

Systemic risk risk that threatens the whole financial system due to the failure of one participant or an event.

T

Term structure of interest rates relationship between interest rates on the same securities with different maturities.

Time value value of an option other than its intrinsic value. The time value therefore includes cost of carry and the probability that the option will be exercised (which in turn depends on its volatility).

Total return swap swap agreement in which the total return of bank loans or credit-sensitive securities is exchanged for some other cashflow, usually tied to Libor, or other loans or credit-sensitive securities. It allows participants effectively to go long or short the credit risk of the underlying asset.

Trading book bank portfolio containing securities that are actively bought and sold for the purpose of making short-term profit, in contrast to the banking book, which generally consists of loans.

Transition matrix an array of transition or migration probabilities from one credit rating to another.

Transition probability probability that the credit quality of a firm will improve or deteriorate; quantifies credit migration; *see* transition matrix

Treasury bond a long-term government security.

Trinomial tree similar to a binomial tree, a trinomial tree is a discrete-time model that describes the distribution of assets. After each time step in the trinomial tree there are three possible outcomes: an up move, a down move or no move in the asset value.

Two-factor model any model or description of a system that assumes two sources of uncertainty or variables – for example, an asset price and its volatility (a stochastic volatility model) or interest rate levels and curve steepness (a stochastic interest rate model). Two-factor models model interest rate curve movements more realistically than one-factor models.

U

Undiversifiable risk amount of credit risk that cannot be diversified away by placing or removing an asset in a portfolio; also called systematic risk.

Unexpected loss (UL) uncertainty in the amount of loss in portfolio value caused by market conditions. This uncertainty, or more appropriately the volatility of loss, is the so-called unexpected loss. Unexpected losses are triggered by the occurrence of default and unexpected credit migrations.

V

Vasicek model an interest rate model that incorporates mean-reversion and a constant volatility for the short interest rate. It is a one-factor model from which discount bond prices and options on those bonds can be deduced.

Value-at-risk (VAR) probabilistic bound of market losses over a given period of time (the holding period) expressed in terms of a specified degree of certainty (the confidence interval). Put more simply, the VAR is the worst-case loss expected over the holding period within the probability set out by the confidence interval. Larger losses are possible but with a low probability.

Value of the firm models propose that the underlying process driving a firm's default (or credit rating change) is the firm's asset value (after Merton, 1974). *See also* credit risk models

Volatility measure of the variability (but not the direction) of prices or interest rates.

W

Warrant certificate giving the purchaser the right, but not the obligation, to purchase a specified amount of an asset at a certain price over a specified period of time. Warrants differ from options only in that they are usually listed. Underlying assets include equity, debt, currencies and commodities.

Weibull distribution an extreme value distribution with unbounded support to the left. Includes the beta and normal distributions. *See also* generalised Pareto distribution

Wiener process *see* Brownian motion

Worst-case (credit risk) exposure estimate of the highest positive market value a

derivative contract or portfolio is likely to attain at a given moment or period in the future, with a given level of confidence.

Y

Yield interest rate that will make the net present value of the cashflows from an investment equal to the price (or cost) of the investment. Also called the internal rate of return.

Yield curve a graphical representation of the term structure of interest rates. It is usually depicted as the spot yields on bonds with different maturities but the same risk factors (such as creditworthiness of issuer) plotted against maturity.

Z

Zero-coupon bond debt instrument issued at below par value. The bond pays no coupons; instead, it is redeemed at face value at maturity.

Index